THE MAN WHO Sold AMERICA

THE MAN WHO

Sold

AMERICA

The Amazing *(but True!)* Story of

ALBERT D. LASKER

and the Creation of the

ADVERTISING CENTURY

JEFFREY L. CRUIKSHANK

ARTHUR W. SCHULTZ

Harvard Business Review Press

Boston, Massachusetts

Library of Congress Cataloging-in-Publication Data

Cruikshank, Jeffrey L.
    The man who sold America : the amazing (but true!) story of Albert D. Lasker and the creation of the advertising century / Jeffrey L. Cruikshank and Arthur W. Schultz.
        p. cm.
    Includes bibliographical references.
    ISBN 978-1-59139-308-5 (hardcover : alk. paper) 1.   Lasker, Albert Davis, 1880-1952.
2.   Advertisers—United States—Biography. 3.   Advertising—United States—History—20th century.
I.   Schultz, Arthur W. II. Title.
    HF5810.L3C78 2010
    659.1092—dc22
    [B]

                                                                                    2010003079

To Mad Men, patient publishers, and wives
who have to listen to the same stories over and over

Contents

Introduction

THE *COLLIER'S* **REPORTER** who interviewed Albert Lasker in Washington in February 1923 was struck by his subject's rapid-fire delivery and elusive logic.

Lasker's brain was a "furious express train," which seemed to run along six or seven tracks simultaneously. The train raced ahead "with every chance that when it reaches the terminal station it will go straight through the back wall."[1]

For Lasker—a forty-three-year-old advertising executive from Chicago who had temporarily transformed himself into a Washington bureaucrat—this was nothing new; he had always lived his complicated life at a breakneck pace. But the second month of 1923 was proving unusually challenging even for the hyperactive Lasker.

He was engaged in a bitter and bruising battle on behalf of the president of the United States, trying to implement a coherent national maritime policy. Two years of hard work were on the line. He was losing.

Meanwhile, his advertising agency, Lord & Thomas—which Lasker had over the previous quarter century built into one of the largest and most influential agencies in the United States—was in financial peril.

At the same time, Lasker was suffering from a nasty case of the flu, which was causing him much discomfort. His only trips outside his Washington townhouse in the first week of February were to the White House, where he spent three successive evenings with President Harding and his wife, Florence. The First Couple, too, had been felled by the flu. They seemed to find the presence of a friend and fellow sufferer—one who was a little farther down the road to recovery—comforting.

1

"I have been making a very determined effort to be just as fashionable as I could be in Washington," the still-bedridden Lasker wrote a few days after his visits to the Hardings, in a sly letter to his friend William Wrigley Jr.

Lasker and the chewing-gum king, both Chicago-based businessmen, maintained an odd relationship, equal parts professional and personal. Together, they owned a controlling interest in the Chicago Cubs. Lasker had enticed Wrigley, who when left to his own devices thought only about gum, not only into baseball, but also into Republican politics. This included tapping Wrigley's substantial fortune on behalf of several Republican candidates, including Warren Harding.

"To be fashionable in Washington is to have the grippe," Lasker continued, tongue in cheek, "and I have had an attack of intestinal grippe, which kept me in bed for practically a week, and away from the office for sixteen days."[2]

By now, Lasker—always a quick study—was an authority on the "grippe," and he enjoyed sharing his newly acquired medical expertise with similarly stricken friends. In a letter to his ailing friend Arthur Brisbane—editor of the powerful *Evening Journal,* William Randolph Hearst's flagship newspaper in New York—Lasker offered tips on combating the flu's miseries.

The real subject of the letter, however, was anti-Semitism. A decade earlier, Lasker and Brisbane had been coconspirators in a nationwide campaign to save the life of Leo Frank, the Jewish factory superintendent in Atlanta, Georgia, who, on scanty evidence, had been convicted of raping and murdering a young factory girl.[3] In that effort, Brisbane and his boss Hearst had established themselves as reliable allies of the Jewish community. But now there was a problem. The *Evening Journal,* still edited by Brisbane, was featuring articles sympathetic toward a presidential run by carmaker Henry Ford: wealthy, famous, and viciously anti-Semitic. Jews in New York and elsewhere expressed their outrage.

Lasker himself had felt the lash of Ford's prejudice less than two years earlier. At that time, the *Dearborn Independent*—a scurrilous rag bankrolled by Ford—had blamed Lasker for the infamous Black Sox scandal, in which members of the Chicago White Sox threw the 1919 World Series in exchange for gambling money.

By then, accustomed to encountering the ugly face of anti-Semitism in his many endeavors, Lasker had simply shrugged off Ford's attacks. But Brisbane lacked Lasker's thick skin. He was receiving a steady stream of angry letters, and he wanted to know if Lasker could explain to him why these particular Jews were so, well, *touchy*.

"Yes, I can," Lasker replied: "The Jew has been persecuted for so many centuries, and he is so fearful that if Henry Ford is President, that persecution will come to him in America, that naturally he is unnerved at any remote incident that might help Ford in that direction, and is particularly unnerved when it comes from a power such as yours, who has always been a staunch supporter of the Jew."[4]

Lasker chose his words carefully. He didn't want to offend his friend. Even more important, he didn't want to risk alienating the powerful Hearst, an invaluable ally as Lasker fought his maritime battle in the nation's capital.[5]

Another more personal problem preyed on Lasker's mind in those early months of 1923. He faced a serious threat to his personal fortune, owing to skullduggery on the part of a client—the California Associated Raisin Company, also known as "Sun-Maid"—to whom Lord & Thomas had advanced large sums of money. And because much of Lasker's personal fortune was tied up in Lord & Thomas's cash accounts, a threat to the agency was also a threat to the Lasker family's opulent lifestyle. The Chicago mansion; the estate in Glencoe, Illinois; the four-month winter vacations; the plans for an even grander country estate—all might be on the line.

Who was this Albert Davis Lasker, whose energy and imagination ran in so many directions at once, and who was (in his own words) "driven by a thousand devils"?[6]

His friends considered him charming, brilliant, thrilling, and exhausting. *Time* magazine observed, not approvingly, that "the current he generates is seldom grounded."[7] Arthur Andersen, head of the accounting firm that bore his name, once commented, "When I go into the room with Lasker, I can hear the dishes break."[8] His subordinates admired him enormously—and dreaded his arrival at the office and the tumult that inevitably ensued. Clients quickly learned that there was no such thing as a half-embrace of, or by, Albert Lasker.

He pursued life with a fervor that offended and alienated many people. "A lot of people can't stand me," he once admitted, "because they think I'm too aggressive and too dynamic."[9] Little men (to use his terminology) were driven off by it. Big men, such as RCA's David Sarnoff and American Tobacco's George Washington Hill, drew energy from it. They looked forward to fighting with Lasker. They learned from him.

"He is the only man I felt I'd like to murder, every now and then," Herbert Field confessed, almost twenty years after being pushed out of his senior position in Lord & Thomas's Chicago headquarters, then adding, "There isn't a finer man living."[10]

"I'd like to kick him in the back," said a former associate who left the New York office under duress, but similarly added, "I have never met a man as colorful and virile and as personable as Mr. Albert Lasker. Never."[11]

Lasker's energy and passion infused both his personal and professional lives—and sometimes those two lives converged. One Monday morning in 1939, his top lieutenants gathered for their weekly "state of the agency" meeting. This was no ordinary Monday, however: it was the first such meeting after the very public unraveling of Lasker's second marriage—a disastrous union with a Hollywood starlet that fell apart even before their shipboard honeymoon ended. Everyone in the room knew the salacious details. All were eager to see how the boss would handle the situation.

The door from Lasker's private office opened, and he walked in and took his customary seat at the head of the table. "Gentlemen," he intoned, "in his life, every man has a right to make one mistake. *I* have made *mine*."[12] The meeting began.

Lasker, often referred to as the "father of modern advertising," exerted an enormous influence on his industry. Before he arrived on the scene, advertising agencies were mostly brokers of space in newspapers and magazines. With Lasker's prodding—and with contributions from pioneers at a handful of other agencies—the industry became a creative force and began earning substantial commissions.

Lasker worked his magic by relying on the power of *ideas*. The list of companies and brands that he helped launch or revitalize—in large part through the selective amplification of powerful ideas and in part through his own instinct for drama—is unparalleled in the history of advertising.

Lasker spearheaded the transformation of an obscure soap produced by a Milwaukee manufacturer into a dominant national brand: Palmolive. He rescued two faltering Quaker Oats breakfast cereals as Puffed Wheat and Puffed Rice—"foods shot from guns!"—and sparked a thirtyfold increase in sales. He invented the "Sunkist" and "Sun-Maid" brands, and prompted huge increases in the consumption of oranges and raisins.

He quadrupled Goodyear's tire sales in less than four years. He plotted out how Kimberly-Clark could market the first sanitary napkin (Kotex)—a previously unmentionable product—as well as the first disposable handkerchief (Kleenex). In the space of three years, he increased sales of Lucky Strike cigarettes from 25 million a day to 150 million a day. Already a self-made millionaire, in the 1920s and 1930s he helped build the tiny Pepsodent toothpaste company into an international powerhouse, making himself far wealthier in the process. He at first resisted the new medium of radio; soon enough, though, he embraced and mastered it. His most celebrated show was *Amos 'n' Andy*; his most famous pitchman (for Pepsodent) was a hitherto obscure comedian named Bob Hope.

Although Lasker enjoyed making and consorting with stars—and in one case, marrying them—he remained largely unimpressed with them. One day, the head of Lord & Thomas's broadcast department reported to Lasker that Hope was grumbling about his contract with the agency. "Mr. Lasker," the subordinate said, "Bob is very unhappy. He says he just can't put the show together for $4,000 a week. He must have $6,000." "Just between us," Lasker replied dryly, "I'd rather have Mr. Hope unhappy at $4,000 than unhappy at $6,000."[13]

Lasker invented a particular kind of ad agency: one that delivered high service to a relatively small number of key accounts—most often driven by a personal relationship between himself and the head of the client company. At Lord & Thomas, relatively little was invested in prospecting or conducting market research on spec. The result was high margins, and—for Lasker—enormous personal wealth.

He maintained close relationships with dozens of powerful businesspeople and applied the insights he gained in one context to give advice in others. Well before McKinsey & Co. began offering strategic counsel in the 1930s, Lasker performed the same role for leading firms across the country. "Give him an equal knowledge of the facts," said RCA's legendary head David Sarnoff, "and I'd rather have his judgment than anybody else's I know."[14]

Using many of the same tools he had developed in advertising, Lasker also helped shape the infant field of public relations. He masterminded the "idea side" of two key political campaigns, helping Warren G. Harding win the presidency in 1920 and thwarting muckraking author Upton Sinclair's 1934 bid for the governorship of California.

Sometimes Lasker failed, and failed spectacularly. In the notorious Leo Frank case (1913–1914), he and his media allies (including not only Arthur Brisbane but also Adolph Ochs of the *New York Times*) so infuriated Georgians that Frank's death at the hands of a lynch mob became almost inevitable. He failed to persuade Congress to transform the maritime industry in the early 1920s. And his attempts to replace the New Deal with an economic compact of his own devising came to nothing.

But he always rebounded. When he finally left advertising, he applied his extraordinary skills in entirely new contexts. His third wife, Mary, introduced him to a new world—philanthropy—which at first proved resistant to Lasker's outsized visions. But he used the tools he had embraced in the commercial context, including radio, to change the way the nation thought about cancer and other diseases. Organizations like the American Cancer Society, Planned Parenthood, the National Institutes of Health, and the National Institute of Mental Health all benefited enormously from the Laskers' energetic advocacy. Reshaping philanthropy and expanding medical research in America—achievements still embodied today in the annual awarding of the Lasker Prizes—are among Lasker's most enduring legacies.

By the time of his death in 1952, Albert Lasker had not only redefined advertising, public relations, politics, and philanthropy but also had exerted a major influence in sports and the arts.

After selling his interest in the Chicago Cubs to Bill Wrigley, for example, he turned his attention to golf. At his splendid 480-acre estate in Lake Forest, Illinois—maintained by a staff of fifty-five—he supported an experimental "grass station," run by the United States Golf Association, that investigated various kinds of turf. He employed the celebrated golf-course architect William S. Flynn to create one of the best courses in America: eighteen holes set on 180 acres. He offered a prize of $500 to anyone, professionals included, who could break par on the Lake Forest course; it took seven years for someone to claim the prize.

Almost incidentally, he assembled one of the world's most significant collections of Impressionist oils, watercolors, and etchings. At one point, he was the owner of multiple Renoirs, nine Matisses, Van Gogh's *Zouave* and *White Roses,* seventeen Picassos, and twenty-four Dali watercolors. He commissioned Dali to paint cityscapes of four Italian cities, and dined with the aging Henri Matisse at his studio in Nice.

Lasker's scope and impact were nothing short of astounding—and he knew it. "There wasn't a living American in so many ways each day partially responsible for people doing as many things as I was," he once commented, in his hurried and distinctive syntax, "That is provable."[15]

He was right.

As the *Collier's* writer observed in those frantic early months of 1923, Lasker was blessed, or cursed, with an extraordinarily high energy level. But there was another side to this intensity: Lasker suffered most of his adult life from a major depressive illness. In 1907, at the age of twenty-seven, he experienced a complete mental and emotional collapse. "I could do nothing but cry," he said. And unfortunately for Lasker, the pattern set by this first breakdown persisted for most of his life: "I always say [that] I got over all my breakdowns except the first one."[16]

He slept poorly. As a teenager and young adult, he drank heavily. Under the influence, he once attempted to drive a horse-drawn sleigh into a Grand Rapids, Michigan, barroom. He suffered from dramatic mood swings and sometimes indulged in impulsive behaviors. But for the most part, Lasker dealt with his affective illness admirably, even heroically. At that time, there was no effective treatment for depression: no electroshock therapy; no psychoactive medications. Although Freudian theory had taken root in the sophisticated circles in which the Laskers traveled, it manifested itself mostly in the form of jargon that was thrown around lightly and only partly understood. In the larger world, meanwhile, mental illness was still perceived as shameful—something to be hidden—and psychotherapy was viewed as an exotic form of quackery.

Drawing on his reserves of energy, self-awareness, and determination, Lasker fought back against his illness. He survived—and flourished. His rare ability to put troubled geniuses to work on challenging problems—legendary advertising talents like John E. Kennedy and Claude C. Hopkins—grew in part from the fact that he himself had been driven by "a thousand devils."

In his final years, Lasker developed an "absolute passion for anonymity in anything he did."[17] He killed off the autobiography that his first wife had begged him to undertake. Only reluctantly did he let his third wife put his name to a foundation. (And only after his death did she put his name on the "Albert Lasker Awards.") Little by little, Lasker became invisible. The curtain that Lasker created between himself and the pages of history became almost impenetrable.

This book parts that curtain to reveal the man behind it—the real and extraordinary Albert Davis Lasker: the man who sold America.

Chapter One

The Orator and the Entrepreneur

*A*LBERT LASKER'S ninth birthday party—on May Day, 1889—provides a glimpse of life in Victorian Galveston, Texas, as lived by a fortunate and precocious child.

That afternoon, at 5:00 p.m., in response to a written invitation from "Master Albert Lasker," more than fifty children assembled on the rolling lawn of his father's house. His parents, Morris and Nettie, supervised games for the first hour of the party: the ritual May Pole dance followed. Next came the crowning of the May Queen, which (according to a reporter in attendance) was of great interest to the girls, whose hearts went "pit a pat" with anticipation: "A large chair, garlanded with beautiful flowers, and arranged in the center of the lawn, answer the purpose of a throne, upon which the queen reigned during her coronation, Master Albert Lasker encircling her brow with a floral wreath, after making a very flowery speech full of spring poetry and beautiful sentiment."[1]

Albert Lasker's story is rooted in the bustling port city of Galveston. There he was raised and schooled. There he got his first exposure to the tantalizing and disreputable world of journalism, and also to its staid and slightly more respectable cousin: advertising. There he first stretched his entrepreneurial wings and developed passions—including baseball, drama, poker, politics, and power—that would endure.

But the broader story of Lasker's life begins in the small Prussian town where his father, aunts, and uncles were born, and in Germany, where Albert was born in 1880 while his parents were visiting Europe. His business acumen, his entrepreneurial drive, and his desire to make a difference in the world can all be traced back to the traditions and values of his extended family.

Those characteristics also reflect the conflicting legacies of his father Morris and his uncle Eduard. Born ten years apart, these two brothers pursued strikingly different paths. Eduard established himself as one of the most renowned and controversial German politicians of the nineteenth century; Morris made his mark as a pioneer and entrepreneur in the American Southwest. Eduard died a bachelor; Morris fathered six children.

But they shared more than a name. Both were ambitious. Both experienced major triumphs and devastating defeats, and both suffered from extended periods of profound mental distress. And although their two lives were very different, the shadows of both can be seen in Albert Lasker's life.

Eduard Lasker was born to Daniel and Rebecca Lasker in 1829. The family lived in Jarocin, a largely Catholic town that had a sizeable Jewish community of around 160 families. Daniel was the proprietor of a nail shop and also part-owner of a glass store and a refinery. But as Jews, his family remained distinctly second-class citizens.

The family had a strong tradition of scholarship; many of Daniel's ancestors had been respected rabbis and teachers. Eduard was a highly intelligent child, with a special talent for Talmudic studies, and the family hoped that he, too, would become a rabbi. But Eduard drifted away from the religious life and at age sixteen left home to attend the University of Breslau, where—during the revolutions of 1848—he became a political activist. At one point he quit school to publish several issues of a radical periodical, *Der Sozialist*.[2] After several years of law study in Breslau, Eduard left for London in 1853, his personal protest against the stifling political climate of Prussia, which was then halfway through the twenty-one-year rule of the deeply conservative King Frederick William IV.

Exile changed Eduard. The more time he spent away from his native country, the more nationalistic his tendencies became. Convinced that his talents should be put to use in the service of his state, he returned to Prussia in 1856, and took a job as a court lawyer in Berlin.

In 1861, following Frederick William's death, his younger brother William ascended to the throne. A year later, he appointed as his prime minister the aristocratic and conservative politician Otto van Bismarck. Over the next three decades, Bismarck pursued an aggressively nationalistic strategy of German unification and also sought to expand Prussia's influence over the unifying states. Successful on both counts, Bismarck not only created the

German empire but also helped define its character. Pessimistic and defensive, he saw chaos along the unruly fringes of his emerging empire, and repressed it whenever and wherever he could.

In 1865, Eduard made his first foray into politics, winning a seat in the Landtag, the Prussian lower house of government. Two years later, he was also elected to the national German parliament, the Reichstag. Eduard supported Bismarck's unification policies, but strongly opposed most of Bismarck's domestic and economic policies. Eduard advocated a state guided by the rule of law rather than by administrative fiat, and this philosophy soon placed him on a collision course with the autocratic Bismarck.

Unyielding—even rigid—in his public life, Eduard was a study in contradictions in his private life. "His personal appearance is . . . flawed by a lack of dignified calm," wrote one of his peers. "He is always in rapid motion."[3] At other times, though, he was nearly immobilized by depression. His drastic mood swings did not impede him in politics, where he won recognition as a skillful orator and forceful personality. "Without a doubt," a colleague commented in 1874, "he was the best known and most popular member of the Reichstag when I entered that body."[4]

As a politician and statesman, he achieved remarkable success, especially in a society that actively marginalized Jews. But as the decades passed, Eduard found himself increasingly isolated on the left fringe of Prussian politics.[5] He became a frequent target of attacks by Bismarck, who referred to him as "the sickness of Germany."[6] Bismarck even instructed his own son, Herbert, to run against Eduard in an election in Lasker's home district in 1879. Eduard trounced Herbert, which only further antagonized the Iron Chancellor.

This victory was the high-water mark of Lasker's political power. Although he remained in the Reichstag, he slid into political eclipse, and his physical and mental health deteriorated. For several years, his friends had been worrying about a "nervous fever" that periodically seemed to overtake and disable him.[7] In the spring of 1883, in an effort both to restore his mind and body—and to renew his relationship with his younger brother Morris—Eduard set off on an extended tour of the United States.

Eduard and Morris, separated by ten years, grew up in two different families. Their mother Rebecca died soon after Morris's birth, and Morris was raised by a stepmother with whom he clashed regularly. Twelve years later, Morris lost his father to the cholera epidemic of 1852, and for the next four years he lived with an elder sister and her husband while attending the local school.

Although a highly intelligent child, Morris did not share Eduard's intellectual ambitions. At sixteen, he boarded a ship bound for America. His relatives in Jarocin wouldn't hear from him again for twenty years.

After a brutal, storm-buffeted Atlantic crossing that lasted thirteen weeks, Lasker's ship limped into Fortress Monroe, Virginia. The young adventurer traveled twenty miles south to Portsmouth, where he got a job clerking in a dry goods store. Next he traveled north to New York, where he scraped by until the financial panic of 1857 wiped out his meager savings.[8]

Morris then again headed south—first to Florida and then Georgia, where he met and became friendly with a young man named Philip Sanger. Lasker spent three years in Georgia and the surrounding states, peddling goods in the country and serving as a distributor for importers based in the coastal towns and cities. He endured many long hours traveling by wagon to small towns and backwoods homesteads, and took advantage of those slow hours to read voraciously. Years later, he would tell his children of the times his horse and cart wound up in a roadside ditch because he was focused more on the book in his hand than on the road ahead of him.

Morris also told them of a Christmas dinner he ate on a plantation in North Carolina. In the rigid Southern social hierarchy of that time, peddlers ranked above the slaves who labored on those plantations, but far below their customers. Forbidden to eat with the family, Morris was offered a seat in the kitchen. He happened to overhear the daughter of the family lamenting the lack of Latin and Greek tutors to help her prepare for an upcoming exam. After the meal, he boldly made his way into the dining room and offered his services as a tutor—a proposal that the family accepted.

Perhaps in telling that story, Morris Lasker hoped to teach his children the value of an education. Perhaps he was also telling them that an adventurer in a new world needed to see things in new ways, apply his skills creatively, and even break the rules.

Tantalized by tales of limitless opportunity in faraway Texas, Morris decided to travel into the wilder reaches of his adopted nation. He hopped a train to New Orleans and then boarded a steamer to Shreveport, Louisiana. From there, he took an overland stage to McKinney, Texas, about thirty-five miles north of a small outpost called Dallas. He carried a letter of introduction to the firm of Baum & Sanger, written by Philip Sanger to his brother Isaac, a joint owner of the company.

But when Morris arrived in McKinney—probably in the early months of 1860—he was told that Baum & Sanger had moved to Weatherford, a small frontier town some sixty miles west of Dallas. Weatherford had only been in existence about four years, but because it was well situated on the crest of a divide between the Trinity and Brazos river valleys, it already boasted a thriving business community.[9] Here the firm of Baum & Sanger was carving out a strong position by offering fair prices and ready barters to its customers.

Lasker quickly found employment at Baum & Sanger. On his new employee's first day on the job, Isaac Sanger instructed him in his routine—walking to the post office and picking up the mail, then minding the store while Sanger went out for breakfast.

A few days later, that daily walk to the post office almost got Morris killed. A local competitor, determined to ruin Baum & Sanger, had secretly been writing letters to a Mrs. Hendricks, proclaiming his passion for her and begging her to write to him at Post Office Box 10—Baum & Sanger's box.

When Mr. Hendricks discovered the letters, he burst into the store just after Morris had retrieved the mail and Sanger had departed for breakfast. Hendricks demanded that the young clerk confirm the store's mail box number. "Number 10," Morris innocently replied—at which point the wild-eyed man pulled out a Bowie knife and ordered Morris to "get on his knees and pray," as he had but seconds left to live.

Hendricks charged; Morris leapt for the door. Luckily, just at that moment, a local army officer walked into the store. He subdued the enraged husband and soon convinced him that Morris—who had only recently arrived in town—couldn't possibly be guilty of any wrongdoing.

It was a startling introduction to life on the frontier.[10]

Morris quickly demonstrated his worth to Baum & Sanger. But larger events were overtaking him: the smoldering regional divisions that had afflicted his adopted country for decades were now intensifying into civil war. Casting the first ballot of his life, Lasker voted against secession. But Texas voted overwhelmingly to leave the Union, and when the terrible national conflict began, Lasker joined the 2nd Texas Cavalry Regiment, under the command of Colonel John G. Ford. The young German immigrant recorded almost nothing about this period of his life, but we know he saw active service in the battles to retake the port cities of Galveston and Sabine Pass from Union troops and also participated in successful campaigns in Louisiana.

At the end of the war, Lasker renewed his acquaintance with Isaac Sanger, who tried to convince him to peddle dry goods for him and offered to loan him enough goods to get started. While Lasker was considering this offer, however, he met up with a man looking for a partner to invest in a store in Galveston. Lasker bought in, and that move paid off handsomely, quickly turning his $150 investment into $1,500. But Lasker became worried about his partner's ethics, so in the early months of 1866, he abandoned Galveston and again went into business with the Sangers in the town of Millican, some 135 miles inland.[11]

Several profitable months later—probably in the spring or early summer of 1867—he sold his interest with the intention of returning to Galveston, where he planned to set up a wholesale grocery business. But this plan was disrupted by an outbreak of yellow fever. Although many plagues had swept through Galveston and other Southern coastal cities, none was as virulent as yellow fever, a mosquito-borne virus that often proved fatal. A particularly wet spring and summer, as well as the presence of large numbers of people in the city (including occupying federal troops) who had never before been exposed to the "yellow jack," caused a terrifying infection rate and death toll. One-third of Galveston's population fled the city. Of those who stayed, three-quarters caught the disease, and more than a thousand died between July and September.[12]

Morris Lasker hoped to wait out the epidemic in Millican, but yellow jack soon engulfed that town as well. Both Elias Baum—cofounder of Baum & Sanger—and his wife Dorethea died there. The postmaster closed the post office, fleeing along with most of the rest of the town's population. " . . . 'Twill be useless to send mail matter to this place from this date," he wrote to his superiors, "as no one will be here to receive it."[13]

Lasker and the Sangers decamped to Bryan, about twenty miles to the northwest, but the disease followed them there. Two of the Sanger brothers fell ill and died almost immediately, leading to the extended family's effective imprisonment—euphemistically described as a "quarantine"—in their own store. (A waiter from a nearby hotel brought meals to the door, and cautiously retrieved the used dishes.) The local people were so terrified, Lasker later recalled, that they "made it very difficult for us to complete the necessary arrangements for [the Sanger brothers'] burial."[14]

Finally the first hard frosts of fall arrived, killing the mosquitoes and temporarily ending the scourge. Morris Lasker packed his bags, bade goodbye to the Sangers, and once again made his way to Galveston.[15]

In 1876, Morris married the niece of a wealthy Galveston businessman who was also in the wholesale business. Nettie Davis, a stunningly beautiful young woman with deep-set brown eyes, was one of nine children of German and Russian immigrants living in Rochester, New York. While visiting her relatives in Galveston, she caught Morris's eye. Her father was a tailor who found it difficult to support his large family, and when Lasker asked for her hand, permission was quickly granted. Morris was then thirty-five years old; Nettie was just seventeen.

About the time that Morris and Nettie had their first child (Edward, born in 1877), Morris decided that it was time to reestablish contact with his German relatives.[16] Those relatives, including older brother Eduard, had long since concluded that Morris was dead. Morris sent a letter to Eduard, regaling him with tales of his business success and his settled family life.

From that point on, Eduard and Morris made efforts to stay in touch. Morris visited his ancestral home a few years later; according to family legend, he appeared at his family's door in knee-high cowboy boots, a bright red shirt, and a sombrero. He had a hard time convincing his family that this gaudy stranger was indeed the long-lost Morris.

Nettie suffered from bouts of poor health, and when she became pregnant with her second child in the fall of 1879, Morris decided that she and the family should spend the last months of her pregnancy in Germany, near a spa, so that she would be closer to skilled doctors if anything went wrong.

The precaution was unnecessary: Albert Davis Lasker was born uneventfully on May 1, 1880, at the home of an uncle in Freiburg.[17] When Nettie was sufficiently recovered, the family made the long journey back to Galveston.

Eduard Lasker's first visit to the United States, which began in the summer of 1883, lasted more than half a year. Eduard was surprised and pleased to find that in the United States he was considered a major German political figure. He received a warm ovation from German Americans at the opening session of Congress. He gave speeches to enthusiastic groups across the country, and in September served as one of several dignitaries who helped inaugurate the Northern Pacific Railroad's transcontinental service to San Francisco.

He also visited his younger brother in Galveston. There he became reacquainted with his three-year-old nephew, Albert, whom he had only seen as a newborn.

This was to be the last time that uncle and nephew would meet. The fifty-five-year-old Eduard returned to the East Coast, where he resumed his ambitious schedule of speaking engagements, addressing, among others, an audience at New York's Mount Sinai Hospital on New Year's Eve on the subject of the Jewish philanthropy. On the evening of January 4, 1884, he suffered a massive heart attack on a New York City street and died.

"German liberalism loses one of its most distinguished leaders," lamented the *New York Tribune*. But on instructions from Otto von Bismarck, not a single emissary of the German government, federal or state, attended his funeral in Berlin. The U.S. House of Representatives attempted to send a message to the Reichstag, offering condolences on the death of Lasker, whose passing was mourned by "lovers of liberty throughout the world." Bismarck returned the message to the German ambassador in Washington, noting coolly that he disagreed with the judgments it contained. A minor diplomatic uproar ensued, which Bismarck shrugged off with a caustic question: "Am I to make myself my enemy's postman?"[18]

By the time Eduard Lasker visited Galveston in 1883, the city was almost fully recovered from the devastating effects of the Civil War and had been free of yellow fever for a decade. It was the largest city in Texas—twenty-two thousand residents—and jockeyed with Houston to be the state's commercial center.[19] The city's main role in the later years of the nineteenth century was as a transshipment point for the agricultural goods of Texas: Galveston's merchants bought products from farmers and resold them to customers in Europe and elsewhere. Products flowed in the other direction as well, with Galveston's traders importing supplies for merchants to sell to the farmers.[20]

By far the most important product to pass through Galveston was cotton. The city was America's fifth-largest cotton exporter in 1882, but like many Southern cities, Galveston failed to industrialize, in part because of its geographical situation. Galveston—an island connected to the mainland by bridges—sits on a narrow, low-lying, twenty-five-mile-long sandbar that juts out into the Atlantic Ocean and divides Galveston Bay from the Gulf of Mexico. The island has been battered by powerful storms as long as records have been kept, and northern investors were reluctant to put their factories and people in harm's way.[21]

Because Galveston couldn't attract capital, local industry languished. In 1880, the year Albert Lasker was born, Galveston's biggest industry was printing, which employed a modest 107 people and represented a capital investment of only $287,000.[22]

The harbor presented another obstacle to Galveston's growth. It wasn't deep enough to accommodate large vessels; as a result, many ships had to anchor well offshore and be loaded and unloaded by barges—a cumbersome and expensive process. Huge sums were spent dredging the sand on the harbor floor in an effort to deepen the ship channels and make the port more competitive.

At the same time, though, Galveston possessed natural advantages. Principal among them were its spectacular white-sand beaches, which began to attract tourists after the Civil War. In 1877, a Galveston company built a network of streetcar lines to transport bathers to the beaches. In 1881, the same company completed construction of an elaborate two-story "pavilion" on the beach—the first building in Texas with electric lights—and two years later, the opulent Beach Hotel opened.[23]

This was the setting in which Morris Lasker built his wholesale grocery business during his first decade in the city and in which he founded the Lasker Real Estate Company, which soon became the umbrella for his increasingly varied business interests. He owned and operated the Texas Star Flour Mills, founded several decades earlier by Austrian immigrants, which was by the 1890s the largest enterprise on Galveston Island. The Texas Star Mills were the first in Texas to adopt an eight-hour day, which earned Lasker the goodwill of working people (and the enmity of manufacturers) around the state. He also bought interests in flour mills in Waco, Wichita Falls, and Wolf City. Morris also dabbled in railroad building—a savvy investment for a coastal trader.

Briefly, Morris Lasker entered the political arena. In April 1895, he was elected to succeed deceased Texas state senator Miles Crowley. While serving out Crowley's term in the Senate, he helped introduce and pass a bill regulating fishing and oyster-harvesting practices, and also cosponsored a major drainage bill.[24] Unlike his brother Eduard, however, Morris found political life distasteful and declined to stand for reelection. But his growing stature in the Galveston business community, as well as other parts of the state, kept him an influential figure in Texas politics well after his departure from the Senate.

Influence led to more influence. Morris became president of the Galveston Cotton Exchange, established the Island City Savings Bank of Galveston, and served as vice president and chairman of the Finance Committee of the First National Bank of Galveston. He received $5,000 a year for each of his bank presidencies, and $3,000 a year for his lesser banking roles, all of which added up to a princely income. Lasker took to wearing a silk hat on Sundays: a distinction reserved for the very wealthy.[25]

Although a sharp-eyed businessman, Morris Lasker also was community minded. Along with a business partner, for example, he donated $30,000 to set up the first classes in "manual training and domestic science" in the Galveston public schools. In 1912, he gave $15,000 to an orphanage, which was subsequently renamed the "Lasker Home for Homeless Children" in his honor.[26] Morris also proved to be a steady hand when calamity struck. In1900, a devastating hurricane—one of the worst natural disasters in U.S. history—struck Galveston, killing more than forty-two hundred citizens and washing away much of the city. Morris Lasker was one of a handful of local men elected to direct recovery efforts.

Although not a particularly observant Jew, Morris was always connected to the Jewish community, both locally and farther afield. Toward the end of his life, one of the causes dearest to his heart was the National Farm School, located twenty-six miles north of Philadelphia. This institution trained immigrant Jews—many fleeing the bloody Russian pogroms of the late 1800s—as farmers, and equipped them to build better lives for themselves. Lasker donated almost $100,000 to the school in 1916 to erect a "Domestic Building" in his name.[27]

A few years earlier, Morris wrote to Albert about the school, saying that he had been pondering how his son could best equip himself for his "aim to benefit mankind, and thus to receive the only truest satisfaction in life, and real compensation for living." If Albert got involved in the affairs of the school, Morris continued, "the field for doing good through that idea could be developed to nearly an unlimited extent."[28]

Although he never got Albert involved with the National Farm School, Morris exercised enormous influence over his son. He directed his career choice, withheld and then granted permission for him to get married, loaned him money for a wedding ring, and was the voice of conscience that whispered in his son's ear. Ralph Sollitt, one of Albert Lasker's closest friends and business associates, said that Morris's words exerted a powerful and abiding influence on Albert: "I have never seen any of the letters from his father . . . but my goodness, I heard by the hour what was in those letters. . . . The effect was tremendous, they were words from the oracle, and [if] the father wanted him to go to Atlanta and tilt with windmills, he did it . . ."[29]

Morris also exerted his influence by example. Charismatic, demanding, endlessly energetic, and frequently absent, he was a challenging father whose children viewed him with a combination of fear, awe, and love. They rebelled against his harsh rules, but struggled to live up to his ideals. As Sollitt further observed: "Either from his father or from this Jewish thing that is in him; the deep thing with him is that he ought to do good in the world. And his whole life has been this struggle somehow or other, to find out how to do this good . . . A man has to justify his existence, and after all business didn't really justify his existence."[30]

The other enduring influence on Albert's life was his Uncle Eduard, so frequently held up to Albert and his siblings as a paragon of hard work and selfless public service. For many years, Eduard's name remained iconic in the German-Jewish expatriate community. When Albert sought to marry, for example, consent came more easily from the young woman's family because Albert was a blood relative of the hallowed Eduard Lasker.

Throughout his life, therefore, Albert measured himself against one man who had gone toe-to-toe with the Iron Chancellor, and another who had braved the privations and horrors of the Civil War, epidemics, and hurricanes and made several fortunes in a foreign and sometimes hostile land.

Orator and entrepreneur, statesman and pioneer, depressive and overachiever: These conflicting legacies would advance Albert Lasker's career, shape his emotions, and dictate his dreams.

Chapter Two

The Galveston Hothouse

*I*N LATE APRIL 1892, the *Galveston Free Press* heartily endorsed the candidacy of George Clark—an attorney from Waco with extremely close ties to the railroads—for governor of Texas.

Clark was running for the Democratic nomination against incumbent James Stephen Hogg. A notable milestone of Hogg's first term had been the creation of the Texas Railroad Commission—a powerful body modeled on the Interstate Commerce Commission that administered the state's railroad-related laws. The legislation that created the Railroad Commission allowed the governor to appoint its three members. Clark ran against the Commission as a "constitutional monstrosity," and called for the popular election of Commissioners.[1]

Citing Clark's progressive and tolerant spirit, the editorial writer enjoined Texans to support him:

> *The office of the governor already has enough power without being given that of the appointment of three railroad commissioners who are invested with authority to make and unmake the greatest corporations in the state. Such power held in the hands of the governor invites suspicion, favoritism, and, worst of all, corruption . . . Judge Clark will add a spirit of tolerance and progressiveness foreign to the nature of the present executive. By all means let Judge Clark head the ticket and Texas will experience a change that will be "what she has sought and mourned because she found it not."[2]*

The editorial was remarkable not so much for its arguments—although they were cogent and sensible enough—but for the fact that its author, Albert D. Lasker, was still nine years away from being old enough to vote. On the day that these opinions appeared in print, Albert Lasker—writer, editor, and owner of the *Galveston Free Press*—was a day short of his twelfth birthday.

The *Free Press*, which Lasker published for more than a year, was a four-page weekly that commanded a yearly subscription price of $1. In addition to editorials, the newspaper ran theater reviews, social notes, and other local news. It also contained advertisements for local businesses, all written and laid out by Lasker. The only aspect of newspapering that Lasker did not undertake personally was the collection of payments from subscribers and advertisers. This, Lasker felt, was beneath his dignity. To dun deadbeats, Lasker hired a boy even younger than he was.

The formula worked. From the operations of the *Galveston Free Press*, Lasker netted around $15 a week, at a time when $60 a month was a respectable salary for an adult in Galveston.

Albert Lasker was one of six children. He had an older brother, Edward, a younger brother, Harry (his mother's favorite, whom Albert loved to torment), and three younger sisters—Florina, Etta, and Loula.

The Galveston of Lasker's childhood was a lively, sociable, and relatively liberal Southern port. The city's most fashionable residences faced the Gulf. The Lasker house was almost at the geographic center of the Galveston peninsula, although several blocks from the water. It was a stately red Victorian on the corner of Broadway and 18th Street that Lasker's first biographer described as "a castle—or prison—out of Grimm . . . a crenelated, gabled house . . . built of bright red sandstone, with sturdy masonry, a white window trim, round copings . . . iron balconies, Corinthian columns, triangular porches, and ornate glass bulges set at improbable angles."[3] It sat atop a small hill, and was usually surrounded by well-tended flowers.[4]

The opulent façade bespoke the very comfortable lifestyle within. Lasker recalled a childhood home in which there were "always lots of servants, and lots of maids, and a butler."[5] Albert's sister Loula was somewhat more precise: there were three servants and a full-time gardener, of whom the maid was white, and the other three staffers were African American.[6]

Nettie Lasker, although the junior partner in her marriage, was nevertheless a commanding presence. "I used to think when I was a girl that she was the most beautiful woman I had ever seen," recalled one of Lasker's schoolmates. "She had that cameo loveliness, that expression. Deep brown eyes, and a beautiful figure, and was very stylish."[7] On Saturday mornings, the family walked to the local synagogue in their best outfits, herded along by Nettie. Mortified by her husband's lack of attention to his dress, Nettie compensated by making sure that the rest of the family was immaculately turned out.

Through the florid hand of a ghostwriter in the 1930s, Lasker later recalled these outings as among the worst memories from his childhood. As they paraded down the street in their Saturday finery, they drew jeers and taunts—including the racial insult of "sheenie"—from their schoolmates:

> We wore Eton collars; sensitive, quiet Edward, three years my senior, had a watch in his breast pocket, and the chain of gold which advertised this fact seemed to me a kind of badge he wore as my father's first born. Our flaring bow ties were silken plaids. Truculent, round-headed Harry, who had come into the world two years after me, had his arms immersed in hand-made lace to the elbows of his jacket, although not of his free will. The vamps of his shoes were of patent leather; the rest of the uppers were the natural shade of kid. My suit had tight little pants that ended gracelessly at the knees. On our heads we wore bowler hats, an indictable offense in the sight of other boys, I guess, but the high crime was what we carried in our hands, silver mounted walking sticks. We would have been better off with baseball bats . . . [8]

On every day but Saturday, the Lasker children mixed easily with the youth of Galveston, but Lasker later said that this weekly encounter with intolerance taught him to "live without having intolerance to any human being in the world."[9]

⸺⸻◦⟨◉⟩◦⸻⸺

Albert's childhood was rife with contradictions both subtle and pronounced. In the local business community, his father's status commanded respect, but the family's religion kept them at the margins of society. Life at home also carried contradictions; while the family was well off financially, at least in the early years of Lasker's's life, the children were not always happy. John Gunther, Lasker's friend and biographer, condemned Morris as a "complete tyrant, a dictator," and claimed that neither Morris nor Nettie ever gave Albert the unconditional love that he craved.[10] Through his early adulthood, Albert struggled to live up to his father's expectations. As a child, though, he feared his father, and lied to him to avoid confrontations.

Morris first beat Albert when he was about nine. The boy was spending all his afternoons at the building site for his family's new home—the grand manse on Broadway and 18th.[11] Albert would fetch and carry when he could, and talk with the workmen. One summer afternoon, when the crew had completed the framing-in of the roof, they took Albert aside and explained solemnly that it was a Texas tradition that the builders be treated to a barrel of beer when they reached this milestone. Albert rushed home to convey this news to his father, who immediately arranged to have a keg delivered to the construction site. When Albert reappeared there shortly thereafter, he was greeted as a hero. As the workmen gathered around the keg, one of them handed Albert a mug, and told him to help himself. An hour later, thoroughly drunk, the boy stumbled home. Even through his first-ever alcoholic haze, he resolved that he would not breathe a word to his mother about what had happened.

But Nettie saw immediately that something was wrong with her slurring and staggering little boy. In a panic, she summoned their next-door neighbor, a physician. Albert later recalled what happened next:

> I can hear my mother frantically telling the doctor that I must have had sunstroke or something had gone wrong with the brain. The old doctor came over to me, smelled my breath, and said, "Has anyone given this child liquor?" And then my mother remembered the [keg] of beer, and my father came home and he gave me a tremendous licking, and he made me do something that he never did . . . before, or after. He made me eat for a whole day in the kitchen where the negro servants ate.[12]

The punishment rankled. Even at that tender age, Albert had a keen sense of justice, and he felt that his severe "licking" and subsequent humiliation were unfair.

Thus began a cycle of pranks, lies, and punishments that came to define Lasker's relationship with his father. When the *Galveston Free Press* got into financial trouble—apparently, its twelve-year-old publisher incurred a printing bill he couldn't pay—he led the printer to believe that his father would cover all of his obligations. When asked by Morris if he had made such a representation to the printer, Albert lied. The truth came out, and Albert got another "licking" in the attic.

The family's privileged lifestyle was threatened, quite suddenly, by the Panic of 1893. Across the country, entrepreneurs were crushed by the economic upheaval, so Morris's story is unusual only in its details. He had decided to go into real estate, founding the Lasker Real Estate Company in 1880. Seeing great potential in central Texas and the Panhandle, he went to London in 1888 to solicit partners in an ambitious development venture. A London banker bought Morris's pitch, and loaned him $250,000: a huge sum, which he invested in San Angelo—a brand-new town some four hundred miles northwest of Galveston—as well as in a Houston subdivision.[13]

Then disaster struck. The mighty Reading Railroad failed, sparking a collapse of other railroads and banks across the United States. The panic quickly spread across the Atlantic, hitting banks in London especially hard. Texas's all-important cotton crop became almost worthless as mills in England and the United States locked their doors. All across cotton country, land values collapsed.

By this time, Morris had interests in flour mills and other commercial properties throughout Texas, and he had placed mortgages on all of these properties to pay for his development projects. He was severely overleveraged, and cash was short. Rather than force his family to live in reduced circumstances, Morris sent his wife and younger children to Germany for a year. By this time, Morris's oldest son, Edward, was away at school in North Carolina, so only Albert remained at home in Galveston with his father.

It was a bad arrangement, with surreal consequences for Albert. While he slept, or pretended to sleep, his father would stealthily enter his bedroom and pace. Albert recalled: "I would see a wraith-like, nightgowned figure. It would be my father, sleepless from worry . . . Sometimes for hours I would be aware of the pat, pat, pat of his bare feet pacing the room. Sometimes I would become wide-awake from more disturbing sounds. Behind him he would smack the palm of one hand against the hairy back of the other, then re-clench them, and groan."

If Albert gave any hint that he was awake, his father would launch into an obsessive rehashing of the chain of disasters that had led to this nightmare: "If I sat up, he would talk to me. He was a lion at bay, bewildered by misfortunes that threatened to be overwhelming. What caused him anguish was no ordinary fear of losing money. All his dreams, all his midnight terrors, were caused by the prospect of being unable to meet his business obligations. To him, a debt you could not pay was in a class with murder."[14]

Albert was both terrified and fascinated. He hungered for more attention from his father, "for some little show of his appreciation of what stirred inside of me." Now he found himself in the role of confidante and wished he could escape it. On the rare occasions that Morris was able to sleep, he was beset by dark dreams. During the night, Albert could hear his sleeping father's fingernails raking through the rug next to his bed. Within a few months, Morris had clawed his way through the rug's thick fibers and laid bare a patch of flooring.

Was this simply the anguish of a merchant facing ruin, or was Morris suffering through the kind of affective disorder that had plagued his brother, and soon would afflict his son? Some of Morris's symptoms—the insomnia, the obsessiveness, the intermittent inability to take action, the inclination to simplify his life through a self-imposed solitude—hint at the kind of emotional distress that has surfaced across the Lasker generations.

Gradually, Morris turned his business affairs around and regained his financial and emotional footing, thanks largely to the general economic recovery. For Albert, however, the memory of those sleepless Gulf nights never fully receded: "I received the full impact of the panic as a lesson. Throughout my business life, I never borrowed; I never asked a living soul to lend to me on the premise that I perceived some way of making money."[15]

At the same time, Morris's travails had a nearer-term impact: they made Albert all the more impatient to make his own way in life.

In 1892, Albert Lasker entered high school. Ball High School, founded in 1884 through a $50,000 bequest from Galveston businessman George Ball, was the first public high school in Texas. It was an impressive structure, with a central domed core flanked by two Italianate wings. The course of study was even more impressive for that time: English, history, algebra, arithmetic, economics, geography, Latin, civil government, trigonometry, physics, political economy, chemistry, philosophy, and physiology.[16]

Lasker, however, was too restless to do well in high school. "School is too slow for a mind like that," his childhood friend Ann Austin later observed.[17] Lasker recalled that he was "bored to death" by the teachers and found most of his classwork either irrelevant or too easy to take seriously.[18] He took the economics course during his second year; it was taught by the grammar teacher, a "lovely old lady" who had been teaching in the Galveston schools for a quarter of a century. Her ignorance of economics was "colossal," recalled Lasker—who found that he had a natural bent for the subject—and he soon knew more about the dismal science than she did. After the first class, he took his textbook home and read it from cover to cover in one night, quickly absorbing all the main lessons.

In other subjects, such as Latin, Lasker proved a far less gifted student. He became (as he later recalled) "weaker and weaker" in school. He developed an addiction to dime novels. He passed his classes only with the help of "ponies"—contraband copies of tests that were passed from student to student—or through the application of his relentless charm.

Although neither an athlete nor a stellar student, Lasker exhibited a drive and appeal that won others over to his causes—and he almost always had a cause to promote. For example, with the encouragement of his principal, Lasker organized and edited the *B.H.S. Reporter*, a school magazine that was first published in April 1893. The magazine, recalled a childhood friend, required advertising support from downtown merchants, and the hunt for ads earned Lasker special privileges: "The one picture that stands out today [is that] after we got the little magazine started, [Albert was] darting out first thing in the morning after these ads, with this great bundle of stuff under his arms . . . And we all envied him because he was allowed to run the streets while we had to study."[19]

Because he was younger and smaller than most of the children he went to school with, he needed to have people meet him on his own terms. "Some of the boys were more than twice my size," he later commented. "Consequently, playing with them meant that I got knocked about and they had the fun. I did not like the percentage." He had to live by his wits, pick his battles, and be assertive. This did not always come easily to him. "My forwardness," he concluded later, "came from the fact that I have been shy all my life."

"With me," Lasker once wrote, "everything always had to be dramatic. I don't mean that it had to be . . . distorted, but all my life I have believ[ed] there is drama in everything and that the fun of life, or the fullness of life, is to find where that drama is."[20] When he told a story, he wanted that story to be spellbinding. It was not enough that it be funny; it had to be *hilarious*. It couldn't be merely interesting, but *thrilling*. It couldn't be just touching; it had to be *deeply moving*. Little stories got bigger and gained momentum.

It's not surprising, then, that his stories of his Galveston childhood became more and more colorful over the years. One such story involved the legendary African American fighter, Jack Johnson, who was born two years before Lasker and grew up in Galveston. From the vantage point of more than a century later, it's unclear how, or even if, Lasker knew Johnson. One story suggests that Johnson's mother, Tina, took in washing for the Laskers.[21] Another asserts that Johnson worked as a custodian for the Galveston Athletic Club, of which Lasker supposedly served as secretary.

As Lasker told the story in later years, he had arranged for an out-of-town heavyweight to come to Galveston and fight a local favorite as a fundraiser for the club. The club's boosters, including Lasker, sold out the house for the night of the fight, only to discover that their local hero had panicked at the sight of the formidable out-of-towner and skipped town. Lasker said he persuaded Johnson to put down his broom and put on a pair of gloves, step into the ring—for the first time in his life—and go several rounds with the champ.[22]

Other accounts are more detailed, and more obviously inaccurate. One has Lasker inviting veteran boxer Joe Choynski to town to fight a local pugilist whom Lasker had backed with his own money. Supposedly, Lasker persuaded Johnson—who in this version of the story had worked for Lasker's uncle—to go four rounds with Choynski, thereby saving Lasker's investment and launching his own boxing career.[23]

There isn't much truth in any of these stories. According to Johnson's biographer, the future world champion did work in a gym and did fight Joe Choynski—in 1901, three years after Lasker had left Galveston for good. Johnson carved out his early boxing career with little or no help from Lasker—or anyone else, for that matter. He fought a tough, 235-pound out-of-towner named Bob Thompson in the summer of 1895—when Lasker was fifteen—making it through four rounds, but he did so in response to Thompson's open challenge: *$25 to anyone who can go four founds with me.*[24]

Lasker served as editor of his school magazine for only a semester or so before handing it off to another classmate. By that time, he had set his sights on a bigger prize—the *Galveston Daily News*, the region's primary newspaper— to which he found himself inexorably drawn:

> I have forgotten what excuse I had for my first invasion of the editorial department of the Galveston News; perhaps I went there to seek advice about my own small paper, possibly I carried there an announcement of some high school activity for which I was responsible. But I shall never forget my sensitive alertness, my admiration for everything in that elongated room. If only I might justify my continued presence there, I felt that I'd have nothing more to ask in life . . . I yielded every day to my desire to mount the iron staircase into that

Heaven. I would sneak up there and then hang around for hours, as wistful, as eager as a stray dog.[25]

One night, Lasker saw his chance to break into heaven. The city editor, G. Herbert Brown, was a grumpy character who tolerated Lasker because he was flattered by the boy's unqualified admiration. On the night in question, Brown complained that he had to review a play, and this would prevent him from going to a party. Lasker jumped at the opening, suggesting that he cover the play in Brown's stead. Brown agreed, and Lasker's career as a theater critic began that night.

From there, he gradually built up his responsibilities at the paper—first covering all local theatrical events, then reporting on the local baseball team, and then collecting testimonials for patent medicines produced by the Peruna Company. Peruna wanted testimonials from people "in all walks of life" in Galveston, and was willing to pay $5 for each.[26] This was grand money for a high school student, and it was money that Lasker now badly needed. Hanging around with older reporters, Lasker had found that he was expected to "stand treat" at the local bars for his senior colleagues.

After barely graduating from high school in 1896, Albert went to work for his father.[27] He quickly improvised a kind of shorthand that allowed him to serve as Morris's private secretary. He also picked up some rudimentary accounting skills and got a feel for how money flowed in and out of his father's complex enterprises. But his heart remained in newspapering. At the end of the workday at his father's office, he would escape to the offices of the *News*, picking up stray assignments. He boasted that he was the "third reporter" at the *News*, neglecting to say that the paper only *had* three reporters.

Lasker's first scoop—a story that, as he told it, cemented his position with the *News* and seemed an augury of a brilliant reporting career—came about through serendipity. The Brotherhood of Locomotive Fireman, a national union, was holding its biennial convention in Galveston in September 1896. Early in the conference, statements were made that impugned the honesty of union leader Eugene V. Debs. Debs—for twelve years the secretary and treasurer of the Brotherhood—had broken with the union in 1892, and gone on to found the American Railway Union. He became well known on the national stage when he was imprisoned for six months for his part in the railroad strikes of 1894.[28] When an Associated Press dispatch detailing the allegations against Debs reached him at his home in Indiana, he immediately set out for the convention to clear his name, arriving in Galveston on Friday evening, September 18, 1896.[29]

The two leading Galveston newspapers, the *News* and the *Tribune*, resolved to scoop each other by landing a first-person interview with Debs— but Debs wasn't talking. Because he considered his differences with the Brotherhood a private matter, he dodged the press.

As Lasker liked to tell the story, he discovered that Debs was staying at a boardinghouse only three blocks from the Lasker mansion, and just across the street from the synagogue that the Laskers attended. He says he went to the Western Union telegraph office and badgered a friend there into loaning him a messenger's coat and hat.[30] Then he headed down the street to the boardinghouse. Not daring to wear the borrowed uniform in broad daylight, Lasker hid in the synagogue until dusk. Then he donned the hat and coat, ran across the street, and began ringing the bell vigorously.

A man finally answered, and asked Lasker his business. "I have a telegram for delivery to Mr. Eugene V. Debs," Lasker shouted.[31]

"Give it to me," the man replied, blocking the doorway, "and I'll give you a receipt."

But Lasker kept insisting that his instructions were to give it only to *Mr. Eugene V. Debs himself*. As Lasker had hoped, Debs himself finally appeared in the hallway and accepted the telegram. Debs opened it, and read:

> *I am not a messenger boy. I am a young newspaper reporter. You have to give a first interview to somebody. Why don't you give it to me? It will start me on my career.—Albert Lasker.[32]*

Debs chuckled, invited Lasker inside, and made a short statement on the spot. It was front-page news, Lasker later said, adding that he made hundreds of dollars as his story was picked up by newspapers around the country. He said the *New York Sun* even offered him a job on the basis of on this journalistic coup.

What really happened?

Assuming that the nonbylined article printed on page 8 of the Sunday paper was by Lasker, the sixteen-year-old stringer (in the story, "The News man") knocked on the door of the rooming house in midafternoon and asked to see Debs. A young African American woman, a servant at the house, claimed to know nothing about anyone named Debs. Lasker then circled the building several times "without making any discoveries." He befriended two delegates to the convention, who stayed to talk with him. About half an hour later, the owner of the rooming house arrived, and Lasker asked him to take his card in to Debs. A few minutes later, the owner reemerged and invited Lasker and his two new acquaintances in to meet with the "great leader":

> They were ushered into a small room opening upon the front gallery. It was twilight, the shutters were closed, and the interior had a very uncertain and ghostly appearance . . .
>
> From what the reporter could discern in the darkness Mr. Debs is a man about six feet tall, holds himself erect and is well knit. He is clean shaven and bald headed. He was attired in light brown garments. His face, from his full forehead down, is full of intelligence, but throughout the interview Mr. Debs seemed ill at ease and kept his lips parted in a nervous smile the whole while.

The labor leader declined to say why he had come to town but pointed out that he had attended all but one or two of the firemen's past conventions. His business in Galveston was purely of a "personal nature," and his conversations with the firemen's union, if any, would be kept private.

"This ended the interview," Lasker wrote, "and the reporter was ushered out."

One more anecdote, also involving journalism of a sort: as Lasker told the story, he had the job of reviewing the opening-night performance of James A. Herne's *Shore Acres* at the Galveston Opera House. He had already seen the play several times, and tonight he had better places to be: on a date with a young woman in Houston. So Lasker wrote up his review before he left, arranged to have it dropped off at the newspaper offices at the appropriate time, and was on his way to Houston well before the curtain went up on *Shore Acres*. The review was printed the next morning.

Lasker claimed the deception would have gone off without a hitch except for one small detail: just before the curtain rose on *Shore Acres* (as Lasker told the story) the Opera House burned to the ground. Lasker said he didn't even bother to go back to the *News* to pick up his paycheck. Instead, he skipped town—heading first to New Orleans, and then to Dallas, to pursue a career in newspapers.

There are two problems with this account. "As a matter of fact," Lasker's biographer wrote, "this experience, or experiences closely similar to it, are a legend in the newspaper business."[33] But it didn't happen to Lasker. There was no Galveston theater fire in the 1890s. The Tremont Theatre—long Galveston's preeminent venue—closed in 1895, a year after the opulent Grand Opera House opened on Postoffice Street.[34] The Grand is still in business today. James Hernes's *Shore Acres* was performed, without incident, at the Grand on February 11 and 12, 1894.[35]

It is also impossible to conceive of Morris Lasker letting his son escape to degenerate New Orleans.

Lasker did have one professional interlude during his Galveston years that was both satisfying and portentous. In 1896, at the age of sixteen, he worked on Republican Robert B. Hawley's congressional campaign.

Hawley, whom Lasker described as "the handsomest man I ever saw in my life," was a wealthy Galveston sugar manufacturer and a close friend of Morris Lasker.[36] From a political standpoint, the two made an unlikely pair: Hawley the ardent Republican and Morris the lifelong Democrat; Hawley a protectionist and Morris a proponent of free trade. But in the public debate over the gold standard—a divisive issue in the election of 1896—the two men found common ground. Morris voted for Hawley—the first and last Republican he ever supported.

Early in the campaign, Hawley approached G. Herbert Brown at the *News* and asked if the city desk editor would recommend someone who could travel with him and report on his speeches. Brown suggested Albert, and Morris (somewhat surprisingly) agreed to the proposition. At least once a week, Hawley would hit the road for the outer reaches of the district, and Albert would go with him, reporting on the impromptu talks that Hawley gave in the back country, mostly in rural grocery stores.

Hawley evidently had a unique appeal: he was the first Republican elected to Congress from Texas, and he would remain the only Texas Republican elected to Congress for another quarter century. As a consequence of traveling with Hawley, Albert joined the Republican Party, of which he would remain a member until late in his life.

When Hawley won the election, he offered Albert a job in Washington. Morris refused to let him go, feeling that his son was too young to accept a position so far from home. Albert had to return to his dreary life in his father's office. For Albert, it was like going back to jail. He wrote letters, did office chores, and ran errands, all of which he considered "degrading."

If it were up to him, of course, he would have continued his forays into the world of journalism. "Every urge in me," he recalled decades later, "was to be a reporter."[37] But Morris strongly disapproved of journalists and journalism, convinced that they would lead Albert into a life of drunkenness and debauchery.[38] There was ample evidence close at hand to support his contention: several of the reporters in Galveston had started their careers in prestigious posts such as New York City, and had gradually drunk their way down. "They drifted into smaller and smaller towns as they became more derelict," one of Lasker's close friends observed, "and about the last place these brilliant men got was Galveston."[39]

In desperation, Albert—barely eighteen years old—announced in the spring of 1898 that he was going to enlist in the Army to fight in the war that had just broken out with Spain. Morris seems to have ridiculed the notion. Albert soon gave up on the idea of enlisting, but remained determined to escape from his father, from his office, from Galveston. He found himself in increasingly open rebellion against a powerful authority figure, and he wanted to prove himself somewhere where he wouldn't be in Morris's shadow.

Morris finally came up with a solution that was acceptable to them both. Years earlier, he had been instrumental in helping a Chicago advertising agency, Lord & Thomas, out of a difficult situation involving a major local debt to the agency. Daniel Lord, who had traveled to Galveston to protect his agency's interests, was both relieved and grateful. He promised Lasker that if he could ever return the favor, he would.

Now, full of concern about his son's future and determined to keep him out of the newspaper business, Morris remembered that promise. He had only a vague understanding of what the advertising business was, but he guessed that it had to be better than journalism. He bargained hard with his son: "You go and try that," he insisted, "and if that doesn't work, I'll give you my blessing to go into reporting."[40]

Out of devotion to his father, Albert agreed. "He didn't know," he would later say, "what a hurt it was to me." From hanging out with the hard-drinking crew in the newsroom, Albert had learned to despise the business side of the shop. "To ask a reporter to become an advertising man was as if a father had asked a daughter to enter a life of shame! I thought, 'My father doesn't know what he's asking of me, but I'll do this. I'll go for a few weeks.'"[41]

Chapter Three

Success in Chicago

ALBERT LASKER arrived in Chicago on May 30, 1898, with $75 in his pocket—the money his father had given him to launch his new life.[1] May 30 was Decoration Day (now called Memorial Day), and to a young man from a striving but still modest Southwestern city, the boisterous streets of Chicago—lined by soaring buildings festooned at street level with flags and bunting—were an astonishing and confounding spectacle. As he elbowed his way down Wabash Avenue to the offices of Lord & Thomas, Lasker wondered if the circus was in town.[2] When he arrived at the agency, he found the doors locked for the Monday holiday.

Still, there was much to impress him in the neighborhood. The Trude Building, home to Lord & Thomas, was located on the southwest corner of North Wabash Avenue and East Randolph Street. Most of the rest of the large city block to the immediate southwest was occupied by Marshall Field's magnificent department store, then growing into one of the largest and most important businesses in the Midwest.

A soaring sixteen stories tall, the Trude Building was owned by Alfred S. Trude, Chicago's leading criminal lawyer, who maintained his offices there. So did an organization called the Social Democracy of America, whose recently named chairman was Eugene Debs—the very man who had given Lasker his first Galveston newspaper scoop less than two years earlier. Another tenant was the Chicago Business College, which enrolled several hundred students each year.

Towering skyscrapers, sidewalks packed with prosperous-looking crowds, the elevated railway clattering by on Wabash, the smell of money and commerce in the air even on a national holiday—this was nothing like provincial Galveston.

By the time Albert Lasker began exploring his newly adopted city, almost three decades had passed since the terrible fire of October 1871, which had burned 2,124 acres of the city's center.[3] In that conflagration, hundreds of people had been burned to death or asphyxiated. Some 17,450 homes had been destroyed, and destruction of property totaled more than $200 million. In the wake of the fire, stunned local leaders looked to New England and the East Coast (where many transplanted Chicagoans had come from) for the capital needed to rebuild. Their exaggerated claims about Chicago's magnificent prospects—yarns that began to be spun while the embers of the ruined business district still smoldered—reinforced the city's reputation for unabashed boosterism and first earned it an unflattering nickname: the Windy City.

And yet, Chicago *was* an important economic engine—for the Midwest, and for the nation—with seemingly unlimited prospects. Perched at the southwestern tip of Lake Michigan (and, by extension, the vast inland waterway of the Great Lakes) and home to one of the largest and most active rail hubs in the country, Chicago was one of the nation's most important transportation centers. Thanks to the railroads, thousands of prairie towns supplied raw materials to Chicago's factories and also served as a ready market for the city's manufactured goods.[4]

Following the great fire, Chicago had reestablished itself as a magnet for immigrants. Some of those newcomers were Easterners who saw more opportunity in a wide-open "frontier" city than in settled cities like Boston, New York, and Philadelphia (the nation's "second city" until overtaken by Chicago in the census of 1890). Others arrived on trains from those small towns on the prairie, desperate to escape from the drudgery and boredom of life on the farm. Still others poured in from the crowded cities of Europe, taking mostly low-paying jobs in the mills and malodorous stockyards. (As early as 1870, Chicago had the highest percentage of immigrants—48 percent—of any place in North America.[5]) Chicago became a city of newcomers, homesick and ambitious, eager to get on with their new lives.

This surfeit of immigrant labor, compounded by the Panic of 1873, drove down wages and touched off the first of the riots that would punctuate Chicago's history for the next quarter-century. A rebellion by socialists in response to railroad wage cuts in 1877 was brutally suppressed by the police. Bombs were set off in train stations and on the front steps of homes of several judges in January 1886; the following month, workers called a strike against the McCormick reaper factory. Three months later, a large rally supporting striking workers in the downtown Haymarket area came to a bloody end when a Nihilist bomb killed seven police officers and injured another sixty bystanders. Police opened fire on the crowd and killed a number of the protesters.

The terrified downtown business community—not convinced that the city's police force could protect them and their property—offered six hundred acres of prime Highland real estate to the federal government to establish a permanent military presence there. Washington agreed, and Fort Sheridan was hurriedly constructed. The next time the city erupted in protest—in the spring and summer of 1894, when factory workers went on strike against railroad-car manufacturer George Pullman—federal troops descended on the city and helped quash the rebellion. Eugene Debs, the head of the American Railways Union, was thrown into jail.[6]

Throughout the 1880s and into the 1890s, Chicagoans were publicly proud of their democratic, antipatrician traditions—and privately embarrassed about their city's reputation for boorishness and provincialism. Theirs was, in the words of novelist Henry B. Fuller, "the only great city in the world to which all its great citizens have come for the avowed purpose of making money."[7] In *Letters from a Self-Made Merchant to His Son*, one of author George Horace Lorimer's fictional characters proclaims, "We don't have much use for poetry in Chicago, except in streetcar ads."[8] Both assertions were uncomfortably close to the truth. The plutocrats who built their grand homes on Prairie Avenue hungered for financial success and little else; when they aspired to sophistication, they were mocked by their eastern cousins.

Chicago aggressively pursued the World's Columbian Exposition—the World's Fair—of 1893 in part to prove to the world that it was a world-class metropolis. The assertion was greeted with a mixture of scorn and indifference in places like New York. Charles A. Dana, editor of the *New York Sun*, suggested that New Yorkers should pay no attention to the "nonsensical claims of that windy city." Ward McAllister, the self-appointed arbiter of New York society and social mentor of Mrs. William Astor—grande dame of that society—contributed a series of columns to the *New York World* giving tips to Chicagoans about how to throw a proper party. It would be, McAllister suggested, a difficult climb for most of the Midwestern poseurs, who should not:

> . . . *pretend to rival the East and Old World in matters of refinement. Their growth has been too rapid for them to acquire both wealth and culture . . . The*

leaders of society are the successful Stock Yards magnates, Cottolene [a brand of lard shortening] manufacturers, Chicago gas trust speculators and dry goods princes. These gentlemen are undoubtedly great in business but perhaps in some cases unfamiliar with the niceties of life and difficult points of etiquette which constitute the society man or woman.[9]

The World's Fair, which officially opened on May 1, 1893, proved a smashing success, drawing some 27.5 million visitors. It was visually distinguished by an invention by Pittsburgh bridge-builder George Ferris: a 260-foot-high vertical steel wheel that accommodated sixty people in thirty-six cars, and rotated every ten minutes to give its riders a breathtaking view of the city. The fair was architecturally bold, unabashedly commercial, and larger than life: the Manufacturers Building, which displayed manufactured goods, was the largest building in the world at that time.

Slowly, Chicago was coming into its own. Architects John Wellborn Root and Daniel H. Burnham figured out how to anchor "rafts" of steel rails and concrete in the muck that underlay most of the city and perfected the art of steel-beam construction; these advances allowed for the design and construction of ever-taller buildings downtown. Their twenty-two-story Masonic Temple at the corner of Randolph and State, completed in 1891, was briefly the tallest building in the world.

For the first time, a community of local artists and writers began to emerge and flourish in Chicago. In 1898, for example, a forty-two-year-old author named L. Frank Baum printed in his own workshop a book of verse in a limited edition of ninety-nine copies. The following year, he published a collection of nursery rhymes entitled *Father Goose*, illustrated by William Wallace Denslow. *Father Goose* was the most popular children's book of 1899, selling an astounding 175,000 copies, and its success led to another collaboration between author and illustrator, who worked together in Denslow's studio in the Fine Arts Building, six blocks south of the Trude Building. In 1900, they published the result of that joint effort: *The Wonderful Wizard of Oz*.[10]

With the city's growing success, of course, came excess. Chicago was known internationally as a "shock city," likely to present rude surprises to the unwary traveler. To a disproportionate degree, it was populated by rootless and unmarried men.[11] Not surprisingly, a robust red-light district—the Levee—sprang up, with hundreds of brothels, pawnshops, dance halls, and saloons crowded into a few square blocks. In *Sister Carrie*, Theodore Dreiser depicted the life of a young country girl corrupted by Chicago's evil ways, and in *Chicago,* Carl Sandberg famously wrote that "They tell me you are wicked and I believe them, for I/have seen your painted women under the gas lamps/luring the farm boys."[12]

Its city government, too, was famously corrupt. One alderman declared that only three of the sixty-eight members of his board weren't "ready and willing to steal a hot stove." He was forced by his colleagues to issue a public retraction, but a subsequent study by the Civic Federation concluded that in fact, fifty-seven of the sixty-eight aldermen were demonstrably engaged in graft. Ambrose Thomas—Albert Lasker's future employer—served briefly on the city's Board of Assessors but then quit, telling a newspaper reporter that "the present system is rotten to the core and should be changed . . . this will continue until the whole system is radically changed and put on a good businesslike footing."[13]

Amid the boosterism and the relentless striving, concerns were starting to be raised about the costs of the city's rapid industrialization. A *Chicago Tribune* special report focused on one particularly distressing aspect of life in the city:

> *Filthy streets, dirt-imbued water, and sickening Stock-Yards odors are not the only uncorrected municipal evils the people of Chicago are enduring with what patience they have left under the present administration. There is the smoke.*
>
> *From hundreds of chimneys in the downtown district, columns of soot-laden fumes rise all day long. The sun is shut out of the streets by the clouds. The lungs of the people are filled with the tiny black flakes. The clothing and faces and hands are soiled, and the fabrics on sale in the marts are damaged if not ruined.*[14]

One of the several dozen buildings singled out for criticism in the article was the Trude Building, which although "not so generous in its delivery of smoke" as some other prime offenders, "continually smudges the vicinity with soot and smoke." Meatpacking magnate-turned-banker Samuel W. Allerton, interviewed for the story, suggested that Chicago had to "take off its coat and get down to work, like a businessman, or we are going to lose." The noxious odors and smoke, he predicted, would deter people from moving to Chicago, and drive away people who were there already.

Meanwhile, though, Chicago's near-term prospects continued to allure. The real estate market was rebounding, buoyed by U.S. naval victories against Spain and the recent announcement that the Schlesinger & Mayer department store was planning to build a million-dollar marble-faced edifice at State and Madison.[15] And perhaps most important of all, the wheat crop promised to be the best in years. The thirteen leading wheat-producing states produced 340 million bushels in 1897; this year, it looked as if they would produce more than 400 million bushels—enough, the *Tribune* noted approvingly, to pay the entire anticipated cost of the Spanish-American War.[16]

Albert Lasker, locked out of Lord & Thomas, wandered the streets that Decoration Day, and then went back to his boardinghouse. The next day, he returned to the agency's offices. His new employer occupied two floors of the Trude Building. Taking the elevator to the twelfth floor, Lasker stepped out onto a bare wooden floor awash in light from the walls of windows on three sides of the building. In front of him he saw a cashier's cage joined to a railing that ran all the way to the west wall, with a swing gate near the cage. A handsome man with iron gray hair and a silk cap sat at an oak desk next to this barrier. Lasker later learned that the man's name was Paxton, and that he (like Lasker) was being paid $10 a week.[17]

Cubicles ringed the floor, with partitions made of oak wainscoting about four feet high, with a horizontal band of frosted glass above the oak. In the corner were two offices about twice the size of the cubicles: the offices of Mr. Lord and Mr. Thomas. On the floor above was a small print shop and a large area housing floor-to-ceiling files, in which were stored copies of every major newspaper in America for the previous several months.[18]

Here on the twelfth floor, behind the railing, were several desks for "overflow"—human overflow—and it was toward one of these desks that Lasker was first steered. Paxton then escorted him to Daniel Lord's office. The co-owner of the agency had a large bald pate and luxuriant mutton-chop whiskers that framed a ready smile. He was a New Englander who had started in business in New York in 1868, then relocated to Chicago to work on a Presbyterian newspaper, the *Interior*, before launching his first advertising agency under the name "Lord, Brewster & Company." (Brewster departed sometime in the 1870s, and Ambrose Thomas took his place in 1881.)

Now, seventeen years later, Lord was responsible for the agency's finances, which in those days mainly meant keeping a watchful eye on clients to be sure they were on a solid enough financial footing to pay their next bill.[19] Thomas was in charge of day-to-day operations, so Lord escorted the new hire into Thomas's office.

"From the moment I saw him," Lasker later said of Thomas, "I loved him . . . He was a short-set man, [a] born horse trader, full of Yankee shrewdness and full of kindness. And still with the Yankee twang."[20] Born in 1849 in Lewiston, Maine, Thomas had relocated to Boston as a young man to work in the advertising department of the *Boston Traveler*. He moved on to the Evans & Lincoln agency in Boston, then launched his own agency, enjoying immediate success. But seeing more opportunity in the "Northwest," Thomas moved to Chicago in February 1881.

After introductions were over, Thomas told his young charge to spend a couple of days talking to people in the office to learn the business. Toward that end, he introduced Lasker to Elmer Bullis, who maintained the firm's directory of newspapers and magazines and wrote up estimates for clients, and Charles Touchlin, who was in charge of the agency's school accounts.

Both men happily shared their knowledge with Lasker. Touchlin even took his young protégé into his home and rented him a room. "The Touchlins had a little brick house on the South Side, at Sixty Second and Monroe; it seemed far in the country," Lasker later recalled. "Mrs. Touchlin was sweet, extremely pretty and graciously considerate of my comfort. I ate breakfasts and dinners with the Touchlins, paying $6 a week for board, lodging, and my laundry."[21] The importance of this warm embrace to Lasker—then on his first extended trip away from home, already suffering from overwhelming bouts of homesickness—can't be overstated.

Bullis, too, helped anchor the uprooted young man. The seasoned advertising veteran lived a few blocks north of the Touchlins, and on many occasions during Lasker's early months in Chicago, the three men gathered at the end of the day on the front stoop of Touchlin's house, talking shop, watching the passersby, and waiting for cooling breezes on warm summer evenings.[22]

No doubt they also talked about the evolution of advertising and the firm they worked for. The industry was still young, and it was evolving quickly. Advertising had once been the exclusive province of circuses and patent-medicine vendors, a tarnished legacy that contributed to its unsavory reputation. Gradually, though, a number of factors converged to make advertising a necessity—and therefore increasingly acceptable.

One factor was the flood of complicated and specialized manufactured goods that began pouring out of America's factories toward the end of the nineteenth century. The tonnage of raw steel produced in the United States increased from 4.4 million short tons in 1891 to 11.2 million in 1900; much of that steel went into a profusion of goods that needed new avenues of distribution.[23] Previously, regional markets were enough to sustain a shovel maker or even a carriage maker; now, though, producers of more expensive products needed broader markets to survive.[24]

Another factor was the development of a national transportation network—principally the railroads, which in the 1870s expanded their total trackage by an astounding 41,453 miles. The railroads' total ton-miles nearly doubled in the decade in which Albert Lasker reported for work: from 76,207 in 1890 to 141,597 in 1900.[25] Intracoastal shipping—port to port on the seacoasts and on the Great Lakes, the Mississippi, and other inland waterways—also prospered. (Great Lakes dry-bulk tonnage alone increased from 35,298 in 1900 to 80,015 in 1910.[26]) Other kinds of networks grew up alongside the transportation infrastructure: the census found 54,000 phones in the United States in 1880, 234,000 in 1890, and 1.4 million in 1900.[27]

Lagging notably far behind was the nation's road system, which consisted of only 154,000 miles of surfaced roads in 1904. Cars, trucks, and other self-propelled vehicles weren't yet a factor in commerce. By 1900, Chicago had issued only 189 permits for cars (90 electric-powered, 55 gasoline-powered, and 44 steam-powered). In a city of nearly 2 million people, ten women held driver's licenses.[28]

An army of intermediaries also arose to help distribute the flood of new manufactured goods: department stores, mail-order houses, and the like. Chicago was the epicenter of that activity—home not only to Marshall Field, but also to national catalog giants Montgomery Ward & Co. ($8.7 million in sales in 1900) and Sears, Roebuck and Co. ($10 million in sales in 1900). In 1900, Montgomery Ward built an impressive new headquarters at the intersection of Michigan and Madison, and by 1904, the company was mailing out more than 3 million copies of its six-hundred-page, four-pound catalog annually.

The final factor contributing to the rise of advertising—and, of course, made possible by that advertising—was the emergence of national magazines and newspapers. The circulation of daily newspapers in the United States jumped from 254,000 in 1860 to 2.2 million in 1900.[29] The circulation of the *Saturday Evening Post*—which began life as a newspaper and evolved in the late 1800s into one of the nation's leading magazines—grew from 90,000 in 1855 to 1 million in 1908, and 2 million by 1913. The *Ladies' Home Journal*, launched in 1883, attracted 25,000 subscribers in its first year; by 1893, it boasted 700,000 subscribers. The page of *Journal* advertising that commanded $200 in 1883 sold for $4,000 ten years later.[30]

As advertising became a necessity, a new trade arose to meet that need. The nation's first two agencies were both founded in 1842: one by a Philadelphian named Volney B. Palmer, and the other by a New Yorker named John Hooper. Both considered themselves "newspaper agents," rather than advertising agents, meaning that they worked for newspapers rather than the companies who advertised in them. The next seminal figure in the industry was an entrepreneur named George P. Rowell, who produced the first comprehensive directory of newspapers in the United States and cemented his reputation late in life by producing a charming volume of reflections on the early years of the industry.[31]

Rowell also earned a footnote in advertising history by turning down a job applicant named J. Walter Thompson, who—by assembling a stable of several dozen prestigious magazines under exclusive contract to him—built the biggest agency in New York. Other agencies in New York, including Charles Austin Bates's firm, Calkins & Holden, and the George Batten Newspaper Advertising Agency, competed for both local and national accounts. But by the end of the nineteenth century, the nation's leading advertising agency was indisputably the Philadelphia-based N. W. Ayer & Son. (In a deft marketing ploy, Francis Wayland Ayer, the agency's founder, named it for his father, thereby implying both continuity and a salutary family influence.[32]) Its total billings increased from $132,000 in 1877 to $1.4 million in 1900.[33] And again, this success reflected a huge and rising tide: In the second half of the nineteenth century, the total volume of advertising in the United States increased from $50 million to $500 million, and advertising expenditures grew from .7 percent to 3.2 percent of the gross national product.[34]

It was no coincidence that Daniel Lord and Ambrose Thomas both hailed from Maine; indeed, a number of other major advertising figures of the day did as well. Mail-order advertising had taken root there, largely owing to the outsized influence of a publisher in Augusta named E. C. Allen, whose magazines combined popular fiction and mail-order ads and were among the most widely circulated in the country in the 1880s.[35] Mail-order advertising reached a frenzied pitch toward the end of the century—about the same time that Lasker arrived at Lord & Thomas—driven largely by the roaring success of the patent medicine companies.[36]

As Lasker was soon to discover, Lord & Thomas—and indeed, most advertising firms in the late nineteenth and early twentieth centuries— served mainly as intermediaries between advertisers and publishers, and were little more than brokers of magazine and newspaper space, sometimes taking responsibility for the appearance and production of the ad. Early promotions for Lord & Thomas emphasized these limited roles. A Lord & Thomas display ad in the agency's 1892–1893 "Pocket Directory" of U.S. newspapers boasted of the agency's skill at producing ads with "proper display, typographically."[37] An 1895 advertisement for the firm stressed a sensible division of labor between agency and client: "If you employ us to prepare and place your advertising you will find it more profitable than taking up your own time with the details."[38] In his book *The Mirror Makers*, Stephen Fox tells the story of the time that Daniel Lord ventured to tell an advertiser how to improve his ad. "Young man," that client told Lord, "you may know a lot about advertising, but you know very little about the furniture business."[39]

Originally, the more successful advertising firms had spheres of influence within which they dominated their trade. J. Walter Thompson, for example, controlled space in the nation's leading women's magazines. Ayer controlled agricultural publications. Lord & Thomas's original niche was religious publications. These boundaries were somewhat permeable, of course; but an advertiser who believed that a product would sell well to a religious audience was likely in the 1880s to hire Lord & Thomas to broker the advertisement.

Gradually, advertising became a competitive free-for-all, with agencies focusing less on selling space and more on winning clients. When the Bissell Carpet Sweeper Company introduced its breakthrough cleaning device, for example, representatives from Thompson, Ayer, and Lord & Thomas traveled en masse to Bissell's headquarters in Grand Rapids, Michigan. There, as a group, they would meet with the appropriate executive—perhaps Melville Bissell himself—who would dictate the specifications for the ads he planned to place in the coming year. (He might even have the "cuts," or text and rudimentary artwork for the ads, on the table in front of him.) The agencies would then bid for the Bissell account. Whenever possible, they would steer ads toward the publications they controlled, on which they would receive the highest commission: 15 percent of the cost of the ad.

Even in this rough-and-tumble competitive environment, however, the winning advertising firm did little more than broker space in publications. Like its competitors, Lord & Thomas rarely wrote the copy for the ads it placed. "As a matter of fact," Lasker recalled, "the agencies at that time were painfully shy in accepting responsibility for creative work."[40]

Agencies such as the National Advertising Company and Ayer began providing copy to their customers in the late 1880s, and Ayer hired its first full-time copywriter in 1892. But copywriting at these and other leading agencies remained a distinctly secondary activity—well behind rustling up business.[41]

Lord & Thomas, certainly, remained "shy." When Lasker started working there, the agency's creative staff consisted of a graphic artist and a half-time writer who worked mornings for Lord & Thomas and afternoons for Montgomery Ward. Lasker was not much impressed by the writer. "We did Hannah & Hogg whiskey," he said, "and he got his pay mostly in sampling the whiskey."[42]

Much later in his life, Lasker liked to say that he became an advertiser because of a staggering gambling debt incurred early in his three-month probationary period at Lord & Thomas. He claimed that he was deep in debt to dangerous characters and had to borrow money from Ambrose Thomas to pay them off, effectively rendering him an indentured servant until he paid Thomas back.

This account of his fall from grace fudged a key detail. Lasker did indeed incur a large gambling debt—about nine months after he arrived at Lord & Thomas—and that misstep helped bind him to the firm. In the previous half-year, however, his departure for New York was delayed several times by spectacular successes in a trade that he found increasingly intriguing.

Lasker was only a few weeks into his apprenticeship when his first stroke of good fortune occurred. Lord & Thomas had received an order from Rubens & Marble, a local manufacturer of knit underwear for infants, for twenty-four lines of space in one of the magazines within the agency's sphere of influence. The clothing manufacturers included a check with their order. Under normal circumstances, the matter would have ended there. But Elmer Bullis—perhaps responding to Lasker's ambition and charm, or perhaps looking to give his young colleague some experience in the art of selling—suggested that Lasker go and talk to the head of Rubens & Marble to explore whether the company could be convinced to increase its advertising budget. This appeared to be a most unpromising gambit, but Lasker was grateful for the opportunity—and remained so for the rest of his life. Decades later, he would say that Bullis, "was the fellow who was interested in him, and watched for a chance and when a prospect came up . . . gave him his chance."[43]

And so Lasker headed over to the corner of Adams and Clark Streets. Rubens & Marble had been founded in 1890 by a Mr. Rubens, a German immigrant who had come up with a new design for a baby shirt that could be folded two different ways and buttoned in the back. At this first meeting, Rubens, a thin, graying gentleman with a thick German accent—Lasker likened him to a wasp[44]—posed a series of probing questions about the advertising business. Not satisfied with Lasker's answers, he complained aloud, "They think because this is a baby business, they have to send *children* over here!"[45]

But Lasker, himself not too far removed from Germans and Germany, repeated his entire pitch to Rubens—*in German.*[46] The crusty old clothes-maker was won over by the boyish salesman. Over dinner with Lasker that night, he increased his advertising budget to $800. This unexpected success "electrified" the office (Lasker's term) when he walked in with the order.

Another piece of luck soon came Lasker's way. A very junior representative from *Collier's Weekly* arrived one day at the office, looked around, and then walked over and introduced himself to Lasker. Lasker inferred that the young man was inexperienced, didn't want to expose his ignorance to the office graybeards, and preferred to deal with someone who looked even younger than he did. The young publisher's rep had been approached by a company interested in advertising liquor in Chicago, and needed someone to manage the account. With no effort, Lasker had landed another account.

It was these early successes that convinced Lasker to delay his move to New York. "I was quite a hero by this accident," Lasker later recalled, "and I was having fun."

<hr />

Ambrose Thomas took note of Lasker's unexpected talents. He began inviting him into his office for chats, and liked what he heard. When the three-month probationary period ended, Thomas asked Lasker to stay, and Lasker—influenced by the substantial raise that Thomas put on the table—readily agreed. Lasker was becoming quite attached to Thomas. This affection was mutual, even though Thomas was often taken aback by his young colleague's unconventional views and methods. When Morris Lasker came to visit his son in Chicago, some eighteen months after Albert began working at Lord & Thomas, Thomas told Morris that his son was "either a genius, or crazy."[47]

Thomas, therefore, was responsive when one of his associates, Charlie Stoddard, suggested that Lasker be given another opportunity. A Cincinnati-based manufacturer of liqueurs and cordials, Rheinstrom Brothers, was planning to spend a major sum—a princely $10,000!—on advertising. The high-powered New York agent Charles Austin Bates was meeting with the Rheinstroms in two days. Barring a miracle, Bates surely would get the business. Another Lord & Thomas representative had already met with the Rheinstroms but had failed to impress them. *Why not send Lasker down there*, Stoddard suggested, *and see if he has better luck?* The train trip would be free—a standing deal between Lord & Thomas and the railroads—and the potential reward was enormous. Finally, Stoddard pointed out, the fact that both Lasker and the Rheinstroms were Jewish might help.

Lasker found the idea of capitalizing on his Jewish heritage offensive. But there *was* another consideration: his younger brother Harry was traveling through Cincinnati at that time, on a layover between Virginia Military Institute and Galveston. The Rheinstrom pitch presented a free way to meet up with Harry, so Lasker hopped on the first sleeper to Cincinnati.

The Lasker brothers met for a very early breakfast the next morning. Albert was anxious about the task that lay ahead of him: "I remember, really, literally and figuratively shaking so my whole body was perspiration, my hands were clammy, every nerve of my body as if I had St. Vitus Dance—it couldn't have been tougher. It was hard for me to talk, because I then realized that I let them fool themselves that there was any chance, and here was I, a kid [who] didn't know anything about advertising. I felt I was going to disgrace myself."[48]

He made his way by streetcar to the Rheinstrom company headquarters on the Cincinnati riverfront. It was an imposing three-story brick building with big double doors. As Lasker entered, he noticed a man with a reddish mustache standing at the bookkeeper's counter, opening and sorting the mail. Lasker knew that he must be the firm's owner, and approached him.

When Rheinstrom barked out a gruff, "What do *you* want?" Lasker could only hand him a card mutely. Rheinstrom's response was immediate and fierce. "I wouldn't expect a young boy like you to have any sense and consideration, but your firm ought to. You have had a man here, I have told them

I am not interested, and here you come on a Monday morning before I have opened my mail and you want to talk to me about advertising? *Get out.*"[49]

Lasker fled to his hotel. There he talked the matter over with Harry, and formulated another plan: "I said, 'The fellow is a German, Harry . . . and he will go home and eat a good lunch, and I am going to take a chance that at two o'clock, he is going to leave to go back to his office after his nap. I am going to look at his home number.'"

A little before 2 p.m., Lasker phoned Rheinstrom and blurted out his revised pitch: "Don't hang up the telephone; you may be affecting the course of your whole life. I am the young man who came to see you from Lord & Thomas, I am not asking for an order, but I will lose my [place]—at least let me talk to you for a few minutes. Treat me as you want to treat your young son, or your young nephew."

Rheinstrom told Lasker to come back down to the office, no doubt intending to grant only a perfunctory interview to the nervous young man from Chicago. But what Rheinstrom didn't know was that, on his way back to the distillery, Lasker suddenly discovered that his fear had left him. He decided that he could represent Lord & Thomas as well as anybody, because at least as far as *he* could tell, nobody in his office really knew anything much about the business they were in: "So little was known about the principles of advertising [that] I had as good a right to talk about them as anyone."[50] Several hours later, Rheinstrom was sold.

Fireworks burst within him, Lasker wrote later. He had looked failure squarely in the eye and realized that he very much wanted to succeed at this new venture. He had to admit it: he was having fun, and the sums that he was now bringing into the office were beyond anything he might have imagined. "I was on the way to building up a clientele of $25,000 a year," he later recalled, "and that was enormous. That was *respectability.*"

Soon after agreeing to hire Lord & Thomas, Rheinstrom took Lasker into a back room to meet his brother Ike. Ike looked Lasker over, and asked if he was by any chance related to a *Morris* Lasker of Galveston, Texas. Rheinstrom Brothers was one of Morris's clients, and this connection, had it been revealed earlier, might have been every bit as persuasive as Lasker's four-hour pitch. But *that* kind of success "would have been bitter in my mouth," he later admitted.

Lasker had now firmly established himself as an advertising salesman at Lord & Thomas. But he never got over the fright he felt when meeting new clients. Long after he had earned a reputation as a pioneer and giant in the advertising field, he would shake with fear before that first meeting.

This was more than stage fright. Throughout his life, Lasker lived with a fear of getting called out as a humbug—of being discovered as unqualified for the task in front of him. Contemplating a job with the Shipping Board in the early 1920s, for example, Lasker confessed to "a feeling of deep inadequacies, a feeling that I was going to be very unhappy because I was untrained and inadequate, a feeling that I was a four-flusher attempting to do something that I knew I wasn't competent to do."[51]

Perhaps because of the enormous stress he was putting on himself, Lasker resumed the bad habits that he had picked up back in Galveston, including drinking with newspaper reporters. There are hints, too, that he kept company with an actress he had met in Galveston who occasionally performed in Chicago.

Weekend antics were a welcome, even necessary antidote to the increasingly demanding, high-stakes work that he did during the week. When he wasn't drinking with the newspaper crowd, he was gambling with his work colleagues; it was in fact Charles Touchlin who introduced Lasker to the Griddle Club and arranged for Lasker to become a member.

The Griddle, located on the top floor of an old four-story building, was a favorite gathering place. It was here, one evening, that Lasker met an affable man who invited him to join a poker game. Lasker had left the Touchlins' house that evening with $50 in his pocket. He sat down at a round table in the back room of the club, and was dealt in. The cards did not break his way, but he kept at it—and then kept at it some more. By the end of the evening, Lasker owed $500. It was a third of his annual salary, and more than many at Lord & Thomas earned in a year.

Lasker realized that he had been taken in by a card shark, but this excuse would not appease his father. Desperate to keep his secret from his family, Lasker approached Ambrose Thomas the next morning. He begged his employer to lend him the $500, saying that learning of the debt would "kill" his father.

Thomas's expression through much of this appeal was unpromising. He sat with his chin in his hand, eyes fixed on the ceiling.[52] Lasker, seeing his future collapsing in front of him, envisioning a much-dreaded return to

Galveston in disgrace, pulled out even more stops. "I will promise you this," Lasker went on. "I don't want any salary . . . I will go out on the road and I will work as no one ever worked for you. I will work so there can't *be* any temptations."[53]

Thomas declined Lasker's offer to work for free, keeping him at his recently increased salary of $30 per week.[54] The card shark was paid off.[55]

The misadventure at the Griddle Club proved to be a turning point. Lasker learned that he was *valuable*. He had escaped the long shadow of his father, and an exciting path was open to him. For this lesson, $500 was a modest price to pay.

Several months after the gambling incident, Lasker learned of a territory that was opening at the agency. Determined to work his way up—both to repay his debt more quickly and to satisfy his growing ambition—he applied for the job.

The territory comprised Indiana, Ohio, and Michigan. It had been the turf of William R. Emery, the salesman who had failed to impress the Rheinstrom Brothers in Cincinnati. Lasker asked Ambrose Thomas for the opportunity to "practice" on the sleepy accounts.[56] In fact, there wasn't much real risk in Lasker's proposition, given that Emery hadn't been particularly productive in recent years, so Thomas was inclined to grant Lasker's request. But the decision wasn't his alone: he had to convince Daniel Lord to go along with the plan. Lord told his partner that he was skeptical—Lasker was only nineteen years old, and looked even younger than his years. He also observed that Lasker needed some help with his wardrobe. Years later, Lasker told the story to his office staff: "Ambrose Thomas was tactful. By repeating some of Mr. Lord's points in opposition, he gave me valuable steering. The first thing I did when I left the office that day was to hustle to the tailoring establishment of H. M. Stephenson. I knew Marshall Field had his clothes made there, and that Wilton Lackaye, the actor, came from New York to have fittings. I asked for haste in the making of two blue suits of serge."[57]

Newly fitted out, Lasker was ready to conquer new lands. Near the top of his list was Kalamazoo, Michigan, where several food-processing companies looked like promising clients. Lasker headed to Kalamazoo armed not only with his extraordinary energy but also with a new feeling of calm determination: "That was *my* territory, do you see? I had this tremendous feeling of responsibility. It just fell on me like a mantle, and I grew to maturity on that

ride, and I have been mature ever since and have never been without responsibility. Mr. Thomas trusted me."[58]

Lasker felt a strong "presentiment," as he rode northward on the train,
that he was destined to remain with Lord & Thomas for a long time. His first
working day in Kalamazoo must have reinforced this conviction. His prede-
cessor, William Emery, had been working closely with several potential
clients and had built up substantial good will toward Lord & Thomas.
(Emery was, in Lasker's subsequent estimation, "a fine man, but he wasn't a
closer."[59]) Thanks to Emery's spadework, Lasker was able to sign a $3,000
contract with the Kalamazoo Pure Food Company on his first day in the
north woods—and he landed almost $50,000 of additional orders over the
next several months. The boyish salesman from Chicago quickly became (as
he later put it) "the talk of the line."

All of this was enormously gratifying, even intoxicating. But Lasker
understood better than anyone else that he had already harvested most of
the low-hanging fruit left behind by William Emery. Meanwhile, he was
beginning to suspect that advertising agencies, certainly including his own,
were leaving an enormous amount of money on the table.

Emboldened by his successes, Lasker pushed Ambrose Thomas to think
more broadly about the *creative* aspects of advertising. But Thomas and his
partner Lord were content to continue on as the middlemen they always had
been. "That was the line," Lasker later reflected. "They felt fine if they could
do good copy, but it never occurred to them that copy could make a tremendous difference . . . If you put your name on it, mentioned your goods, had a
pretty picture—that was advertising."[60]

Lasker pushed for a broader conception of advertising. In part, this was
self-interest. He realized that if he kept doing business the way Lord &
Thomas was accustomed to, he was trapped. "I quickly saw," he said, "that I
would get nowhere under the status quo, because it took so much of my
time to handle the business Lord & Thomas *already* had in the territory when
I took hold."[61] And much of that business was only marginally profitable. He
once spent an entire day driving fifteen miles in a sleigh to a school in Indiana
that had an advertising budget of $300 a year. Such an account would land a
10 percent commission for Lord & Thomas—thirty dollars, minus expenses.

Lasker felt sure that he could build the business, and boost Lord &
Thomas' commissions, if he could improve the agency's copywriting. Before

the year was out, therefore, Lasker asked Ambrose Thomas to put him in charge of a few accounts that were not making any money so he could practice copywriting. With little to lose, Thomas agreed.

Lasker teamed up with newspaperman Eugene Katz, whom he had met in Galveston and who had relocated to Chicago. Together, they made an unorthodox proposal to one of Lord & Thomas's clients: the Louisville, Kentucky–based Wilson Ear Drum Company. Wilson, which manufactured a primitive hearing aid out of paper cones, was then paying a 6 percent commission—well below the industry standard of 10 percent, and even further below the 15 percent that industry-leading N. W. Ayer almost always commanded. Lasker, determined to close these gaps, proposed that his firm write the copy and develop the artwork for future ads. If the new ads showed good results, the advertiser would then agree to pay a 15 percent commission.

Company owner George Wilson, agreed. Lord & Thomas's graphic artist—whom Lasker later said looked like the "deafest man you ever saw"— had a picture taken of himself cupping his hand to his ear. The headline read, "You Hear! When you use Wilson's Common Sense Ear Drums."

"Much to [George Wilson's] surprise and ours," Lasker later recalled, "it worked."[62] Wilson increased its monthly ad budget from $2,000 to $6,000, and—more important—agreed to pay the 15 percent commission that Lasker demanded. Instead of making $1,440 annually on the account, Lord & Thomas would now earn $10,800.[63]

From that point on, Lord & Thomas offered two tiers of service. Clients who wrote their own copy and wanted only space brokering would pay a 10 percent commission; clients who wanted their copy written by Lord & Thomas would pay 15 percent.[64]

Gradually, Lasker built up a cadre of six copywriters. Both Ambrose Thomas and Daniel Lord encouraged him in these experiments; on the other hand, they resolutely stayed away from the side of the business that eventually became known as "creative."[65] This hands-off stance gave Lasker room to operate, but it also put more pressure on him to resolve his uncertainty about the *substance* of advertising. What, exactly, was good advertising?

Lasker felt compelled to discover the essence of advertising. "If somebody had handed me the money to pay back the five hundred dollar debt," he said a half-century later, "I couldn't have quit. I had to find out what advertising was about."[66]

Chapter Four

Salesmanship in Print

SHORTLY AFTER arriving in Chicago, Albert Lasker wrote a letter to his father. He was worried, he confessed, because he couldn't resolve his fundamental confusion about the advertising business: "The great force of advertising has been shown to me in the short time I have been here. People are spending what to you and me are inconceivable sums. They are getting results, or they could not keep it up. Yet I haven't been able to find the man who could tell me what advertising is."[1]

Lord & Thomas's slogan was "Advertise Judiciously." But no one at the firm could explain exactly what that meant. "Well, spend your money carefully, in the right papers," his colleagues told him.[2] At the rival N. W. Ayer agency, the corresponding slogan was "Keeping Everlastingly at It Brings Success." Lasker sat down with a counterpart from Ayer one day, and grilled him on the meaning of *this* slogan:

> *"Now," I said, "here, let me ask you this. Supposing I start wrong and I keep everlastingly at it. Where is that going to get me?"*
>
> *"Well," he said, "what they meant was, keeping everlastingly at it* right *would achieve success."*
>
> *"Well," I said, "What is 'right' in advertising? Can't you define it for me?"*
>
> *"Why," he said, "keeping your name before the people."*
>
> *"Well, I said, "supposing I can't live that long. Supposing I go broke; that I can't keep my name before the people. There must be something else to this thing."*[3]

Lasker started scrutinizing all the ads in newspapers and magazines and on the new advertising phenomenon—billboards. Most of what he saw only puzzled him further, because there appeared to be no underlying theory. Advertisers seemed to have no plan. Lasker loved *ideas*, and his industry seemed bereft of them:

> *Well known advertisers were the Gold Dust Twins, that showed a picture of a couple of little cupids and said, "Let the Gold Dust Twins do your work." Another was a picture of a nice little girl, and it said, "How would you like to have a fairy in your home? Use Fairy Soap . . .*
>
> *Another was Armour's "Ham what Am." The Negro would say, "The ham what am—Armour's." And the next time you would see that ad, it would be an Italian, and he said, "The ham was ees—Armour's." The next time you saw him, he would be a German, and he said, "The ham vat iss—Armour's" . . .*
>
> *Well, that was what advertising was, do you see, keeping the name before the people. And of course, in the competition to keep it before the people, most of them got to kidding their own names—about the worst thing you can do.*
>
> *That was advertising: sloganizing.*[4]

Gradually, though, Lasker became aware of the work of a Chicago-based competitor: the Charles H. Fuller Company. Fuller had recently signed up breakfast-food maker C.W. Post, and the advertising that began to appear in support of Postum and Grape-Nuts struck Lasker as decidedly different from the vapidity of the Gold Dust Twins. Fuller wrote and ran ads that looked exactly like newspaper copy—in the same typeface as the newspaper—and told stories about happy users of the products in what Lasker called a "newsy" way.

Maybe, Lasker speculated, that's the answer: *Advertising is news.*

Then again, maybe it wasn't. Other departures in advertising also intrigued Lasker. A patent medicine firm in Racine, Wisconsin—Dr. Shoop's Family Medicines—was running an ad with a provocative headline: "What Tea-Drinking Does for Rheumatics." Every time he saw this ad, Lasker stopped and read it, even though he didn't use patent medicines, didn't have rheumatism, and didn't drink tea. Why was that concept so striking? It wasn't "newsy," exactly. So what was it?

One evening in May 1904, around 6:00 p.m., Lasker was in Ambrose Thomas's office discussing the business of the day. A messenger boy came into the office and handed Thomas a note. The older man scanned the note, chuckled, and tossed it across the desk to Lasker.

Written in a striking hand, the note read:

I am in the saloon downstairs. I can tell you what advertising is. I know you don't know. It will mean much to me to have you know what it is, and it will mean much to you. If you wish to know what advertising is, send the word "yes" down by the bell boy.—John E. Kennedy

Thomas dismissed the note as the work of a crank, and suggested that Lasker ignore it. But Lasker, intrigued, sent his response back downstairs: *Yes.*

He retreated to his office and awaited the arrival of his visitor. Within a few minutes, a man strode in looking every bit as striking as his handwriting—six feet tall, with piercing blue eyes and a heavy blond mustache. Kennedy's wavy dark blond hair crowned an expansive forehead—a physical characteristic that Lasker considered a sign of high intelligence. Although he was then in his late forties, he looked years younger. Lasker thought his guest to be "one of the handsomest men I ever saw in my life."[5]

Lasker got straight to the point: "Well? What *is* advertising? Tell me."

But Kennedy was not forthcoming. In subsequent years, Lasker told the tale of this initial meeting many times, and each version was slightly different. Reminiscing in 1938, Lasker recalled that Kennedy was "reluctant" to answer the question. Before giving anything away, Kennedy made it clear that he wanted to strike a business arrangement with Lord & Thomas—and that he "wanted to make it guaranteed."[6]

So Kennedy bought time and fueled Lasker's curiosity by telling stories in a commanding tenor voice about his allegedly colorful past:

The caller told me that for several years previous, he had been in the Canadian Northwest Mounted Police. And for reasons unfathomable to me, he had become interested in advertising.

Vivid in my mind are his tales of long, lonesome days and nights in the snowy emptiness of Northern Canada. Meditative days and nights spent in academic concentration. Not on the externals of advertising copy. Not on the by-products of advertising. But in deep, scholarly contemplation to isolate a fundamental concept of true advertising—which is copy.[7]

In a conversation some years later, Lasker elaborated on the theme: "He carried himself in a military way—spoke his words in a short, choppy manner. He impressed you as a man who had lived alone, and within himself, as a man there in those northern vastnesses would have to do . . . He was a typical lone-wolf type . . ."[8]

Much of this, it later turned out, was malarkey. Subsequent inquiries failed to turn up any "John E. Kennedy" among the ranks of the Mounties. Kennedy *was* Canadian by birth, but it appears that the closest he ever got to the "snowy emptiness of Northern Canada" was the Hudson's Bay Company's department store in Winnipeg, for which he wrote some undistinguished copy at the turn of the century. He subsequently bounced around—working on a Montreal newspaper, writing ads for a shoe company in Boston, and even promoting his own designs for shoes and clothing.[9] He did some work for cereal-maker C.W. Post in 1903, although it is unclear whether he worked for Post directly, or through the Charles H. Fuller agency.[10]

Lasker was intrigued, in part because it emerged that the handsome stranger across the desk from him had written the ads for Dr. Shoop's Restorative. Now he was all the more determined to learn Kennedy's definition of advertising. When he pressed him, Kennedy countered by asking Lasker what *his* conception of advertising was.

"It is news," Lasker replied.[11]

"No," Kennedy said. "News is a technique of presentation, but advertising is a very simple thing. I can give it to you in three words."

"Well," Lasker exclaimed impatiently, "I am hungry! What are those three words?"

"*Salesmanship in print,*" Kennedy said.

A century later, this doesn't sound like a particularly powerful insight. But to Lasker's ears, it was a revelation. He knew about salesmanship: he was an excellent salesman. Advertising, Kennedy was telling him, was simply a stand-in for *him* when he wore his salesman's hat. Great advertising did the same work as a great salesman. Advertising multiplied the work of the "salesman" who wrote it a thousand-fold. "The minute he told me that," Lasker later recalled, "the very second he told me that, I understood it."[12] Finally, there was an *idea* on the table which Lasker could work with.

While Lasker was thinking through this insight, Kennedy dropped another thunderbolt: a letter to Lord & Thomas from Dr. Shoop. The letter stated that Kennedy was under contract to his patent-medicine firm for the balance of 1904 at an annual salary of $16,000—a staggering sum. (Lasker's six copywriters were then commanding something like $1,400 a year for their full-time services.) Shoop wrote that both he and Kennedy wanted to end the arrangement, and proposed that if Lord & Thomas would take over the contract for the balance of the year—$8,000—he would contribute half of that sum, or $4,000.[13]

Lasker agreed to take the proposal to Ambrose Lord and Daniel Thomas the next day. He told Kennedy that he "couldn't conceive" that they would turn him down.[14] With a tentative deal struck, Lasker and Kennedy then continued their discussion until well past midnight.

Lasker guessed that Ambrose Thomas (whom he called a "Scotch Yankee") would be astounded at the price tag, but unable to resist the 50 percent subsidy offered by Shoop. He was right: Thomas agreed to the deal, but on one condition—that he "never have to see the fellow." During the subsequent two years, Thomas had almost no contact with the high-priced talent that Lasker had brought under his roof.[15]

As soon as Kennedy signed on, Lasker asked him for a tutorial in the theory of advertising. He confessed that he felt like "the fellow who uses electricity but doesn't know what force it is. Sometimes he doesn't get the right results; sometimes he does."[16] Kennedy agreed, and so for the next year, they did their respective jobs during the day—with Kennedy mostly writing at home—and met for "classes" after hours. Kennedy was uncomfortable speaking to groups, but he was a superb teacher one-on-one. No doubt it was gratifying to Kennedy's considerable ego to have a brilliant student catering to him and hanging on his every word.

Somewhere along the line, the lessons turned into short essays written by Kennedy. The first essay defined advertising as "salesmanship in print."[17] The second focused on the application of this principle—a lesson that Kennedy called "Reason Why in Copy." Advertisers, Kennedy wrote disapprovingly, seemed to believe consumers should buy their goods because it was good for the *advertisers*—and this arrogant attitude came through loud and clear in their copy. Nonsense, said Kennedy: advertisers had to give consumers a "reason why" they should buy the advertised goods.

Again, more than a hundred years after the fact, this sounds elementary. And it was far from a new idea: the patent-medicine vendors had for many years been concocting spurious reasons why consumers should purchase their dubious products. (One ad for *Dr. Chase's Recipe Book*—an 1867 book aimed at "merchants, grocers, saloon-keepers, physicians, druggists, tanners, shoe makers, and harness makers," among others—was titled "Reasons Why."[18]) Like everyone else who had trained in the patent-medicine field, Kennedy understood that "medicines were worthless merchandise until a demand was created."[19] And reasons why created that demand. Lasker, who craved "the Big Idea," felt that he was gaining profound insights into his trade, and this gave him newfound confidence.

That confidence came in handy when, not many months later, J. Walter Thompson—the legendary head of the New York agency that bore his name—demanded an audience with Lord & Thomas. Thompson had seen an article in *Judicious Advertising*, the Lord & Thomas house organ, celebrating the hiring of Kennedy at $16,000 per year, and felt the need to straighten out his Chicago-based competitors.

Thompson arrived at Lasker's office, "white whiskered [and] fiercely mustachioed."[20] As a starstruck Lasker later recalled the encounter, Thompson delivered a stern lecture: "He said, 'Young man, I have come out here with no interest for you, but because it happens that our interests are identical. I have got to give you good advice to save myself. What is all this foolishness that you are doing—paying $16,000 to a copywriter! Now, you are just going to ruin the line. There isn't any copywriter born ever worth over $3,000!'"[21]

But Lasker, believing that he was on the right track, wasn't intimidated. When he was with Kennedy, he felt he was "in the presence of a great man." Yes, Kennedy was "eccentric, egocentric, utterly inconsiderate of everyone else"—and expensive—but he held the key for which Lasker had been searching. And history ultimately proved that Lasker's faith in the power of copy was well placed. The J. Walter Thompson agency, as Lasker noted years later, was eventually taken over Stanley and Helen Resor, "than whom there have never been greater copywriters."[22]

———————⊙———————

Sometime in the early summer of 1904, Lasker heard that the Nineteen Hundred Washer Company—a manufacturer of washing machines in Binghamton, New York, that sold exclusively by mail order—might be shopping for a new ad agency.[23] Lasker and Kennedy sat down and analyzed the company's recent campaigns.

Washers in that day were clumsy, hand-cranked machines—only slight improvements over tubs and washboards (some "washing machines," in fact, were little more than tubs with washboards attached). Motorized machines were still several years in the future. Doing the family wash, therefore, was hard labor, requiring hours of exertion and leading to aching muscles and chapped hands. Monday was washday in many households—the origin of the phrase "Blue Monday."

The main selling point of the Nineteen Hundred machine was a set of "perfectly adjusted ball-bearings" that supposedly minimized wear and tear on both the housewife and her family's clothes. To Kennedy's eye, the company's ads were dreadful. They depicted a haggard-looking woman, hair askew, who appeared to be dragging a washing machine behind her, by means of an enormous chain attached to the small of her back. *"Are you chained to the wash tub?"* demanded the headline. "Whether a housekeeper does her own washing or not, the worry and work connected with 'Blue Monday' literally chain her to the wash tub. *We can sever the chain."*

Kennedy ticked off the many failings of the concept. The chain metaphor was negative and would drive away any woman who didn't want to think of herself as an oppressed drudge. The ad said almost nothing about what the Nineteen Hundred could do—it provided no *reason why*—and had no news interest. And finally, it offered the washer on an installment plan, of which most consumers were still highly suspicious. "Otherwise," Kennedy sniffed, "it is all right."[24]

Lasker and Kennedy talked their way through alternatives. Then they took a train to Binghamton, where Lasker successfully sold the account. During that trip, Lasker and Kennedy learned that Nineteen Hundred was "keying" its advertisements to different newspapers to show the response rates pulled by different ads in different areas. *None* of their current ads, company officials complained, were paying for themselves. If things didn't turn around soon, they told the team from Lord & Thomas, Nineteen Hundred would be in trouble.

Back in Chicago, Kennedy struggled to come up with a new approach. Lasker, watching the master at work, discovered that writing did not come easily to Kennedy:

He had to think everything out laboriously, with labored pains. I imagine he corrected an advertisement . . . 25 to 50 times before he would release it. And to write his key ad, which is the first ad of the campaign, might take him a month or six weeks. . . .[25]

He would be lost to the world for two hours, thinking out a paragraph of 50 or 60 words. Then, laboriously, he would underline and scratch out until . . . maybe half or three-quarters of the words were taken out. He would hunt for *the shading of a word, and then seek to polish the sentence so that its impact was not to be resisted.*[26]

When Kennedy's concept for the Nineteen Hundred finally arrived, it was brilliant. The new ad still featured a woman and a machine. This time, though, the woman sat in a rocking chair next to the washer. Her hair was perfectly arranged in a Sunday-go-to-meeting bun. Her face was serene—eyes closed, as if in prayer. Her right hand sat languidly on the machine's crank. "Let this machine do your washing free," read the headline. Then followed some thirty paragraphs of detailed description, in two parts. The first described how the machine *actually worked*—with "motor springs" and paddles doing all the hard work "in from *six to ten minutes* by the clock." The second part attempted to rehabilitate the concept of installment-plan buying, arguing that having the housewife send 50 cents a week until the machine was paid for was actually less than *"what the machine saves you every week."*

The ad was stiff and wordy by today's standards. But the paragraphs and sentences were short and studded with the underlined and capitalized words that emerged as Kennedy's trademarks. Reasons why abounded: *Do twice the wash in half the time. Let our machine pay for itself. Use the washer four weeks at our expense.* And a concluding note of urgency: "This offer may be withdrawn at any time it overcrowds our factory."

Kennedy's ad ran in selected publications for a total of $715. In the first seven days, it generated 1,547 inquiries, for a per-inquiry cost of 47 cents. The Nineteen Hundred Company, accustomed to paying upwards of *$20 dollars* per inquiry, was ecstatic. In addition, the *quality* of the inquiries was unprecedented. From the pile of more than 1,500 responses, the Nineteen Hundred Washer Company's treasurer, R. L. Bieber pulled 200 at random. Of those, 119 asked the company to send a washer with no questions asked.

What did Lasker think of this coup, which increased his client's business sixfold in four months, and more than validated his faith in the mysterious stranger from the North? "I had *learned*," he said.[27]

One of the things that he learned from Kennedy—which the Canadian in turn had learned from his days in the patent-medicine trade—was the power of *keyed* advertising, which used coupons, unique return addresses, or other devices to track responses. It wasn't enough simply to write what you thought was great copy; you had to *test* that copy to see if your instincts were right. Kennedy had enormous confidence in his abilities; nevertheless, he believed that talent and intuition weren't enough. *Put your best ideas out there,* he argued, *and then see what works.*

Briefly, Lord & Thomas ran parallel ads for the Nineteen Hundred washers in the same magazines—one ad written by Kennedy, and one not—to see which pulled better. (On a cost-per-inquiry basis, Kennedy's were five times as effective.) Kennedy welcomed this kind of scrutiny, and he and Lasker tried a similar approach with several other accounts. Using keyed ads, they experimented with different copy approaches and carefully tracked responses. Lasker began assembling what came to be called his "Record of Results." The information contained in that wall of black filing cabinets served as the basis for training generations of copywriters.

Kennedy then began writing the first of a series of twelve short essays for publication in *Judicious Advertising.* The premise of the essays was that *all* advertising should be tested in these ways. Each article began with a fairly specific challenge—how to test mail-order advertising, for example—and offered ways to respond to that challenge. In most cases, the proposed solution involved pitting the advertiser's current ads against "reason-why" advertising that would be prepared, naturally enough, by Lord & Thomas. At the end of each article came a pitch for the agency: "Let us talk the Saving process over together, in a personal interview."[28]

This writing exercise proved to be more difficult than anticipated. Lasker believed that his resident genius could crank out a dozen essays on advertising with little difficulty. After all, wasn't Kennedy the world's leading expert on the subject? But Kennedy's genius quickly ran dry. As one Lasker associate later commented: "I think he was to do twelve articles for *Judicious Advertising.* He wrote five of the twelve. He could find nothing new or any resourcefulness in his makeup to enable him to carry on."[29]

It is unclear who wrote the remaining articles. What *is* clear, though, is that Lasker ultimately put them to very effective use. He gathered the articles together and published them in a pamphlet titled *The Book of Advertising Tests.* He then persuaded a number of friendly magazines and newspapers to donate space, which he used to advertise the availability of the pamphlet to anyone who was interested. The response, according to Lasker, was overwhelming: "In response to these advertisements, it was nothing for us to receive hundreds of letters a week from leading manufacturers all over the United States. I doubt if there were 10 percent of the big manufacturers and advertisers of America who didn't write us at that time."[30]

Like Lasker, America was hungry to learn more about advertising. Lasker used the outpouring of interest generated by *The Book of Advertising Tests* to change the Lord & Thomas client base:

> *I immediately switched our business . . . Kennedy and I agreed to get mail order business, and we got it to the extent of about 35 percent of our volume.*
>
> *We kept a record of the results. Every week, the clients would send us the papers and how they paid, and every Tuesday morning we would go over how the papers were doing, and order repeat insertions or not, depending on how the paper paid out.*

In other words, Lasker and Kennedy refined their craft on the client's nickel, and delivered increasingly effective advertising to those clients. Lasker later referred to this early mail-order effort—which tracked the agency's work for some three hundred accounts—as a "great laboratory," and it was one of the foundations upon which Lasker's genius as a business consultant was based.[31]

Ultimately, however, it proved to be a self-limiting experiment. After about six years, Lasker quietly shut down his laboratory. Mail order, he had decided, was like working summer stock—good practice, but only a warm-up. "The reward," he concluded, "is on Broadway."[32]

The flood of inquiries that resulted from *The Book of Advertising Tests* overwhelmed Lord & Thomas's small copy department. The agency had offered itself up as an expert, and the world had responded eagerly—but Lasker couldn't meet its demands.

Kennedy's unpredictability heightened the challenge. When it came time to negotiate his contract for 1905, the gifted Canadian announced that he was willing to sell only three days a week of his time to Lord & Thomas, as he wanted to reserve the balance for freelance activities. Lasker took what he could get. He gave Kennedy a $4,000 raise—to $20,000—and then prorated that figure to $10,000 to reflect Kennedy's half-time status. Somewhat astoundingly, Kennedy then began advertising his freelance services in *Judicious Advertising*:

After January 1st, half my time is my own. The other half belongs to Lord &
Thomas, Chicago. I am reserving half my time to write Copy for a few adver-
tisers who are willing to pay for Results.[33]

Kennedy's half-time status put a strain on the copywriting department, which was compounded by Lasker's awareness that he should get out of the writing end of the business. He knew that his strengths lay in editing rather than writing.[34] He had assessed his copywriting skills, as compared with Kennedy's, and decided that he wasn't good enough.

Still another factor squeezed the agency's copywriting resources: the creation in 1905 of the "Outdoor Advertising Department." This specialized group sold ad space inside streetcars, on billboards along streetcar lines, and on the main roads traversed by carriages. Although this was primarily a selling effort—approximately a dozen men sold these ads from offices in New York and Chicago—there was still writing involved, and the new department put even more pressure on Lasker's small staff of writers.

So Lasker approached Ambrose Thomas with yet another bold request: to expand the copywriting department:

I said, "I have been upstairs and I have measured that we can take out all the
files against the north windows and all the files against half of the west win-
dows, and we can make nine offices eight by ten each. I want you to let me put
up nine offices that will cost about $2,000 to build the partitions, and advertise
for nine young newspaper men, and Kennedy and I will start training them,
because out of the nine we might only get three or four."[35]

Although Thomas remained skeptical of the power of advertising copy, he couldn't deny the business generated by Lasker and Kennedy. They discussed the price tag associated with this daring new venture—primarily the additional copywriters—and Lasker came up with an estimate of up to $5,000 a head.[36] Thomas gave his blessing, and Lasker set out to recruit his copywriters.

In subsequent recountings of this episode, he often claimed that Lord & Thomas was the first agency to set up a copywriting department, but this was another case of Lasker's enthusiasm overwhelming the facts. N. W. Ayer established its "Copy Department" in 1900, a few years before Lasker built up his expanded staff.[37] Cincinnati-based Procter & Collier began claiming in 1896 that it had copywriting "specialists" on its payroll.[38] But at this early date, the top agencies were only dipping their toes in the copywriting waters. Even at the end of the decade, Ayer was cautioning against the industry's "tendency toward copy exaltation."[39] Lasker felt no such reticence, and pursued his vision with a particular ferocity. By 1906, Lord & Thomas had nine copywriters—nominally headed by Kennedy, but directed by Lasker. Because Kennedy was awkward in front of even small groups, Lasker conveyed the master's insights to them. "We had a class at least twice a week, for three or four years," Lasker later recalled, "and the sessions would last four or five hours at a stretch."[40]

The department was the "sensation of the advertising world," Lasker boasted. But from the inside, it often looked less than sensational. Kennedy's inability to work with groups hampered Lasker, who had account-servicing responsibilities that often took him out of town. Not surprisingly, the department's output sometimes proved unsatisfactory. There was no easy way to replicate the Kennedy magic. "It was less easy than I anticipated," Lasker admitted, "to implant the genius of Kennedy in other brains . . . Whenever Kennedy did it, it was perfect, but where the other nine men tried, we failed, nine times out of ten, and they failed ridiculously. It was one thing to have a technique, and another thing to learn the application."[41]

Turnover was high, and having high-priced talent coming and going resulted in a lot of stomach-churning for Lasker. Too often, the best of these young people were stolen by competitors who offered them up to five times their Lord & Thomas salary. Meanwhile, of course, the bad ones—the ones who "failed ridiculously"—had to be let go. That job fell to Lasker, who despite his energy and brashness hated confrontation. "It made a terrible strain on me," Lasker later admitted.[42]

A related strain was riding herd on his resident genius: "I had been working overwhelmingly, establishing this copy department. And this man Kennedy! If I had nothing else, just managing him was a man-breaking job, because you just had to sit on top of him to get the work out. He had very long lapses when he couldn't work at all."[43]

Kennedy turned out to be a basketful of contradictions. On first blush appearing to be an extrovert, he was in fact bashful, sensitive, and introverted—"hard to know, hard to talk to," according to Lasker.[44] Lord & Thomas's half-time genius lived a life of extremely productive highs and miserably lows. He lost interest in accounts almost as soon as he had solved their initial challenge, leaving Lasker to struggle with the client, whose expectations now had been elevated by Kennedy's talent. "He was like a bee," Lasker complained. "He went and sipped the pollen out of a flower, and if he got it, his interest was gone. He wanted to try another flower."[45]

As with many aspects of the Lasker story, alcohol played a prominent role. Kennedy was "pickled in liquor," Lasker recalled—a "champion drinker."[46] He would work almost nonstop several days running, then disappear on a binge for weeks on end. Caring little about money but enamored of sailboats and other expensive luxuries, Kennedy often required advances even on his princely salary.

Alcohol fueled Kennedy's eccentricities. One time, Lasker went looking for his troubled and inebriated genius, finally tracking him down at a shooting gallery on South State Street. Kennedy agreed to return to work, but first insisted on demonstrating his sharpshooting prowess to his boss. Right-handed, he hefted a rifle in his left hand, turned one eye away from the metal pigeon targets that were rolling by on a track—and picked off every one of them.[47]

Finally, Kennedy was suspicious and paranoid—"a man whom it was impossible to get along with," as Lasker put it. In fact, Lasker believed that he was the *only* person who ever got along with Kennedy. "But that was my business—to get along with him," added Lasker. "And it was worth the price to me."[48]

The price eventually became too high. When Lasker most needed a reliable ally, bulwark, and stand-in, Kennedy proved to be fundamentally unreliable. He "couldn't be managed," Lasker concluded. Sometime in 1906, Kennedy and Lord & Thomas parted company. Given the enormous impact Kennedy had had on Lasker, it is remarkable how little time he actually spent at the firm. He arrived in Chicago in mid-1904, cut himself back to half-time in 1905, and left in 1906 to take a position with the advertising firm of Ethridge-Kennedy in New York.

The parting appears to have been reasonably amicable. When Lasker opened a Lord & Thomas office in New York in 1910, Kennedy rejoined the payroll there—a "re-recruitment" coup that Lasker later boasted about. But Lasker sensed that Kennedy had peaked and the magic was gone: "He had one big message to give, and from the day he left, he retrogressed steadily. He had done his big work. It is like some animals you read about who reproduce themselves . . . and then lie down and die."[49]

Kennedy, Lasker concluded, was not a "born advertising man." That was one reason why he had to work so hard at his copywriting. Of course, not being born into the business gave Kennedy advantages, as well. It forced him to articulate the business for *himself* and, by extension, for Lasker, Lord & Thomas, and the larger advertising community. It fell to others to extend Kennedy's powerful concepts, and put them to their fullest use.

Kennedy eventually relocated to Los Angeles, where he became involved in real estate. He died in 1926, long forgotten by most people in the advertising industry. But he was not forgotten by Lasker, who for the rest of his life referred to Kennedy as the "father of modern advertising"—a title that he could reasonably have claimed for himself.

Chapter Five

Growing Up, Breaking Down

*A*LBERT LASKER arrived in Grand Rapids, Michigan, late on a blustery November night in 1900. Although only twenty years old, he was already a highly successful advertising salesman—making $3,600 per year, and on a productive day placing $800 worth of ads.[1]

He had spent the day with a manufacturer out in the country, and didn't get back to his hotel until after 10 p.m. In those days, most travel was done by train and horse-drawn wagons. As soon as the streets in the northern reaches of the Midwest acquired their five-month mantle of snow, the wheels were removed from horse-drawn vehicles and replaced with runners. Travel that was already slow got slower, and the life of a salesman got harder.

Gratefully ducking into the lobby of his Grand Rapids hotel to escape the blizzard outside, Lasker wore his Elks pin prominently displayed on his lapel. He had no interest in the Elks, but he had discovered that a surprising number of hotel clerks were Elks. Wearing his pin often got him better accommodations than he could secure otherwise.

Tonight the lobby was crowded, with scores of men seated in lounge chairs, smoking and talking, making the steamy air even more stale than usual. A short, chubby young man spotted Lasker's pin and enthusiastically gave him the Elks handshake. The young man introduced himself as Arthur Warner. He was a salesman from Buffalo, and wanted to have a drink with his fellow Elk. Lasker could tell that Warner—like himself, little more than a teenager—had already had a drink or two. He declined, saying that he was tired and wanted to go to bed, but Warner persisted.

"I thought that I would teach him a lesson," Lasker later recalled. "Not that it was my business to teach him a lesson."

Off the lobby was a poolroom with a huge bar, which on this wintry night was doing a booming business. Lasker walked Warner up to the bar, and said he would drink with him if Warner would match him drink for drink. Warner agreed. Lasker then called for two beer glasses and a bottle of whiskey. Filling his own glass with whiskey—eight ounces' worth—he challenged Warner to fill the other glass and drink it "bottoms up."

"I figured he wouldn't do it," Lasker admitted, "and I would be rid of him."

The challenge attracted the attention of many of the bar's patrons. The pool players put down their cues, crowding around the two Elks at the bar. Warner lifted his beer glass and chugged its entire contents. Lasker, now remembering that he hadn't eaten anything in many hours, did the same.

The huge slugs of alcohol soon swamped their brains, and what followed was a long night of half-remembered antics. "We Elked all night long," Lasker recalled ruefully.

They staggered outside and ran into an elderly cabman, and soon both Lasker and Warner were reduced to weeping at the realization that this poor old fellow had to wait outside in the subzero temperatures while they sat inside drinking. Lasker pressed a few dollars on the cab driver—a large sum, in those days—then took the reins of the carriage, the better to show Grand Rapids to his fellow Elk.

At one point deciding that they needed another drink, Lasker spied a bar that looked promising. Like many saloons of that era, this one had two sets of doors—one a pair of swinging shutters, and behind them, a pair of glass doors. Sending Warner ahead on foot to open the inner doors, Lasker then attempted to drive the carriage into the bar: "I do distinctly remember getting the horse through the swinging doors, by golly, and the fellow who was running the place threw a knife at us, and we went away."

The two Elks stumbled back into their hotel as the sun was coming up. Lasker was fine, but Warner felt deathly ill. Lasker concluded that his suffering companion needed food, and ordered two enormous breakfasts: fruit, bacon and eggs, toast, and coffee. When the food arrived, Warner became violently ill—"the sickest boy I ever saw in my whole life," Lasker later remembered. "I never saw a man that ill."

Lasker ate both breakfasts and went off to his nine o'clock appointment. For the rest of the day, whenever he had a free moment, he checked in on the ailing Warner. This solicitude—as well as his cast-iron stomach—earned

Lasker the lifelong admiration of Arthur Warner: "He kept writing me letters, and he would write me at great length. Sometimes I wouldn't answer the letters, or sometimes I would just drop him a few lines. But the fact that I could eat that breakfast always made him think that I was the greatest living male in America."

Everything about the experience seemed to relegate it to the closet of embarrassing tales from the road. To Lasker's surprise, that proved not to be the case.

About a month later, on the Saturday night between Christmas and New Year's Eve of 1900, Lasker was seated in the Munro Baths in Cincinnati, a city he often visited to service the Rheinstrom account. In a Turkish bath, travelers rented rooms without separate bathing facilities, and met downstairs in the common baths for the steam and the male camaraderie. Lasker had gotten to know a number of the young single men who frequented the Munro Baths fairly well. Many were Jewish, like himself. They called each other by nicknames, and engaged in easy banter.

In the previous few weeks, Lasker had been doing some serious soul-searching. He had been at Lord & Thomas for two years. He no longer dreamed of leaving for New York to become a reporter; now he aimed to "conquer advertising," make a lot of money, and then go *buy* a newspaper.

But there were at least two obstacles. The first was that by his own estimation—perhaps tinged with some fresh guilt—he was reckless and irresponsible. The antics in Grand Rapids weren't an isolated incident but part of a recurring pattern. "I wasn't getting rid of them," Lasker admitted.

The second problem was that he was terribly lonely in Chicago. During the Thanksgiving holiday a little more than a year earlier, he had acted on his loneliness in an almost desperate way:

> I remember going to my room and crying in a paroxysm of tears. Within an hour, I went down to the station and took the train for Galveston, which at that time was a 48-hour trip from Chicago. I wrote a note to Mr. Thomas, and just told him that my homesickness had grown so nostalgic that I couldn't resist it. Maybe he'd understand it, and maybe he wouldn't. Would he send me a wire whether or not I could come back to work?

Thomas reassured his troubled young colleague that he was welcome to come back to work. But the isolation that Lasker felt in Chicago soon closed in around him again and reinforced his tendency toward obsessive thinking: "I was very introspective on certain things. And I made up my mind that what was the matter with me was that I was just sheer lonesome, and if I had a home, I could get ahead, and I would settle down."

On this particular night, downstairs in the Turkish baths, Lasker and his cronies were playing poker and drinking. The members of the group were between half a decade and a decade older than Lasker, and regarded him as a precocious teenager. It was now 3:00 or 4:00 in the morning: an hour when troubled young men are sometimes given to startling confessions. On this night, Lasker didn't disappoint: "I said, 'This is all foolishness—my staying up like this. I am only going to be young once, and every day counts. I want to make my youth accumulate experience, and this thing that I am doing isn't good for me, and anyway, I have done it enough . . . If I could meet the right type of girl, I'd get married.'"

His companions egged him on. *What kind of girl, Lasker? What would she look like?* Lasker obliged with a detailed description of his ideal woman. *Well, we know just the type of girl you described,* they responded. *She's visiting here at Elsie Bernard's, and we can take you over there this afternoon.* But this unexpected opportunity confronted Lasker with another problem. Although he was nearly twenty-one years old, he was insecure with women: "I wasn't much for going socially with girls, and I was always self-conscious that I wouldn't know how to conduct myself. It was all right with the males, but I didn't know how to sell a female, and I guess my lack of confidence telegraphed itself to them."

Lasker may have known more about women than these comments suggest. Photographs of him in his late teens and early twenties show an intense, handsome young man with wavy black hair and deep-set, expressive eyes—certainly attractive enough, especially considering his sparkling wit and ready cash. During his theater-reviewing days in Galveston, for example, Lasker happily caroused with the choruses of touring theater companies, including the actresses. "I'd party with them," Lasker recalled, "which no boy in Galveston had ever done."[2] But this kind of experience hardly prepared him to court a socially appropriate woman.

To make matters worse, Elsie Bernard—a prominent young socialite in Cincinnati's affluent German-Jewish community—had met the awkward Lasker on one of his previous trips to town and made it clear that she didn't much like him. Lasker decided that, if only to aggravate Bernard, he would go meet the out-of-town visitor staying at her house.

Later that afternoon, Lasker's cohort of gregarious young companions arrived at the Bernard house. Lasker, still feeling the effects of the previous night's carousing, now had second thoughts about this adventure. Those misgivings vanished, however, the moment he was introduced to Elsie Bernard's guest. He promptly forgot her name, but he didn't forget much else about her:

She weighed about 108 pounds, just as thin and straight, with that boyish figure that later came into popularity, but at that time you were supposed to be considerably plumper. She had the biggest eyes I had ever seen, before or since, coal black, and coal-black hair, and I remember she had on a blue dress with white dots, and coral beads, and her hair hung in a loop on the back of her head.

She had an infinite amount of charm, of gentility, of kindness, of breeding. You could tell that she was beautifully reared, and well educated, sensitive, and artistic. And, my! I hadn't seen her one minute that I fell like a thousand.

The young woman soon was whisked off, and Lasker now felt excruciatingly out of place. In his oddly sheltered life, he had never before been in a social setting anything like this. He couldn't bring himself to say a word to anyone: "Just everything I had in me closed up."

He sat down on a piano bench, and to his surprise, the beautiful young woman with the enormous eyes sat down next to him. She again told him her name—Flora Warner—and said that she was nineteen years old; this was her first trip away from Buffalo. Remembering his escapade in Grand Rapids, and startled by the unlikely juxtaposition of "Warner" and "Buffalo," Lasker found his tongue. He asked if she was related to *Arthur* Warner.

Why, *yes*, she replied, surprised. Arthur was her first cousin, and lived next door to her in Buffalo. They had grown up together since birth, and were virtually brother and sister. When she finally excused herself to rejoin her friends, Lasker sat there dumbfounded:

The minute she was called away, that whole place was empty for me. I was just a lovesick calf . . .

All I knew, from that second, I knew I loved that girl. I had never had a girl, but I knew I loved that girl, and I knew that girl could supply what I lacked.

He sought out his friends and told them that he was ready to leave. When they asked what he had thought of the visiting socialite from Buffalo, he told them, "I am going to marry that girl."

⸻ ◈ ⸻

Aside from the fact that Flora had no notion of marrying *him,* there were some major impediments to this New Year's resolution. First, he needed to get his father's consent to court a young woman. (He could no more get married without his father's permission, he explained, than he could go out and commit a robbery.) That night, in his cramped quarters at the Munro Baths, he wrote Morris a long letter, explaining his intentions and asking for Morris's blessing.

The letter he received in response—on January 4, 1901—brought an unwelcome message. There was nothing Morris wanted more than to see his son happily married. At the same time, certain facts weighed heavily on his mind. He knew his son had been drinking a great deal and, in his opinion, Albert had no right to ask a decent girl to marry him. Therefore, he would withhold his blessing until his son had abstained from alcohol for six months.

Albert wrote back immediately, agreeing to the terms. He then began taking steps to increase his chances of success in the larger campaign. First, he resumed his correspondence with Arthur Warner. Concurrently, he also approached Ambrose Thomas with a proposition. The Pan-American Exposition—the World's Fair—was then under way in Buffalo. It was a celebration of industry and commerce, with awards of all sorts being passed out to exhibitors. At the Frankfurt World's Fair in 1891, Lord & Thomas had come up with a plan whereby, for a modest fee, the agency would help award-winning U.S. manufacturers trumpet their successes by sending press releases to selected newspapers. Lasker proposed to revive this program for the Buffalo exposition—only this time, for a much bigger profit. Instead of the $1,200 or $1,500 that Lord & Thomas had charged for the service previously—a fee that already had included a "big profit"—now the firm would charge between $3,000 and $4,000. Thomas readily agreed. And even though Buffalo was not in his territory, Lasker got himself assigned the Exposition job, which would give him ample reason to visit Buffalo at the firm's expense.

Lasker kept his promise to his father, refraining from taking a drink for the entire first half of 1901. It was probably a difficult challenge. Lasker once admitted that he "drank heavily for years." He owned up to getting drunk with the hard-bitten newspaper reporters back in Galveston; he also commented that during his early days in Chicago, "all advertising men drank a great deal." He was constantly surrounded by alcohol and alcoholics, and life on the road was often lonely.

In June, Lasker wrote Arthur Warner to say that he was coming to Buffalo on Wednesday evening, July 3. He would be staying until Sunday night, and hoped to spend the evenings and the holiday with him. Arthur wired back that he would be delighted to host his friend.

Lasker took a train up to Buffalo from Cleveland, arriving at around 9:00 p.m. Warner met him at the train station, and exclaimed excitedly that they were going to have a "great time tonight."

Now, though, Lasker confessed to Warner that he had come to win the hand of Warner's cousin, Flora. Warner, laughing, said that Flora had been engaged for several years, and it was only a matter of time before she married her Buffalo beau. Lasker asked if this was a *formal* engagement; Warner admitted that it was not. In that case, Lasker replied, there was no problem:

> I said, "Oh, that makes no difference to me, if she isn't [engaged], I'll tend to that . . . But you have met other fellows. If you think I am earnest, and think I am going to get along in the world—if you think you are doing your cousin a favor—I want you to direct me to her."
>
> He said, "Why, I know you are going to be a success, and I know I am doing my cousin a good turn. I love her as much as anybody can love anybody. I'll do anything you ask me to do."
>
> So we went out that night and had quite a time. And that night, that part of my life was buried, and never rose again.

The following morning—Thursday, the Fourth of July holiday, 1901— Lasker arrived at Arthur's house on Main Street. There he found a unique living arrangement: Arthur's and Flora's fathers were in business together, lived in identical and adjacent frame houses about fifteen feet apart, and drew from a communal financial pot. In a chair on the front porch of Flora's house was a woman—a "lovely motherly looking old lady," to Lasker's eyes— Flora's mother.

Arthur and Lasker casually wandered over and inquired where Flora might be. The woman replied that she was out playing tennis and wasn't expected back before lunch. Arthur leaned over and whispered something in her ear, and she got up and went inside. Shortly thereafter, a young boy emerged and sped off on his bicycle. And not too long after that, Flora arrived on her bicycle, wearing a long white tennis dress. She shook Lasker's hand politely, excused herself, and went inside.

Once in the house (Lasker later learned) a furious Flora confronted her mother. Who did this Lasker think he was, interrupting her tennis game? Flora's mother scolded her, and sent her back outside to be hospitable to the nice young man who had come visiting all the way from Chicago.

Over the next seven weeks or so, Lasker arranged to be in Buffalo four times on business, each trip lasting three or four days. He pressured Flora to break whatever engagements she had and to spend time with him:

> With Art's connivance, we arranged it all around, he telling her, and I rehearsing with him what I wanted represented as my fine points. We put a little glamour to me, and a little mystery to me, and made me on the one hand very attractive, and—on the other hand—just put in enough about my being a boy of the world to a girl of that type [to] be intriguing.
>
> I would send her little things from the towns I went [to], that she couldn't get otherwise, and I made no concealment that I was enamored beyond measure. And at the same time, made no forward move, wasn't bold, held back, and was plainly bashful and worshiping in her presence, but plainly that behind that, that I could get aggressive if I wanted to.
>
> That is the only piece of salesmanship I ever did study, and I went at it as an actor would, to create a part. I saw she was very romantic, and I didn't have any romance in me. But I put on an act that would appeal to a romantic girl.

Calculating he may have been, but the more he learned about Flora, the more he loved her. Although she was Jewish, she had been educated in a Buffalo convent. Influenced by these two faiths, Flora had a strong moral streak. And although she had told him she was nineteen when they first met, she was in fact twenty-one, a year older than Lasker—a fact that caused her great embarrassment.[3] She made him promise never to reveal this to anyone, even to the three children they eventually raised together.[4]

A letter to his father from August 1901 suggests that Albert did not control the courtship quite as deliberately as his comments above would imply: "I am in that state of constant mental worry—a hell on earth—where I must take some immediate action. I won't enter into any extravagant phrases as to how deeply I love—all I know is, I must end this mental torture or I don't know what will happen."[5]

Lasker again asked for his father's blessing. In remarkably plain logic and language—good reason-why advertising copy, in fact—he laid out his case before his father:

> In considering this matter please remember:
>   First: I was never overly wild.
>   Second: The girl shall know the whole situation.
>   Third: My earning capacity is sufficient.
>   Fourth: I know I am settled.
>   Fifth: I propose a year's engagement.
>   Sixth: How I love this girl.
>   Seventh: That I'm not worth a dam [sic] to anyone until I get this settled.

Morris telegraphed his response to the Hotel Iroquois in Buffalo, where Albert was staying: *Go ahead. I am with you. She must be a good girl or you could not love her so much.* He also loaned his son $125 for an engagement ring. Albert promised to pay back the $125 before the wedding, should it take place.

On the evening of August 30, Lasker took Flora to have their fortunes told by Julius and Agnes Zancig, a celebrated pair of fortunetellers on the midway at the fairgrounds. According to Lasker, both he and his beloved were under "equal strain" because of the large, unspoken topic on their both of their minds:

> There was a beautiful full moon, and the setting was quite exotic at the fair . . . And she looked up and said, "Couldn't you just love a moon like that?"
>
> And I said, "Why, if you have love to spare, do you give it to an inanimate thing like the moon? Why don't you give it to me?"
>
> And she turned to me and in all seriousness said, "Are you by any chance proposing?"
>
> "Indeed I am—I'm asking you to be my wife," I said. "What is the answer?"
>
> And she said, "Why, I have never given it any thought. I'll have to think it over."
>
> And I said, "I can't give you an option. I'm a young man trying to get along in the world. I have a career in front of me that I want to share with you, and if you get someone to tell you about it, you will see that I am hard-working, and have already taken too much time coming here . . . You will have to tell me yes or no, because I have to get along with my career."

At that moment, they arrived at the fortune-tellers' door. They entered and sat down together for their reading. Agnes Zancig told Flora that she would have a long and serious illness from which she might never fully recover. And, she continued, Flora would be going on a long and joyous journey. Flora turned, looked at Lasker, and asked, "Are we?"

And that was how Albert Lasker and Flora Warner became engaged. Lasker was thrilled:

> I had never called her anything but "Miss Warner," up to that moment. And more than anything else in the world, I wanted to kiss her, to seal the bargain . . . We were both trembling, and mind you, she was a girl [in] the spirit of [the] mid-Victorian[s]. Never did anything without her parents making the decision, and here she had gotten herself engaged.
>
> And here I proposed that we go on the roller coaster, on which you come to a dark spot. And when we came there, I put my arm around her, because I had never thought of it, I put my lips to hers, and said, "May I, Miss Warner?"
>
> I want to say, there is all the romance there has ever been in life, before or since—that is all the romance.

Fortunately, the Warners didn't stand in the way of the match.[6] Flora's father, half Hungarian and half Austrian, actually knew Lasker's celebrated Uncle Eduard, and that was enough of a reference for him. Morris Lasker traveled to Buffalo to meet his prospective daughter-in-law, and again gave his blessing.

The wedding took place in Buffalo on June 9, 1902. The delay resulted from the fact that Albert had promised his father a long engagement, and also from the fact that Morris's family was still in Europe, where he had sent them in his efforts to economize, and they couldn't get back any sooner. Flora wanted a large wedding, to which Lasker very reluctantly agreed. But he was pleased that a large number of his Chicago colleagues came—including Ambrose Thomas, who in response to a request from Lasker had agreed to give him a 40 percent raise, to $5,000 per year. "You're entitled to a lot more," Thomas had said. "Say it now, if you want more." Lasker declined.

The couple had planned a two-week honeymoon. They went first to the Savoy Hotel in New York for several days. While in New York, though, Lasker began to get agitated about being away from his office for so long. "There was no organization," Lasker later explained, "to keep my work going." His anxiety rose to intolerable levels.

Flora, aware of her husband's mounting distress, suggested that they cancel their planned ten-day trip to the Delaware Water Gap and instead return immediately to Chicago. They arrived in Chicago in mid-June, and Lasker plunged back into his work. Almost immediately, he rushed off to Battle Creek, Michigan, to take part in a strange new kind of "gold rush": the boom in packaged breakfast foods sparked by two local entrepreneurs named C. W. Post and W. W. Kellogg.

Flora set up housekeeping at the Chicago Beach Hotel: a lakefront establishment that had been built to accommodate visitors to the 1893 World's Fair. She lived an isolated existence. She knew no one in Chicago, and her husband traveled extensively. She made friends with some of the hotel's residents, but she was alone a great deal of the time.

Lasker grasped the difficulty of his wife's situation, and about six weeks into their marriage, he suggested that she go home to Buffalo for a few days. He would keep his appointments in New York and Battle Creek, and then pick her up in Buffalo. She agreed, and they went off by train in different directions.

Several days later, Lasker was working in his room at the Post Tavern in Battle Creek. The once-sleepy Michigan town had been transformed almost overnight by the national craze for packaged breakfast foods, and Lasker had positioned himself well:

> I was a big figure there, because in the boom, the hotels were overrun with people who wanted to sell cotton to the manufacturers, with people who wanted to sell machinery to the manufacturers, with people who wanted jobs as salesmen, who wanted to put in processes. And among them, of course, every newspaper in America had its representatives there, and magazines and streetcar companies and billboard companies—they wanted the advertising, and they would look me up when I came.

Lasker often returned to his hotel room at night to find a stack of twenty or thirty telegrams waiting for him. On one particular night in August 1902, a friend was helping him open the telegrams. Lasker spotted one from Buffalo. Gripped by the premonition that it contained bad news, he asked his friend to open it. It was from Flora's father. *Come to Buffalo at once,* it read. *Flora has typhoid fever.*

This was decades before antibiotics became available to treat bacterial infections. And although the dreaded typhus bacillus killed only between 10 and 20 percent of those whom it infected, it incapacitated almost all who survived. Frantic, Lasker arrived in Buffalo the next day. But there was nothing the distraught husband—then only two months into his marriage—could do for his stricken wife, already bedridden. She would not get out of bed for sixteen months.

Lasker was compelled to return to Chicago, leaving his beloved Flora behind. For more than a year, he lived alone at the Chicago Beach Hotel, visiting Buffalo almost every weekend during the long months of Flora's illness.

Typhoid fever has an incubation period of between seven and fourteen days, so Flora almost certainly contracted the disease in Chicago.[7] A disease caused by poor sanitation or poor personal hygiene, typhoid fever swept across the nation at regular intervals, often striking Chicago with particular ferocity. (In 1891, for example, the typhoid death rate in Chicago was 166 per 100,000 persons—75 percent higher than the national average.[8]) The city was especially vulnerable because of its high concentration of food-processing industries, as well as its woefully inadequate water and sewer systems.

Upton Sinclair's novel, *The Jungle*—which highlighted the disgraceful and unsanitary conditions in Chicago's meatpacking industry and led to sweeping reforms at both the local and national levels—was still three years from publication. Chlorination of the Chicago water supply, which would finally end the threat of typhoid fever and other scourges, was still fifteen years in the future. Meanwhile, Chicagoans from all walks of life took sick. Many died, and many more were disabled.

Albert Lasker now faced thousands of dollars of unexpected medical bills. Mortified, he went back to Ambrose Thomas and asked for another raise—his second in two months. Thomas increased Lasker's salary to an astounding $10,000 per year. This helped, but four months later, his father-in-law's jewelry-case business failed, and Lasker found himself supporting the entire family.

Throughout this period, Albert found it achingly difficult to be separated from Flora. But as her condition worsened, it was just as wrenching to be near her: "Complications set in. The poison got into her blood, her veins were distorted to many times their natural size, her glands were all distorted; for months her legs were up in the air. At the end of 14 months, Dr. Rosewell Park operated on her for adhesions which had formed all through her legs."

Flora's initial bout with typhoid fever—which normally runs its course in three or four weeks—was followed by phlebitis, which brought on some of the complications that Lasker referred to: "The joints of both legs were affected, and became frozen, as in a severe case of arthritis . . . the bones of her toes and ankles had to be broken, one by one, reset, and locked in casts. She was one of the first patients in medical history to benefit from the modern orthopedic technique of traction; if this treatment had not been successful she might never have walked again."[9]

At about the same time that the leg surgeries were performed, Flora told Albert that her nurse—one of the most highly regarded nurses in Buffalo—was beating and otherwise abusing her at night. When Lasker reported these accusations to her physician, he was told that Flora was hallucinating, and that he should not worry about it. Shortly thereafter, however, the nurse was caught stealing silver from the Warner house. According to Albert, she subsequently made a shocking confession: "[She] admitted in the note that she had been a dope fiend, and had been giving my wife injections of dope, and it was those injections which the doctors didn't know about which had evidently retarded her so. The nurse was evidently one of these people who seemed sane and wasn't sane."

As a result of her immobility for more than a year, as well as the various complications of her illnesses, Flora gained more than seventy pounds. Even when she finally was able to get out of bed—in the fall of 1903—she was barely able to walk. Once she had been an accomplished tennis player and dancer; now she found it so painful and frustrating to shuffle around her bedroom that she preferred to stay in bed. The doctors told Lasker that unless he could get Flora walking again, the adhesions would return to her legs: "She just made up her mind she couldn't walk. So, in desperation—I came only weekends—she said to me I had to do something about it. So I asked her to go driving, and I got a horse and buggy, and took her into the park. And I had arranged with the driver to stop by a bench . . . in a romantic little spot. It was the first time we had had alone together in 16 months."

Lasker had the driver drive 150 feet farther down the road, taking Flora's crutches with him:

We had a nice visit. And she said, "Oh—the carriage is down there; ask him back."

I said, "No, Flora; you have to walk there." And that was the first big scene we ever had. She went into hysterics in the park . . . my heart was breaking. I was only a kid of 23. This was in November, and it was getting darker, and it was cold. But I knew we were at a turning point, because the doctors had said, "You are going to have a bedridden invalid all your life, if this isn't done now, and done drastically."

I had told them my plan, and they had approved of it. Oh, how my heart broke . . . And the fact that her nerves had been shattered was first revealed to me then. And I remember how she had to drag herself, and at each step she upbraided me, and cried. And I remember a man coming up and wanted to beat me. He came up and my wife cried to him to make me [stop], and he . . . thought I was a brute, and grabbed me, and I shoved him aside and I said, "Let me alone! I know what I am doing! This is my wife!"[10]

Flora never fully regained the use of her legs. Lasker had married a young woman who moved, he said, like a fawn—full of grace, with a spring in her step. That woman was gone forever.

Gone, too, was the relatively carefree young man whom she had married. "The minute my wife took sick," he later said, "I reached full maturity. I never had a kiddish moment." Up to now, Lasker had never cared much for money; now he desperately had to have it. "From then on, I had to concentrate on work, and from then on, I knew I was fooling myself that I would ever get out of advertising."

Flora—who returned to Chicago in November 1903—was determined to have children, despite medical advice to the contrary.[11] As Lasker recalled: "She had this craze to have children . . . The doctors said she must not have a child, but she kept after me so much to have a child that I just felt I didn't have to right [to say no], particularly when I was away from her almost all the time, and she was alone."

The extreme varicosity of the veins in Flora's legs required that she remain on her back for most of her pregnancy. This worked against her long-term recovery, and preyed on Lasker's mind.

The baby was delivered at the family's rented home in Woodlawn, near the University of Chicago's campus, in September 1904. She was a healthy girl, whom her parents named Mary. Flora appeared no worse off physically, but her physician warned her that if she attempted to have another child, he would no longer attend her.

Upon returning to Chicago, Flora attempted to make friends and establish a social circle. Inevitably, conversations turned to the subject of livelihoods:

What does your husband do for a living? When Flora told them that Albert was in "advertising," her newfound friends were baffled. The concept of modern-day advertising simply hadn't penetrated the public consciousness yet. *Does he paint billboards?,* one of them asked Flora. *Does he wear a sandwich board?,* asked another. Another invoked the disreputable realm of elixirs, painkillers, and other magic compounds: *Is he connected with the patent-medicine business?*[12]

Flora went downtown one day to open a charge account at Marshall Field. The clerk asked where her husband worked. "Lord & Thomas," she replied. This was reference enough for the department store, and the account was opened. She recounted the episode to her husband that evening, and, combined with Flora's stories about her friends' reactions to his profession, it provoked a strong response in him:

> Well, I had never thought of being employed by anybody, or working for anybody, and I [had] distinctly two reactions . . . One was that I was going to work all the harder and make it a business of which my wife wouldn't be ashamed, and one which wouldn't confuse people as to the type of man she had married. And the second thing was that never again should they ask my wife who her husband worked for . . . And of course during the time of her sickness, that wasn't a pressing thing. But I had made up my mind that when she returned, I would be in business for myself—either as a partner in Lord & Thomas, or in some other work.

He had a strong hand to play. Only five years into his tenure at Lord & Thomas, he was one of the agency's most valuable assets—he was generating more business than the rest of the agency's sales force combined. Years later, he estimated that with the notable exception of the Ayer agency's legendary Henry N. McKinney—"he occupied the first ten places, and I occupied the eleventh"—he was the most successful ad salesman in the world.

Traditionally, in the last quarter of the year, the salesmen of Lord & Thomas (and almost every other sizeable agency) fanned out across their territories in an effort to sign up their existing clients for the ensuing year.[13] As Lasker made his rounds in the final months of 1903, one-year renewal contracts in hand, he met with little resistance, since his clients were thrilled with the results he had produced for them. His last stop was in Indianapolis, where he had a meeting scheduled with Frank Van Camp, the head of the Van Camp Packing Company. The meeting took place in Lasker's room at a downtown Indianapolis hotel. After Van Camp signed his contract, Lasker asked him to accompany him to the mailbox in the hotel lobby. Van Camp, puzzled, watched Lasker drop the envelope containing the signed contract into the mailbox.

Then Lasker explained why he had wanted Van Camp to watch him put the contract in the mail: "You are the last account that Lord & Thomas has entrusted to me that [remained to be] signed up for 1904, so nothing that I can say to any of them or you can change your relationships, because you are legally bound to them. Now I feel I owe it to unfold something to you . . . I am going home tonight to resign, and [go] into business for myself."

Lasker felt that Ambrose Thomas had made implicit promises to him that hadn't been kept—including a partnership in the agency. He felt that all he could honorably take away from Lord & Thomas was the experience that he had gained in the previous five years. On the *other* hand—he said pointedly— if any of the clients whom he had just re-signed felt unhappy with Lord & Thomas at the end of the upcoming contract period, he would be happy to take them on in 1905.

Lasker also mentioned that he had discussed his plans with a senior colleague, Charles R. Erwin, but with no one else at Lord & Thomas. In truth, his discussions with Erwin were far advanced. Lasker "dreaded" going into business alone; he wanted a partner to share the risk, and he believed Erwin could lend credibility to the new venture: "He was a man of fine appearance, who could give confidence to anyone. Lovely shock of hair . . . And he was a good deal older than I was, [and] he understood a great deal of figures. I still had the feeling that the head of the house had to do what Mr. Lord did— open the mail, go to the bank if we needed it. I never had any contact with that end, so it all seemed very important to me."

Lasker offered Erwin a fifty-fifty partnership in his proposed new agency—and Erwin immediately accepted. "That is the only thing I ever did in business of which I am ashamed," he later admitted. "I don't believe that I had the right to win one of my coworkers away."

In response to these revelations, Frank Van Camp volunteered very little.

The next morning, back in Chicago, Lasker approached Ambrose Thomas's secretary, Kate Grady, and asked to see Thomas. Grady told Lasker that Thomas was in a meeting with Mr. Van Camp and could not be disturbed.

It is difficult to imagine the anxiety Lasker must have felt upon hearing this news. That anxiety must have increased exponentially, hour by hour, as

Thomas and Van Camp remained behind closed doors all morning. Finally, Thomas sent word to Lasker to meet him at the bar in Chicago's Wellington Hotel at the end of the day.

Standing at the bar, drink in hand, Thomas revealed that Frank Van Camp had called an emergency meeting, taken the train to Chicago, and repeated everything that Lasker had said to him. Moreover, Van Camp had informed Thomas that he fully intended to jump to Lasker at the end of the upcoming year, and that he suspected that every other one of Lasker's accounts would do the same. The only thing for Thomas to do, Van Camp said—the only way to hang on to Lasker and his accounts—was to make Lasker a partner.

Thomas told Lasker that he had decided to take Van Camp's advice and make both Lasker and Erwin partners in the firm. He had already approached cofounder and partner Daniel Lord and induced him to resign to make room for Lasker and Erwin. They had put a value of $200,000 on the business, which meant that Lord's half-interest could be acquired for $100,000, with $30,000 down. Stunned, Lasker accepted the proposal.[14]

Then came the hard part: finding $30,000. Lasker scraped together $10,000 in loans from friends and family members—not including his father—and Erwin came up with $5,000.[15] This left them $15,000 short. In an astounding display of bravado, Lasker then demanded that Ambrose Thomas make him a *gift* of the remaining $15,000, arguing that going into business on his own would cost Lasker far less than $15,000, and that Thompson was trading a more or less inactive partner (Lord) for two active partners (Lasker and Erwin).

On February 1, 1904, Albert Lasker became a one-quarter partner in Lord & Thomas. His peculiar road to partnership created tensions between himself and his mentor. One Saturday night in the early months of 1906, for example, Lord & Thomas held a firmwide dinner at the Stratford Hotel. At the end of the evening, Lasker rose and toasted Ambrose Thomas. "Whatever the business is," he proclaimed, "it owes to Mr. Thomas, because of his tolerance, and the fact that he gives everyone opportunity. The remarkable progress we are making is through the confidence and encouragement he lends to all of us."[16]

After the dinner, Charles Erwin suggested that the three partners head down to the hotel bar for a nightcap. Even though it was now past midnight, Lasker and Thomas agreed. After downing several drinks, Lasker recalled,

Thomas suddenly addressed him in the "meanest tone" that the elder man had ever used on him:

"Why did you make that talk tonight?" Thomas demanded. "You know you never meant a word of it."

Lasker, "hurt to the quick," protested strenuously that he had. And then he fought back:

> Mr. Thomas, ever since we started the new firm, you have changed. Instead of being to me, in a personal way, like you were before, you have done nothing but be offensive. You have done nothing but humiliate me with myself, and I can't stand another humiliation.
>
> This is Saturday night. I'll not be down to work on Monday. You can have my stock. This time, I'm going to start up in business across the street. I can't stand it anymore. I owe you a great debt, but I don't owe you my self-respect.

At this point, Thomas turned to Erwin and demanded that he back him up. Instead, the normally placid Erwin rose to the defense of his younger partner. If Lasker quit, Erwin concluded, he would be out the door with him.

Thomas backed down immediately. He apologized to Lasker, and sometime after 2:00 a.m.—tired, tipsy, but with the hatchet mostly buried—Thomas and Lasker boarded the same Illinois Central train to return to their homes in Woodlawn.

For the next six months or so, into the late fall of 1906, Thomas was wary around his junior partner. Lasker later remembered this interlude as the most difficult period in his relationship with Thomas, even worse than the months of abuse that had preceded it: "He tried to show his extreme[ly] tender feeling for me, until I could no longer be natural in the office, and hated going to the office . . . That isn't what I wanted from Mr. Thomas. He always was the boss, and the chief, to me. I was perfectly willing for him to order me to do something. I even preferred to have him cross with me. I felt unnatural."

Once again, Lasker decided to leave the firm. He resolved to hand over his interest in Lord & Thomas to his senior partner and—acting on his long-deferred dream—go into the newspaper business. The best way to make his break, he concluded, was to ask Thomas if they could walk to work together the next morning: November 10, 1906. On that walk, Lasker would quit. The pretext that Lasker gave to Thomas over the phone was that he wanted to show him a red rug that he had seen that day at Carson, Pirie, Scott on State Street. Lasker proposed to buy the rug to decorate Thomas's new office, he said, but wanted to make sure Thomas approved of the choice. Could they stop at the furniture store on the way into work, Lasker asked? Thomas agreed.

From Lasker's point of view, the walk couldn't have gotten off on a worse note. Thomas told Lasker that the younger man needed to take some time off. "No one can work the way you are working," he said solicitously. Then he suggested that Lasker take Flora, their two-year-old daughter Mary, and a nurse to Japan for six months, at the firm's expense. Lasker had always dreamed of visiting Japan.

Presented with this extraordinarily generous gesture, Lasker lost his resolve. Curtly, he told Thomas he didn't need a vacation.

Now they arrived at Carson, Pirie, Scott. They took the elevator to the rug department on the seventh floor, and sat on a sofa while a salesperson went off to retrieve the red rug. Thomas again urged Lasker to take an extended vacation. "If you *don't* take this vacation," the fifty-five-year-old Thomas continued, addressing his twenty-six-year-old partner, "we will bury you by the time you are thirty-six."

Those were the last words Thomas ever uttered. At that moment, he gasped for air, and fell dead onto Lasker's shoulder, the victim of a massive heart attack.[17] A physician who happened to be nearby tried unsuccessfully to revive the stricken executive, while members of the sales force threw up a screen to conceal the scene from curious onlookers. Lasker wandered back home while the store manager took responsibility for notifying Thomas's family. "I couldn't take any part in it," Lasker later admitted.[18]

In the wake of Thomas's death, there was no way Lasker could abandon Lord & Thomas. By the terms of the partnership agreement, Thomas's interest in the firm now was divided equally between the two surviving partners.[19] At the age of twenty-six, Lasker was the leader and half-owner of the second-largest advertising agency in the United States, with billings in excess of $3 million. The "Lord & Thomas" name remained unchanged. (Lasker wanted to take advantage of the agency's accumulated goodwill, and even at this early age, he saw advantages in adopting a low profile.) Charles Erwin became the new president of the company, but no one was confused about who was running the firm.

The business pressures that Lasker was already finding onerous before the fall of 1906 now became unbearable. And now, pressure began mounting from another direction, as Flora continued to suffer from a range of ailments. Early in 1907, her condition worsened, with the glands in her neck swelling to an alarming degree. Phlebitis, her continuing affliction, was not well understood, but it was known to be a sudden killer.

In April 1907, Lasker—heretofore a sometimes fragile but generally high-functioning individual—experienced a total collapse. He looked at his world and couldn't stop crying:

I had a terrible breakdown . . . I just couldn't work . . . I couldn't keep going anymore . . .

My wife, of course, was never well—she was an invalid all through our 35 years of married life—and this was a tremendous burden on her, in her condition, because I could do nothing but cry. Literally. I lost control to do anything but cry.

I had done nothing but work from the time I was 12. I married, and my wife was ill, and I never had taken off any time to play, excepting the type of play that did me hurt. And the reason I did that type of play, I imagine, was that it was so digested, concentrated, and I could do a lot of [it] in a hurry.

I just had a good old-fashioned breakdown. And in fact, my life ever since has been a struggle from breakdowns, because I never fully—I always say I got over all my breakdowns except my first one.[20]

Lasker operated at a high energy level. He was frequently expansive, irritable, highly verbal, intensely creative, and insomniac—all symptoms of a condition that today would be called hypomania. He never ascended to the level of mania that is generally associated with manic depression, or—again in today's vocabulary—a bipolar I disorder, although he sometimes behaved erratically, especially under the influence of alcohol.[21] Most likely, he was afflicted by a bipolar II (or "unipolar") disorder.

Recent research suggests that there is an increased risk of bipolar II disorder among people whose family members suffer from the disorder. Eduard Lasker, Albert's uncle, clearly had depressive episodes. Morris, too, may have experienced depressions; his rollercoaster financial affairs may have had their root, in part, in some sort of affective illness.

Finally, that diagnosis is supported by Lasker's age when the ailment overtook him. Bipolar I—the depression that is accompanied by wild, manic excess—usually first manifests itself in the teenage years, while the unipolar form of the illness often stays masked until the mid- or late twenties. Lasker was stricken at age twenty-seven. Abraham Lincoln, whose depressive symptoms closely resemble Lasker's, was twenty-six when his first attack overtook him. Both Lasker and Lincoln had their second major breakdown a half-decade after their first.[22]

In both Lincoln's and Lasker's case, the ailment was episodic. "Most people who have manic-depressive illness are, in fact, without symptoms (that is, psychologically normal) most of the time," writes psychiatrist Kay Redfield Jamison.[23] Jamison also puts forward the provocative hypothesis that bipolar illness is often bound up with creativity. Although her study of madness and creativity focuses on artists, it is intriguing to examine Albert Lasker (and indeed, Abraham Lincoln and others outside the "artistic" realm) through this same lens: "It is the interaction, tension, and transition between changing mood states, as well as the sustenance and discipline drawn from periods of health, that [are] critically important; and it is these same tensions and transitions that ultimately give such power to the art that is born in this way."[24]

Lasker assumed that he had succumbed to the pressures of his life. Those pressures surely were mounting in the winter of 1906 and spring of 1907. But recent psychological research suggests that the search for causality in depression may be fruitless. Certainly, having a surrogate father die in one's arms and being forced to watch a beloved wife deteriorate were crushing burdens. Most likely, though, Lasker's illness arrived on its own timetable. And now Lasker—the man who did everything in a hurry, in "concentrated" form—was immobilized.

No effective therapies for depression existed at that time. Sigmund Freud's "talking cure" was known only to a small medical community and was still highly controversial. Electroconvulsive therapy didn't come into common usage until the 1930s, and the efficacy of lithium and other drugs in treating mental illness remained unknown until the 1950s. In 1907, the only option for an individual who couldn't stop crying was to retreat from the world.

So that is what Lasker did. Putting the business in the hands of Charles Erwin, Lasker left for Europe with Flora, in search of peace of mind for himself and expert medical care for his wife.

The Laskers' first stop was a sanatorium on the edge of Germany's Black Forest. The *ruhe* ("retreat") was owned by a cousin—a physician also named Albert Lasker. He had built several guesthouses on the property, where he offered a restful environment for people who had suffered nervous breakdowns. The American Lasker found the place congenial enough, but far from therapeutic: "I just rested in bed and took the baths, and walked through the forest, do you see? And then, because I wanted to get my money's worth, we did considerable traveling on the Continent, which sent me home not much recovered from what I had started."

By now, Lasker had been away from the office several months, and his anxiety was mounting. The Laskers, still suffering from their respective illnesses, cut short their trip and returned to Chicago.

───────── ◦◉◦ ─────────

Perhaps the question is not why Albert Lasker crumpled in the spring of 1907, but rather, how he held up as long as he did.

From the outset, his mental health was fragile. After relocating to Chicago, he was isolated—in part by his brilliance, and in part because he had physically removed himself from everyone he loved and who loved him. Leaving Galveston, he not only cut himself off from parents to whom he felt closely bound, but also denied himself a gradual transition to adulthood. Overnight, he was thrown into an adult world, largely populated by rootless men and heavy drinkers. He drank heavily himself, further insulating himself from the world.

Lasker was deeply introspective: a trait that sometimes helped him. Seeing self-destructive tendencies in himself, for example, he found and methodically courted a mate. But in an astoundingly cruel twist of fate, Flora became permanently disabled less than two months after their marriage. The financial burdens, psychological upset, and guilt imposed by her illness were staggering.

The melodramatic death of Ambrose Thomas pushed him closer to the edge. Now he was running the business that he had planned to run away from. He was trapped—by the business and by the grinding financial needs of his family. By April 1907, Lasker couldn't stop crying.

It was only the first of many such episodes, which—on their own schedule—broke into his world and stole him away.

Chapter Six

The Greatest Copywriter

FOR LORD & THOMAS, and for Albert Lasker in particular, Frank Van Camp—the head of the Indianapolis-based Van Camp Packing Company—was an extremely important client. Van Camp's confidence in his young account manager had led directly to a major shake-up at Lord & Thomas, to Daniel Lord's abrupt retirement in 1904, and to Lasker getting his original ownership stake in the agency.

Van Camp was also a *demanding* client. When the gifted but erratic John E. Kennedy, copywriter for the Van Camp account, left Lord & Thomas in 1906, Van Camp insisted that Lasker come up with a writer who was as good as Kennedy—or better. This was a formidable challenge, and Lasker didn't know how to meet it.

The Van Camp Packing Company was founded by Gilbert C. Van Camp in 1862. Gilbert and his wife Hester ran a small store in Indianapolis, selling fruits and vegetables that they canned themselves. Gilbert, an accomplished tinsmith and tinkerer, gradually built up the business, improving his canning techniques and constructing one of the nation's first cold-storage warehouses.[1] Gilbert's and Hester's three sons—Frank, George, and Cortland—all joined the business, although Cortland soon departed to start a hardware company. Although tinned foods had been produced for nearly a century, cost and quality-control problems restricted their use mainly to the military. The perfection of new canning techniques—especially ways of preventing solder from getting into the food—and the advent of new distribution channels opened up unprecedented opportunities in the 1890s. Now, food companies like Franco-American and H.J. Heinz began producing an array of canned goods aimed at consumers.

In 1894, George figured out a way to can pork and beans in tomato sauce, thus broadening the company's base beyond its standard vegetable, chicken, and turkey products.[2] Frank, meanwhile, put a half-dozen salesmen on the road to push Van Camp canned goods, and commissioned some rudimentary advertising.[3] Also in 1894, the Joseph Campbell Soup Company, headed by the visionary John T. Dorrance, introduced a line of canned condensed soups. Dorrance invested $5,000 in streetcar ads in 1899; the results were so gratifying that the company increased its ad budget by 50 percent within six months. By 1905, Campbell's was selling 20 million cans of soup a year.[4]

Albert Lasker wrote some of Lord & Thomas's early copy for Van Camp. That work—including the "Ludwig and Lena" campaigns, which featured cartoons of two children in Hansel-and-Gretel outfits holding cans of pork and beans—was forgettable, at best. ("It's the intangible, subtle element which has taught you to think Van Camp whenever you think of pork and beans," the text of one ad ran.[5]) "I confess that I was responsible for Ludwig and Lena," Lasker later said ruefully, "who prated some kind of nonsense in the Van Camp advertising."[6]

Together, Kennedy and Lasker helped solved a knotty problem for Van Camp. Just after the turn of the century, the company had gone into the evaporated-milk business. Evaporating (or condensing) milk meant putting raw milk into large vacuum pans and removing two-thirds of the water. This condensation process, which involved high temperatures, also sterilized the milk and prevented it from spoiling. Housewives could use the product undiluted as a substitute for cream, or could add two pints of water to turn it back into an approximation of milk.[7]

Kennedy started searching for ways to market Van Camp's milk, which was generally a weak competitor, trailing Borden's and other leading brands. He came up with an ad that featured a bold headline—*Now a cow in your pantry*—and a picture of an eye-catching creature: a cow with Van Camp milk cans for its body and legs, can openers for horns, and a serving spoon for a tail.[8] Even Lasker, who generally disapproved of illustrations (because they were a distraction from the copy), acknowledged the power of this concept.

Lord & Thomas persuaded Van Camp to run test campaigns in Peoria, Indianapolis, and Jacksonville, and these tests revealed a problem. Van Camp's Evaporated Milk—like its competitors—didn't *taste* very good. Housewives, seduced by the prospect of a "cow in their pantry," were willing to try Van Camp's tinned milk, but most disliked the scalded aftertaste.

Lasker and Kennedy first persuaded Van Camp to change the name of its product from "evaporated milk" to "sterilized milk." Next, they proposed that Van Camp simply own up to the slightly objectionable taste of the product and recast it as a *virtue*. As the Lord & Thomas case history—probably dictated by Lasker—later put it: "We tried to find something that would nicely describe that scalded taste, and we finally hit upon, 'Be sure and taste the milk and see if it has got the almond flavor. If it has not the almond flavor, it is not the genuine.'"[9]

"It is like telling an Aladdin fairy tale," the account history bragged, "to tell you how it went."[10] Van Camp quickly displaced Borden as the leading evaporated milk in key markets like New York City. "No one else had a chance with milk [in New York]," one of Lasker's business associates later commented, "while [Lasker] was carrying on his campaign."[11] Van Camp's overall sales soared 30 percent between 1904 and 1905.[12]

With this success, of course, came greatly increased billings for Lord & Thomas. Frank Van Camp, Lasker recalled, "had made up his mind that the world was his if he advertised well, and widely."[13]

The problem for Lasker now was that the mercurial John E. Kennedy had departed, and Frank Van Camp knew it. The Indianapolis packer wanted to put substantial resources into marketing his company's old standby: pork and beans. Up to this point, he had restricted his pork-and-bean advertising to selected magazines, assuming that there was only a limited market for the product. Now he was willing to double or even triple his advertising dollars—in fact, he was willing to make the huge leap to national newspaper advertising of pork and beans—but only if Lasker could find an outstanding copywriter to replace Kennedy.

"So I was up against it," Lasker later recalled.

Sometime in 1907 (as Lasker told it), he was riding on a train. Seated across from him was Cyrus H. K. Curtis, the powerful founder of the Curtis Publishing Company, whom Lasker considered to be a shrewd judge of advertising. A former ad salesman, Curtis had launched a weekly magazine, the *Tribune & Farmer*, in 1879. His wife Louisa's popular column in that periodical led to a spin-off in 1883—the *Ladies' Home Journal*. In 1896, Curtis bought a broken-down publication called the *Saturday Evening Post* with ad revenues of less than $7,000 per year; by the time he was sharing a train compartment with Albert Lasker, the *Post* was bringing in $1 million a year.[14]

Lasker at first didn't recognize the celebrated publisher, who was partially concealed behind his newspaper. After they finally exchanged greetings, Curtis told Lasker that he had just read an extremely effective ad in his newspaper. "Lasker," Curtis supposedly said, "I am just about to order a bottle of beer as a result of an advertisement that I read, and you ought to go get the man who wrote that advertisement for your advertising business."[15]

Lasker knew that Curtis was a near-teetotaler who didn't permit the words "beer" and "wine" to appear in his *Ladies Home Journal*.[16] Now, here he was, heading off to the bar car in search of a beer. *Which* beer, exactly? Lasker looked at the ad that had caught Curtis's eye. "Poor Beer vs. Pure Beer," the headline read. It was an ad for Schlitz—a second-tier competitor to mighty Anheuser-Busch of St. Louis, which happened to be a Lord & Thomas account. "The beer that made Milwaukee famous," read the tag line below the prominent Schlitz logo. Lasker read the copy with interest:

> Both cost you alike, yet one costs the maker twice as much as the other. One is good, and good for you; the other is harmful. Let us tell you where the difference lies.

Poor beer, the copy claimed, involved "no filtering, no sterilizing, [and] almost no aging, for aging ties up money." Pure beer, by contrast, "must be filtered, then sterilized in the bottle," and must be "aged for months, until thoroughly fermented, else it causes biliousness."[17] Schlitz's product was a pure beer, and therefore a "healthful" beer. One proof was the Schlitz brewery, with its plate glass windows that gave visitors a clear view of the brewing process. "You're always welcome to [visit] that brewery," the ad concluded cheerily, "for the owners are proud of it."

Lasker was amused and intrigued. Without exactly saying so, the copywriter had effectively accused Schlitz's competitors of being unsanitary and inducing in beer drinkers the nasty-sounding "biliousness." The copy had suggested that Schlitz welcomed *scrutiny* of its brewing process in a way that other brewers could not. Schlitz, the beer that made Milwaukee famous, had nothing to hide!

Upon returning to Chicago, with the urgent demands of Frank Van Camp very much in his mind, Lasker began making inquiries: *Who is writing the Schlitz campaign?* The answer came back: an odd duck named Claude C. Hopkins.

Much of what is known about Claude Hopkins's early years comes from *My Life in Advertising*, his charming and maddening autobiography. Written in 1927 and today considered a classic, this slim volume's appeal grows out of its idiosyncratic authorial voice:

> *I do not know the reactions of the rich. But I do know the common people. I love to talk to laboring-men, to study housewives who must count their pennies, to gain the confidence and learn the ambitions of poor boys and girls. Give me something which they want and I will strike the responsive chord. My words will be simple, my sentences short. Scholars may ridicule my style. The rich and vain may laugh at the factors which I feature. But in millions of humble homes the common people will read and buy.[18]*

At the same time, *My Life In Advertising* frustrates because it is so remarkably devoid of facts. Perhaps Hopkins had no records at hand as he sat down to write. Or perhaps he saw no particular advantage in making it easy for his readers to connect the dots in ways that might reflect unfavorably on him or his family. In any case, it would be hard to find another autobiography with such a shortage of people, places, and dates.

We know from other sources that Hopkins was born on April 24, 1866.[19] He grew up in Hillsdale, Michigan, until his father—Fernando F. Hopkins, a college-educated printer—bought a partial interest in a weekly newspaper based in Ludington, Michigan, which Hopkins described only as a "prosperous lumbering city."

In his writings, Claude Hopkins claimed that his mother was "left a widow" when Claude was ten years old, but the sketchy available evidence suggests that Fernando may have abandoned the family. In either case, for the next decade, Hopkins struggled alongside his mother to keep the family housed and fed. He sold his mother's silver polish door-to-door. He cleaned two schoolhouses at the beginning and end of each school day. He delivered the *Detroit Evening News* to sixty-five houses before dinner. On Sundays he worked as a church janitor, and during summer vacations he did farm work. For the rest of his life, even after becoming an extraordinarily wealthy man, he feared slipping back into the desperate poverty of his youth. As a result, he maintained a seven-day-a-week, twelve-hour-a-day work regimen: "If I have gone higher than others in advertising, or done more, the fact is not due to exceptional ability, but to exceptional hours. It means that a man has sacrificed all else in life to excel in this one profession. It means a man to be pitied, rather than envied, perhaps.[20]

Sometime around 1883, Hopkins graduated from high school and became a minister and teacher. Neither profession satisfied his aching ambition. Perhaps a year later, he enrolled at Swensburg's Business College in Grand Rapids, which he later dismissed as a "ridiculous institution."[21] But it led him to a job keeping the books—and sweeping the floors, and cleaning the windows—at the nearby Grand Rapids Felt Boot Company.

In the course of what may have been a year at the Felt Boot Company, Hopkins met Melville R. Bissell, president of the Bissell Carpet Sweeper Company. In 1876, Bissell had patented his carpet-cleaning device—which he had invented to lift sawdust off the rugs in the small crockery store that he and his wife operated—and by 1883, he was constructing his first factory. Bissell offered Hopkins a bookkeeping job at his new factory for substantially more money than he was making at the boot factory.

Once at Bissell, Hopkins again went looking for opportunity. One day, a mediocre draft for a new brochure arrived at the factory, written by a celebrated advertising man who had not bothered to learn much about carpet sweepers. Hopkins asked for the chance to rewrite the text on his own time. His skeptical superiors said yes, and Hopkins beat out the celebrated out-of-towner with a much-improved text.

He then began figuring out ways to drum up demand for his company's product. First, he pushed carpet sweepers as Christmas presents—a notion that had not occurred to anyone before—and generated a staggering one thousand orders through a combination of letter writing and store displays. Next, he hatched a scheme to offer Bissell Carpet Sweepers in a dozen different woods, "from the white of the bird's-eye maple to the dark of the walnut, and to include all of the colors between."[22] Using both the carrot and stick with the company's dealers—and again overcoming the deep skepticism of his colleagues in Grand Rapids—Hopkins sold 250,000 exotic-woods carpet sweepers in three weeks.

In the parlance of the day, Hopkins had become a "scheme man," and a marketing talent like this would not remain in Grand Rapids for long. Sometime in 1891, when Albert Lasker was still an eleven-year-old boy down in Galveston, Lord & Thomas got in touch with the dazzling young talent up in Grand Rapids and offered him a job. As Hopkins recalled:

> They had a scheme man named Carl Greig, who was leaving them to go with the Inter Ocean to increase the circulation. Lord & Thomas, who had watched my sweeper-selling schemes, offered me his place. The salary was much higher

than I received in Grand Rapids, so I told the Bissell people that I intended to take it. They called a directors' meeting. Every person on the board had, in times past, been my vigorous opponent. All had fought me tooth and nail on every scheme proposed. They had never ceased to ridicule my idea of talking woods in a machine for sweeping carpets. But they voted unanimously to meet the Lord & Thomas offer, so I stayed.

Not for long, however. Probably later in 1891, Hopkins saw an ad for a position as advertising manager at Swift & Company, in Chicago. He got the job and moved to Chicago, only to find that the huge packing firm viewed his profession—and by extension, him—as a necessary evil. Founder Gustavus Franklin Swift, a transplanted Yankee from Massachusetts who had founded the packing company a half-decade earlier, regarded business as a form of warfare and advertising as an expensive distraction from the business of war-making. As Hopkins put it: "I was more unwelcome than I supposed. Mr. G. F. Swift, then head of the company, was in Europe when I was employed. It was his first vacation, and he could not endure it, so he hurried back. When told that I was there to spend his money, he took an intense dislike to me, and it never changed."[23]

Hopkins's first big challenge was to promote a Swift product called Coto-suet, which was a mixture of cottonseed oil and beef suet, packed in tin pails and used as an inexpensive substitute for lard and butter. It was no different from, or better than, or cheaper than, its entrenched competitor, Cot-tolene. Hopkins struggled to come up with a way to push Cotosuet on an indifferent public. He soon settled upon a scheme to bake the "world's biggest cake" using Cotosuet, and put it on display in a new department store that was about to open in downtown Chicago. Traffic stalled on State Street as huge crowds flocked to behold the monstrous dessert. Over the course of a week, more than 100,000 people climbed four flights of stairs to see it. They were encouraged to try a sample and to win prizes by guessing the weight of the cake—but only after buying a pail of Cotosuet. "As a result of that week," Hopkins wrote, "Cotosuet was placed on a profit-paying basis in Chicago."[24]

Next, apparently in 1895, Hopkins left Swift and began a six-year stint in Racine, Wisconsin, working for Dr. Shoop's Family Medicines—the manufacturer of patent medicines that subsequently employed John E. Kennedy.[25] In later years, Hopkins looked back with some embarrassment on his efforts to promote remedies that were either ineffective or dangerous, but he never stopped thinking of that experience as the "supreme test" of the copywriter's skills. "Medicines were worthless merchandise," he wrote, "until a demand was created."[26] Hopkins came up with various "pull-through" schemes to compel druggists to carry Dr. Shoop's elixirs.

In 1902, Hopkins was contacted by Chicago-based entrepreneur Douglas Smith, who had made a small fortune manufacturing the Oliver typewriter. While building a typewriter factory in Toronto sometime around 1898, Smith had learned of a supposed germicide—Powley's Liquified Ozone— that came highly recommended by local users. Smith picked up the product for $100,000, changed its name to "Liquozone," and started marketing his new product through the newly formed Liquid Ozone Company, which he headquartered in Chicago.

Four years and four ad managers later, he was desperate to find a way to sell the stuff. Hearing that Hopkins was the best scheme man and copywriter in Chicago, Smith approached him with an unusual proposition: If Hopkins would sign on with Liquozone and agree to work for no salary, Smith would give him a quarter of the company. After a great deal of anguish about leaving his comfortable perch in Racine for a situation where he would be living off his savings while trying to rescue a dying company, the deeply conservative Hopkins took the plunge. In February 1902, he moved to Chicago and began promoting another product nobody much wanted.

"Night after night I paced Lincoln Park," Hopkins wrote, "trying to evolve a plan."[27] The plan he came up with resembled one he had developed earlier for Dr. Shoop. The company would offer a fifty-cent bottle of its germicide *free* to anyone who responded to a newspaper ad. (Getting the consumer to *ask for* the sample was a key part of many schemes devised by Hopkins.) Liquozone would send a coupon redeemable at a local druggist, where the recipient of the free sample would also be offered a money-back guarantee on five $1 bottles of the product. Beginning with a test market—Hopkins believed fervently in testing his "schemes" before asking his client to plunge—the company found that requests for free samples cost 18 cents to generate. Thirty days later, it was clear that the average coupon redeemer was spending 91 cents on Liquozone. Over the next three years, Smith and Hopkins gave away 5 million free samples. By 1904, Liquozone was advertised in seventeen languages and sold around the world, and Hopkins was a rich man.

Here the chronology again starts to get tangled. Beginning sometime in the early years of the twentieth century—probably while he was still with Dr. Shoop's—and continuing through his days at Liquozone, the peripatetic Hopkins moonlighted as a freelance copywriter for the Chicago-based J. L. Stack Advertising Agency. Stack was a Lord & Thomas–trained ad man who, around the turn of the century, had gone into competition with his former employers.[28] He recognized the copywriter's formidable talent, and put him to work with a number of key clients, including Montgomery, Ward & Co., and—notably—Schlitz.

Hopkins toured the Schlitz brewery in Milwaukee and was impressed. When he asked his clients why they didn't boast of their pure water, their white-wood-pulp filters, their filtered air, their four separate washings of their bottles, the Schlitz executives responded that *everyone* brewed beer in this way. No matter, said Hopkins. If you tell a good story, and tell it *first*, it will be *your* story:

> So I pictured in print those plate-glass rooms and every other factor in purity. I told a story common to all good brewers, but a story which had never been told. I gave purity a meaning . . .
>
> Again and again I have told common facts, common to all makers in the line—too common to be told. But they have given the article first allied with them an exclusive and lasting prestige.
>
> That situation occurs in many, many lines. The maker is too close to his product. He sees in his methods only the ordinary. He does not realize that the world at large might marvel at those methods, and that facts which seem commonplace to him might give him vast distinction.[29]

On the strength of Hopkins's efforts to "give purity a meaning," Schlitz jumped from fifth in sales to a near-tie with mighty Anheuser-Busch in St. Louis.

<hr>

On the day that Albert Lasker read Claude Hopkins's Schlitz ad on the train in 1907, Hopkins was no longer working for Liquozone. In fact, for the first time since he was ten years old, he was not working at all.

In *My Life In Advertising,* Hopkins says that he signed on with Doug Smith's company in 1902 and worked there for five years—in other words, almost up to the day Lasker spotted him. We also learn that he had a breakdown toward the end of those five years, which forced him to consult a doctor in Paris. The French doctor told Hopkins that the only thing that could save him would be for him to go home and rest. Hopkins (who lived out of hotels, and didn't *have* a home) retreated to the sleepy town of Spring Lake, Michigan, near the eastern shore of Lake Michigan, where he had worked as a farmhand decades earlier. There, he spent three months "in the sunshine, sleeping, playing, and drinking milk."[30]

What Hopkins does not mention in his autobiography, and which surely must have been a contributing factor to his breakdown, is a series of events that surely represented calamity to the one-quarter owner of the Liquid Ozone Company. The disaster kicked off on October 7, 1905, when *Collier's* magazine carried an article entitled "The Great American Fraud" by an enterprising young writer named Samuel Hopkins Adams. Adams was one of America's first investigative reporters, and he was extremely good at his trade. "This is the introductory article to a series which will contain a full explanation and exposure of patent medicine methods, and the harm done to the public by this industry," Adams began, "founded mainly on fraud and poison."[31]

At the end of the article, Adams apologized in advance that he would not be able to expose *all* of the vile potions and elixirs that were out there, bilking Americans of some $75 million per year and discouraging them from seeking legitimate medical help. There were simply too many of them, and "many dangerous and health-destroying compounds will escape through sheer inconspicuousness." But Adams promised he would go after the worst offenders in each of several categories: the alcohol stimulators, the opium-containing soothing syrups, the headache powders, and the "comparatively harmless fake, as typified by that marvelous product of advertising and effrontery, Liquozone."[32]

A subsequent installment in the series was devoted to Liquozone. In his attack, Adams combined wit, scorn, and science in roughly equal measures. A typical passage mocked the Liquid Ozone Company's claims that their product consisted of "liquid oxygen": "Liquid oxygen doesn't exist above a temperature of 229 degrees below zero. One spoonful would freeze a man's tongue, teeth, and throat to equal solidity before he ever had time to swallow. If he could, by any miracle, manage to get it down, the undertaker would have to put him on the stove to thaw him out sufficiently for a respectable burial."[33]

In fact, as Adams compelled the Liquid Ozone Company to reveal, their product was 98 percent water, with trace amounts of sulfuric and sulfurous acids. *Collier's* paid the Lederle Laboratories in New York to test Liquozone's efficacy against anthrax, diphtheria, and tuberculosis (all of which supposedly were warded off by the internal or topical use of Liquozone). In every case, *all* of the test animals—those treated with Liquozone and those not treated—contracted diseases.

Nor did the senior executives of the Liquid Ozone Company escape Adams's scourging. Douglas Smith was dismissed as a "promoter" with a "keen vision for profits." Adams called Claude Hopkins the "ablest exponent of his specialty in the country," and admitted that he might not be the *most* culpable in a generally guilty group:

> *An enormous advertising campaign was begun. Pamphlets were issued containing testimonials and claiming the soundest professional backing. Indeed, this matter of expert testimony, chemical, medical, and bacteriologic, is a specialty of Liquozone. Today, despite its reforms, it is supported by an ingenious system of pseudoscientific charlatanry. In justice to Mr. Hopkins, it is but fair to say that he is not responsible for the basic fraud; that the general scheme was devised and most of the bogus or distorted medical letters arranged before his advent.*[34]

This was a public-relations disaster of the first order, and it kept getting worse. No matter that Hopkins believed in Liquozone—and believed that its use had saved his daughter's life. In response to the *Collier's* revelations, North Dakota banned the sale of Liquozone. So did San Francisco and Lexington, Kentucky. In 1906, partly owing to the public outcry caused by Adams's articles, Congress passed the federal Food and Drugs Act, which compelled manufacturers to state exactly what was in the preparations they were selling to the public.

It is not surprising, then, that Claude Hopkins called his five years with Liquozone "strenuous," and that by the spring of 1907, he was on a milk diet along the quiet shores of Spring Lake.

———

Albert Lasker was well aware of the troubles plaguing the Liquid Ozone Company. In fact, he had had a similar experience. Early in his tenure at Lord & Thomas, the agency represented a patent-medicine concern called the Kalamazoo Tuberculosis Remedy Company. The company was exposed as a fraud, and as soon as Lasker took the reins at Lord & Thomas, he steered the agency out of the patent-medicine business.[35]

Lasker had followed the Liquozone campaigns carefully, going so far as to cut out a particularly effective ad and study it "a hundred times."[36] He admired the company's clever use of coupons, which made Lasker think of the Liquozone writer as a "kindred spirit."[37] Now, as he made his discreet inquiries in 1907, he discovered that the same person—Claude C. Hopkins—was behind both the Schlitz ads and the Liquozone campaigns.[38]

He learned this from a friend, Stephen Hester, who owned a small stake in Liquozone. Lasker asked Hester how he might persuade Hopkins to come work for Lord & Thomas. Hester—an invalid who rarely left his Chicago hotel rooms and had both the time and the inclination to conspire with Lasker—came up with an elaborate ruse for recruiting Hopkins, whom he regarded as "a quiet man, a highly sensitive man, a man who is stingy with money in small things."[39]

Hopkins, Hester explained to Lasker, had spent nearly his whole life in advertising. By most accounts, he was the greatest advertising man alive—and yet, he was now "disgraced, and disheartened." And to further complicate things, Hopkins was worth something like $1 million, so he didn't need to work. Rumor had it that Hopkins was going to get out of business and become an author.[40]

Hester proposed to introduce Lasker to Hopkins at lunch. Lasker would tell Hopkins about his problems with Frank Van Camp, and explain that he would consider it a great personal favor if Hopkins would compose a few ads just to get the new campaign started. Hester strongly advised Lasker *not* to offer to pay him. Instead, Hester said, he should offer to buy a new electric automobile for Hopkins's wife. "His wife wants an electric automobile for $2,700," Hester told Lasker, "and he won't give it to her. This will solve the most pressing problem he has." Lasker agreed to the scheme.

He may have been surprised, on the day of the luncheon, at the relatively unprepossessing manner and appearance of his man. Slightly foppish, with a thin mustache and protruding front teeth, Hopkins spoke with a lisp, so that when he introduced himself as "C. C. Hopkins," it came out as "Thee-Thee." (This became his nickname around the office for the next seventeen years, although to his face, Thee-Thee was always addressed as "Mr. Hopkins.") Lasker followed Hester's script to the letter, and Hopkins agreed to jumpstart the Van Camp campaign.

Hopkins's account of that lunch adds some interesting details. He recalled Lasker showing him a contract for $400,000 from the Van Camp Packing

Company, contingent on satisfactory copy being submitted to Frank Van Camp. According to Hopkins:

> Mr. Lasker said, "I have searched the country for copy. This is the copy I got in New York, this in Philadelphia. I have spent thousands of dollars to get the best copy obtainable. You see the result. Neither you nor I would submit it. Now I ask you to help me. Give me three ads, which will start this campaign, and your wife may go down Michigan Avenue to select any car on the street and have it charged to me."
>
> As far as I know, no ordinary human being has ever resisted Albert Lasker. He has commanded what he would in this world. Presidents have made him their pal. Nothing he desired has ever been forbidden him. So I yielded, as all do, to his persuasiveness. I went to Indianapolis that night.[41]

Shortly afterward, Lord & Thomas publicly announced that it had retained the services of Claude C. Hopkins. Lasker assembled the office staff one morning and told them about the new hire, who would be paid the astounding sum of $1,000 per week—more than twice what John Kennedy had commanded only two years earlier. "My instinct for showmanship was fully gratified," Lasker later remembered, "when I heard a voice at the rear of the crescent-shaped clustering of our people repeating with awestruck emphasis, '—a week!'"[42]

That same morning, in conversations with groups of staff members, Hopkins began imparting his theory of copywriting. We should never brag about a client's product, he said, or plead with consumers to buy it. Instead, we must figure out how to appeal to the consumer's *self-interest*. The group we call "everybody" is actually a collection of individuals, each mainly concerned about him- or herself. "We must get down to individuals," he stressed. "We must treat people in advertising as we treat them in person."[43]

Hopkins had begun his adult life as a teacher, and he saw himself as a teacher still. But he was also a *doer*—and the task at hand was pushing pork and beans.

Van Camp presented some interesting challenges, including the fact that its pork and beans product was undistinguished. (At the Van Camp factory, Hopkins laid out a spread of a half-dozen rival brands with no identifying labels; no one could figure out which was Van Camp's.) But this wasn't the most pressing concern. As Hopkins soon discovered, something like 94 percent of housewives cooked their own pork and beans and weren't interested in a canned alternative. So Hopkins decided that he first had to soften up that uninterested 94 percent of the potential market: "I started a campaign to argue against home baking . . . I told of the sixteen hours required to bake beans at home. I told why home baking could never make beans digestible. I pictured home-baked beans, with the crisped beans on top, the mushy beans below . . . Then I offered a free sample for comparison. The result was an enormous success."[44]

⸻ ❖ ⸻

Next, Hopkins set about "differentiating" Van Camp's product from the competition:

> We told of beans grown on special soils. Any good navy beans must be grown there. We told of vine-ripened tomatoes, Livingston Stone tomatoes. All our competitors used them. We told how we analyzed every lot of beans, as every canner must. We told of our steam ovens where beans are baked for hours at 245 degrees. That is regular canning practice . . . We told just the same story that any rival could have told, but all others thought the story was too commonplace.[45]

Hopkins then acted on an observation he happened to make on the streets of downtown Chicago. At the restaurants and lunch counters into which Hopkins poked his head, a large number of the men at the tables and counters were consuming factory-baked pork-and-bean products. This, of course, was simply semantics: by definition, commercial establishments couldn't provide "home-cooked" meals, so diners who liked pork and beans for lunch took what they could get. But Hopkins realized that many housewives were ready to quit the onerous, sixteen-hour process of making pork and beans from scratch. He told them that their "men folks were buying baked beans downtown," and "told them how to quit easily."[46]

Soon, Van Camp was able to command a premium for its unremarkable pork and beans, and emerge as the dominant national brand.

An overlapping story begins in 1908, when the head of the American Cereal Company, Henry Parsons Crowell, got in touch with Lord & Thomas. Crowell—a devout Christian who went into business to serve God after recovering from a childhood bout with tuberculosis—had bought the run-down Quaker Mill in Ravenna, Ohio, in 1881. One of the first manufacturers to start packaging and selling oats directly to consumers, beginning with its

"Pure Quaker Oats" in 1884, Crowell had created one of the nation's most successful branded cereals. In 1901, he joined forces with three other cereal magnates to found American Cereal (henceforth "Quaker"), headquartered in Chicago.[47]

Over its early history, Quaker employed a variety of ad agencies.[48] Quaker felt that it didn't need Lord & Thomas's help in selling its flagship oats; on the other hand, as Crowell informed Hopkins at a 1908 meeting, the company had a portfolio of products that were only bumping along. Impressed with Lord & Thomas's recent string of successes, he offered to put $50,000 into promoting a Quaker product of Hopkins's choosing.[49]

Hopkins soon settled upon two odd products—Puffed Rice and Wheat Berries—which had been introduced as novelties at the 1904 World's Fair in St. Louis. They were manufactured by a similar process: Raw grains were placed in long metal cylinders that looked something like rifle barrels. Hot compressed air was then injected into these tubes, and the kernels of grain expanded to something like eight times their original size. When the cylinder was opened, the compressed air exploded out, carrying with it the "puffed" cereal.

Hopkins loved it. It was visual, counterintuitive—and *patented*. Quaker controlled the puffing machinery, and for the time being, at least, nobody else could make puffed cereals in just this way; this made it a far better business than corn flakes. Into Hopkins's head popped the soon-to-be-immortal phrase: *Food shot from guns.*

Of course, Lord & Thomas still had to lay the groundwork for a successful campaign. Looking at the economics of cereal manufacturing and distribution, Hopkins and Lasker realized that the rice and wheat products had to be sold together to justify the cost of advertising them. This meant that Wheat Berries needed a new name: "Puffed Wheat." Quaker agreed. Next, Lord & Thomas argued for a price increase: from 10 cents to 15 cents a box for Puffed Rice, and from 7 cents to 10 cents for Puffed Wheat. Quaker worried that this would kill sales of two products that were already in decline; Lord & Thomas argued that the price increases would pay for the advertising needed to drive up sales.[50] Once again, Quaker acquiesced. The agency contacted retailers and suggested that they stock up *before* this price increase, which had the welcome effect of driving up sales.[51]

Then Hopkins went to work. He invented a personality, Professor Alexander P. Anderson—in fact, the real-life Quaker Oats technician from the

University of Minnesota who had developed the puffing process—to explain the science behind puffed cereals. ("Personalities appeal," Hopkins observed, "while soulless corporations do not."[52]) He lovingly wrote up the process (*125 million steam explosions in every grain!*). He described the puffed grains (*eight times their original size!*). He hammered away at the theme of "foods shot from guns"—a theme that elicited howls of derision from the advertising community: "That idea aroused ridicule. One of the greatest food advertisers in the country wrote an article about it. He said that of all the follies evolved in food advertising this certainly was the worst. The idea of appealing to women with "Food shot from guns" was the theory of an imbecile."[53]

Not so: Puffed Wheat and Puffed Rice were soon the most profitable breakfast foods on the market. Quaker, astonished, retained Lord & Thomas to promote its flagship Quaker Oats and other products.[54]

Hopkins later admitted that Lord & Thomas made some mistakes with Puffed Wheat and Puffed Rice. They pushed for newspaper advertising—a mass medium—for a product that the masses couldn't afford. (The agency soon retreated to magazine ads only.) They distributed millions of samples "promiscuously," Hopkins recalled ruefully. ("It never pays to cast samples on the doorstep," he later concluded. "They are like waifs."[55]) One series of ads offered a box of Puffed Wheat free to anybody who bought a box of Puffed Rice. ("The offer was ineffective . . . it is just as hard to sell at a half price as at a full price to people who are not converted."[56]) But the agency learned from its mistakes, and when the next consumer product came through the door, Lord & Thomas was far better prepared.

Hopkins never ceased being the scheme man who had taken Grand Rapids and Chicago by storm, and at Lord & Thomas he persisted in his promotional ways. These, combined with Lasker's powers of salesmanship, continued to generate marketing miracles.

One such scheme involved the creation of an "advisory board" in the Chicago offices of Lord & Thomas. This lofty-sounding body was actually sixteen Lord & Thomas employees, over whom Hopkins presided. Using *Judicious Advertising* and other vehicles, Hopkins heavily advertised the existence of this board, which was available to help anyone with an "advertising problem."

As Hopkins wrote in a 1909 Lord & Thomas publication called *Safe Advertising*: "Here we decide what is possible and what is impossible, so far as men can. This advice is free. We invite you to submit your problems. Get the combined judgment of these able men on your article and its possibilities. Tell them what you desire, and let them tell you if it probably can be accomplished."[57] Several hundred entrepreneurs came to the advisory board's table. Some 95 percent of them—those with what Hopkins called "dubious prospects"—were told to give up on advertising. The remainder, of course, were good prospects for Lord & Thomas.

Two visitors not sent packing were B. J. Johnson, head of the Milwaukee-based B.J. Johnson Soap Co., and his newly appointed sales manager, Charles Pearce, who appeared before the advisory board one morning in 1911.[58] The company had been founded a half-century earlier, in 1864, and was mainly known for its Galvanic laundry soap. But even in 1911, the laundry-detergent field was a cutthroat arena, and the advisory board advised against a Galvanic campaign.

Do you have anything else, the board asked? Yes, Johnson and Pearce said, they did have another product—a bar soap made from palm and olive oils. The soap, which had been on the market since 1898 and had a nearly undetectable market share, was called Palmolive. The delegation from Milwaukee had low expectations for their obscure bar soap, but the Lord & Thomas board felt differently.

After internal discussions, they proposed to Johnson that the company mount a small test. Galvanic was then sold mainly through grocers. Lord & Thomas would approach these retailers in test markets and ask them to participate in a promotion called "Johnson Soap Week." During Soap Week, shoppers who purchased a tin of Galvanic would be given a bar of Palmolive. Grocers who agreed to purchase Palmolive in advance would be listed in full-page advertisements telling consumers where they could get their "free" bar of soap. Johnson agreed to the scheme, and the promotion proved successful, establishing a "solid trade" in the obscure Palmolive brand.[59]

The real challenge, though, was to get Palmolive out from under the skirts of Galvanic and into drugstores, where it could stand on its own. The agency proposed a novel campaign in Grand Rapids for $1,000. When Johnson objected to the price, Lord & Thomas proposed a scaled-down experiment—for $700—in the lakeside town of Benton Harbor, Michigan. Johnson agreed.

The agency ran a series of ads touting the "beauty appeal" of Palmolive, and announcing that the manufacturer would "buy a cake of Palmolive for every woman who applied." The next ad contained a coupon good for a ten-cent cake of soap at any store. The dealer, according to the coupon, would then charge Palmolive ten cents.

The notion of a dime changing hands, or at least *appearing* to change hands, was central to Hopkins's scheme. (In fact, the dealer would be buying the sample bars at wholesale prices of less than a dime, thereby receiving a guaranteed profit on each bar sold.) The coupon gimmick also helped persuade dealers to stock the product. Lord & Thomas mailed a copy of the coupon in advance to local retailers, pointing out that every household in the vicinity would soon be getting one of these coupons—worth a dime, back in a day when a dime was worth something—and that consumers would certainly redeem them *somewhere*. The threat was clear: existing customers might go elsewhere. "We gain[ed] by this plan universal distribution immediately at a moderate cost," Hopkins boasted.[60]

At a cost of approximately $700, Lord & Thomas persuaded several thousand Michigan women to try Palmolive. The product was good—the essential building block, according to both Lasker and Hopkins—and repeat sales in Benton Harbor paid for all advertising costs even before the bills came due. "We knew we had a winner," wrote Hopkins.[61]

A subsequent test in Cleveland (where Palmolive sales had up to that point averaged about $3,000 per year) generated $20,000 in sales. Consumers redeemed twenty-thousand coupons, costing Johnson $2,000. With an additional $1,000 for newspaper advertising figured in, the campaign cost a total of $3,000, or about 15 percent of gross sales.[62]

From then on, it was simply a matter of ratcheting up the scheme in a series of ever-larger markets. When every local test returned the same results, Lord & Thomas persuaded Johnson to take Palmolive national. Buying a full page in the *Saturday Evening Post*, Lord & Thomas drew up an ad that made essentially the same offer that had been made in Benton Harbor. Then the agency sent out letters to fifty thousand druggists and retailers all over the country, explaining what was about to happen. More than $50,000 worth of orders poured in for a soap none of these retailers had ever seen. As an internal Lord & Thomas account put it:

It is an astonishing fact that on this circular alone, before the advertising appeared, over $50,000 worth of the soap was sold and the resultant sales in the four weeks following the appearance of the advertisement totaled almost

$75,000. Almost 200,000 coupons were redeemed and the advertiser had gained a foothold on a national basis that had never before been contemplated. The astonishing thing was that the soap orders came from over 300,000 cities, towns, and hamlets in the United States and Canada.[63]

A juggernaut was now in motion. A similar ad four months later in the *Ladies' Home Journal* generated a huge response. Dealers began placing ads—totaling some $30,000—announcing that they would redeem the Palmolive coupons. Johnson sold more than $100,000 worth of soap *before* the ad appeared. A year after the advertisement appeared in the *Journal*, Johnson was still redeeming up to two thousand coupons per month. An astonishing 99 percent of drugstores stocked Palmolive and ordered new stock on an average of between three and four times a year.[64]

Palmolive was now the best-selling soap in the world. One reason was that, despite the costs associated with advertising, Palmolive (at ten cents a bar) remained the lowest-priced "beauty soap" on the market. Competitors that traditionally had sold high-end soaps for as much as twenty-five cents a bar were forced to cut their prices to stay competitive.[65]

In 1916, B.J. Johnson Soap changed its name to the Palmolive Company.[66] Lord & Thomas promoted a variety of products under the Palmolive brand—including shampoo and shaving cream—with great success, and the account remained with the agency until the 1930s.

Now comes one of the stranger stories from the Lasker-Hopkins heyday, drifting into the darker realms of commercial espionage and betrayal.

The melodrama begins in 1907, shortly after Hopkins's arrival at Lord & Thomas. The Goodyear Tire & Rubber Company—an Akron-based tire manufacturer founded in 1898 by Franklin A. Seiberling and his younger brother Charles—was an established Lord & Thomas client with a consistent annual ad volume of about $40,000. Although this was a respectable figure for the early years of the twentieth century, Lord & Thomas proposed a significant expansion of the tire manufacturer's advertising. After prolonged debate, Goodyear agreed to increase its ad budget to $250,000. This sum was twice as much as the company's entire profits from 1906 and represented an enormous gamble.[67]

The huge expansion of the Goodyear account occasioned a memorable moment at Lord & Thomas. Robert Crane, then a young copywriter, was talking with Hopkins in Hopkins's office: "Suddenly the door opened, and in rushed Lasker. Hopkins was standing up with his back to the wall, about two or three feet away from the wall. And Lasker doubled up his fist, and hit Hopkins in the chest, and said, 'By God, Hopkins, we *landed* it!' And Hopkins bumped his head against the wall, and his eyes bulged out, and he didn't crack a smile. And said, 'Isn't that gratifying?'"[68]

But a problem soon emerged. After visiting Akron and prowling around the Goodyear plant, Hopkins confessed that he couldn't figure out the merits of the tire that Goodyear was then promoting: the Straight Side tire, introduced in 1906.[69] Who cares if a tire has "straight sides," he asked? Don't all tires have more or less straight sides? Goodyear's technicians rushed to straighten him out. This patented construction, they told him, meant that size for size, Goodyear tires had 10 percent greater air capacity. Just as important, they could not be cut by the rim of the wheel in the wake of a puncture.

Hopkins listened, pondered, and came up with a plan: "I coined the name 'No-Rim-Cut Tires.' Across every ad, we ran the heading, 'No-Rim-Cut Tires, 10% Oversize.' The results were immediate and enormous. Sales grew by leaps and bounds. Goodyear tires soon occupied the leading place in tiredom."[70]

According to Lord & Thomas records, sales of the No-Rim-Cut tire doubled in four months. Goodyear's business increased from $2 million in 1906 to $9.5 million in 1910, reflecting both effective promotion and a huge surge in car production (from 33,200 cars produced in the United States in 1906 to 181,000 in 1910).[71] By 1911, the company's Akron plant was operating twenty-four hours a day to keep up with demand.[72]

Competitors soon imitated the No-Rim-Cut design, so Hopkins moved on to another angle: the tire's patented, diamond-pattern antiskid tread, first introduced in 1908. He decided that this should be called the "All-Weather" tread. Again, sales boomed. Goodyear became the nation's leading tire maker. Ad budgets grew from $250,000 a year—a sum that Goodyear had ventured with some trepidation—to an astounding $2 million.

But all was not well between Lord & Thomas and Goodyear. "I lost it," Hopkins later wrote of the Goodyear account. His explanation was characteristically vague: "There developed a desire for institutional advertising which I could never approve."[73]

Actually, the account left the Lord & Thomas fold for several reasons, including dramatic changes then taking place within the agency. In 1912,

Albert Lasker decided that he had to get rid of his sole remaining partner, Charles R. Erwin. Lasker had muscled his way into his ownership position at the agency in 1904 with Erwin's support. Over the next eight years, however, he became frustrated with Erwin's minimal advertising skills. Erwin was a "business-getter," in Lasker's estimation, but not an ad man. Hopkins, too, had little use for Erwin. "He liked Mr. Erwin tremendously," Lasker later commented, "[but] had nothing but the most supreme contempt for him on advertising, which he realized Erwin didn't grasp at all."[74]

In 1910, Lasker opened a Lord & Thomas office in New York, at Fifth Avenue and Twenty-Eighth Street, putting added pressure on himself to build business in two cities.[75] By 1912, Lasker's irritation with Erwin came to a head, and he announced that he wanted out. "I went back to Erwin," he later recalled, "and told him that I wanted to split partnership with him . . . that I realized that I was a lone wolf, that I couldn't be in a partnership."[76]

Erwin took the bad news graciously. He knew Lasker was the true driving force behind the business, and generously suggested that Lasker should take more than half of the agency. Lasker made a counterproposal: "No, Mr. Erwin, that is totally unfair . . . I am going to make you a proposal. I will give you $400,000 for your half interest, and you agree not to go into the advertising business. Or, I will take $200,000 for my half interest, and I will agree not to go into the advertising business."

It was a clever formula that Lasker used several times in his life: offering to buy out the other party for a certain sum or to be bought out for half that amount. Erwin chose to be bought out and arranged to stay on at the agency for five years as a non-partner. The changes were not divulged publicly. Erwin retained his title of president and an annual salary of $18,000.

By the end of 1914, however, Lasker had had enough. "I still had to pull my punches," as Lasker later explained it, "[so] I asked him to go." Lasker felt that he had done right by Erwin, but later admitted that Erwin never forgave him for forcing him out of Lord & Thomas.[77]

Soon enough, though, Lasker had his own reasons for feeling aggrieved. Several years earlier, Erwin had hired a young man named Louis Wasey. In Lasker's estimation, Wasey was one of the ablest recruits ever to join Lord & Thomas. One day in 1915, Wasey advised Lasker to fire a colleague named W. T. Jefferson, whom Wasey described as a "bad influence." Lasker did so, giving Jefferson a generous severance package. About two months later, Wasey resigned from Lord & Thomas and went into business with Jefferson.

In those interim two months, however, Lord & Thomas salesmen noticed that whenever they went out in response to a prospective client's call, they ran into representatives from "Jefferson & Wasey" pitching to that same company. Lasker's hardnosed lawyer, Elmer Schlesinger, decided that Lord & Thomas's switchboard operator was slipping information to the rival agency. He arranged a fake inquiry from a friendly firm, and—sure enough—Jefferson & Wasey showed up. The switchboard operator was fired and shortly thereafter turned up as Jefferson & Wasey's switchboard operator.

At about this time, Charles Erwin also joined the new agency, which was renamed Erwin, Wasey & Jefferson.

Meanwhile, there was the problem of Goodyear. The tire company was originally Erwin's account, but it had been built up mainly by Hopkins. When Erwin left Lord & Thomas, Goodyear stayed with Lasker's agency, even though Goodyear cofounder Frank Seiberling felt less comfortable with Lasker than with Erwin. Seiberling's discomfort was heightened by his increasing irritation with Hopkins, who disdained the kind of institutional advertising that Seiberling was now demanding. "Seiberling wanted to be glorified institutionally," copywriter Mark O'Dea explained, "[and] Hopkins and Lasker wanted to tell why the tires were better."[78]

All of these factors converged, and a crisis erupted one day in this tumultuous year of 1915. Seiberling called a summit conference with Lasker and demanded that Hopkins be taken off the Goodyear account. "That put me on the spot," Lasker recalled. Lasker agreed with the client in the particulars of the case, but felt it was "one of those stubborn places" where he couldn't influence Hopkins. And humiliating Hopkins by bumping him from the Goodyear account might lead to disaster. "I knew I'd lose [Hopkins] for everything else," said Lasker, "and that left me no choice."[79] He refused to move Hopkins. As expected, Goodyear fired Lord & Thomas and retained Erwin, Wasey & Jefferson.

As a rule, Lasker didn't mind when his subordinates left Lord & Thomas and went into competition with him. Later in his life, in fact, he took great pride in the fact that thirty-nine agencies had been founded by Lord & Thomas alumni. But he believed in *honorable* partings of the ways, and he felt that Wasey had behaved dishonorably. "He is the only man that ever I was connected with," Lasker later commented, "that did something that was studiedly wrong." Although Lasker rarely held grudges, he resented Wasey for the rest of his life.

Claude Hopkins earned every bit of his legend, and he was incredibly *productive*. "Hopkins could photograph the thing instantly," Lasker later commented. "Three days after he would take over the thing, he would have an immortal campaign written." In fact, Lasker sometimes sat on Hopkins's output for days or weeks, fearing that the client wouldn't value a product that had been generated so quickly.[80]

Hopkins enjoyed no forms of amusement, Lasker recalled; he worked incessantly, although, like Kennedy, he was a "prodigious drinker."[81] As Mark O'Dea wrote, he was also a hard man to fraternize with:

> Hopkins was always difficult in conversations. His intimacies were few. He was far from a social being . . . never a mixer. In many ways, he was Lasker's opposite, for the latter was cosmopolitan, gay, voluble, and won a countless host of friends from Presidents to caddies. Whereas Lasker was versatile, Hopkins was single-traced. His one subject was advertising copy. For music, books, politics, sports, plays, personalities, he had little concern.[82]

Although in later years he preferred to work out of his house in Spring Lake—only coming into Chicago every ten days or so—Hopkins exerted a huge impact on the firm. His presence and his success changed the status and stature of copywriters at Lord & Thomas. Before Hopkins's arrival, copywriters proposed, but the solicitors—the salesmen on the street—disposed. Under Hopkins, the copywriters became kings.

He also worked effectively with Lasker in a process they called "staging." A solicitor would get a foot in the door and speak glowingly of "Mr. Lasker," the magical, driving force behind the Lord & Thomas phenomenon. Then Lasker would take the next round with the prospective client, living up to his own advance billing and all the while singing the praises of the astounding "Mr. Hopkins." By the time the client met the master himself—the Merlin of Lord & Thomas—the effect could be intoxicating.

After the account was landed, Lasker and Hopkins continued to work the client. Lasker recalled how he and Hopkins played their own version of good cop/bad cop:

> I always said [to Hopkins]: "We will divide up this way . . . Whenever I find you are going to differ with them, I am going to agree with them, not to be the

diplomat, but so we can explore the difference . . . You stand for our viewpoint, Mr. Hopkins, and I will get on his side. As it develops, I will make up my mind . . . If I think he is right, I will argue it up with you, and I will have no trouble convincing you. If I finally think he is wrong, I will turn to him and say, 'Mr. Blank, I guess we are both *wrong.'"*[83]

And what of Lasker's own role? Even more than in the Kennedy era, Lasker was the extraordinary manager of an extraordinary talent. He grasped Hopkins's unique gift for identifying the Big Idea and nurtured that gift. He went in ahead of Hopkins, and—as in the case of Goodyear—also stood behind him.

At the same time, he was quick to point out that Lord & Thomas had even greater successes *after* Hopkins left the company in the 1920s. He was offended by Hopkins's account of his years at Lord & Thomas—in a book that he claimed, implausibly, he never read—because he felt that Hopkins had slighted him in it: "He mentioned me casually, just like ships that pass in the night . . . [but in] all that period of Lord & Thomas where he says he did it, it was Hopkins and myself. No doubt that he created all the creative part. [But] there is also no doubt . . . that I did the selecting, and told him what to develop . . . and what not to develop in the creative end."[84]

"Creating all the creative part" was an indispensable factor in Lord & Thomas's success, and Lasker compensated Hopkins accordingly. Although Hopkins's stated starting salary was a staggering $52,000 a year—a figure that Lasker trumpeted far and wide—Hopkins in many years made at least three times that amount, counting bonuses. In fact, Lasker had to steer accounts away from his prodigious copywriter so that there would be work and bonuses for others in the shop.

Despite their falling-out in the 1920s, Lasker always gave Hopkins full credit for his enormous contributions to Lord & Thomas. "I never knew a finer, more earnest man than Mr. Hopkins. No greater advertising man lived or ever will live."[85]

Arguably, Lasker could have claimed that distinction for himself. But of the several master copywriters whom the master of Lord & Thomas discovered and nurtured, Hopkins was far and away the most versatile, productive, and durable.

Chapter Seven

Orange Juice and Raisin Bread

7OWARD THE END of 1904—the year Albert Lasker bought his initial stake in Lord & Thomas and the gifted but erratic John E. Kennedy arrived on the scene—a delegation from the Southern California Fruit Exchange (SCFE) made its way to the Trude Building. They were there to hear Lord & Thomas's proposal for a campaign to promote California citrus products.

By that time, Lasker was the leading rainmaker in the agency, so it is safe to assume that he helped shape the presentation that was made to the SCFE that day. Perhaps he also helped deliver it.[1] If so, it was one of his rare failures.

That day, Lord & Thomas proposed a test campaign aimed at promoting oranges in Iowa. The choice of target was not as arbitrary as it might sound. More than the residents of any other Snow Belt state, Iowans took winter vacations in California and were accustomed to eating the relatively exotic fruits that the SCFE hoped to promote. Perhaps Iowans would respond to an effort to build demand for oranges on their home turf.

The $30,000 price tag for the campaign struck the SCFE delegation as far too high. The Californians said no and went home, temporarily giving up on their dream of persuading Midwesterners to eat oranges.[2]

Oranges and lemons had come to California along with Spanish missionaries in the 1700s. During the Gold Rush of the 1840s and '50s, interest in citrus fruits was spurred by the discovery that they could prevent scurvy, a vitamin-deficiency disease that in this case erupted when the incoming stampede of miners overwhelmed the local food supply. But the first real boom in orange production came with the introduction into California of the navel orange in the 1870s. Sweet, seedless, and visually striking, the navel quickly swept across Southern California. The summer-ripening Valencia orange came next, complementing the November-to-May harvest season of the navel.[3]

This move toward year-round production appealed not only to the growers, but also to the railroads. The 1885 arrival of the Southern Pacific and the Atchison, Topeka, and Santa Fe lines in Los Angeles linked that city by rail to Eastern markets for the first time. Technological advances—such as the ventilated freight car (1887) and the "ice-bunker" car (1889)—further promoted the shipment of citrus fruits and other perishables. Land-rich railroads like the Southern Pacific had another compelling reason for promoting Southern California: they wanted to sell some of their landholdings to easterners. The depiction of California as a veritable Garden of Eden could only help the cause.

But from the grower's perspective, all was not well in paradise. During the last two decades of the nineteenth century, agents and shippers had transferred most of the risk inherent in the citrus trade to the growers. Prices were set at daily auctions in major cities in the Midwest and East, and—because demand was relatively flat—those prices were driven entirely by supply.

Beginning in the late 1880s, California's orange growers began organizing into cooperatives to enhance their bargaining power, increase their financial returns, and—from their perspective—share risks more equitably. The economic recession of 1893 put enormous pressure on farmers across the nation, and in August of that year, the Southern California Fruit Exchange was born to advance the interests of California's orange growers. Lemon growers joined in 1896, and in 1905, growers from the San Joaquin Valley north of Los Angeles joined the exchange. At this point, the cooperative changed its name to the California Fruit Growers Exchange (CFGE).

Several of the CFGE's leaders were convinced that better marketing was critical to the Exchange's long-term success. By 1907, something like thirty thousand boxcars of oranges (or about 10 million boxes) were being shipped out of California—five times the 1893 total—and in peak harvest seasons, oversupply was pushing prices so low that many growers were operating at a loss.[4] And the future looked worse: past success had led to the planting of thousands of acres of new groves, and as these new trees began to bear fruit over the next several years, the orange supply might well double.[5] Either supply would have to be reduced—a difficult task in a cooperative made up of some six thousand independent-minded farmers—or demand would have to be increased through advertising.

But what, exactly, was to be advertised? The "California Fruit Growers Exchange" would not be an easy sell. Of course, one could sing the praises of California oranges, but (as skeptical CFGE directors pointed out) this would also benefit the growers who were *not* CFGE members—and who would have a cost advantage because they weren't advertising.

Cost remained an issue, as well. The CFGE was a tightfisted, low-overhead operation. With this constraint in mind, the CGFE's president approached his counterpart at the Southern Pacific Railway in the early months of 1907. The Southern Pacific was not a natural ally, given its history of price-gouging on freight rates. Nevertheless, the two presidents struck a deal: for every dollar the CFGE spent on advertising to promote citrus products, the Southern Pacific would throw in a dollar to support the campaign. With this incentive in hand, the CFGE board authorized an expenditure of $10,000 to test the effectiveness of advertising. This meant that up to $20,000 would be available to run a bold experiment: the first large-scale advertising of a perishable commodity.

Lasker's agency was a natural choice to run the experiment, since Chicago was a major terminus for railroads running to and from the west coast, and it was there that the CFGE maintained its General Eastern office, responsible for its marketing efforts. In the spring of 1907, Lord & Thomas and the CFGE struck a deal for an exploratory campaign. It was a relatively small effort, but it got Lasker's attention:

> I remember vividly my first contact with the California Fruit Growers Exchange, over thirty years ago. The vice president in charge of traffic of the great Southern Pacific Railroad came into our office and said that the railroad was interested in seeing the demand for oranges and lemons increased, so that they could get the added tonnage . . . This railroad official introduced us to the head of the newly formed Citrus Cooperative . . . An initial venture of $3,000 in Iowa—a test campaign—marked the entrance of Sunkist oranges into advertising.[6]

Lasker's account compresses several stages in the new account's evolution. In July 1907, for example, copywriter R. C. Brandon proposed using the name "Sunkissed" to bring the many CFGE brands under one marketable umbrella.[7] A month later, the agency had a revised recommendation: *Sunkist*, a made-up word that would be easier to defend as a trademark. The CFGE's growers were intrigued, but couldn't bring themselves to embrace a single trademark that would subsume all of their individual orchards' trademarks.

Once again, the campaign was aimed at California-friendly Iowa, and was scheduled to roll out in early March 1908, coinciding with the peak of the navel crop. Still lacking a compelling brand to market, Lord & Thomas fell back on pushing the generic concepts of "California" and "oranges." For its opening salvo, the agency prepared a full-page ad for the *Des Moines Register* that declared the first week in March to be "Orange Week in Iowa," supposedly coinciding with a week of parallel festivities in California. (The truth, of course, was that most orange growers were far too busy that week, as their valuable crop came in, to stop and celebrate anything.) "Now," the ad proclaimed, "Iowa will celebrate 'Orange Week' . . . by receiving direct from the beautiful groves of California hundreds of carloads of the choicest oranges grown in the world."[8]

In a departure from most of Lord & Thomas's work, the centerpiece of the ad was a cartoon by the then-popular J. N. ("Ding") Darling. (Lasker—who disdained illustrations of all sorts—lost this argument.) The cartoon depicted a little girl in a bonnet and summery dress (labeled "Miss California" on the hem) feeding a half-peeled orange to a second little girl wearing a winter hat, leggings, gloves, and a heavy coat labeled "Iowa."[9] Also surprising was the fact that the ad was published in three colors—orange, green, and black—an almost unheard-of luxury, for newspaper advertisements of the day.

The ad appeared on Monday, March 2, 1908, as part of a larger campaign of advertising and public relations. Reflecting its two sponsors, the campaign had two distinct but complementary themes. As the Sunkist corporate history puts it: "Fruit was shipped to Iowa in special bannered trains, and prizes were offered for articles that could be used in advertising California oranges and lemons. Southern Pacific posted billboards throughout Iowa to display such slogans as, 'Oranges for health—California for wealth.' A prominent lecturer was employed to tour Iowa's larger cities to elaborate on California's many advantages, especially its orange industry."[10]

Estimates of the cost of this initial campaign vary, ranging from Lasker's $3,000 to a $15,000 estimate made by a former CFGE manager. But there was no confusion about the success of the campaign. While the Exchange's business increased by an average of 17.7 percent elsewhere in the country during 1908, it shot up by 50 percent in Iowa.[11]

Could perishables be advertised on a large scale? The answer was a resounding yes.

Thereafter, the CFGE began taking Lord & Thomas's advice more seriously. In April 1908, it formally adopted the Sunkist brand to identify the best fruits produced by its member growers.[12] The growers still weren't ready to give up on their colorful and distinctive packing labels, which had evolved into a high form of commercial art. But they were ready to compromise. According to the cooperative's official history, some 6 million "Sunkist orange" stickers (and 1 million "Sunkist lemon" stickers) were ordered in the fall of 1908, to be pasted on top of the growers' own labels.

Everyone agreed that the advertising had succeeded beyond all expectations, and—in anticipation of the 1909 growing season—the CFGE's board increased its advertising budget to $25,000, and instructed Lord & Thomas to begin blanketing the northern half of the country with ads for citrus products.[13]

Now Lord & Thomas had a brand—*Sunkist*—that it could work with. At this point, though, a strange wrinkle arose: there was no easy way to attach the product's name to the product. The CFGE's growers wanted to make sure that their advertising dollars generated returns for *them*, rather than for rival growers in California or much-despised Florida. But once the grocer took the oranges out of their separate boxes, who was to know which fruit was the Sunkist? What was to prevent a grocer from selling a cheaper Florida orange as a Sunkist, and pocketing the difference?

Lord & Thomas argued for a paper wrapper, stamped with the Sunkist logo, that would accompany each piece of CFGE-packed fruit from the packing house to the merchants' counters, and the growers agreed to this solution. During the 1909 season, however, it became clear that unscrupulous merchants were throwing away the wrappers and calling *all* of their oranges "Sunkist," in an effort to unload inferior products (as well as Sunkist oranges) at premium prices.

A Lord & Thomas publication recounts the solution that the firm hit upon:

> To force the retailer to retain the wrappers on the fruit, we suggested to the Exchange that they advertise that they would give a Sunkist Orange Spoon to any one who would send them twelve Sunkist wrappers and 12 cents to partly pay the cost. In this way, the consumer would ask for the wrappers from the retailer and force him, whether he wished to or not, to keep the wrappers on the fruit. The trade was also circularized on this fact, impressing on him the value of keeping the wrappers on for the benefit of his trade, and also that fruit kept in wrappers was more salable and held its appearance much longer than if left unwrapped.[14]

The spoon gimmick proved an immediate and astounding success. No matter that the flatware ("in the exclusive new 'California Blossom' pattern," according to one ad[15]) was not particularly distinguished. In the first year of the promotion alone, consumers snapped up a million spoons, with orders coming in at the rate of five thousand a day. At Lord & Thomas's urging, Sunkist expanded the flatware line to fourteen pieces, comprising everything from gravy ladles to iced-tea spoons. "The entire planning of this premium feature," Lord & Thomas recorded a few years later, "the designing of the individual pattern and all negotiations were made by us."[16] By 1910, more than 2 million pieces in the California Blossom line had been distributed, making the CFGE the largest single purchaser of flatware in the world.[17]

Even Lasker's self-confident firm had failed to anticipate this volume. Lord & Thomas had guessed that the twelve-cent cash payment would offset some of the costs of the premium. But when volumes soared, and the CFGE began buying silverware by the carload, the flatware trade began making money for the CFGE—something like a $40,000 profit, in the first year—presenting a welcome sort of problem for the Exchange, which by the terms of its charter was supposed to be a nonprofit.[18]

Meanwhile, the real business at hand—selling oranges at a profit—continued. Lord & Thomas developed a second brand, Red Ball, for lesser-quality fruit produced by CFGE growers; Red Ball produce was marketed in sections of the country that proved unwilling to pay a premium for the highest-quality produce. In 1910, Lord & Thomas noted, there was "not a single shipment of Sunkist or Red Ball oranges on which the grower has not made a profit"—a dramatic turnaround for an industry that often failed to find a way to make money.[19] The firm also developed plans for particularly tough or competitive markets, and these, too, met with success. "We have devised plans and carried same out which has produced results in such territory," a Lord & Thomas publication proclaimed in 1911, "and out of 400 towns in which their advertising appears, but four of them do not show a handsome profit."[20]

The growers rewarded Lord & Thomas by increasing their advertising budget dramatically: from $40,000 in 1909 to $100,000 in the following year. Because of the ever-increasing volume, the per-box cost of advertising remained relatively low—something like one of the seven cents per box that the Exchange charged its members. "During the last three years," the CFGE's general manager told his directors and members in August 1912, "your advertising campaign has added about one cent to your expenses which, in my opinion, is the best investment you have ever made."[21]

The evidence for this assertion was compelling. By 1914, Americans were consuming forty oranges apiece per year: up almost 80 percent from the comparable 1885 figure.[22] In 1915, the Exchange increased its advertising budget to $250,000.[23]

<hr>

It would be a mistake to conclude that Lord & Thomas had all the answers and that the CFGE simply blessed and paid for the Chicago firm's insights and innovations. In fact, the Exchange had an extensive and sophisticated distribution network, which included a number of talented marketers.

One of these was a young man from Lansing, Michigan, named Don Francisco. Francisco was later described by Lasker's biographer as "bland, cheerful, outgoing, and a good executive"—in other words, "altogether different" from Albert Lasker.[24] A graduate of the Michigan Agricultural College, Francisco signed on after college as a Chicago-based fruit inspector for the CFGE. In that role, he checked shipments of fruit arriving in Chicago, protecting the growers from unfair claims of spoilage during shipping. In the summer of 1914, Francisco took a new job with the Exchange, circulating among the grocers and other retailers who sold Sunkist products:

I started calling on retailers as a matter of curiosity, to see what kind of oranges people asked for, and how many they bought at a time, and how they selected them, and so on . . . I tabulated these findings that I made, and gave

them to the [CGFE's] advertising manager, and he was very much interested,
and asked me to do this in other cities, on a larger scale . . .

I picked up a lot of ideas on how the smart dealers increased their sales of
oranges and lemons. And, as I would go about this work, I would pass on these
ideas to other dealers . . . to tell the retailers how they could increase their
sales.[25]

One of the things that Francisco learned in his travels was that soda-fountain attendants hated to make fresh-squeezed orange juice or lemonade. Extracting the juice from the fruit made too big a mess and took too much time. As a result, many retailers simply priced these drinks out of reach or served a substitute beverage.

To Francisco, this hinted at a far bigger problem. Wouldn't people in their houses encounter exactly the same problems and look for something else to drink? Or, phrased more positively: wouldn't it be good for orange sales if, instead of encouraging people to eat half an orange with a spoon, you could persuade people to consume the *juice* of a whole orange—or even two or three whole oranges?

Working with manufacturers in 1915, Francisco first developed a heavy-duty electric juice extractor for use in soda fountains—"to make it simple for the clerk to prepare it," Francisco later explained, "and convince the consumer that it was made from the real thing."[26]

At the same time, the ad hoc team developed both a scaled-down electric extractor and a simple glass extractor for home use. A glass company agreed to produce a million of these glass extractors—with the "Sunkist" name prominently displayed in raised glass letters along its sides—to be sold by fruit retailers for a dime apiece.

Francisco, working closely with Lasker's agency, had invented orange juice.

All of this, of course, was a preamble to an advertising campaign, and Lord & Thomas happily pounced upon Francisco's innovative work. In 1916, the agency introduced the classic campaign that later became known as "Drink an Orange."

"Nature's finest beverage," read the headline of an early ad in this series, "pure orange juice." The ad depicted a woman spoon-feeding orange juice to a jolly, pink-cheeked baby. Orange juice, claimed the ad, "is regularly prescribed for the diet of *tiny babies* because physicians know its purity and food value." The fruit from which this healthful juice was derived was produced by eight thousand growers "whose sole purposes in organizing [were] to produce *better fruit* and distribute it so economically that every family may obtain it at a reasonable cost." The ad instructed readers to look for glass Sunkist extractors at their favorite store or to send sixteen cents in stamps to receive one direct from Sunkist.[27]

Again, the response was astounding. The campaign resulted in sales of something like 70,000 commercial juicers, 140,000 electric juicers for home use, and more than 3 million glass juicers. Independent glassware manufacturers jumped into the market with their own juicers, extending the impact of the Sunkist push. On the strength of this campaign alone, orange consumption per serving in the United States soared from a half an orange to between two and three.[28]

In 1916, at the request of the CFGE, Lord & Thomas opened a branch office in Los Angeles to service the burgeoning Sunkist account. Robert P. Crane was named head of the new office, and Don Francisco—now the CFGE's advertising manager—also relocated to Los Angeles, in part to keep working closely with Crane. Francisco produced the growers' newsletter, the *Sunkist Courier,* and helped develop new campaigns in support of oranges. Crane and Francisco also ended the premium program and shifted to advertising that emphasized the fruit itself—most often, beautiful full-color portraits of oranges or lemons—and increasingly focused on the health benefits of consuming citrus fruits.[29]

Crane, meanwhile, rode herd on an increasingly far-ranging office. Two years earlier, in 1914, the runaway success of the orange campaigns had convinced the California raisin industry to hire Lord & Thomas. Then, in 1915, the CFGE began aggressively advertising lemons. As part of this campaign, Lord & Thomas pushed lemon pie, lemon in tea, lemon garnishes, and lemon juice as a hair rinse. Of particular concern to the CFGE was competition from imported Italian lemons, which in that year commanded about half of the U.S. market; accordingly, Lord & Thomas stressed the advantages of *California* lemons. By 1924, California lemons—mainly Sunkist—had captured almost 90 percent of the domestic market.[30]

In 1917, the California Walnut Growers association signed on, and between 1917 and 1923, consumption of California walnuts increased from just under 40 million pounds to almost 50 million pounds.[31] Similar stories could be told of avocados, apples, butter, eggs, grapes, honey, lima beans, milk, olives, peaches, pineapples, plums, prunes, and nectarines—all of which Lord & Thomas promoted in the early decades of the twentieth century.

By and large, these promotions were not only successful, but were accomplished at a reasonable cost.[32] In the case of oranges, for example, the incremental cost of advertising was about 4.5 cents per box of oranges and 7 cents per box of lemons (or between one-quarter and two-fifths of a cent per dozen). Advertising of oranges averaged about 1.07 percent of the freight-on-board (FOB) value of the Sunkist orange crop between 1908 and 1924.[33] Stated differently, the CFGE during these years spent less than one cent per year per customer, while the FOB returns increased from $11.8 million to $50.5 million.[34]

Advertising of fruits also brought benefits to consumers, and not only in the realm of improved diets. As growers invested more and more dollars in their collective brand, they were more inclined to protect that brand from self-inflicted wounds. Traditionally, for example, orange growers whose orchards suffered a heavy freeze rushed to harvest and ship their crops immediately, before the frost damage became visible. The frustrated consumers who ate the damaged product—tasteless and dry—would conclude that *all* California oranges must be inedible. By the mid-'teens, Sunkist's growers had learned that their long-term interests lay in disposing of damaged goods. "In the Sunkist trademark," Don Francisco observed, "they had a definite asset to protect."[35]

Lord & Thomas's relationship with the California citrus industry, and specifically its ties to the CFGE, was remarkable for its durability and relative tranquility. The agency's relationship with California's raisin growers presents a far different picture. This story includes financial shenanigans, mutual accusations of betrayal, threats and counter-threats, and firings and rehirings.

The saga begins in 1913, with the adoption by Congress of language (in the form of a rider on an appropriations bill) that prevented the Department of Justice from using antitrust laws to prosecute farmers who acted cooperatively to extract higher prices for their products. The Clayton Act, passed a year later, exempted certain kinds of agricultural cooperatives—for example, non-stock associations—from the antitrust restrictions of the Sherman Act of 1890, and the CFGE reorganized itself as a non-stock organization to bring itself into compliance with the provisions of the Clayton Act.

Not so wise were the California raisin growers, who incorporated themselves in 1912 as the California Associated Raisin Company (CARC). CARC's founders put a cooperative "face" on their enterprise, in part to persuade skeptical growers to sign up. But it was in fact a traditional corporation, structured to provide ready infusions of capital because the company intended not only to gain control over the supply of raisins (i.e., horizontal control), but also over the processing and packing of raisins (vertical control). This vertical integration required a strong capital base, and CARC's capital stock increased from $1 million in 1912 to $5 million in 1919.

From the start, therefore, CARC was very different from the CFGE. Heavily influenced by local banking interests, it first paid dividends to its shareholders and paid its growers afterward. Stock ownership was not restricted to growers, and by 1919, more than half of CARC's stock was held by non-growers.[36] As a result of these and other factors—especially its push toward vertical integration—CARC risked provoking the federal government into initiating antitrust action against it.[37]

Meanwhile, CARC also faced many of the same issues confronted by CFGE, the most urgent being the need to stimulate demand. Shortly after its incorporation in 1912, CARC came up with the brand name "Sun-Made," which played off the highly successful Sunkist brand; the company also invented the soon-to-be-familiar image of a pretty girl in a sunbonnet holding an overflowing basket of grapes. But these first steps failed to go far enough, largely because of continued overproduction by the growers. In 1913, the industry produced 132 million pounds of raisins but sold only 110 million pounds, creating a "carryover" of 22 million pounds that threatened to depress 1914 prices drastically. At this point, CARC took yet another cue from CFGE. Impressed by the orange growers' successes, the California Associated Raisin Company hired Lord & Thomas to stimulate demand for its own commodity.

Wylie M. Giffen, president of CARC and a veteran of the raisin wars that had led up to its founding, sold the idea of advertising to his board and also persuaded the board to allocate $100,000 for advertising beginning in 1914. Lord & Thomas's Robert Crane made an immediate and obvious suggestion: change the brand name from "Sun-Made" to "Sun-Maid," thereby strengthening the trademark potential of the name and its inherent pun.

An orchestrated campaign to drive up raisin consumption opened on several fronts. CARC, which set up offices and hired sales forces across the country, began marketing a five-cent box of raisins through cigar stores and drug stores. The new package met with instant success: something like 16 million boxes were sold within three months of its introduction. "You'd see that five-cent package on every cigar counter and [in] every drugstore," Don Francisco later recalled. "They were under foot all over town. You'd see the used cartons [where] hikers and fishermen went up to the mountains."[38]

Meanwhile, Lord & Thomas pushed what it referred to as "carrier foods," including raisin bread, raisin pie, and raisin toast, among others. A typical ad (from the December 1915 *Ladies' Home Journal*) depicted a young girl handing a grocer her shopping list: "Give me a loaf of California Raisin Bread. Also a package of Sun-Maid Raisins." The accompanying text emphasized that raisin bread was "delicious, nutritious, digestible, and slightly laxative." It suggested that housewives "serve it daily . . . at every meal," so that their children could "satisfy, in the most healthful way, their natural desire for sweets." In relatively small type at the bottom, the ad encouraged the reader to "send your grocer's name and address" to receive a "beautiful book showing ways to use Sun-Maid Raisins—in cereals, sandwiches, salads, pies, puddings, cookies, cakes, sweetmeats, and frozen desserts."[39]

Through steady increases in advertising expenditures, CARC and Lord & Thomas pushed up per capita consumption of raisins. At least up until 1921, this joint effort eliminated the carryover of raisins from one year to the next, and thereby protected growers' income. This was a remarkable achievement, in light of the fact that between 1914 and 1920, the statewide raisin crop nearly doubled, from 91,000 tons to 174,000 tons.[40]

Then came 1922, when the raisin industry got into trouble again—and this time, took Lord & Thomas along for the ride—a story we'll return to later.

Chapter Eight

Fighting for Leo Frank

ON THE MORNING of Sunday, April 27, 1913, at about 3:30 a.m., a night watchman named Newt Lee discovered the lifeless body of thirteen-year-old Mary Phagan in the basement of the Atlanta-based National Pencil Factory. Sawdust, pencil shavings, and soot covered the young factory girl. She had bruises and cuts on her face.[1] A subsequent medical examination revealed that Phagan had been strangled and sexually abused.[2]

Police investigating the crime scene discovered two notes—later to become known as the "murder notes"—amid the debris that littered the floor near the dead girl's head. They read:

he said he wood love me land down play like the night witch did it but that long tall black negro did boy his slef

mam that negro hire down here did this I went to make water and he push me down that hole a long tall negro black that hoo it wase long sleam tall negro I wright while play with me[3]

These notes pointed to Newt Lee as the murderer, because he matched the description of a "tall black negro." Lee—also a suspect because he had discovered the body—was arrested immediately and taken to the local jail for questioning.

At 7:00 that Sunday morning, in response to a request by the investigating officers, factory superintendent Leo Frank arrived at the scene. Born in Texas and raised in Brooklyn, Frank—then twenty-nine years old—had been living in Atlanta for five years. He had married a local Jewish woman and had recently been elected president of the Atlanta chapter of B'nai B'rith, cementing his position as a prominent member of the local Jewish community.

Initially, he told police he did not know anyone named Mary Phagan, but it soon emerged that he was the last person known to have seen her alive.[4] Shortly after noon on the previous day, Phagan had visited the factory to collect her paycheck before heading off to watch the Confederate Memorial Day Parade. According to Frank—his memory now refreshed—she came into his office, he handed her wages to her, and she left his office.

Newt Lee had come in two hours early for his Saturday-to-Sunday shift, arriving at 4:00 p.m. Oddly, Frank instructed Lee to leave the factory and return at his usual starting time of 6:00 p.m. Then Frank telephoned Lee from home at around 7:00 p.m. to see if everything was in order—a call that Lee found strange, since Frank had never before called him from home.[5]

Increasingly, the investigators became interested in Superintendent Frank.

There were then three daily newspapers in Atlanta: the leading *Atlanta Journal*, the *Atlanta Constitution*, and the *Atlanta Georgian*. William Randolph Hearst had bought the anemic *Georgian* the previous year, and immediately set out to boost its circulation. The murder of Mary Phagan presented Hearst—as well as his competitors—with a golden opportunity.

A reporter for the *Constitution* had the good luck to be at police headquarters when Lee's emergency call came in, and he covered the murder exclusively in a Sunday morning extra edition. But the competition intensified on Monday, when the *Journal* "borrowed" and printed the murder notes: a stunning breach of police procedure that prevented any fingerprint analysis from being performed. Not to be outdone, Hearst's *Georgian* published a morgue photograph of Phagan's battered face crudely pasted onto a picture of a live girl's torso, along with an inflammatory five-page article.

On the Monday after the murder, Hearst offered a $500 reward for "Exclusive Information Leading to the Arrest and Conviction of the Murderer." On Tuesday, a bidding war erupted between the *Constitution* and the *Georgian*, with the *Georgian* offering $1,800 by midday.[6]

Albert Lasker, the lapsed journalist, later described the effect of this sensationalism on Atlanta readers:

> They [the Georgian] weren't doing very well. So they had all their northern editors and they had to take what at that time was the big city yellow journal method. They had to find some sensation, and just imagine when, on a Sunday

morning in a town that had surely not seen an 'extra' since the Civil War, they came out with an eight column streamer about this murder...

That [sensationalism] . . . grew up gradually in the north. It didn't come overnight—but here it came overnight, and can you imagine the shock of that impact in the community, and how it excited them? Human beings [being] what they are? And so the stage was all set.[7]

Yellow journalism sold papers. By the end of 1913, the *Georgian* had the largest circulation of any southern daily newspaper.[8]

A shocked public demanded that the murderer be discovered and punished. Leo Frank, anxious about the sloppy police work in the case, hired the celebrated Pinkerton Detective Agency to perform an independent investigation. The factory superintendent had reason to be concerned. Among other things, the investigating officers had given away the murder notes, lost a board smeared with bloody fingerprints, and failed to issue a report on the bloody fingerprints on Phagan's jacket.[9]

On the morning of Mary Phagan's funeral—Tuesday, April 29—Frank was taken into custody, largely because he had been the last person to see Mary Phagan alive and had appeared extremely nervous in the presence of the police. The coroner conducted the largest inquest in Georgia's history, summoning every employee of the National Pencil Factory to give testimony.[10] Over the course of this inquiry, two very different pictures of Leo Frank emerged. One was of a model citizen with a Cornell diploma and a responsible job, occupying a prestigious place in his community. The other was of a vicious fiend who preyed on working-class girls—*Christian* girls.

The fact that Frank was Jewish was never far from people's minds, and the more difficult Frank's circumstances became, the more aggressively Atlanta's Jewish population defended him. To some extent, their efforts paid off. The *Georgian*, for example, reversed its course and emerged as "pro-Frank," in large part because of the Atlanta Jewish community's unhappiness with Hearst's initial anti-Frank coverage.[11]

Nevertheless, the tide was running against Frank. On May 24, he was formally indicted for the murder of Mary Phagan. To the delight of Hearst and his competitors, the case kept throwing up bizarre new twists. On the day that Frank was indicted, for example, an African American sweeper at the factory named Jim Conley confessed to having written the murder notes for him. Police had arrested Conley two days after Frank's arrest when he was observed washing blood from a shirt.

The big surprise to most Atlantans following the case was that a black factory sweeper could read and write. Conley had remained mum about those abilities, he told investigators, because he was hoping to extort a large sum of money from Frank to keep the murder quiet. Within a week, Conley produced three affidavits swearing that he not only had written the notes, but also that he helped Frank move the body to the basement. Despite glaring inconsistencies in Conley's accounts and his suspicious behavior, police considered his testimony to be conclusive evidence that Frank was guilty. "The Mary Phagan murder is no longer a mystery," they declared.[12]

Frank, now fearing for his life, stopped talking to the press. Predictably, the newspapers punished him for his lack of cooperation, dubbing him the "Silent Man in the Tower"—as the Fulton County Jail was popularly known—and hinting that his silence was somehow incriminating.[13]

Frank's trial lasted a month, making it the longest criminal trial on record in Georgia. On August 25, 1913, he was convicted of the murder of Mary Phagan. Breaking his silence, he simply declared: "I am as innocent as I was one year ago."[14]

Frank was sentenced to hang on October 10. His lawyers immediately moved for a new trial, arguing that the guilty verdict was both unlawful and contrary to the weight of the evidence.[15]

Although the murder and trial dominated the newspapers and conversations of Atlanta for four months, they received minimal coverage outside of Georgia. Three short articles appeared in the *New York Times* in May of 1913, focusing on tangential aspects of the case. The *Times* also reported on the sentencing of Leo Frank, his motions for a new trial, and the efforts of several Cornell alumni to free him.

The first significant coverage of the Frank case in the *Times*, four columns' worth, ran on February 18, 1914, when the Supreme Court of Georgia denied Frank a new trial.[16] Frank's story now became an obsession for the *Times*, which produced more than a hundred articles—about the case, the prisoner, and his fight to stay alive—over the next year and a half. When the *Times* weighed in, other publications took note, so *Times* owner Adolph Ochs was largely responsible for stirring up a national media frenzy about an obscure local case that had already been decided and its verdict upheld.

And it was Albert Lasker who persuaded Ochs to take up the seemingly lost cause of Leo Frank.

Atlanta's Jewish community felt that anti-Semitism had played a major role in the decision of the jury that convicted Frank. One of the factors contributing to this sentiment, they believed, was a scurrilous weekly newspaper, *The Jeffersonian*, written by a politician-turned-publisher named Thomas E. Watson.

The Frank case opened new vistas for Watson, just as it had for Hearst and his competitors. Watson began by asking his readership rhetorical questions—"Does a Jew expect extraordinary favors and immunities *because* of his race?"—and quickly escalated from there.[17] His simplistic editorials, touching a nativist nerve, became wildly popular. Watson intensified his attacks on Frank, depicting him as a northern Jew whose main goal was to savagely exploit young southern women.

Lasker, himself a master manipulator of public opinion, was appalled. "This paper [*The Jeffersonian*]," he later said, "was devoted to hatred of Catholics and Negroes, and when the Frank case came up, he jumped in and added Jews."[18]

Rabbi David Marx, a close friend of Frank's and one of his most passionate defenders, considered the trial an American version of the Dreyfus Affair—the celebrated court martial of a French Jew that fifteen years earlier had torn apart that country. "The feeling against the Damned Jew is so bitter," Marx wrote, "that the jury was intimidated and feared for their lives, which undoubtedly would have been in danger had any other verdict been rendered."[19]

Hoping to gain support for a movement to free Frank, Marx visited New York City. While there, he contacted Louis Marshall, a highly successful lawyer, champion of Jewish rights, and president of the American Jewish Committee. Although he was concerned about Frank's plight, Marshall refused to make Frank's case an official cause of the Committee.[20] He believed that a behind-the-scenes appeal for financial and legal aid would minimize southern resentment toward northern—and Jewish—intervention, and therefore be more successful.

Marx then attempted to meet with Adolph Ochs, hoping to focus media scrutiny on the case. Marx's timing wasn't good—at the time, Ochs was traveling in Europe. But in any case, the Frank case was not a cause that Ochs normally would choose to embrace—he had gone to great lengths to prevent the *Times* from appearing to be a "Jewish paper."

The missing ingredient, soon to be supplied, was Albert Lasker.

During this period, Lasker's recurring emotional distress was interfering with his ability to work. He fell back into depression in 1912, and took almost half of the year off for an extended trip to Mexico. He became "tired," he said—so much so that he disappeared from Lord & Thomas's expanded offices in the Maller Building at Addison and Wabash and hid himself away from his colleagues: "I had gotten so tired that I had three floors below built a hideaway office with a private phone going out, where I could see people by appointment without any stenographer or secretary. It was the only time in my life I did anything eccentric."[21] Given his state of mind, Lasker probably would have ignored the Frank case entirely, had it not been for a letter from his father in the later months of 1913.

It is not clear how Morris Lasker became entangled in Leo Frank's cause, but by November 1913, he was serving as a clearinghouse—in the Jewish community of Galveston, and beyond—for news related to Frank. Morris did not share Louis Marshall's or Adolph Och's fastidiousness about Jews advancing a Jewish cause. On the contrary: he believed that Jews *had* to take action when confronted with a challenge like the Frank case. And he felt, further, that his increasingly influential son ought to be among those leading the way.

Albert initially hoped to sidestep the whole affair. After getting his father's letter, he contacted Arthur Brisbane—the celebrated editor of Hearst's New York newspaper, the *Evening Journal*—and called in a favor. He told Brisbane: "It will satisfy my father entirely if I'll say to him that Brisbane is looking into it first. The great Brisbane with his trained mind, and second, it equals getting a review from the Hearst papers. Would you do that for me? Send me a long telegram, I'll send it to my father and the whole thing will be dismissed, and I'll have satisfied my father."[22]

In New York, Brisbane met at length with David Marx, and the following evening, he sent Lasker a telegram. "Spent four hours with a rabbi," Brisbane wired. "The thing concerns us both. I am taking the train for Atlanta tonight and expect you to meet me there the day after tomorrow morning."

Lasker's escape plan had backfired. He later described this trip to Atlanta with Brisbane:

> He and I went and talked to the District Attorney. We went and talked first to every one of the prosecution, and then we went and talked to the defense, and we talked to the prisoner. Both he and I took a tremendous prejudice against the prisoner. Like so many, all this publicity had gone to his head—he became a megalomaniac . . .
>
> But we were determined in our minds that he was innocent and that this was a big frame-up. Then we were dejected, Brisbane and I, what we were about to do. I never got back to my desk in nine months.

Lasker soon decided that his skills as a "propagandist" might prove decisive:

> [The Frank case] struck deeply into me for several reasons. First, it was the first thing my father had ever asked me to do. He had never asked me anything in his life, and I felt when he asked me to tend to it that it was just an old man being imposed upon, and then putting the burden on me. I was resentful.
>
> When I found . . . that there was no legal base for finding [Frank] guilty, then I felt guilty in my feeling of resentment toward my father, and I felt I had an obligation. Then also, I was a reporter and a propagandist, and when I made up my mind this was a legal crime that they were committing . . . I wanted to both run down the facts and spread them to the public—with the same instinct that has kept me going in my whole career . . .
>
> Then of course I was deeply moved directly and personally because of the anti-Semitism involved.[23]

Lasker was not a particularly observant Jew. In fact, according to his youngest daughter, Francie, he was "very antireligion." He didn't need a middleman between himself and his God, he used to tell his children.[24] Although he had encountered anti-Semitism in his childhood and throughout his professional career, he had either ignored it or deflected it.

At the same time, he was proud of his Jewish heritage, and was an active member of the Chicago Jewish community. Throughout his adult life, he raised money for the Associated Jewish Charities of Chicago. Every Wednesday night and Saturday afternoon, he sat down to a poker game with his local cronies—the "Partridges"—all of whom were Jewish. (They also made a point, Francie recalls, of playing poker together every year on Christmas

Eve.) And in an unguarded moment, Lasker might even admit that he was prejudiced in *favor* of the Jews:

The Jews are a superior people, I have a hard time hiding that; I feel we should be patient with non-Jews, that we should be understanding because we have gone through all that suffering ourselves that makes you cultured and civilized . . .

I deeply believe that no Christian civilization can last that removed from it the Jews. That it is the Jew that brings them the pollen.[25]

Lasker understood that the three most salient facts about Frank—that he was a mill superintendent, a northerner, and a Jew—all counted against him. "I would say it was split three ways," he concluded, "in three equal parts."[26] But it was the anti-Semitism that spurred Lasker to action. He possessed a keen sense of justice, and he had a boundless admiration for his uncle Eduard, who had fought for religious tolerance in Germany. And of course there was his father's example, as well as his request. "Broadminded in all things, his benefactions, the extent of which only himself knew, were restricted by no creed, race, or factional lines," the *Galveston News* editorialized at the time of Morris's death in 1916. "He was always ready to help the helpless."[27]

By the time Lasker got back to Chicago from his unscheduled Atlanta trip, he had decided to help Leo Frank.

***

Late in 1913, Lasker quietly donated $1,000 to Frank's cause. He also arranged for his father and his friend Julius Rosenwald—the chairman of Chicago-based Sears, Roebuck and Company—to make equal (and equally quiet) contributions. In response, Frank sent a personal note to each of them, thanking them.[28]

Lasker decided that he had to raise the stakes, in part by focusing an intense media spotlight on Georgia. David Marx and Louis Marshall had been trying to get on Adolph Ochs's calendar as soon as he returned from Europe. Lasker joined Marx's and Marshall's cause, and—toward the end of 1913—he secured the all-important meeting with Ochs, as well as an audience with Mark Sullivan, the influential editor of *Collier's Weekly*:

I came up north [after visiting Atlanta with Brisbane] and I called on two men—Adolph Ochs and Mark Sullivan . . . If I could get those two to crusade

I didn't have to take care of any other thing, that it would be quite spontaneous combustion. I have got the type of mind that works that way, if you start a fire it will spread—the thing to do is get the fire started away from a firehouse—[so] instead of scattering, I made up my mind to concentrate on them.[29]

Lasker, ever the salesman, delivered a powerful pitch to the skeptical head of the *Times*:

"Mr. Ochs," I said, "they are about to hang a man in Atlanta, Georgia, who in any event isn't legally guilty, and that is legal murder, and you have a duty, Mr. Ochs."

Mr. Ochs, far from being intrigued, was annoyed . . . First, I saw in that interview that no man could love a thing more preciously than he loved America, and he said such a thing couldn't happen in America, and he really acted as if he thought that I was a traitor to our country.

The second thing was, he was a southerner, and he loved the South, and his idea of southern fairness and southern fair play was shocked—that I brought that charge against the South.

The third reason was that he was a Jew, and Frank was a Jew, and I was a Jew, and he thought I was coming to him and trying to use his paper, which he really tried to keep free of any entanglements . . .

He was very impatient with me . . . Seeing I was getting nowhere, I turned to him and said, "Mr. Ochs, when this man dies, and afterward, you will [be an] accessory to the fact of this legal murder, because you can't get away from [the fact] that I came here and notified you.

"I don't propose to you to bring to you any proof but the record of the trial, and the record of the Supreme Court; if you read that, and tell me as an American, that this man is legally guilty, then I will say to you not only that I won't put any more pressure on you, but I will withdraw from the case, because I have more confidence in your objective judgment than I have in my own . . ."

Well, that appealed to him . . . He said, "You come in tomorrow morning at eleven o'clock." . . .

I came in at eleven o'clock the next morning and Mr. Ochs was there with tears streaming down his cheeks. He said, "I have read that record. I stayed up until four o'clock in the morning, and I read every word of it. I never believed that could happen in America. Of course, this man is legally not guilty."

He said, "So far as calling the nation's attention to it, you leave that to me. I am sending my best man down there today."

On February 17, 1914, the Georgia Supreme Court denied Frank's appeal for a new trial. For the first time, thanks to the *Times,* the story commanded a national audience.[30] From February to May, the *Times* reported on all major and minor developments in the Frank case, treating many as front-page news. Behind the scenes, Lasker exulted: "They had that case all quieted. The Supreme Court had dropped it; there was nothing left but to execute him. The northern papers had hardly printed anything about him. And in four weeks, I had it every day in every paper, [and] it was on every breakfast table in the country. So it wasn't a bad job."[31]

At the same time that he was wooing Ochs and the *Times,* Lasker was also cultivating Mark Sullivan. "He came to *Collier's* with reluctance," Sullivan later recalled, "because his advertising agency was throwing business [our] way."[32] Lasker used the same strategy with Sullivan that he had used with Ochs, putting the documents in front of Sullivan and trusting that the editor would respond with moral outrage. It worked: "I was deeply stirred by it," Sullivan said.

Lasker knew that there were still at least two more fronts to be opened. First, he had to break down the government's case against Frank. On Ochs's advice, Lasker retained a celebrated detective, William J. Burns, to poke holes in the prosecution's case. With great fanfare, Burns arrived in Atlanta on March 14, 1914.[33] Entirely without fanfare, Lasker had slipped into Atlanta a few days ahead of him. This visit constituted the "second front" in Lasker's overall campaign, whereby he would rehabilitate Frank's image. Frank could no longer afford to play the "Silent Man in the Tower." He had to swing public sentiment in his favor—no small challenge, given that he had been convicted of raping and murdering a child.

The day after the Georgia Supreme Court denied Frank's appeal, Frank made what the *Times* called "a remarkable statement to the public," which included declarations of his innocence and his unshaken faith in God. The statement, scripted by Lasker, focused on *truth,* and incorporated a core slogan: a technique that characterized all of Lasker's advocacy and political campaigns. "I stake all on the truth," Frank said in his statement. "The truth will out . . . The truth is on the march."[34]

The *Times* did its part, reporting that the previously inaccessible Frank had decided to open up to the media:

> *Until then Frank himself was a riddle. He had spoken only through his attorneys and had received no visits from reporters. Silence seemed wisest, and he*

was as hard to spy as an Irish banshee. But suddenly word was given that Frank was ready to see questioners, and to answer all the queries they could put. Since then he has been under daily cross-examination, and his air of mystery has given way to definite impressions of Frank as an individual.[35]

Overnight, with a lot of help from Lasker, the Silent Man in the Tower began exhibiting an unexpected eloquence. In those daily media sessions, Frank reiterated Lasker's slogan. "I, again, say that truth is on the march," he told the assembled reporters. "Truth is coming like a dawning day, and the first pink signs of it can be seen in the East."

Lasker was rarely on the scene. He visited Atlanta two or three times, staying three or four days each time. "I did my work up North, and I surely did it well, too."[36] On the same trip that he advised Frank to start speaking with reporters, for example, Lasker and Hearst editor Arthur Brisbane persuaded the *Atlanta Journal* to publish an editorial—on March 10, 1914—asserting that Frank was not guilty. According to a historian of the Frank case, this editorial created a sensation, and proved to be the "most dramatic appeal for Frank."[37]

Lasker was thrilled: "And by God, it was one of the biggest sensational things in journalism in the South . . . They came out with a two-column editorial, which they had never had in Atlanta—in the *Atlanta Journal* demanding a pardon or a new trial for the man. We had then the authority of the largest leading newspaper in Georgia, because the *Journal* was the largest circulation paper in Georgia, [and] the only evening paper in Atlanta."[38]

But the *Journal*'s bold stance had crossed a line that both Louis Marshall and Adolph Ochs had worried about. Angry Georgians criticized it as having been "bought with Jew money." Stung, the *Journal* waited another year before it dared to write favorably of Frank again.[39]

Lasker bankrolled the effort to save Leo Frank, but it is not clear exactly how much he spent on the cause. He paid the $4,500 retainer to Burns in the beginning of March 1914. He also paid Burns's fees beyond that $4,500— although not always happily. In late April, for example, Lasker sent defense attorney Herbert Haas a pointed note: "Believe me, my dear Mr. Haas, there is a limit to the money that can be raised, and unless Burns proves something direct, there is a limit that can be paid him. If he is going to follow every lead to an indefinite conclusion, I can well see how he can keep on for years, and run up a bill of $100,000."[40]

In this same letter, Lasker offered $10,000 more from himself and his father. He enclosed the first $5,000 directly and told Haas he could have the other $5,000 whenever he needed it. As of this point, it appears, Morris and Albert Lasker together had contributed $16,750. Haas had estimated that an additional $25,000 had to be raised outside Atlanta. Lasker felt that he could collect at least $5,000 in Chicago (with the help of Julius Rosenwald and others) and expected that "as New York had given nothing," they could raise $10,000.

Two days later, though, in an apparent change of heart, Lasker wrote to Louis Wiley of the *New York Times* that he would underwrite the entire $25,000.[41] This was certainly welcome news: Haas soon reported that the $5,000 that Lasker had sent on April 20 had already been expended to pay for Burns's time, legal fees, medical experts, and other costs.[42]

In this case, as in so many other episodes in his life, Lasker assiduously covered his tracks. He got others to go along with him in concealing his role in the affair. Burns dutifully played the Sphinx. In May 1914, prosecutor Hugh Dorsey asked Dan Lehon, an assistant to Burns, to identify the financier of Burns's investigation. Lehon identified Herbert Haas as the primary source of funds—which was true enough, as far as it went.

Investigator Burns was a showman; he loved the spotlight and enjoyed making a splash. His predisposition, combined with the *Times*'s determination to publicize the case, generated blizzards of headlines: "Burns Says He Can Solve Frank Case," "Burns to Extend Frank Case Inquiry," "Praise for Burns's Work," and "Conley Notes Show Guilt, Says Burns," among others.[43]

Lasker focused his efforts on persuading other influential newspapers—such as the *Chicago Tribune, Washington Post,* and *Baltimore Sun*—to cover the Frank case.[44] Meanwhile, he kept his eye on his expensive investigator, and he didn't like what he was reading. From his advertising experience, he knew the perils of claiming too much. As he wrote to Haas:

> *Referring to Burns: I do not know what effect it has in Atlanta, but when he was in the North he gave out statements that he knew who the murderer was. He gave it out in such a way that people up here expect that he will produce either a confession from the real murderer, or at least direct evidence. Failing to*

do that, the people up here will be very disappointed, and, to be very frank with you, I fear if he does not do something like that, it will hurt us and may do the case more harm than if he had not entered into it at all.[45]

Burns's provocative statements also caused trouble closer to the front lines. On May 2, he traveled to Marietta, Georgia—where Mary Phagan's family lived—and was set upon by an angry mob. The *New York Times* wrote: "The detective's declaration that Frank was not guilty and that James Conley, a negro factory sweeper convicted as an accessory after the murder, alone was responsible for the crime, aroused intense feeling here."[46]

Watson's *Jeffersonian,* fulminating against northern intruders, helped to fuel these "intense feelings." Just two weeks before, *The Jeffersonian's* headline read: "The Leo Frank Case: Does the State of Georgia Deserve This Nation-Wide Abuse?"[47] Georgians were becoming increasingly defensive. They resented the interference of northerners—including the flashy Burns—as well as a national publicity campaign in which they were depicted as ignorant racists.

In mid-April, Lasker persuaded a pair of defense lawyers, John Tye and Henry Peeples, to file a motion in the Fulton County Superior Court arguing that Frank had been deprived of his constitutional right of due process because he was not present when the jury returned the verdict. The motion not only delayed Frank's execution, but—because it dealt with an alleged violation of a constitutional right—also provided a potential avenue into the United States Supreme Court.

Because the ruling on the motion was not expected until mid-autumn, the Frank case was out of the *New York Times* for most of the summer.[48] But as September arrived, Lasker launched another energetic national publicity campaign in anticipation of a possible U.S. Supreme Court case.

Now Lasker's cultivation of *Collier's* editor Mark Sullivan began pay off. Sullivan assigned a celebrated journalist, Christopher Powell Connolly, to write an article in *Collier's.*[49] Frank's defense team supplied Connolly with exclusive information and court documents once he reached Atlanta. In the first week of December, Connolly sent Frank a letter telling him that he would write an eighteen-thousand-word article on the case and would align himself with Frank and the defense. Moreover, *Collier's* would distribute the article to ten thousand newspapers "with permission to write in full."[50]

On November 14, 1914, the Supreme Court of Georgia denied the Tye-Peeples motion on the grounds that the appeal was not made directly after Frank's conviction. Louis Marshall now joined Frank's defense team, and the team approached the U.S. Supreme Court individually, including the distinguished Justice Oliver Wendell Holmes. In a written opinion, Holmes agreed that Frank had not received a fair trial, and argued that the trial took place "in the presence of a hostile demonstration and seemingly dangerous crowd, thought by the presiding Judge to be ready for violence unless a verdict of guilty was rendered."[51] Holmes's opinion garnered national media attention, but the U.S. Supreme Court denied the writ of error on December 7.[52]

After the failure to reverse the conviction, a new execution date was set: January 22, 1915. Throughout December, Ochs and the *New York Times* kept the spotlight on Frank. The defense made one last attempt to get the case in front of the U.S. Supreme Court, filing a writ of habeas corpus on December 17. That same day, *Collier's* published the first part of Connolly's article. It argued, among other things, that Frank "did not have a fair trial; that his conviction was the result of popular passion, which demanded a victim, and that all the facts point, not to Frank's guilt, but to his innocence and to the negro Conley as the murderer."[53]

Connolly emphasized the mob qualities of the trial. He implied that Georgians were anti-Semitic, and willing to legally murder a Jew for the sake of "politics, prejudice, and perjury." When the second part of the article appeared the following week, the Frank case once again became a national obsession. People across the country became overwhelmingly sympathetic to Frank, concluding that Georgia was determined to execute an innocent man.

Now Lasker gained a powerful new ally, as William Randolph Hearst aligned all of his papers with Frank. In a letter to a friend, Lasker reveled in the success of his stealthy campaign: "Outside the state of Georgia, the press of the United States, including the leading papers of every city in the South, are editorially agitating public sentiment for the unfortunate Frank. Daily, hundreds of papers are editorially crying that Frank's execution would amount to judicial murder."[54]

On December 28, the Supreme Court agreed to review the Frank case. "The Supreme Court of the United States," Justice Joseph R. Lamar wrote, "has never determined whether on a trial for murder in a state court, the due process clause of the federal Constitution guarantees the defendant a right to be present when the verdict is rendered."[55] Because the case would not be heard for eight weeks, Frank gained a new stay of execution.

The review began on February 25, 1915. Louis Marshall now managed Frank's defense. "I am glad that Mr. Marshall is taking hold of the matter," Lasker wrote to Frank.[56] But on April 19, by a vote of seven to two, the Supreme Court upheld the conviction: "In our opinion, he is not shown to have been deprived of any right guaranteed to him by the Fourteenth Amendment or any other provision of the Constitution or laws of the United States. On the contrary, he has been convicted and is now held in custody under 'due process of the law' within the meaning of the Constitution. The judgment of the District Court refusing the application for a writ of *habeas corpus* is affirmed."[57]

On May 10, Judge Benjamin H. Hill of the Fulton County Court set Frank's execution for June 22.

Frank's last hope rested in the hands of the governor of Georgia, who had the authority either to set aside Frank's conviction—a highly unlikely outcome—or commute the death sentence. Frank's defense team had hoped that the presumably sympathetic governor-elect, Nathaniel H. Harris, would make the commutation decision, but they had to make their appeal to lame-duck governor John M. Slaton, who would hold office until June 26.

Lasker launched yet another campaign of petitions and letters demanding the commutation of Frank's death sentence. In a single week in Chicago, more than 400,000 people signed a petition supporting the prisoner. Prominent citizens ranging from Thomas Edison to Jane Addams spoke out in Frank's defense.[58] Senators and governors from fourteen states wrote to Governor Slaton, and groups of supporters traveled to Atlanta in the last week of May to present millions of signatures in person.[59]

On June 12, Slaton initiated the final hearing in the Frank case, coming under enormous pressure from both sides as he made his momentous decision. Years later, Lasker recalled that the formidable William Randolph Hearst himself had lobbied the governor: "Brisbane did that—got Hearst to come down to go to the Governor . . . The only reason that the Governor didn't pardon him completely, they all became so convinced that he was legally innocent that the Governor was afraid of race riots and said, 'It is much better to let him stay in the penitentiary for a few years, then he will be pardoned.'"[60]

After a week of mounting tension, Slaton commuted Frank's sentence on the grounds that new evidence introduced after the trial undercut the testimony on which the conviction was based. Frank was transferred from his cell in the Tower to the State Prison Farm in rural Milledgeville.[61] In a brief telegram to the New York Times, Frank responded to the commutation: "Deeply moved and gratified by Governor's action, though innocent and suffering for a crime I did not commit, I await the complete vindication and exoneration which is rightfully mine. In the future I live to see the day when honor shall be restored to me."[62]

Georgians, meanwhile, reacted to the commutation with fury. A crowd of a thousand demonstrators gathered outside the governor's country home. Slaton declared martial law and surrounded himself with a Georgia National Guard battalion. In Marietta, the governor was hanged in effigy, alongside a sign reading "John M. Slaton, King of the Jews and Georgia's Traitor Forever."[63]

The nation remained intensely interested in Frank, creating enormous media pressure for more words from the prisoner. Haas advised against this strategy, believing that it would only inflame local passions and embolden Frank's enemies. But Lasker encouraged Frank to keep issuing statements in his own defense.[64]

On Saturday, July 17—just four weeks after Leo Frank was remanded to the Milledgeville prison—a fellow prisoner used a kitchen knife to carve a seven-and-a-half-inch-long gash in Frank's throat. Bleeding profusely from a severed jugular vein, Frank was rushed to the prison hospital. He survived, but just barely. Lasker paid Frank's medical bills, again taking care to disguise the source of those funds.[65]

The Times report on the murderous assault was considerably shorter and more matter-of-fact than previous coverage, reflecting controversy at the newspaper about how much attention had been paid to Frank. But Adolph Ochs remained determined to keep the spotlight on the prisoner. At his insistence, the paper ran an article in late July condemning "the hideous mob spirit."[66]

The article proved horribly prescient. On August 16, 1915, Frank was discharged from the prison hospital and sent back to his cell. Just before midnight, a mob of at least two dozen men, many with links to the Ku Klux Klan, cut the telephone and telegraph wires connecting the prison to the outside world, broke into the prison, and seized Frank.[67] They then drove 125 miles to Marietta, and there, in the early morning sunlight, they lynched Leo Frank, hanging him from a tree in a grove where Mary Phagan had played as a child.

While the *Constitution*, the *Journal*, and the *Georgian* condemned the lynching, the *Macon Daily Telegraph* pointed to the role of outside influence in inflaming the passions of Georgians. An editorial entitled "Finis" asserted:

> *Thus was Leo Frank caught between the upper and nether millstones—the foolish, calamitous propaganda by alleged friends and the natural and justified resentment in Georgia against this outside interference, allied with the propaganda of Watson, and his life was taken—he was killed as an unclean thing is killed and left for the buzzards.*
>
> *Such a thing can never happen again in Georgia. It would never have happened had the rest of the nation left this State to mind its own business, which would have been infinitely better for Frank, better for Georgia, better for the Jewish race in this State.*[68]

The editorial captured the most common local interpretation of the lynching: that it was caused by outside interference, which intensified previously latent anti-Semitic feelings. Asserting that newspaper coverage had failed to present the Georgian point of view, a circuit court judge who had been involved in the lynching offered an explanation: "The Jewish element are a very thrifty element, as a rule law-abiding. They do lots of advertising. I believe that had a great deal to do with the attitude of the presses."[69]

In the wake of Frank's murder, Adolph Ochs instructed his staff to write an editorial condemning the horrific act of vigilantism, and then sent the piece to all of Georgia's newspapers, assuming that they would dutifully print the editorial from New York. None did. In fact, the offended editor of the *Macon Daily Telegraph* wired Ochs that it was the "outside interference of the Jews"—including Ochs—that had made Frank's death inevitable. He concluded by suggesting that the *Times* mind its own business.[70]

Albert Lasker poured his heart, soul, and wealth into the defense of Leo Frank. In a typical letter to his father, sent six months before the end, he wrote, "The Frank case is taking practically all my time, and leaves me sorely pressed to even keep up with my business in a most superficial way."[71] The case had upset his mental equilibrium: "The amount of work and time consumed by it [the Frank case] you cannot imagine—it's letting now—five and six hours daily—I have to spend all next week in New York on it. Added to this not only my regular work—but some charities of large proportions I am reorganizing—and I am as near to a breakdown from overwork as ever I was in my life."[72]

Now, despite all those costly efforts, Frank was dead, and Lasker concluded that his own relentless efforts had helped *cause* that death. He had inflamed deep racial prejudices, and once that evil genie escaped from its bottle, no one could put it back in: "I was seeing the ugly side of it; I was seeing what Macaulay saw, when he said, 'The public is a great beast.' And then the editors in working it up . . . ran editorials constantly with headlines like this: 'The Crime of Georgia' . . . We put the whole state of Georgia on trial, and we did what is so often done: in the cure that we gave for the disease, we increased the disease."[73] Reluctantly, Lasker conceded that a quieter campaign probably would have been more effective. "We handled it badly, Brisbane and I," he said. "We got him lynched instead of hung."[74]

From the Frank case, Lasker learned a lesson that he would remember for the rest of his life, which he summarized in an aphorism: "Very often the art of public relations is the art of private relations."[75] But it was a lesson learned at the cost of a man's life.

Under the circumstances, though, Lasker was far too hard on himself. True, Frank ultimately was "lynched instead of hung." A case can even be made that Lasker helped revitalize the Ku Klux Klan.[76] But if the alternative was inaction, Lasker *had* no alternative. In response to his father's repeated entreaties and his own impulses, he fought to protect a man who was in peril in part because of his religion—a Jewish man, from Texas, four years younger than himself, who like himself had made his own way in life.

In the tradition of his father and his uncle, Lasker acted to help the helpless. Perhaps the fight for Leo Frank was poorly fought—but it was fought, as Lasker later observed, by honest and inspired dreamers.[77]

Chapter Nine

Into the Tomato Business

A DVERTISING COMPLEMENTS a business, and sometimes even overshadows a business, but it is not the business itself. Documenting the successes of an advertising agency risks creating a distorted picture, by implying that the marketing of a product is more important to the success of that product than the product itself. Albert Lasker knew that wasn't true. He told his clients that good advertising couldn't rescue a bad product or a bad company.

He also understood that building and operating a thriving enterprise was an incredibly complicated proposition. Sometimes—as in the case of the Van Camp Packing Company—he was reminded of that firsthand.

The story begins in the summer of 1911, when a bumper crop of tomatoes hit the wholesale markets in the northern United States. For companies that processed and sold tomato-based products, it was a moment of opportunity and peril. The ever-ambitious Frank Van Camp—instrumental in Lasker's rapid rise within Lord & Thomas—decided that because his company both grew and owned futures in tomatoes, it was in his interest to shore up their wholesale price. With a number of Indianapolis businessmen and a Baltimore-based consortium, he set out to buy up surplus tomatoes and establish a price floor under the crop.

It was a huge gamble, but Van Camp was, in the words of a fellow Indiana businessman, a "plunger."[1] He liked to think big, and make big bets.

Lacking sufficient cash to accomplish this ambitious end on his own, Van Camp approached Lasker for a loan. Lasker was then worth about $600,000, mostly in the form of cash surpluses in Lord & Thomas's accounts. "I never had a financial mind," Lasker once admitted, "[and] I didn't know how to invest it."[2] Lasker agreed to lend Van Camp Packing $440,000 at 5 percent interest until the bumper crop could be liquidated. "It was the proudest and happiest moment of my life," Lasker recalled.[3] Barely thirty years old, he could loan a huge sum of money to an older friend who happened to be one of his agency's most important clients.

But something went wrong. The money from the liquidation did not come in as scheduled. When Lasker asked Van Camp what was happening, Van Camp remained cordial, but he was evasive. Sometimes he didn't respond at all.

One day toward the end of 1911, or perhaps in the first week of 1912, Lasker was returning home to Chicago on an overnight train from Toledo. At around 7:30 a.m., he stepped off the train at the suburban Englewood station, where he was astonished to see his wife waiting for him on the platform. Because of Flora's poor health, this almost never happened. His first panicked thought: *Something has happened to baby Mary.*[4] But no; Flora told him that she had received an urgent phone call from a group of bankers in Indianapolis. They had discovered that Frank Van Camp had been making false statements regarding the packing company's financial condition and that the business was "hopelessly broke."[5] The bankers had called a summit conference, and they urgently needed Lasker—Van Camp's single largest creditor—to take the next train to Indianapolis. Flora was to drive him to a station across town, where he could jump on the next train for Indiana.

Lasker thought about it for a moment. Then he turned to Flora: "'Well,' I said to her, '[if] after almost twenty years of working I am wiped clean, I might just as well take the noon train, and go home and take a bath and see the baby.' Which I did. I mention this because I do think that my wife was prouder of me that minute than any minute in my life."[6]

Arriving in Indianapolis that evening, Lasker went into a series of emergency meetings in Frank Van Camp's office. It was an odd cast of characters: Van Camp and his brother Cortland, who had left the family canning business to launch a hardware-supply business; Otto N. and John P. Frenzel, the president and vice president of the Merchants National Bank in Indianapolis; and W. D. Campbell, representing the New York investment banking firm of Hollingshead & Campbell.[7] All faced huge losses if Van Camp went down, but none as large as Lasker's. They were, he recalled, "the gloomiest bunch of men I ever saw."[8]

The group first agreed on a critical point: they were in too deep to allow Van Camp Packing to go under. Their previous loans to Van Camp would have to be converted to equity, and each investor would have to put in more money to give the company some running room. The disgraced Frank Van Camp had his 100 percent ownership of Van Camp Packing reduced to six thousand shares out of thirty thousand—a 20 percent position. Lasker, Cortland Van Camp, and Hollingshead & Campbell each got six thousand shares, and the Frenzels split the final 20 percent. All received seats on an expanded board of directors. The group also agreed to incorporate a new wholly owned subsidiary, Van Camp Products, to serve as the distributor of the parent company's products. Finally, the new owners agreed not to discuss Frank's misdeeds publicly. They liked the buccaneering executive and saw no advantage in humiliating him; it was in the new owners' self-interest, moreover, to speak highly of their company and maintain the Van Camp name.[9]

The emergency huddle in Indianapolis marked the relaunch of what Lasker later called "a strange company," formally organized on February 26, 1912. A group of bankers, a hardware-store owner, and an ad man set out to direct the affairs of a fast-growing enterprise of national scope and importance. But with the exception of the demoted Frank Van Camp, no one in this new group of owners knew much about manufacturing.

Nor could the packing company's new ownership structure be kept secret. As soon as that new structure came to light, the revelation affected Lasker in unexpected ways. As he explained:

> When it became known that [Frank] Van Camp was relegated to the background and only had a fifth, and as I was the up-and-coming advertising man of the country, any account I went after, [my competitors] tried to assassinate me by saying, "Look what he did to Van Camp. He gets people's confidence, loans them money, pulls the string when it isn't possible for them to meet their obligations, and then he goes in, owning the business." It did me untold hurt.[10]

By "hurt," Lasker meant not only professional damage, but also personal insult. (Reading between the lines, particularly in the "money-lending" theme, the whispers also conveyed anti-Semitic undertones.) Characteristically, though, Lasker shrugged off the smears and the hurt. All such talk, he said, just made him "dig my teeth in, and say we have got to be that much better than anyone else."

But he was digging his teeth into an unfamiliar business, and tenacity alone could not guarantee success.

In 1914, Frank Van Camp sold his shares in the packing company to Columbus, Indiana, native William Glanton (W. G.) Irwin. Irwin was easily the most prominent resident of Columbus, a small city of some eight thousand residents, forty-five miles southeast of Indianapolis. Early on, he displayed a rare talent for business, parlaying a modest inheritance from his father into a much larger fortune.

His most enduring business success took root in 1919 with the founding of the Cummins Engine Company. Irwin had long been interested in new technologies, and the diesel engine seemed to be on the verge of sweeping the transportation industries. Irwin staked Clessie Cummins—a self-taught mechanical genius who had attached himself to the Irwin family as a part-time mechanic and chauffeur—to the capital needed to build diesels in Columbus. For the next nineteen years, the company lost money while Clessie Cummins struggled to perfect his innovative diesels. Today, Cummins is one of the largest manufacturers of diesel engines and power-generation systems in the world.[11]

Irwin's first invested in Van Camp in the fall of 1912, when he purchased some of the Van Camp Products Company's preferred shares that were issued in February.[12] He liked what he saw, purchased Frank Van Camp's stake in the packing company, and took a seat on the Van Camp board. Almost immediately, Irwin made it clear—for example, in a March 1914 letter to a Van Camp manager—that he did not intend to be merely a passive investor: "At the time of the purchase of the stock from Mr. Frank Van Camp, he mentioned that you got out a balance sheet each month showing the condition of both the Packing Company and the Products Company. I would appreciate it very much, if it will not be inconsistent with the regulations, to have a copy of these sheets as they are made each month."[13]

Soon Irwin was receiving not only balance sheets but also year-over-year comparisons of sales-to-date and orders placed, as well as summaries of cash flows. Aside from raw materials, salaries, and dividends, one of the company's biggest outlays was for the advertising campaigns that Lord & Thomas ran on its behalf. As of May 1914, for example, Van Camp was spending an average of about $23,000 a month on magazine advertising, or a total of nearly $300,000 per year.[14] The advertising budget waxed and waned depending on the fortunes of a very cyclical business. In 1915—a "bum" year for the company, as Irwin confessed—the company made no profit on its condensed-milk business, and bean sales dropped off significantly.[15] By mid-1916, the board had decided to suspend all advertising.

Albert Lasker believed that this strategy was shortsighted, and (in 1917) lobbied Irwin to help get the moratorium lifted: "The advertising is, to my mind, the best move we have made in two years. I feel that it was an overwhelming error ever to have been cut. We must rise or fall on good goods and acquainting the public with same. We will have a remarkable campaign that ought to make itself felt about mid-winter."[16]

But involving W. G. Irwin in the specifics of advertising cut both ways. While Irwin didn't consider himself to be expert in any aspect of advertising, he didn't hesitate to suggest changes in ad copy or illustrations. Irwin worried in particular about Claude Hopkins's tendency to stretch the truth, and he communicated those concerns to Lasker. Sometimes Lasker simply acquiesced—"I think your point well made," he wrote at one point, agreeing to tone down a Hopkins claim about the wonderful pastures in which Van Camp butter allegedly got its start.[17] At other times, however, he stood his ground. In the fall of 1917, for example, Irwin objected to the illustration in a proof that had recently crossed his desk: "Does it not seem to you that it would be objectionable to the fastidious housewife to see that the college cook uses the cooking kettle as something against which to lean? However, probably they will not know that it is a cooking kettle he is leaning against?"[18]

Lasker refused to make a change. "The chemist is not leaning up against the kettle," he replied, "he is lifting it. It must be poorly drawn to give you that impression, but none to whom I have shown it seemed to interpret the drawing other than as it was intended."[19] At the same time, despite his inexperience on the operating end of a food-processing business, Lasker freely offered up his advice on a range of subjects. Responding to a sales slump in the first half of 1914, for example, he urged an increase in output from the factories: "I believe that the inrush of business this fall will make up for the loss of the first six months, as we were crowded with business last year in the first few months. If we get an increased business the last few months, as we surely will in handsome measure, then it means that [factory superintendent W. G.] Mann must have our factories in such shape that we can promptly fill this inrush of increased business . . ."[20]

The "inrush of business" never materialized, and this foray illustrates the problems inherent in having Lasker actively involved in mapping the strategy of a company like Van Camp. First, it was a *complicated* business—or more accurately, several complicated businesses under the same roof. The canned-beans business, for example, called for shrewd purchasing of agricultural products in highly cyclical markets. Frank Van Camp was humbled when he got this aspect of the business wrong just once.

The canning of tomatoes and beans called for nailing down current orders in the early spring, and "futures" (orders today for goods tomorrow) in the fall. A skilled sales force could sign up twenty thousand new retail customers—as the Van Camp salesmen did between mid-1915 and mid-1916—but this effort could be undercut if the company cut back on its promotional activities, as it did when it suspended advertising in 1916.

Cash flow was lumpy. The company expected to lose money the first quarter of every year and make up for the deficits in subsequent quarters. The canning of foods also required significant manufacturing skills, with dire consequences (including dead customers) if something went wrong. In 1919, a botulism-tainted can of olives killed seven people at a country club in Canton, Ohio, and the entire California olive-canning industry—a Lord & Thomas client—languished for a decade.[21] Van Camp set up branch plants to handle peak demand periods, but protecting quality levels at those plants proved very difficult.[22]

Then there was the challenge of procuring cans. Without an adequate supply of cans at a reasonable price, Van Camp couldn't get its products to market profitably—or at all. "I feel we ought to arrange to build a can plant this coming year," Lasker wrote to Irwin toward the end of 1916. "It is ruinous to keep paying the can company a profit which I am sure would equal all the common dividend we could pay."[23] This challenge could intensify overnight, as it did when the United States declared war against Germany on April 4, 1917, and Washington imposed controls on the national can supply. Of course, the company could set up its own can-making operation, as Lasker advocated, but that entailed a whole new set of complexities, beginning with the challenge of getting the necessary tin from the tin czar in Washington. And because beans were needed by both soldiers overseas and consumers on the home front, the bean czars in the nation's capital controlled both production and pricing.

In April 1917, the federal government prohibited the packing of both pork and beans. In November, it prohibited the packing of pork *with* beans, but not beans alone. When Irwin visited the Washington bureaucrat in charge, a Mr. Bentley, he was told that the goal of the ban was to save on *tin*, rather than pork, and that any step-up in production by Van Camp—if it could find the necessary canning materials—would incur the government's wrath. "I am satisfied that the best thing we can do," a somewhat shaken Irwin wrote to Lasker, "is to stay away from Mr. Bentley."[24]

A letter written to Irwin a year later by a Van Camp manager detailed the difficulties of doing business in wartime. At that point, the factory had orders for forty-two thousand cases of goods that it couldn't fill. Pork and beans were being held up for lack of cans (the American Can Company couldn't get tin plate). Van Camp couldn't pack peanut butter for lack of glass jars. Kidney beans were behind schedule because the company had been unable to buy enough high-quality beans. Hominy corn, tomato-based chili sauce, and chicken soup were delayed for the same reason: lack of raw materials. (The company needed between 12,000 and 15,000 pounds of chicken per week; it was then averaging about a tenth of that amount.) Worse still, the delayed 42,000 cases were holding up another 60,000 cases of goods that could only be shipped in full carloads.[25]

One final hurdle: the canned-foods industry was populated by highly skilled competitors. Borden, Campbell's, and Helvetia—to name just a few— were all focused on the same goal as Van Camp: to become the dominant national brand.

Despite all these obstacles, Albert Lasker had great faith in himself. This was a mixed blessing: while this trait helped him in his own business, it was less helpful when he ventured onto someone else's turf. His predictions of crops and markets—the economic flywheels of Van Camp—were consistently off. In July 1917, for example, he predicted a "great surplus of beans," which would be difficult to unload.[26] But two months later, Van Camp's sales manager Wilkes was ruing the fact that the company had run out of beans, and wishing (in a letter to Lasker) that the company hadn't sold off ten thousand bushels to the Atlanta quartermaster.[27]

Lasker also believed that his far-ranging business experience had given him a good handle on the near-term direction of the national economy. "I think the present depression will clear the business up, and make it healthier than it ever was," he wrote to Irwin in April 1918. "I am for sticking and play-ing the hand out pat."[28] In fact, things were slowly going from bad to worse, and the *real* recession—the crunching postwar downturn of 1920–1922—was still two years off.

In the early months of 1919, he argued that Wilkes should build up the sales force, despite stagnant sales: "On all these things, whether it is milk, or chocolate, or salesmen, I don't feel that we should run at the first sign of stag-nation. In the earlier days, when pressed for capital, we had to, but the way to build up a permanent business, it seems to me, is, having arrived at our pro-gram, to sit tight and see it through the dark days. As a result, we will gather the harvest when bright days come—and come they always do."[29]

In this communication and many others, Lasker's optimism about busi-ness shines through. Unfortunately, his inclination to "sit tight" and build the business proved misguided. In May 1917, co-owner Campbell, Heath & Co. in New York (the successor to Hollingshead & Campbell) announced that it wanted to sell its Van Camp common for $200 a share—or, alternatively, buy the shares held by Irwin, Lasker, and the Frenzels, and gain control of the company. If Lasker had accepted this offer to purchase, he would have received $1.2 million for his six thousand shares. Since his initial investment was $440,000 and he had already received something like $240,000 in divi-dends from the company, he stood to make a pretax profit of around $1 mil-lion on his original investment. But Lasker persuaded Irwin not to sell—and it was a decision they both came to regret.

A third reason why Lasker's involvement worked against Van Camp's suc-cess was that he was only intermittently available. Sometimes he was too busy to pay much attention to Indianapolis, and sometimes he was incapaci-tated by emotional distress.

Shortly after he was first dragged into an ownership position at Van Camp, for example, he became embroiled in the Leo Frank case. After Frank's murder, Lasker went on a five-month sojourn of Europe for rest and rehabilitation. Upon his return he found that he still couldn't work, and so spent the next four months in Mexico. Then World War I started, with dev-astating effects on Lasker's equilibrium. "I couldn't talk for five minutes with-out starting to weep," he later said. "Finally I had to be left in a sanitarium."[30]

One way that Lasker dealt with the stresses of his life was to abandon Chicago early in the winter—usually around the turn of the calendar year—and move his family to a more congenial climate. In the 'teens, this meant

Southern California, with Lasker using the excuse of his agency's expanding operations in the Golden State to spend up to four winter months out west each year. Almost nothing deterred him from this schedule. In the early months of 1918, for example, the ailing Flora Lasker declined to make the trip to California; Lasker decided to go without her. "Ninety percent of my reason is, I am getting stale in my work, and dread coming to the office," he wrote to a friend. "The other 10 percent is, we have established offices in Los Angeles and San Francisco, which I want to look over."[31]

The following year, writing to Irwin from the Huntington Hotel in Pasadena, Lasker made it clear that he was unavailable, even for emergencies:

> *I have left word with all of my associates in my various interests not to communicate with me on business while I am away. I do not expect to either write or receive a letter for three months. I really need a rest, and my rest is considerably disturbed when I have correspondence to look after . . .*
>
> *I am sure you will understand exactly how I feel. For instance, regarding Van Camps: I do not want to know whether we lose a million or what happens until I get back, because if I know about it, I will start worrying, and if I do not know about it, I have nothing to worry over.*[32]

Again in 1920, Lasker spent thirteen weeks with his family in California—this time at a bungalow he had constructed on the grounds of the Huntington Hotel—and again was in communication only when he chose to be. "I am adhering strictly to my program of loafing while I am here," he wrote to Irwin in February. "I expect . . . to come back so benefited by the trip that I will be full of a double dose of pep on my return."[33]

It didn't work. "Oh—this awful weather," he wrote in a disconsolate letter to Irwin after returning to Chicago in mid-April. "It is enough to break one's heart. It is horrible to come from glorious California to this rotten climate."[34] And even when Lasker was in Chicago—only a short train ride from Indianapolis—he sometimes made himself inaccessible. A letter to Irwin in August 1917, in the wake of negotiations with the Frenzels about the possible purchase of their stock, paints the picture: "I am staying out in my country place for a few weeks' rest. I found I had been going at a pretty stiff pace, and was accelerated beyond the safety point. It was the first time I ever felt that way, and I thought I had better take warning of the signs . . ."[35]

Irwin generally tolerated Lasker's long absences, nonnegotiable demands, and complaints about the weather. Occasionally, he tried to focus Lasker's attention on the business. "I dislike very much to call upon you to cut short your vacation," he wrote in the winter of 1921, "but it seems to me that this is a time that it is necessary that it be done."[36]

The issue was the proposed sale of the business: an outcome that Lasker was now eager to effect. Even so, he told Irwin that he had no intention of curtailing his vacation. He had already spent ten days of his California sojourn on business, and wasn't yet in any shape to attend to affairs in the Midwest.

Irwin understood the value of getting away from it all. (He took long summer vacations at the family compound at Lake Muskoka, Ontario.) He also was accustomed to the extended winter absences of Clessie Cummins—the talented but mercurial president of the Cummins Engine Company—and had grown used to picking up the slack created by the absence of a creative genius. He knew Lasker well and understood that his friend had to pace himself, fending off his recurrent depressions as best he could.

And it sometimes helped to have Albert Lasker far away from the day-to-day affairs of the Van Camp Packing Company.

Irwin, who had become increasingly involved in the operation of the business, soon realized that Van Camp was playing a losing hand. In December 1919, he took a tour of Campbell's Soup's state-of-the-art manufacturing complex in Camden, New Jersey. The tour was conducted by Dr. John Dorrance, the MIT-trained chemist credited with the invention of condensed soups. Irwin grasped instantly just how hard it would be for his slow-moving company to compete with Dorrance's powerhouse. Van Camp's sales volume—about $20 million a year, at that point—was roughly the same as Campbell's, but this Camden facility was light-years ahead of any Van Camp plant. Dorrance casually let slip the news that his company was about to begin packing in the Midwest to minimize freight costs.

"We will have to have our costs right and as low as Campbell's," an anxious Irwin wrote to Lasker, once back in Indianapolis. "He makes good goods."[37] Even Lasker couldn't ignore this. "I can well see the difference in our positions," he wrote back. "We are fast getting to the point where we must do something."[38]

Campbell's Soup did invade the Midwest, and—in the spring of 1920—launched a price war against Van Camp and other local producers of soups and

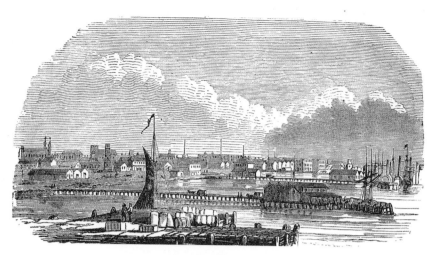

Top: In the early 1880s, Galveston was the largest city in Texas, with 22,000 residents. *Bottom:* Albert Lasker's uncle, Eduard, was a prominent German legislator who crossed swords with Chancellor Otto von Bismarck—and set an example of public service that Albert tried to live up to for much of his life.

Above: The Lasker family home on the corner of Broadway and 18th Street. It was during the building of this mansion that Lasker—then nine years old—got drunk with the construction crew and earned a beating from his father. *Right:* Lasker's small stature and "outsider" status forced him to live by his wits during his Galveston childhood. (Lasker photo courtesy of Chicago History Museum.)

AVENUE, NORTH FROM ADAMS STREET, CH

When Lasker arrived in Chicago in 1898, the city claimed just under 2 million residents. It was the shipping capital of the Midwest, had the highest percentage of immigrants of any city in North America, and was home to one of the largest concentrations of advertising agencies in the United States.

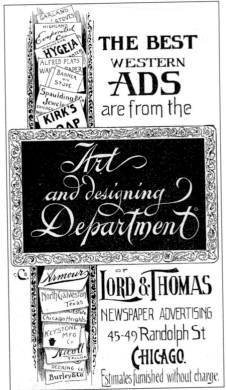

Above: Lasker was puzzled by the slogan of the Lord & Thomas agency. What, exactly, did "advertise judiciously" mean? *Right:* Lacking an adequate answer to Lasker's question, the agency boasted of its typesetting prowess and design skills. *Below:* Like most agencies of the day, Lord & Thomas simply tried to put the client's name in front of an appropriate audience as often as possible. "Get some," urged this early Van Camp's ad. (Van Camp's ad reprinted with permission of ConAgra Foods, Inc. All rights reserved.)

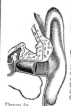
An ambitious Albert Lasker, hoping to help Lord & Thomas earn its full 15 percent commission on ads it placed, decided to run an experiment based on more expansive and persuasive copy. He asked the agency's owners for a chance to reconceive the Wilson Ear Drum Company's ads, and they agreed. The pre-Lasker ad (*above*) relied principally on a bold headline and a technical-looking drawing to make its case. Lasker's revised ad (*right*) included a picture of company owner George Wilson—whom Lasker later said looked like the "deafest man you ever saw"—and extensive copy touted the multiple benefits of Wilson's invention. It worked, and Wilson increased his ad budget from $2,000 to $6,000 a month and agreed to pay the full 15 percent commission. This transition—from "deafness" to "deafness cured"—foreshadowed major changes that Lasker would later effect in his industry.

Above: In May 1904, an exotic stranger named John E. Kennedy arrived on Lord & Thomas's doorstep claiming to know the secret of successful advertising. It was, he told Lasker, *salesmanship in print. Below:* A pre-Kennedy ad for the 1900 Washer Co. (today's Whirlpool), which Kennedy considered dreadful. *Right:* Kennedy's ad, which generated an avalanche of inquiries and reduced the company's per-inquiry cost from $20 to 47 cents. (Ads reprinted with permission of the Whirlpool Corporation.)

Let this Machine do your Washing Free.

There are Motor Springs beneath the tub. These springs do nearly all the hard work, when once you start them going. And this washing machine works as easy as a bicycle wheel does.

There are slats on the inside bottom of the tub. These slats act as paddles, to swing the water in the same direction you revolve the tub.

You throw the soiled clothes into the tub first. Then you throw enough water over the clothes to float them.

Next you put the heavy wooden cover on top of the clothes to anchor them, and to press them down. This cover has slats on its lower side to grip the clothes and hold them from turning around when the tub turns.

Now, we are all ready for quick and easy washing. You grasp the upright handle on the side of the tub and, with it, you revolve the tub one-third way round, till it strikes a motor-spring.

This motor-spring throws the tub back till it strikes the other motor-spring, which in turn throws it back on the first motor-spring.

The machine must have a little help from you, at every swing, but the motor-springs, and the ball-bearings, do practically all the hard work.

You can sit in a rocking chair and do all that the washer requires of _you_. A child can run it easily full of clothes.

*　　　*　　　*

When you revolve the tub the clothes don't move. But the _water_ moves like a mill race _through the clothes._

The paddles on the tub bottom drive the soapy water THROUGH and through the clothes at every swing of the tub. Back and forth, in and out of every fold, and through every mesh in the cloth, the hot soapy water runs like a torrent. This is _how_ it carries away all the dirt from the clothes, in from six to ten minutes by the clock.

It drives the dirt out through the meshes of the fabrics WITHOUT ANY RUBBING,—without any WEAR and TEAR from the washboard.

It will wash the finest lace fabric without breaking a thread, or a button, and it will wash a heavy, dirty carpet with equal ease and rapidity. Fifteen to twenty garments, or five large bed-sheets, can be washed at one time with this "1900" Washer.

A child can do in six to twelve minutes better than any able washer-woman could do the same clothes in TWICE the time, with three times the wear and tear from the washboard.

*　　　*　　　*

This is what we SAY, now how do we PROVE it? We send you our "1900" Washer free of charge, on a full month's trial, and we even pay the freight out of our own pockets.

No cash deposit is asked, no notes, no contract, no security.

You may use the washer four weeks at our expense. If you find it won't wash as many clothes in FOUR hours as you can wash by hand in EIGHT hours you send it back to the railway station,—that's all.

But, if, from a month's actual use, you are convinced it saves HALF th. time in washing, does the work better, and does it twice as easily as it could be done by hand, you keep the machine.

Then you mail us 50 cents a week till it is paid for. Remember that 50 cents is part of what the machine saves you every week on your own, or on a washer-woman's labor. We intend that the "1900" Washer shall pay for itself and thus cost you nothing.

You don't risk a cent from first to last, and you don't buy it until you have had a full month's trial.

Could we afford to pay freight on thousands of these machines every month, if we did not positively KNOW they would do all we claim for them? Can you afford to be without a machine that will do your washing in HALF THE TIME, with half the wear and tear of the washboard, when you can have that machine for a month's free trial, and let it PAY FOR ITSELF? This offer may be withdrawn at any time it overcrowds our factory.

Write us TO-DAY, while the offer is still open, and while you think of it. The postage stamp is all you risk. Write me personally on this offer, viz.: R. F. Bieber, General Manager of "1900" Washer Company, 155 Henry St., Binghamton, New York.

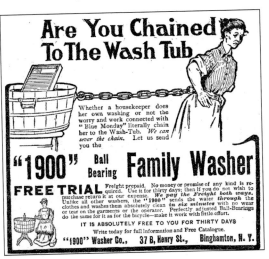

Are You Chained To The Wash Tub

Whether a housekeeper does her own washing or not the worry and work connected with "Blue Monday" literally chain her to the Wash-Tub. *We can sever the chain.* Let us send you the

"1900" Ball Bearing Family Washer

FREE TRIAL Freight prepaid. No money or promise of any kind is required. Use it for thirty days; then if you do not wish to purchase return it at our expense. *We pay the Freight both ways.* Unlike all other washers, the "1900" sends the water *through the* clothes and washes them absolutely clean *in six minutes* with no wear or tear on the garments or the operator. Perfectly adjusted Ball-Bearings do the same for it as for the bicycle—make it work with little effort.

IT IS ABSOLUTELY FREE TO YOU FOR THIRTY DAYS
Write today for full information and Free Catalogue.

"1900" Washer Co., 37 B, Henry St., Binghamton, N. Y.

Rubens
Infant Shirt

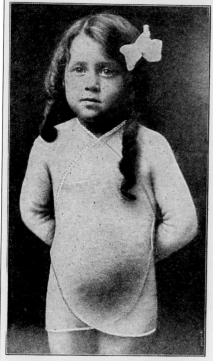

FRONT VIEW.

BACK VIEW.

A Word to Mothers:

The Rubens Shirt is a veritable life-preserver. No child should be without it. It affords full protection to lungs and abdomen, thus preventing colds and coughs, so fatal to a great many children. Get the Rubens Shirt at once. Take no other, no matter what any unprogressive dealer may say. If he doesn't keep it write to us. The Rubens Shirt has gladdened the hearts of thousands of mothers. We want it accessible to all the world.

BEWARE OF IMITATIONS!

The Genuine Rubens Shirt has this signature stamped on every garment —

Rubens

The Rubens Shirt is made in cotton, merino (half wool and half cotton), wool, silk and wool, and all silk, to fit from birth to nine years. Sold at Dry-Goods Stores. Circulars, with Price-List, free.

No Buttons

No Trouble

Patent Nos. 528,988 — 550,233.

Manufactured by RUBENS & MARBLE, 90 Market Street, Chicago

Only a few weeks into his apprenticeship at Lord & Thomas, Lasker got the opportunity to call on the Rubens & Marble Company, which manufactured knit underwear for children. The youthful Lasker made a pitch to Rubens in English, which the company founder disdainfully shrugged off: "They think because this is a baby business, they have to send *children* over here!" Lasker then repeated his pitch in German—and Rubens was won over.

Flora (seated), Lasker's first wife, with daughter Mary and a governess, in Atlantic City in 1910. Flora—a strong-willed woman who exerted great control over her husband for more than three decades—was stricken and made an invalid by typhoid fever shortly after their marriage in 1902. Against doctors' orders, she gave birth to Mary and two other children, Edward and Frances. (Photo courtesy of Chicago History Museum.)

Sunkist was one of Lord & Thomas's most important accounts. Lasker persuaded the six thousand independent growers who made up the California Fruit Growers Exchange to band together under the Sunkist brand—and then used a succession of clever marketing ploys (*right* and *below*) to promote the consumption of California oranges and lemons. (Sunkist is a registered trademark of Sunkist Growers, Inc. Reprinted with permission of Sunkist Growers, Inc. All rights reserved. No use or reuse without the express, written consent of Sunkist Growers, Inc.)

Above: The second of Lasker's brilliant copywriters, Claude C. Hopkins wrote one successful campaign after another for Lord & Thomas. *Left:* Hopkins's first work for Lord & Thomas attempted to differentiate Van Camp's pork and beans from its competitors. In this and subsequent campaigns, Hopkins celebrated an unremarkable aspect of the production process to make the product sound special—a "reason why" the customer should buy the product. "Reason-why" advertising evolved into the "unique selling proposition" of later decades. (Ad reprinted with permission of ConAgra Foods, Inc. All rights reserved.)

Better than jewels
—that schoolgirl complexion

The girl with a clear, smooth skin, radiant with freshness and natural color, should leave jewels to those less fortunate. The charm of a perfect natural complexion attracts far more than elaborate dress and ornaments.

If your complexion lacks the beauty which women envy and men admire, don't depend on clothes and jewelry to draw attention from its defects.

Every woman can transform her bad complexion into a good one, for alluring freshness and clear color isn't a gift of Nature, but a matter of care.

How to have a perfect skin

No girl need be afflicted with a bad complexion, for improvement is simple and easy. Daily cleansing, gentle but thorough, is the secret.

You must use soap, for nothing else will remove the dirt, oil and perspiration which collect in the pores and cause most skin trouble.

Choose Palmolive, because its action is soothing. Harsh soap should never be used for washing the face.

Massage the smooth, creamy lather gently into the skin until it removes all clogging deposits. Don't forget your neck and throat. They are as conspicuous as the face for any lack in beauty.

Careful rinsing leaves the skin stimulated, freshened and free from the accumulation which enlarges the pores, causes blackheads and carries infection.

Blended from the same oils

Palmolive Soap is blended from the same bland, soothing oils which adorned the sumptuous marble baths of Egyptians, Greeks and Romans.

But although very expensive, the gigantic volume in which Palmolive is produced keeps the price very low. Users profit by Palmolive popularity. The Palmolive factories, working day and night, and the importation of the rare oils in vast quantities, allow you to enjoy this finest facial soap for the modest price of 10 cents—no more than ordinary soap.

THE PALMOLIVE COMPANY, MILWAUKEE, U. S. A.
THE PALMOLIVE COMPANY OF CANADA, Limited, TORONTO, ONT.
Also makers of a complete line of toilet articles

Volume and efficiency produce 25-cent quality for only

10c

Take a lesson from Cleopatra

With a world of ancient beauty arts at her command, she depended on cleansing with Palm and Olive oils to protect, improve and preserve the freshness and smoothness of her skin.

Copyright, 1922—The Palmolive Co. (1524)

The Milwaukee-based B.J. Johnson Soap Company brought a little-known beauty soap to Lord & Thomas in 1911. Drawing on their experiences in direct-mail advertising, Lasker and Hopkins came up with a series of promotions designed to get Palmolive into drugstores across the country. Within a few years, Palmolive was the best-selling soap in the world. In 1916, B.J. Johnson Soap changed its name to the Palmolive Company. (Reprinted with permission of the Colgate-Palmolive Company.)

Above, left: Arthur Brisbane, editor of William Randolph Hearst's *New York Evening Journal*, worked with Lasker and *New York Times* editor Adolph Ochs to try to save the life of Leo Frank (*above, right*), a Jewish factory superintendent in Atlanta who was accused of raping and murdering a young factory girl.

Brooklyn Robins' second baseman Lee Magee was acquired by the Chicago Cubs—then co-owned by Lasker and William Wrigley—in 1919 for the relatively low price of $5,000. When Lasker and manager Bill Veeck learned that Magee was a gambler who had "thrown" games, they kicked him off the team and ultimately saw him banned from baseball for life.

Kenesaw Mountain Landis was appointed to the bench of the Northern District of Illinois in 1905 by President Theodore Roosevelt. Two years later, he made a national reputation for himself by fining Standard Oil $29 million for antitrust violations and compelling John D. Rockefeller to testify in his courtroom. He was a Cubs fan—which endeared him to Lasker and the other Cubs owners, and annoyed White Sox fans in his hometown of Chicago. In the wake of the "Black Sox" scandal of 1920, Lasker came up with a plan for a national commissioner of baseball who would have extraordinary power over the game and its owners. Upon receiving his appointment as commissioner, Landis promptly banned the eight "Black Sox" players for life. "At no point," a later commissioner observed, "did [Landis] temper justice with mercy."

Above: Chewing-gum magnate William Wrigley throws out the first ball at a Cubs game, as Lasker (seated to Wrigley's right) looks on. Lasker owned a larger stake in the Cubs than Wrigley, but was happy to let Wrigley be the team's "front man," and thereby reap publicity for Wrigley's Gum. (Picture of Lasker and Wrigley © Getty Images.) *Below:* Lasker and Will Hays at a Washington dinner in 1920. Hays was the political genius who—with Lasker's help—installed Warren G. Harding in the White House.

Left: Lasker and Harding became close friends during the 1920 campaign. Harding recruited Lasker to serve in his administration, although he gave the job that Lasker wanted—Secretary of Commerce—to a rising political star named Herbert Hoover. *Below:* Harding and Lasker both enjoyed poker, golf, and baseball—and on April 24, 1923, met Babe Ruth at Yankee Stadium, where the Yankees were playing the Washington Senators. (Picture of Lasker, Harding, and Ruth © Bettmann/CORBIS.)

Right: Flora, Albert, and daughter Mary Lasker aboard ship. *Below:* Mary Lasker prepares for a golf outing. Mary's willful nature gave her parents many anxious moments—which continued during her brief tenure at Lord & Thomas.

President Harding prevailed on Lasker (front row, fourth from left) to serve as chairman of the United States Shipping Board, which Harding referred to as the "damnedest job in the world." Lasker became only the third Jew in U.S. history up to that time to hold a high federal position.

canned foods. "It means slim profits for us," Irwin wrote gloomily to Lasker, "for whatever length of time he chooses to continue his present plan."[39]

Lasker couldn't decide what he wanted to do about Van Camp. On the one hand, he confessed to Irwin, he would gladly sell out for the $200 a share that Campbell, Heath had previously offered. On the other hand, Flora argued against selling out. "I remember that you once said you believed in woman's intuition," he wrote to Irwin. "She was quite bitter that I would consent to sell at all, and feels it is a mistake."[40]

Meanwhile, the other Campbell—W. D. Campbell, of Campbell, Heath—continued his overtures to the Van Camp directors. When Irwin cut what appeared to be a final deal with Campbell in April 1921, Lasker—once again in Pasadena—expressed his gratitude. "I just can't begin to express to you how happy I am that the deal has gone through," he wrote. "No money is worth while if worry goes with it."

As it turned out, many more months had to pass before the new Van Camp preferred stock could be sold. The depression of 1920–1922 was in full force, and investors were sitting tight. "I WANT TO GET OUT, AND I WANT TO GET OUT QUICK," Lasker wrote to Irwin in January 1922. He was now deeply involved in the next phase of his life—running a federal government agency in Washington—and his family was in turmoil. The week before, his six-year-old daughter, Francie, had nearly died from pneumonia—the second such dangerous episode in a year. ("She almost slipped away from us," Lasker confided.) And now the ailing Flora was headed to Johns Hopkins in Baltimore for several months of observation.[41]

Ultimately, Lasker accepted a financial drubbing as the cost of disengaging from Van Camp. Exactly how severe a beating is unclear, although he later claimed that he "lost everything [he] had in," suggesting a write-off of perhaps a half-million dollars.[42] He also did worse than he absolutely had to: before the final deal was sealed, Lasker bought back much of the preferred stock that he had sold to various friends and family members because he didn't want them exposed to unnecessary risk.[43]

Lasker offered his own biting epitaph for Van Camp: "We managed to make a great failure of it, and [then] we sold out."[44]

He likened his Van Camp experience to his involvement in the Mitchell-Lewis Motor Company—a Racine-based automaker in whose affairs he had immersed himself in this same time period, and which cost him something like $1 million:[45]

> I learned a great lesson there, and in the Mitchell case—that not having expe-rience in manufacturing, I could be poison to any manufacturing business where I had any say in the manufacturing end; that my specialty was publicity and distribution . . . At times when I became impatient with manufacturers because they have strong opinions on my end, I [was] constrained to remember my two great failures when I sat in their chairs.[46]

Lasker's magic definitely faded when he got "down in the weeds." But from start to finish, the Van Camp experience was about people and relation-ships more than manufacturing and money. He was drawn into Van Camp through his friendship with Frank Van Camp, who severely abused that friendship. Lasker, typically, not only forgave him but continued to help him financially as Van Camp set up a tuna-packing operation on the West Coast. Lasker even asked Van Camp to accompany him on his Mexican rest cure, underscoring their close and enduring ties.

By far the biggest benefit that Lasker derived from the experience was his friendship with W. G. Irwin. He considered Irwin one of the finest men he ever encountered, and the mutual respect that they developed for each other in the early 'teens evolved into a close friendship.[47] Their written salutations grew increasingly warm (from "Dear Mr. Irwin" to "my dear Will"). They visited each other's homes, and the Laskers made a special effort to welcome lifelong bachelor Irwin into their family's inner circle. They exchanged gifts, went to ball games together, and helped each other enter new worlds.

As he wrote to Irwin on the first occasion when the sale of Van Camp appeared to be going through: "My profit from the transaction comes from the close contact it has brought me into with you, and the very intimate asso-ciation it has given me with you. Even though we shall not meet in connec-tion with business, I hope we shall always keep alive the friendship which has existed between us and which, to me, shall ever mean much."[48]

That friendship that not only survived but intensified, ending only with Irwin's death in 1943.

Chapter Ten

Saving Baseball from Itself

*A*LBERT LASKER'S impulse to find, hone, and exploit a powerful idea manifested itself in many arenas—perhaps the least likely of which was professional baseball.

His first exposure to the game came in the early months of 1894, when the Chicago Cubs came to Galveston for what was then called "winter training."[1] In that simpler time, Chicago sportswriters didn't bother to travel south to cover the Cubs in training; instead, the Chicago newspapers paid local stringers to write up the exhibition games. Lasker covered the games for multiple papers, earning a dollar per game from each for providing a box score and a few lines of commentary. "Through that," Lasker recalled, "I became deeply interested not only in baseball, but also in the mechanics of how a big league team was run."[2]

Perennially, the Cubs franchise that Lasker covered in Galveston had great potential; just as consistently, it failed to live up to it. The Cubs underperformed so badly, in fact, that in 1898—the year Lasker moved to Chicago—team owner Al Spalding fired legendary manager Cap Anson. These failures and tensions mattered little to Lasker, who was by now a diehard Cubs fan, attending games at Cubs Park and remaining loyal to his notably unsuccessful team.

The Cubs soon rewarded his loyalty many times over. In 1906, with manager and first baseman Frank Chance at the helm, the Cubs finally brought home the pennant. They finished the season with a 116-and-36 record: the best record in the history of baseball.[3] The Cubs went 60 and 15 on the road, and won 50 of their last 57 games. Their "Tinker-to-Evers-to-Chance" double-play combination was immortalized in a 1910 poem composed by a frustrated New York Giants fan.

In October 1906, the Cubs met the White Sox in the first World Series ever to feature two teams from the same city. Charlie Comiskey's White Sox won the series in six, but the Cubs came back just as strong the following season. They took the pennant again, winning 107 games and finishing 17 games ahead of the second-place Pirates. In the World Series that year, they met a Detroit squad headed by the legendary hitter—and brawler—Ty Cobb. But the Cubs proved to have more fight than even Cobb. Frank Chance suffered a broken finger when hit by a pitch during his first at-bat in Game 3; he simply taped it up and kept playing. The Cubs won in five, and their fans—including a rising young ad man named Lasker—gloated.

The Cubs met the Tigers again in the 1908 World Series and again beat them in five games, thereby becoming the first team in baseball history to repeat as world champions. They won the pennant again in 1909, and it looked as if the team Frank Chance had built might go on winning forever.

———————

But it was not to be. The erratic owner of the Cubs, Charlie Murphy, began selling off Frank Chance's stars in 1912, thereby earning the eternal enmity of the team's players and fans. Murphy was also despised by his fellow owners because he sold some of those stars to the "Federal League," which had gone into business in that year. The players Murphy sold helped make that new league viable, and hurt the already established American and National Leagues.

The Federal League owner who benefited the most from Murphy's lone-wolfish behavior was a Chicago entrepreneur named Charles Weeghman, who had made a modest fortune with a chain of low-priced luncheonettes and owned the Federal League entry in Chicago. Weeghman spent $250,000 on a stunning new ballpark at Clark and Addison, on Chicago's North Side, which opened in 1914. He renamed his team the "Whales"—implying bigness—and named the new ballpark after himself.

In January 1915, the Federal League took the two older leagues to court, claiming that they were acting in restraint of trade. Because both the American and Federal Leagues were headquartered in Chicago, the venue was the United States District Court for the Northern District of Illinois. There the disputing parties encountered Judge Kenesaw Mountain Landis, who had achieved a national reputation as a progressive and a trust-buster. If the upstart Federals were hoping for a trust-busting victory in Landis's court, they were disappointed. "Do you realize," Landis at one point asked their lawyer, "that a decision in this case may tear down the very foundation of this game, so loved by thousands, and do you realize that the decision must also seriously affect both parties?"[4] A blow to the game of baseball, he warned both sides, would be regarded by his court as a "blow to one of our national institutions."[5] Landis took the case under advisement and stalled for almost a year in hopes that the squabbling leagues could resolve their problems outside his courtroom.

In early twentieth-century America, football, basketball, and hockey were still college sports; with the possible exception of boxing, baseball was the only professional game in town. And for many fans in the early years of the twentieth century, baseball *embodied* America. Even then, it harkened back to a time when the nation was slower-paced, more rural, and—as the story would have it—more innocent. It provided a stage for acts of heroism in an era when frontiers had closed and wars were discovered to be bloody and brutal.

Baseball owners were happy to propagate these myths of innocence. But the reality was different, especially when it came to the *business* of baseball. In the first two decades of the twentieth century, for example, seventeen of the eighteen American and National League franchises had close ties to federal or state politicians, urban political machines, or gambling interests.[6] Gambling had already elbowed its way into baseball, just as it previously had cast a pall over boxing, horse racing, football, and wrestling. Several club owners were either professional gamblers or openly kept company with gamblers. Baseball was far less innocent than its fans knew.

The disputing parties in Judge Landis's court reached an out-of-court settlement in December 1915. The National and American Leagues paid $5 million to put the Federal League out of business and to absorb its players and assets. For the long-time owners, the deal restored a profitable monopoly. It also got Cubs owner Charlie Murphy off the baseball stage, with Cincinnati-based Charles P. Taft—owner of the National League's Philadelphia franchise and Murphy's original financial backer—taking over ownership of the Cubs on a caretaker basis. Since having one person own competing teams was clearly inappropriate, Taft then sold the Cubs to former Whales owner Charles Weeghman.

Under the terms of the sale, which closed on January 20, 1916, Weeghman merged the Whales into the Cubs and moved them north to Weeghman Park. Some feared that Cubs fans would refuse to follow their team all the way from their dingy West Side Grounds to the North Side. As it turned out, the team's spectacular new ballpark—as well as some of Weeghman's innovations, such as encouraging fans to keep baseballs that were hit into the stands—attracted large numbers of paying customers during the spring of 1916.

Many also feared that Weeghman's ties to the underworld might taint the Cubs. He associated publicly with both Chicago-based gambler Jacob "Mont" Tennes and the notorious Arnold "The Big Bankroll" Rothstein, who ran substantial gambling operations out of New York. These fears, too, proved unfounded.

Weeghman's real weakness lay in his lack of capital. Under the terms of his purchase, Weeghman and his associates set up a company with a capitalization of $1 million—of which half was stock representing the merged teams' assets (principally Weeghman Park and the players' contracts), and the other half was to be new money raised from additional investors. Weeghman's option gave him a year to raise this additional $500,000.[7]

He secured pledges of $50,000 each from chewing gum magnate William Wrigley, meatpacker J. Ogden Armour, and seafood wholesaler William Walker, as well as lesser amounts from other investors. (Wrigley, Armour, and Walker had little interest in baseball but they had cash on hand—and Weeghman's restaurant chain was a valued customer.) By the end of 1916, however, Weeghman had raised only $350,000, and his option was set to expire. Desperate, he approached a wealthy Chicago businessman—a friend of a friend—who was an avid Cubs fan.

That fan was Albert Lasker.

Lasker had never considered *buying* a baseball team, so when Weeghman approached him in January 1917, he was taken aback.[8] He didn't know Weeghman, and didn't know the first thing about assessing or running a professional baseball club. In addition, Weeghman needed a commitment overnight. Lasker told him to keep looking, but also invited him to come back at nine the next morning if he failed to turn up another investor.[9]

That night, Lasker took this strange story home to Flora, who strongly encouraged her husband to buy into the Cubs: "She insisted that I buy that interest, saying that I worked so hard that this would give me an avocation. I saw that she was very determined. I don't think she ever saw a ball game in her life. She was an invalid, and never took any part in my business affairs, but on this she was insistent. She persuaded me to do it."[10]

The next morning, Weeghman showed up once again at Lasker's office. He hadn't found another buyer. Would Lasker consider buying in?

This time, Lasker had an answer. He would take a 15 percent share in the team for the stated $150,000, he told Weeghman, but he had to be "protected." First, one of his own lawyers, Alfred S. Austrian, had to be retained as the Cubs' attorney. Extremely well connected, Austrian boasted a client list that included not only Lasker and other prominent Chicago business leaders, but also Charles Comiskey, owner of the Chicago White Sox. Austrian was an art collector, the owner of a page from an original Gutenberg Bible, and a scratch golfer, and was both extremely intelligent and likeable.[11] This latter quality, Lasker once commented, served his lawyer well: "Mr. Austrian was a man who was very aggressive in that way—a very dominating man—but with a very wonderful personality so that he often got away with it."[12]

Weeghman agreed to hire Austrian. Then came Lasker's second condition: Lasker wanted the right to approve the directors of the franchise. Again, Weeghman agreed.

At the organizational meeting of the team's owners, Lasker announced that he wanted both William Wrigley and Ogden Armour to serve on the Cubs board. Neither man was in attendance at this unimportant meeting, of course; they had sent proxies. Armour's representative made it clear that the prominent meatpacker had no intention of participating in the affairs of a ball club. Lasker then demanded that George Marcey—head of Armour's grain division, whom Lasker knew—be elected instead. Marcey, reached by phone, agreed, and was elected to the board.

Wrigley's representative proved less successful at fighting off Lasker. Lasker announced he was certain that Wrigley—then out of town and unavailable by phone—would agree to become a director, and insisted that the group elect him in absentia. (This was pure bravado on Lasker's part; he didn't even know Wrigley.) Wrigley was elected.

Then the aggressive new minority owner took steps to make the election stick. As Lasker later recalled: "When Mr. Wrigley returned, I went to see him. He had no interest in baseball. I don't think Mr. Wrigley even knew that there were three strikes for an out. I mean that seriously. I'm *sure* he didn't know what a squeeze play would mean. However, he assented when I put my reasons before him. He immediately became intrigued with it as an avocation."[13]

"Intrigued," perhaps, but not particularly involved. So Lasker continued to cultivate Wrigley, whose office was just across the hall from his own "hide-away" suite in the Maller Building. Lasker talked baseball with the chewing gum magnate. He took him to Cubs games. He persuaded Wrigley to allow the franchise to rename Weeghman's elegant North Side ballpark "Wrigley Field," on the grounds that it would be good for business. And when Weeghman's financial condition worsened, Lasker persuaded Wrigley to join him in buying Weeghman out.

Throughout, Lasker—the team's largest shareholder—stayed well behind the scenes. "I am perfectly willing to put you out in front as main owner of the team," he told Wrigley, "and let you get this publicity."[14] Lasker, who judged Wrigley to be a "one-idea man," knew what motivated his fellow owner: "He lived for Wrigley's Chewing Gum."[15] If something could get the Wrigley name in front of the public, that was enough for Will Wrigley. Not until December 1918 did Wrigley attend a Cubs board meeting, although by that time he had been a director for nearly two years.

Gradually, with Lasker's encouragement, Wrigley got more involved with the Cubs. It was his idea, for example, to hire *Chicago American* sportswriter Bill Veeck as the team's general manager—a job at which Veeck proved to be enormously talented.[16] With Lasker pushing from behind, "Wrigley's Cubs" made headlines by buying the outstanding pitcher-and-catcher combination of Grover Cleveland Alexander and William Killifer Jr. from Philadelphia in December 1917 for the then staggering sum of $50,000. "Nobody had ever heard of money like that," Lasker crowed.[17]

In the spring of 1919, Veeck learned that he could buy the contract of Lee Magee—a gifted second baseman with the Brooklyn Robins (soon to be renamed the Dodgers)—for a modest $5,000.[18] Even as the deal was being closed, Veeck confessed to Lasker that he was worried.[19] Magee had passed the Cubs' physical exam with no problems. So why was Brooklyn owner Charlie Ebbets so eager to deal him away?

Magee played only eight games for the Cubs in 1919, in part because of rumors that he was "crooked." Then, on February 10, 1920, Veeck learned the truth: while playing for the Cincinnati Reds in 1918, Magee had tried to throw a game to the Boston Braves. Cincinnati owner Garry Herrmann unloaded his tainted second baseman on Brooklyn, conveniently failing to mention the gambling rumors. When Ebbets got wind of Magee's reputation, he too bailed out, selling Magee to the Cubs.

Lasker and several other members of the team's executive committee discussed the situation with Veeck.[20] They decided that they would refuse to honor their contract with Magee and that they would demand that baseball's all-powerful National Commission—consisting of men who were either the heads of leagues or the owners of clubs—throw Magee out of the game.

There were several complicating factors, including the fact that Cincinnati owner Herrmann was one of the three members of the National Commission. This infuriated Veeck, who was a "very high type of man," in Lasker's estimation.[21] Veeck was incensed that Herrmann—an owner with partial responsibility for the fortunes of America's national pastime—had knowingly dumped a crooked player on a fellow owner.

Not surprisingly, the National Commission wanted to keep the whole affair quiet. "They said, 'Oh, no, baseball can't have a scandal like that,'" Lasker recalled, "'We mustn't have a scandal.'"[22] But Veeck persisted, and on February 20, 1920, the Cubs unconditionally released Magee.

The drama now threatened to spin out of control. Magee announced his intention to sue the Cubs for breach of contract. The National Commission, headed by Ban Johnson—a legendary baseball figure who almost singlehandedly had built the American League into a powerhouse and now controlled the Commission—strongly urged Veeck to settle. If the suit went ahead, they argued, baseball would get a black eye from which it might not recover.

Veeck and the Cubs' executive committee elected to stand on principle. "We all decided, by gum," Lasker explained, "that we'd go through with the lawsuit even if it busted up baseball. We didn't want to be in a thing like that."[23]

In federal court in Cincinnati, the Cubs argued that, "previous to the making of the contract the plaintiff was guilty of betting against the team of which he was a member, and sought to win bets by intentional bad playing to defeat said team." On the witness stand, Magee confessed to having bet on games involving the Reds while he was a member of that team, but argued that his Cubs contract nevertheless should be enforced. The court disagreed. On June 9, 1920, Magee's suit was thrown out, and he was banned for life from organized baseball.[24]

By standing up to Ban Johnson, Veeck and his Executive Committee demonstrated considerable courage.[25] The National Commission exercised enormous authority over the game and had a history of showing favoritism toward compliant owners and punishing uncooperative ones. Among the latter group were the Boston Red Sox's Harry Frazee, the New York Yankees' Jacob Ruppert, the Chicago White Sox's Charles Comiskey, and the Pittburgh Pirates' Barney Dreyfuss, each of whom had battled with the Commission. Comiskey was perhaps the angriest of all, believing that several of Johnson's rulings had unfairly hurt the White Sox.

The story that endures from the 1919 World Series is probably apocryphal. According to legend, a newsboy called out to "Shoeless" Joe Jackson, one of eight Chicago White Sox players accused of throwing the series to Cincinnati, as his hero left the Cook County courthouse in Chicago on September 29, 1920. Jackson had just finished testifying in front of a grand jury. *Say it ain't so, Joe*, the anguished newsboy implored. Jackson—a wonderfully talented outfielder and, according to both Babe Ruth and Ty Cobb, the greatest hitter in the history of baseball—supposedly replied, "It's so, kid."[26]

That a group of professional ball players would conspire to rig the World Series deeply offended America. "The country as a whole," Lasker said, "was almost as shocked as if they had heard that the president of the United States, or members of the Cabinet of the United States, had been bribed."[27]

The facts were both simple and baffling. Charlie Comiskey's Chicago White Sox were the best team in baseball in 1919—probably one of the best teams of all time. (Although Lasker was a Cubs fan, he arranged his business schedule to ensure that he could attend the first game of the Series. "I have never missed an opening game of the Series," he wrote unapologetically to one business associate, who wanted him to be elsewhere that day.[28]) The White Sox went up against Garry Herrmann's Cincinnati Reds, and—astoundingly—lost a best-of-nine series by a score of five to three. Somehow, the White Sox fielders couldn't field cleanly at critical junctures; their winning pitchers mostly couldn't win; their fearsome hitters couldn't come up with timely hits.

For no apparent reason, just as the Series opened, the gambling odds shifted heavily in favor of Cincinnati. Chicago sportswriters—among them the gifted Ring Lardner, a friend of Lasker's—smelled a rat, but no one could point to anything concrete. Rumors of great sums of money being bet on the games swirled in the background, but again, no one could turn up proof that gamblers were influencing the outcome. The eighth game ended with Cincinnati taking the championship trophy home, while angry Chicago fans went into the winter months scratching their heads.

Almost a full year later, in an interview in the *Philadelphia North American,* a shady character known sometimes as Billy "Maharg" (and at other times Billy "Graham") detailed how the 1919 Series was fixed, with the active involvement of Arnold Rothstein and other prominent gamblers. A grand jury was impaneled, and at the end of September 1920, three members of the White Sox—soon to be known in disgrace as the "Black Sox"—confessed that they and five of their teammates had thrown the Series.

Lasker called an emergency meeting with Veeck and told the Cubs' manager that he feared the Black Sox scandal might destroy baseball. Veeck agreed. A loss of public confidence in the integrity of the game was only one concern. Far more ominous was an unrelated case then being appealed by organized baseball in the District of Columbia Court of Appeals. If the lower court's decision was not overturned, professional baseball would be deemed a combination in restraint of trade—a monopoly—and effectively dismantled. The Black Sox scandal could nudge the appellate court judge in the wrong direction.[29]

Lasker told Veeck that the structure of organized baseball—the National Commission—was partly to blame for the fiasco. He had made a similar argument a year earlier, in a reorganization proposal that had been ignored by the Commission.[30] "They have vested interests," Lasker reiterated. "They can't make decisions freely, because they are too involved themselves."[31]

Again, Veeck agreed. But what would an alternative structure look like?

Lasker set out to answer that question. Working closely with his lawyer, Alfred Austrian—who was also the lawyer for both the White Sox and the Cubs, and was deeply involved in the investigation into the Black Sox scandal—Lasker drew up a four-page plan for a new commission, consisting of three independent commissioners: one elected by the National League, another elected by the American League, and a third elected by the minor leagues.[32] These commissioners had to be nationally prominent individuals, outside of baseball, and each had to be acceptable to the other two leagues. Lasker's plan even put forward the names of individuals who he thought would fill the bill, including California's renegade senator Hiram Johnson.[33]

Another name on Lasker's list was that of Judge Kenesaw Mountain Landis. Although Lasker had met Landis once, a decade earlier, he knew the judge mainly by his reputation.[34] Named for the Civil War battle in which his father had received grave injuries, Landis had achieved national celebrity in 1907 by levying a $29 million fine against Standard Oil for multiple violations of federal laws governing interstate commerce. It was the largest fine ever imposed by an American court up to that point, establishing Landis's reputation as a tough and independent-minded jurist. Briefly, Landis was touted as a candidate in the upcoming presidential election—a boomlet that he firmly quashed. "I have the best position in the world," he wrote. "I would not give up the judicial work for three times Mr. John D. Rockefeller's money."[35]

Another qualification that may have helped put Landis on Lasker's list was the fact that the judge was a Cubs fan. (Landis had been booed by White Sox fans during the 1906 Cubs-White Sox World Series.) But Landis, ever the embodiment of probity, made a point of attending American, National, and Federal League games—and accepting free tickets from no one.[36]

Lasker first revealed his plan (and his list of candidates) to the Cubs' Executive Committee. "We are in back of you," they told Lasker. "Go to it."[37] With this endorsement in hand, Lasker signed up New York Giants owner Charles Stoneham and manager John McGraw in a subsequent meeting.[38] Next, a week after the eight White Sox were indicted, Lasker invited representatives of five major league teams to an October 5, 1920, meeting at Austrian's office. These included the owners of the American League's White Sox, Yankees, and Red Sox and the National League's Cubs and Giants. Lasker laid out his plan to them, arguing that the only way to save their game was to give someone from outside of the game "complete power over baseball." Having people with financial interests in the game make key decisions, he told them, was "bound to result in scandal."[39]

Seven team owners agreed to what Lasker dubbed the "Lasker Plan." It was an uncharacteristic bit of self-promotion. "My little boy was madly in love with baseball," he explained, "and I wanted to show off for my little boy."[40] The owners signed the document—although, typically, Lasker himself did not sign for the Cubs.

The signatories included the owners of both New York and Chicago franchises—"where the big money came from," explained Lasker. If the New York and Chicago franchises bolted, the existing American and National Leagues could not survive. He made full use of that leverage. That night, he and Veeck mailed out seven hundred copies of their manifesto to the owners of every major and minor league team in the country, as well as to the sports editors of all major newspapers.

None of this could have come as a surprise to Ban Johnson, since the original meeting was reported on in the newspapers and the proposal generated hundreds of telegrams of support, including more than fifty from minor-league owners.[41] But Johnson chose to downplay the significance of the rebellion. "Who *is* this fellow Lasker?" Johnson asked a reporter. "I've never heard of him."[42]

Lasker felt no personal animosity toward Johnson, whom he considered the "greatest figure baseball ever produced." But he felt that Johnson had become an autocrat and that the National Commission he headed was hopelessly compromised.[43] It was time for a change. When reporters repeated Johnson's question to Lasker—*who is this fellow Lasker?*—he responded coolly, "Mr. Johnson will have heard of me before this is over."[44]

Five American League teams (Philadelphia, Washington, Cleveland, Detroit, and St. Louis) immediately announced that they would support Johnson and the existing National Commission. In the National League, all but Cincinnati Reds president Garry Herrmann sided with Lasker—and soon enough, the Reds too came around, mainly because Lasker went to see Herrmann's financial backers ("friends of mine," he admitted), and they forced Herrmann to sign up with the insurgents. Lasker's allies announced that, if necessary, they would set up a new twelve-team league that would include a new franchise in Detroit, then one of the American League's most lucrative franchises.

The American League (except Chicago, New York, and Boston) shot back, publicly denouncing the Lasker Plan as risky and ineffectual. In the face of this opposition, Lasker worked to shore up the resolve of his National League allies. Brooklyn's Charlie Ebbets, for example, asked how long Lasker and the Cubs would stick with a new league that was almost certain to lose large amounts of money.

"Until Wrigley's lost his last dollar," Lasker replied.[45]

On November 8, the National League teams formally voted to overthrow Ban Johnson and establish a three-man commission of outsiders. As its chairman, they selected a figure already well known to both Standard Oil shareholders and baseball moguls: Judge Kenesaw Mountain Landis.

There are several versions of how Landis's name got put in front of the November 8 meeting.[46] As Lasker told the story, his ubiquitous attorney, Alfred Austrian, summoned Lasker to his office while the National League meetings were in process.[47] Austrian told Lasker that he had offered the top commissioner's job to a qualified individual.

"You've engaged the man?" Lasker repeated, stunned. "What authority have you to engage the man? You have no authority to engage a man. You're our attorney. You're my close personal friend. But certainly, the meeting is going to decide upon who the man is." No, Austrian replied; the owners would do what Lasker told them to do. Still amazed at his lawyer's effrontery, Lasker asked to whom Austrian had offered the commissioner's post.

"Kenesaw Mountain Landis," Austrian replied.[48]

Austrian next revealed that he also had promised Landis a salary of $50,000 a year—an enormous increase from his judge's salary of $7,500. Again, Lasker marveled at his lawyer's nerve, but admitted that the owners could readily come up with $50,000 from World Series gate receipts.

Then Austrian made one final disclosure. He felt strongly that Landis was the right man for the job, but he also had another motivation for pushing Landis.

"And what was *that*?" Lasker asked.

"I want to get the son of a bitch off the bench," Austrian replied.[49]

Ban Johnson resolved to fight the Lasker Plan. "War," he proclaimed defiantly, "is the best cleanser."[50] But his American League allies quailed at the prospect of internecine fighting. Lasker, smelling victory, gave Johnson one more kick in the ribs. "We have made our proposal," he told reporters, "and it's up to the five American League clubs to come in, or we'll forget all about them and go ahead with the twelve-club league."[51]

On November 12, with the American League teams in attendance and Johnson barred from the meeting, the major and minor league owners wrangled over the Lasker Plan. One major change emerged from all this: Lasker's three-man commission was dumped in favor of a single commissioner—a "czar" of professional baseball. Lasker was delighted; he thought it was a far better solution. "We would have proposed it in the first place," he explained, "but we didn't believe we could possibly get it through."[52]

The owners voted to accept Landis as the so-called "high commissioner."[53] In a show of spite, the five American League owners who were still loyal to the deposed Ban Johnson insisted that the deal had changed significantly, and should no longer be referred to as the "Lasker Plan." Lasker quickly acquiesced. "It was much more important to save the faces of the five American League clubs," he concluded, "and let them feel that they had chastised me, than to have a formal resolution passed that this was the 'Lasker Plan.'"[54]

Landis accepted the job, although he briefly held on to his judgeship. (For the duration, his $7,500 judge's salary was deducted from his $50,000 commissioner's pay—although his $7,500 tax-free baseball expense account more than made up the difference.[55]) Formally installed on January 12, 1921, he moved quickly to rid baseball of the elements that he considered undesirable. He suspended the eight arraigned Black Sox on March 13, banned a number of small-fry gamblers, and forced owners to divest themselves of outside holdings that might bring baseball into disrepute. In the first week of August, when the Black Sox jury found the players not guilty of conspiring to defraud the public—a difficult charge to prove—Landis banned the eight players for life.[56] His statement reinforced his reputation as a "hanging judge," and cemented his position as the all-powerful czar of the national pastime: "Regardless of the verdict of juries, no player that throws a ball game; no player that undertakes or promises to throw a ball game; no player that sits in a conference with a bunch of crooked players and gamblers where the ways and means of throwing games are planned and discussed and does not promptly tell his club about it, will ever play professional baseball."[57]

"At no point," a later commissioner observed, "did [Landis] temper justice with mercy."[58] Banning the Black Sox effectively wrecked the franchise of Charlie Comiskey, one of Landis's original backers for the commissioner's job. (The White Sox languished in the bottom half of their division for the next fifteen years.[59]) And his merciless net swept up at least one player—third baseman George "Buck" Weaver—who was probably innocent of wrongdoing. No matter: Landis was, as his biographer phrased it, both judge and jury. He saw himself as protecting baseball from its owners and players, and saving it for America's kids.

In the spring of 1925, William Wrigley's lawyers began encouraging him to take formal control of the Cubs.[60] Wrigley phoned Lasker and asked him if he would sell him his interest in the Cubs, thereby making the chewing-gum magnate the club's majority owner.

Lasker was eager to sell. His interests had moved on: he was now passionately interested in golf, and especially in the design and construction of challenging courses. He also disapproved of the way Wrigley was "consorting" with the players. "I didn't go around with any of the players," he later explained. "While I had a world to say [about the team's direction], it was behind the scenes with Veeck."[61] Wrigley showed no such restraint.

In addition, Lasker felt drained by the drama that he had orchestrated. He later referred to it as the "bitterest, most complex, and most fatiguing struggle" of his life.[62] He was ready to leave that field of battle behind.

A final factor may have been the negative publicity associated with his brief interlude in baseball's limelight. Anti-Semitic tracts published in the fall of 1921 singled out him and Austrian by name. For example, the *Dearborn Independent*, little more than a mouthpiece for the viciously anti-Semitic Henry Ford, sneered at the "Jew lawyer, Austrian," and his "Jewish friend, Lasker," and suggested that the only remedy for baseball's woes was expunging its Jews: "If baseball is to be saved, and there are those who seriously doubt it ever can be restored, the remedy is plain. The disease is caused by the Jewish characteristic which spoils everything by ruthless commercial exploitation . . . There is no doubt anywhere, among either friends or critics of baseball, that the root cause of the present condition is due to Jewish influence."[63]

So when Wrigley made his approach, Lasker agreed to negotiate, and revived a formula he frequently used to recast a business relationship. He offered to pay Wrigley $200 a share for his interest in the Cubs—*or* he would accept $150 a share from Wrigley for his own holdings. When Wrigley began objecting to the $150 purchase price as "too steep," Lasker reiterated his offer to buy out Wrigley for the steeper price. Trapped by Lasker's logic, Wrigley agreed to pay Lasker's asking price.[64] The parting was amicable; Lasker remained on the Cubs board (and retained his box seats) until Wrigley's death in 1932.

For the rest of his life, Lasker took great pride in his contribution to restructuring major league baseball. He was also proud that he'd largely invented the model of an industry "czar"—an outsider who could rescue an industry from its own excesses.[65] Hollywood embraced this model a few years later, in the early 1920s, when it needed a savior of its own, and a new friend of Lasker's—Republican political wizard Will Hays—needed a job.

Chapter Eleven

Venturing into Politics

*A*LBERT LASKER called himself an "ardent Republican."[1] But with the notable exception of his early involvement in Robert B. Hawley's successful congressional race back in Galveston, Lasker was not particularly ardent about his Republicanism as a young man. In the more than two decades since Hawley had won his congressional race, he once asserted, he had "never given any thought to politics, not bothered."[2]

This wasn't exactly true. And larger trends—as well as Lasker's fascination with power and Big Ideas—almost guaranteed that he would try his hand at politics.

The backdrop was both complicated and fluid. In the 1912 presidential elections, the Republican Party had been split by the defection of Teddy Roosevelt's "Bull Moose" Progressives, and the result was the election of the Democrat Woodrow Wilson to the White House and a Democratic Congress. By 1918, the Republicans were tired of being outmaneuvered and disenfranchised. Eager to reverse their fortunes, they went looking for new blood.

They found it in Indiana. There, two years earlier, Republican state chairman Will H. Hays had engineered an astounding sweep: electing a Republican governor and two Republican senators and carrying all of Indiana's Congressional districts. And so in February 1918, anxious Republicans huddling in St. Louis elected the thirty-eight-year-old Hays chairman of the Republican National Committee.

Chairman Hays set up shop in New York City—on the third floor of the Knox Building, at the corner of Fifth Avenue and 40th Street—and began crisscrossing the country in a highly visible effort to sell war bonds. During this extended tour, he met with party elders in key states and asked whom he should include in his brain trust. During a stop in Indianapolis, his friend W. G. Irwin strongly encouraged him to enlist Albert Lasker to handle the Republican Party's public relations in the upcoming off-year congressional elections.

Hays already knew a lot about Lasker. Both in 1910 and 1914, he had brought him into Indiana to make speeches on behalf of local candidates. Hays agreed that it would make sense to involve Lasker in a bigger effort. "I wanted to get the best person, the biggest person in the world, to sit with me on that program," he later recalled.[3]

Sometime in June 1918, Hays, Irwin, and Lasker met, and Hays leaned heavily on Lasker to head up public relations for the Republicans. "Nothing could have interested me less," Lasker later claimed.[4] "I was just as interested as if he had asked me to become chief ballet dancer with the Russians."[5]

But on a deeper level, the unexpected opportunity came at a good time. A half-decade after the Leo Frank debacle, he was still looking for a way to do something of significance on the national level. And Russian ballet dancers notwithstanding, Hays was offering Lasker the very job Lasker had tried and failed to land four years earlier.

Lasker's first tentative ventures into politics since his Galveston days came as a result of Hays's request that he speak at small gatherings in Marion and other Indiana towns. This connection served Lasker and his agency well. Lord & Thomas placed the advertising for the presidential campaign of William Howard Taft in 1912—a plum account.

Lasker's next push into the political realm came in part through the efforts of a colorful character who played an important role in the next two decades of Lasker's life: John Callan O'Laughlin. Originally a newspaper reporter with the Associated Press, O'Laughlin was covering St. Petersburg when war broke out between Russia and Japan in 1904. President Theodore Roosevelt pressed O'Laughlin into service as an intermediary to help broker a ceasefire between the warring nations in 1905—an intervention that subsequently earned Roosevelt the Nobel Peace Prize.[6] O'Laughlin later worked as a Washington-based reporter for the *Chicago Herald*, served briefly as acting assistant secretary of state under Roosevelt, and then accompanied Roosevelt on his celebrated hunting expeditions to Africa and Europe.

How Lasker met up with O'Laughlin is unclear, although Lasker's personal lawyer, Elmer Schlesinger, probably made the initial introductions. In the spring of 1916, Schlesinger enlisted O'Laughlin's help in an unsuccessful effort to get Lasker appointed to the Federal Trade Commission—a job that Lasker was "extremely anxious" to get, according to Schlesinger.[7]

A few months later, in the wake of the Republican convention that nominated Charles Evans Hughes for President, O'Laughlin and Schlesinger tried to get Lasker named chairman of the Publicity Committee of the Republican National Committee. This meant bringing him to the attention of influential senators (including Ohio's Warren G. Harding), and persuading them in turn to write letters to the Committee's heads in support of Lasker's candidacy. To Massachusetts senator W. Murray Crane, for example, O'Laughlin wrote:

> Mr. Lasker is the head and owner of the Lord and Thomas Advertising Agency, the biggest advertising agency in the United States. He is a young man—only 42 or thereabouts—is a Jew, and a millionaire. You will remember the tremendous publicity in the Leo M. Frank case for which he was responsible. Through his advertising agency he is of course in touch with all the newspapers in the United States, and naturally they would be disposed to treat with consideration any suggestion he might make to them.[8]

The effort came to nothing, however, most likely because the Republicans were reluctant to offend other leading advertising agencies. Again, Lasker thanked O'Laughlin for his efforts and withdrew temporarily from the political fray.

"We have not heard the last of friend Lasker," Schlesinger wrote to O'Laughlin. "We are going to land him in the kind of a job he wants some day."[9]

Events on the world stage soon placed Lasker's ambitions in a new context. America's entry into World War I in April 1917 shifted his focus from politics to national service.

> My feeling had been one of rather sympathy for Germany, but I recognized that that sympathy was entirely due to the fact that I came from a long line of Germans, [and] that I had cousins in the war on that side . . .
>
> The minute we went into the war, she was my enemy, but at all times I felt that nothing was going to be settled with this war . . . I began feeling within myself—Golly, am I keeping out of going to that war because I am afraid? Is it the coward in me, the physical cowardice? . . .
>
> And also I knew that . . . if they made a group of men utterly unfitted to serve in war, I was [one of them], because all my life . . . I was no good with my

hands. My physical side and my brain never have coordinated. I have never been able to tell right from left. And if somebody tells me, even today, to go right, I have to see which hand I write with. And I know if they told me to turn right, in the confusion I might turn left . . .

I was one of the controlling heads of the Mitchell Motor Car Company and the Van Camp Company, and as such, had every reason to excuse myself on the grounds that I was making war supplies, but the whole thing just made me bitter with the world and with myself, and it was a mighty trying period for my wife.[10]

Briefly, Lasker thought about selling Liberty Bonds to support the war effort. Next he lobbied for an unpaid post in Washington. Finally, he used family connections to secure a position as an unpaid assistant to Secretary of Agriculture David F. Houston in Washington. The Department of Agriculture had launched a drive in the spring of 1917—the War Garden Conservation Program—to persuade American women to raise vegetables in their yards, and as those crops came in, many of these inexperienced gardeners had to be taught how to can and preserve them. Working part-time out of a large corner office in the Department of Agriculture building in Washington, Lasker orchestrated the publicity for the program, promoting "National Vegetable Canning Week" and similar efforts.

Lasker considered the entire effort an embarrassing failure: "Most of what the women raised exploded in their faces or rotted. It was just a tremendous waste of effort and money. And of course the next year nothing like that was encouraged. But it was all done in the good old name of 'war.' Valuable time and glassware that could have been used for the Allies!"[11]

At least one good thing came out of it, however: a deeper friendship with O'Laughlin. By the end of that summer, they opened their letters to each other with the salutations "Dear Cal" and "Dear Al." Few people got away with calling Albert Lasker "Al"; O'Laughlin was one of them.

Lasker retreated to Chicago, still looking for a way that he could contribute to the war effort. "The government wore me out in my effort to volunteer my services," he observed wryly.[12] He thought about the pros and cons of volunteering to serve in the Army, conscious that service in uniform might one day be important to his still hazy political ambitions. "No matter what one does for the country at this time," he wrote to O'Laughlin, "in after years one's contribution will be more definitely measured if one serves in the army than if one serves otherwise."[13] Several branches of the Army, including the Motor Transport Service, approached Lasker to see if he would consider signing on with them. Still, Lasker hesitated: *If they told me to turn right, in the confusion I might turn left.*

O'Laughlin enlisted early in 1918 to serve on the staff of Acting Quartermaster General George W. Goethals, so by the time Will Hays tracked down his quarry in the early summer of 1918, Lasker was primed to hear about opportunities for government service—even of a partisan stripe.

Hays wanted more than selling; he wanted access to Lasker's organizational talents: "Lasker, right after I was made chairman, set out to organize this country to make a party. [I] had to get a man for that, like I'd get a secretary, or treasurer, or anything else. They got the best man in every way—never in politics before—to do a selling job for a righteous commodity, a righteous cause, that really had the goods."[14]

Hays understood Lasker well, putting several powerful inducements in front of him. First, of course, there was the "righteous cause." Second, Hays said that *Teddy Roosevelt himself* wanted to meet with Lasker, in hopes of persuading him to take the job.

Perhaps Hays knew that Lasker was a "great worshiper of Roosevelt."[15] Perhaps he was simply banking on the fact that almost any American of that era would have been thrilled to get a personal audience with the immensely popular former president, Rough Rider, author, and big-game hunter. In either case, Lasker bit down hard on Hays's hook, and—in the third week of September—Hays drove him out to the Roosevelt compound at Oyster Bay, Long Island.[16]

The legendary "TR," sporting his trademark khakis, was waiting on the front porch at Sagamore Hill to greet his two visitors from the Midwest.[17] "So this is Lasker," he boomed, throwing an arm around his guest's shoulder. "They tell me you're the greatest advertiser in America!"

Lasker, thinking on his feet, demurred. "Colonel," he shot back, "no man can claim that distinction as long as you live!"[18]

An intoxicating afternoon followed. Lasker and Hays lunched with Roosevelt, his wife, Edith, and a daughter-in-law. Roosevelt, "in his own impetuous way," retrieved one of his favorite books and had the group read its preface out loud.[19] Afterwards, Roosevelt took Lasker into his study for some one-on-one arm-twisting. Such a sustained overture from the overpowering Roosevelt (*dynamic*, in Lasker's eyes, and *everything that appealed to any red-blooded man*) proved impossible to resist.[20] Before the afternoon was out, Roosevelt had talked Lasker into signing on.

Lasker relocated temporarily to New York and set up shop in Hays's leased quarters. Together, in adjoining offices, Will Hays and Albert Lasker undertook to sell Republicans to Americans.

⸺ ·«❰❱»· ⸺

Hays gave Lasker a free hand on the "propaganda end" of the operation. "He never once interfered," Lasker said.[21] Once again, Lasker positioned himself well behind the scenes, arranging to have another staffer appointed as the campaign's formal publicity manager. Retreating into the background gave him the freedom to be the "lone wolf" and "do that which I felt should be done." It also ingratiated him to Hays's staff, who appreciated his generosity in letting other people take the credit for work well done. "That always made people work very much harder for me," Lasker explained, "because they saw I didn't want anything out of it in self-aggrandization."[22]

Working behind the scenes also freed up Lasker to be of more direct assistance to Hays as the chairman tackled a series of pressing problems. One was a desperate shortage of funds. Mining magnate William Boyce Thompson had agreed to advance up to $300,000 to underwrite the Republicans' activities, on condition that he eventually would be paid back. Hays's audacious response, as described by Lasker, sounds like a page out of the playbook of Lasker's favorite copywriter and ad-campaign strategist, Claude Hopkins: "Hays very shrewdly announced that the Republicans for this off-year congressional campaign would not accept contributions of over a thousand dollars from anyone. As it was then very difficult for Republicans to get as much as a thousand-dollar contribution, this was making no financial sacrifices and was mighty good public relations."[23]

Hays's staff drew up a list of wealthy individuals who might be inclined to make a thousand-dollar contribution. They went to work, and donors soon started arriving at the Knox Building. Shortly after Lasker took up his post in New York, a buzzer summoned him into Hays's office. "Lasker," Hays said, as his top propagandist came into his office, "I want you to meet our first thousand-dollar contributor—Mr. R. S. Hawley." It was the same Robert S. Hawley for whom Lasker had campaigned decades earlier. Hawley had left politics, entered international trade, and risen to become the head of the

Cuban Cane Sugar Company. As Lasker and Hawley reunited after twenty-two years, each was astonished to encounter the other in the innermost sanctum of the Republican Party.

Lasker also ran interference for Hays. At one point, for example, an expatriate American named Brown traveled all the way from Paris to seek an audience with Hays. Hays decided that this unexpected visitor should be turfed out to Lasker. The Republicans' chief publicist listened carefully to Brown's ideas, which boiled down to a cautionary tale for America about getting embroiled in postwar Continental intrigues, and encouraged Brown to write them up in a pamphlet. Ultimately, Lasker paid something like $30,000 out of his own pocket to have the pamphlet—entitled *After the Peace, What?*—printed and distributed. "We put out millions and millions of those brochures," Lasker later recalled.[24]

"Millions and millions" certainly overstates the real numbers. But the main point remains: Lasker learned that saturating the landscape with pamphlets had a very powerful effect, in this new game of politics, and he filed the technique away for future campaigns.

Yet another challenge faced by Hays and Lasker was the continuing phenomenon of Teddy Roosevelt. Still only in his late fifties, still ambitious and energetic despite being blind in one eye and deaf in one ear, Roosevelt was positioning himself for yet another run at the White House. Lasker concluded that an informal deal had been cut, and that Roosevelt would be nominated in 1920.[25] But Hays, as national chairman, couldn't appear to favor Roosevelt over other possible contenders—nor did he have time, in a midterm election year, to cater to the high-maintenance Roosevelt. He therefore turned over this delicate assignment to a very willing Albert Lasker. Hays told Lasker that whenever Roosevelt called, Lasker should immediately go see him in the former president's combined office-and-residence suite at Manhattan's Leighton Hotel, and carry out whatever assignments Roosevelt might give him.

Minor skirmishing between the Democrats and Republicans continued all summer, but the real hostilities broke out in the fall. On October 25, with the congressional election less than two weeks away, President Wilson—better known for his powerful intellect than his political instincts—committed a major blunder. He issued a letter that asked Americans to vote Democratic to strengthen his hand in the conduct of the war. Although he letter didn't quite impugn the patriotism of Republicans, it came very close. Hays shot back gleefully: "A more ungracious, more unjust, more wanton, more mendacious accusation never was made by the most reckless stump orator, much less by a President of the United States for partisan purposes."[26]

Lasker had Hays arrange a meeting at the Union League Club between Teddy Roosevelt and William Howard Taft. The two former presidents and former political allies—Roosevelt had anointed Taft as his successor in 1908—had only recently ended a bitter six-year feud that dated back to the 1912 election. In advance of the meeting, Lasker composed a statement blasting Wilson, which he wanted Taft and Roosevelt to release jointly. Given the need for an immediate turnaround, Lasker insisted that Hays attend the summit conference in case it went off the rails:

> There were the four of us—Roosevelt and Taft, Hays and me. I will always remember the first words they said to each other—again showing breeding. The two men came in and they put their arms around each other, and the one said, "Hello, Will," and the other said, "Hello, Teddy," and then they immediately got to work.
>
> By the time they finished, there wasn't much left of the document that I wrote. I think the only thing left was, "Our fellow countrymen."[27]

Later that day, Roosevelt asked Lasker to help with a major speech he would be giving at Carnegie Hall in a few days.[28] At the New Amsterdam Theater, Roosevelt had seen a performance by a brilliant young actor whom he thought should be brought into the Republican fold. "That man is destined someday to become a great power in our national life," Lasker recalls Roosevelt declaring. "That man someday is going to fashion the views of millions, and as the head of our propaganda department, I want you to meet him and cultivate him."

Roosevelt proved prescient: the young actor turned out to be Will Rogers, the "Cowboy Philosopher," who through his writing, acting, and stand-up monologues, went on to be a major force in American culture for years to come.

Rogers said that he'd be happy to help Roosevelt out. "In the work I do," he told Lasker, "I'm going to hit each side a lick where it ought to be hit, and boost each side where it ought to be boosted." He emphasized, however, that he was a *Democrat*.[29] If the Democrats came to him for help, he continued in his trademark drawl, he'd *most certainly* help them. Accepting these terms, Lasker asked Rogers to take a look at the opening of Roosevelt's speech, which Lasker disliked. Rogers supplied a gentle jab at President Wilson that Roosevelt wound up delivering at Carnegie Hall.[30]

When the counting was finished after the November 5 election, the Republicans had seized control of Congress, winning a two-vote majority in the Senate and a thirty-four-vote majority in the House. For Wilson, the outcome was a disaster; for Hays and Lasker, it was a triumph.

Hostilities in Europe ended six days after the election.[31] If the Armistice had occurred the week *before* the election, Hays admitted, Wilson would have won a resounding victory.

Lasker derived two unexpected bonuses from his short period of service with Hays in New York. The first, of course, was his friendship with Hays. Diminutive in stature, soft-spoken, and self-effacing, the "Chairman" (as Lasker came to refer to him) looked more like a school superintendent than a kingmaker. He was only a year older than Lasker, and yet he struck Lasker as distinguished and worldly—a larger-than-life figure. By most measures, Lasker had seen far more of the world. But the mild-mannered Hays had tapped into the rushing artery of national political power, and that elevated him out of the ranks of ordinary men. "I had [had] no opportunity to meet great national figures in politics," Lasker later recalled of his life before 1918.[32] Yes, he had done business with the leading manufacturers of the Midwest and further afield. He had taken their measure, and concluded that he was at least their equal. But Hays consorted with past and future *presidents*, the shapers of history.

Lasker's second bonus was his friendship with Ralph V. Sollitt. Sollitt had been a professor and administrator at the University of Indiana, where he had met Hays. Hays, impressed with Sollitt—an accomplished lawyer and a skilled orator, as well as an academic—asked him to serve in New York as his executive secretary.[33] Lasker realized immediately that Sollitt had special qualities:

> I remember no man in my life as beloved by everyone he met as Sollitt. Sollitt was beloved in the university; in the Republican Party every national figure loved him. The little people around the office loved him—the scrub women, everyone from the highest to the lowest . . .
>
> A great friendship sprang up between Sollitt and me until we became the same as brothers in the blood, and I wouldn't know the difference between him and blood brothers.[34]

For decades afterward, both Hays and Sollitt remained important figures, and key mooring points, in Lasker's life. Hays engaged Lasker in the making of a president, and years later introduced Lasker to the woman who would become his second wife. Sollitt served Lasker in multiple executive capacities, including an interlude in Washington and a difficult stint at the helm of Lord & Thomas. "All the years I was gone from Lord & Thomas," Lasker later commented, "and all the things that didn't go forward that should have gone forward . . . will be made up many times over to Lord & Thomas by the coming of Ralph Sollitt."[35]

But just ahead for the trio of Hays, Lasker, and Sollitt were much larger adventures, which would further cement their friendship and mutual respect.

Chapter Twelve

Electing a President

STUNG BY HIS ELECTORAL disaster in November 1918, Woodrow Wilson sailed for Europe in early December to attend the Paris Peace Conference.

Teddy Roosevelt, certain to be nominated by the Republicans at their 1920 convention, fell ill and was hospitalized. On January 6, 1919, at the age of sixty-one, he died of a blood infection from an abscessed tooth—there were no antibiotics yet—and his death left his party without a clear favorite in the presidential race that was soon to begin.

After the 1918 electoral victory, Albert Lasker retained his title as head of the Republicans' public relations department, but this was a job in name only.[1] Determined to come to grips with his business and personal challenges, he moved back to Chicago. For a year or so, he put politics on hold, occasionally stopping by the Knox Building for strategy sessions.

The excitement of the election of 1918, however, persisted. He harbored no ill will toward Woodrow Wilson. He was, however, worried about Wilson's judgment and intentions. The news filtering back from Europe in the early months of 1919 included sketchy details about two documents that Wilson and the European heads of state were hammering out: the Versailles Treaty, formally bringing hostilities to an end; and a "Covenant of the League of Nations," aimed at creating an unprecedented union of nation states. At least in theory, members of the League could invoke its charter to drag U.S. soldiers and sailors into local squabbles overseas—without the prior consent of Congress.

Lasker was an uncompromising isolationist, and in the early months of 1919 he complained to Hays that Senate Republicans weren't speaking out forcefully enough against the League of Nations. In response, Hays organized a dinner at the Shoreham Hotel in Washington so that the senators could hear directly from Lasker. The evening did not go well, from Lasker's perspective:

> *I presented my views, and when I finished, [Massachusetts Senator Henry Cabot] Lodge traced with fine logic what [he and his isolationist colleagues] had been doing. Although later, when I went into the Administration in Washington, Lodge and I became very good friends, I shall never forget the sarcasm and contempt he put into his remarks as he addressed me. The contempt was for an outside young whippersnapper like myself coming down [to Washington] to criticize.*[2]

In fact, Lodge and his fellow isolationists were then plotting an all-out assault on Wilson and his League. Lodge, who chaired the Senate Foreign Relations Committee, used a protracted series of committee hearings over the summer to pick apart the proposed treaties. The embattled Wilson embarked on a twenty-seven-day, ten-thousand-mile cross-country barnstorming tour in September, designed to bring pressure to bear on his enemies in the Senate. The strain of twenty-six major speeches and countless whistle-stop orations—as many as ten a day—proved too much for Wilson. On September 23, as his train passed through Pueblo, Colorado, he suffered a debilitating stroke.[3]

Although Wilson was incapacitated, his League was not dead. Many in positions of power continued to advocate for *some* kind of international organization that could help avoid a repeat of the horrors of World War I. It was against this muddied backdrop that, in the early weeks of 1920, Joseph Medill McCormick—U.S. senator from Illinois—came to see Lasker in his office.

Lasker had known him for years. McCormick, an heir to Cyrus McCormick's farm-machinery fortune, had played an active role in his family's paper, the *Chicago Tribune*, and—with Lasker's help—had helped boost the *Tribune's* circulation. (Among other stunts, Lasker and McCormick in January 1907 devised America's first beauty pageant for promotional purposes.[4]) McCormick was elected to the U.S. House of Representatives in 1916 as a Republican, and two years later Lasker helped him make the leap to the Senate.

In the subsequent four years, McCormick had emerged as a leader among the fourteen "Irreconcilables"—the senators who had declared that they would never be reconciled to a League of Nations. As the 1920 presidential election neared, the Irreconcilables decided that they needed a candidate. They settled on Hiram Johnson, U.S. senator from California.

Johnson had been governor of his home state, and somewhat reluctantly agreed to run on the Progressive ticket in 1912 as Teddy Roosevelt's (losing) vice presidential candidate. He returned to California and the governor's job, but halfway through his second term, in 1916, he was elected to the Senate. An odd blend of free-thinking populist and zealous isolationist, Johnson fancied himself a "bloc of one."[5] The Irreconcilables didn't believe that Johnson could *win*; the goal, Lasker later explained, was "simply to display the strength of our [isolationist] element in the Party."[6] McCormick asked Lasker to help raise money and garner visibility for Johnson. Although he had never met the candidate, Lasker agreed to raise funds for Johnson's Midwestern effort and set up a regional headquarters in Chicago.

Increasingly involved in the Johnson effort, Lasker went to Will Hays and offered to resign from the Republican National Committee.[7] Hays turned Lasker down, but did grant him a leave of absence for the prenomination season.[8] Lasker then jumped into the Johnson campaign with his characteristic passion: "I got into the fray, and gave it *all* my time, and a considerable amount of money, and this is referred to in Harold Ickes' book, *Autobiography of a Curmudgeon*. He refers to the fact that we managed that campaign—he from the political end in helping Hiram Johnson, and I from the publicity end and in raising money. I also established the main headquarters in Chicago."[9]

One way that Lasker raised the money for Johnson was to get William Wrigley involved in the effort. The chewing gum magnate and co-owner of the Chicago Cubs contributed something like $30,000 to the campaign and also made space available for its headquarters.[10]

To the surprise of the politicos, Johnson won five of the first six primaries he entered—several by impressive margins—thereby establishing himself an unlikely frontrunner for the Republican nomination.[11]

The Republican Convention took place in June 1920 in Chicago. The three leading contenders were General Leonard Wood—the late Teddy Roosevelt's friend and fellow Rough Rider—Hiram Johnson, and Illinois governor Frank Lowden. They arrived at the convention with 124, 112, and 72 committed delegates, respectively. The genial Senator Warren Harding, favorite-son candidate from Ohio, had a scant 39.

Although Hiram Johnson had scored significant victories, the hard truth was that he could never be nominated in Chicago. He had, in Lasker's opinion, "too much of a will of his own."[12] He was too tough to do business with. "You could agree with Johnson on a hundred things," Lasker commented, "and if you disagreed on the hundred and first, it was all off between you."[13]

The Republicans in the smoke-filled room decided to offer the presidential nomination to Pennsylvania senator Philander C. Knox, and make Johnson Knox's running mate. Knox and Johnson were friends, and both Irreconcilables, and the power brokers thought the Bloc of One might bite. He did not. Johnson felt, as Lasker put it, that *"he* had made the good fight," and that Knox should be *his* vice presidential candidate.

Next, the operatives settled on Harding. At 2:00 a.m., Harding strode into Johnson's suite: the first time Lasker had ever met the senator from Ohio. Harding wanted to talk to Johnson privately, so they went into the bedroom. As Lasker later recalled: "They talked for five or ten minutes, and when Harding left, Johnson was *livid* with anger. He said, 'I like Harding. I like him very much, but I can't conceive of him being president of the United States. He's done nothing to deserve it. He tells me they have just agreed upstairs to make him president, and *he* came down here to ask *me,* wouldn't I run as vice president? Of course I indignantly refused.'"[14]

The next day, the convention nominated Harding; his running mate was Massachusetts governor Calvin Coolidge. Lasker was deeply disillusioned. "I thought I was completely out of politics," he later recalled. "I was discouraged and disheartened."[15]

In addition, Lord & Thomas once again was calling. "I wanted to get back to my business," he explained several years later, "because the business had been running in a rather loose way."[16] That was an understatement; Lasker had rarely been to the office for the previous year and a half, and in his absence, the agency was adrift.

In conversations after Harding secured the nomination, the candidate and Hays decided they would run a "front-porch" campaign reminiscent of William McKinley's 1896 campaign. Harding wouldn't travel the country; he would let the press—and the country, presumably—come to him. "You are going to out-McKinley McKinley, as sure as you are alive," Hays told Harding.[17]

Harding was quite happy to stay home. "I think myself it develops an unfortunate side of our political activities," he wrote to a supporter, "to have a presidential candidate chasing about the country soliciting support."[18] The strategy also sidestepped Harding's liabilities as a campaigner. Although a powerful orator, Harding was prone to malapropisms. Keeping him on his big stone front porch at 380 Mt. Vernon Avenue, in small-town Marion, Ohio, would minimize those perils.

Having reliable allies in Marion was now a priority for Will Hays, and so, sometime in late June, he called Albert Lasker. Playing to Lasker's vanity, Hays said that he had told Harding that the only other man from headquarters that the candidate *absolutely* had to meet: a brilliant image-maker named Lasker.

A day or two later, Lasker huddled privately with Harding in Marion. Harding asked him to stay on as chief propagandist for the Republicans. Lasker replied that as long as Harding staunchly opposed the League, he could count on Lasker's support. He later recalled the candidate's response:

Mr. Harding was a kindly man. While Mr. Hays was one of the fairest men I ever met, Mr. Harding was the kindliest. That was his weakness. Senator Harding revealed his whole character at our first meeting. After my declaration, he put his arms around me and looked me square in the eyes. He said, "Lasker, let's at the start agree on one thing—that we'll never fall out because we disagree."

That was the key to him. Of course one must fall out on vital issues when there is major disagreement. But Mr. Harding, once he gave his friendship, would forgive anything in a friend.[19]

Lasker also noted that Harding neatly sidestepped the League question. "It confirmed my hunch," he commented, "to be a little disturbed as to what his attitude [toward the League] might be."[20] So Lasker took steps to allay his concerns. One of his roles in subsequent months was to keep Harding "on message," in modern political parlance. Speeches would land on Lasker's desk in Chicago; Lasker would scrutinize them for equivocation about the League. Whenever Harding attempted to straddle the issue, Lasker would "minimize the straddle to nothingness."[21]

Of course, Lasker did more than that for Harding. But by forcing the candidate to toe the isolationist line, Lasker exerted a powerful influence on the direction of the campaign—and by extension, on post-war America.

Meeting in San Francisco two weeks after the Republican Convention, the Democrats nominated Ohio governor James M. Cox for president, and a relative unknown—thirty-eight-year-old Assistant Secretary of the Navy, Franklin D. Roosevelt—for vice president. Even though the campaign would not formally start until August, giving the candidates on both sides an opportunity to recuperate and draw up battle plans, Lasker began his work in early July. For the duration of the campaign, he divided his time mainly between Chicago and Marion, spending about a day a week in Marion, with occasional side trips to the New York headquarters.

One of his first steps was to recruit William Wrigley into the Harding camp. Just as Wrigley's fortune and connections had been tapped during the primaries to benefit Hiram Johnson, now they were marshaled on behalf of Harding.[22] At Lasker's urging, Wrigley was appointed chairman of the Committee on Public Information. "I know that you understand," Hays wrote to a supporter, "that while Mr. Wrigley is chairman of the [committee], it is Mr. Lasker, of course, who does everything that Mr. Wrigley would do."[23]

This preliminary work culminated in a strategy session with Harding in Marion on July 27, attended by both Lasker and Wrigley. The account of the meeting in the *New York Times*—and the fact that the meeting was written up at all—reflects Lasker's behind-the-scenes influence: "The campaign will utilize all mediums of modern advertising, including billboard posters, newspaper and magazine advertisements, and motion pictures. Today's conference was to obtain Senator Harding's approval of the plan. It is understood that the Senator's approval was not given until he, a newspaper and advertising man himself, had placed his O.K. on preliminary advertising copy."[24]

The *Times* alluded to a "twelve-word slogan" that would capture Harding's political beliefs and galvanize the campaign, but spokesman Scott C. Bone—former newspaperman and putative publicity director for the Republican National Committee—declined to reveal it. "That's the secret," Bone told reporters. But once it was revealed, he said, it would be *everywhere*: in the newspaper on your breakfast table, plastered across a billboard on your way to work, and so on.

Here again was Lasker's hand at work: both in the plan itself and in its coy unveiling, calculated to maximize newspaper coverage and public interest. There never *was* a "twelve-word slogan." One bland battle cry—probably favored by the bland candidate himself—gained some currency: "Steady America! Let us assure good fortune to all!" A second, slightly sharper call to arms—"Let us be done with wiggling and wobbling"—was Lasker's personal favorite, and probably his creation; in the later stages of the campaign, he keyed much of the Harding advertising on this phrase.

Early in the campaign, an old rumor gained new currency. Warren G. Harding, according to the whisperers, had black ancestry—a story that had dogged Harding from his early childhood.[25] His olive-colored skin and wiry black hair prompted taunts and fights in the schoolyard—his classmates called him "Nig"—and led to stealthy attacks throughout Harding's career in the ruthless world of Ohio politics. The fact that his wife's father had publicly opposed their marriage on the grounds of Harding's alleged mixed blood didn't help. This was one of the few subjects that could arouse the affable Harding to fury—even though he acknowledged that he couldn't *prove* that he had no black blood. "How do I know, Jim?" he once agonized aloud to a friend. "One of my ancestors may have jumped the fence."[26]

Lasker set out to prove the opposite anyway. He distributed photographs of Harding's grandparents to prove the candidate's "whiteness." He hired a newspaper editor to "investigate" Harding's roots. He commissioned Pennsylvania's prestigious Wyoming Historical and Geological Society to produce a Harding family tree that showed nothing but white ancestry dating as far back as the seventeenth century—a document that was distributed to newspapers across the country.

Ultimately, a principled stand taken by Woodrow Wilson probably saved Harding. The Cox campaign asked the president's blessing for an effort to make political hay out of Harding's alleged mixed blood. Wilson said no. "We must base our campaigns on principles," the enfeebled and wheelchair-bound President said, "not on backstairs gossip."[27] Wilson's high road, combined with Lasker's energetic counterattacks, made it impossible for Democrats to "play the race card" effectively.

There were other whispers about Harding that could not be dispelled, because they were too obviously true: the candidate had an outsized sexual appetite, and indulged himself freely.

Harding's wife Florence ("the Duchess," as he called her) was a determined woman, and she put her considerable energies to work on her husband's behalf: first growing his small-town newspaper into a substantial enterprise and later advancing his political career. But physical affection, it seems, did not rank high on her agenda. Warren Harding, by contrast, was easygoing, affectionate, and—by the standards of the day—handsome. Thanks in large part to Florence's efforts, he was also wealthy. The women in small-town Marion, and later in the nation's capital, found this brew of charm and money all too intoxicating. Florence's recurring illnesses, as well as Harding's frequent out-of-town speechifying—and later his senatorial duties—made assignations easy.

One of the women seduced by Harding was Carrie Phillips, whose husband, James E. Phillips, ran a successful dry-goods store in Marion. Harding and Carrie Phillips first became romantically involved in 1905, when Jim Phillips was recuperating in Michigan from a nervous condition and Florence was recovering from kidney surgery. For years, the betrayed spouses suspected nothing. The two couples even traveled to Europe together in the early months of 1909, and vacationed in Bermuda in 1911.

The affair made Harding, first elected U.S. senator from Ohio in 1914, politically vulnerable, but he took no steps to simplify his life. Indeed, when both Carrie and Florence failed to give him the attention he craved, he took up with Nan Britton, a twenty-year-old Marion woman who had been infatuated with him since she was a thirteen-year old girl. Moving Nan to New York City, Harding found her a job and helped pay her living expenses. They met secretly for a day here, a weekend there. In January 1919, in his inner sanctum at the Senate Office Building, they conceived a child.

Meanwhile, by the summer of 1920, Jim Phillips had discovered his wife's infidelities. Furious, he refused to decorate his three-story brick building on Marion's main street with the requisite red, white, and blue bunting that the town was using to celebrate its front-porch candidate. Because almost every other building on Center Street was so festooned, the Phillips house stood out in eloquent barrenness. With very little else to do, local reporters began asking about the missing bunting, and Hays asked Lasker to intervene.

Sometime in the summer of 1920, Lasker and Carrie Phillips had a heart-to-heart.[28] Lasker told her the campaign would pay her $20,000 and a monthly sum as long as Harding remained in office. He proposed that she and her husband leave immediately for an all-expenses-paid, round-the-world trip, ostensibly to investigate the silk trade that represented a small part of Jim Phillips's dry-goods business. The Phillipses left for Japan before the summer was out.

In their absence, the bunting went up, and a crisis was averted.

In the 1920 election, Albert Lasker played both defense and offense. When on the offensive, his model was the advertising world's scheme man, dreaming up colorful stunts to capture the public's fancy and the press's attention.

Will Hays, too, had his scheme-man impulses. During the 1916 races in Indiana, Hays had hired a cameraman to make short films of key events, which he then sent to theaters around the state to boost his candidates' chances.[29] As early as May 1919, Hays began huddling with movie studio heads to plot out a plan for greatly expanding the use of motion pictures in the upcoming presidential campaign. After Harding secured the nomination, Hays put that plan in motion. On his instructions, and certainly with Lasker's approval, a New York camera crew based in Marion recorded the endless staged encounters on the Hardings' front porch. They also filmed the candidate as he made his way around his hometown: discharging his limited duties at the newspaper that had made him rich, and accompanying his country-doctor father on his rounds in a horse-drawn carriage.[30]

Using this footage, the Republicans produced newsreels featuring Harding that were distributed to movie theaters around the country: a way to get their front-porch candidate in front of millions of Americans. In most cases, these shorts were screened before the evening's feature, with no hint that this was a purely political message. In some cases, a Republican operative on the spot then conducted a poll of the audience.[31] The results of the instant poll would be used to gauge Harding's standing in that area and also to measure the effectiveness of the short film that had been screened.

In July 1920, a short went out that included images of Harding playing golf. Almost immediately, polls and other anecdotal data suggested it was a disaster. It confirmed suspicions that the candidate—portly, affluent, and thoroughly at home on the links—was a member of a rich elite. The golf fiasco was discussed at length at the July 27 strategy session in Marion. At that meeting, Lasker suggested that Harding be placed in a new athletic context. The two principal owners of the Chicago Cubs—himself and Will Wrigley—were in the room. Why not stage some sort of event whereby Harding could be closely associated with the national pastime?

The day after the meeting, Lasker wrote to Harding's private secretary, George B. Christian:

I shall tomorrow start negotiations on that baseball matter, and will undoubt-edly bring it to a successful conclusion, so that the game will be held as we planned before mid-August. I believe we can work it up in such a way as to do a great deal of good. It will give the Senator an opportunity, if he deems it wise, for a fitting occasion to express his views on sturdy sports, and I am sure all the press associations will gladly carry same.[32]

But a staged baseball game in Marion, Ohio, was far easier to dream up than to pull off. Lasker and Wrigley could deliver the Cubs, but finding a sec-ond professional ball club willing to participate in an unvarnished political event proved difficult. The Cleveland franchise expressed interest but then bowed out, citing schedule conflicts. The New York Giants at first agreed to the contest, and then changed their minds. Lasker complained that Giants manager John McGraw "kicked it over at the last minute because of his polit-ical alignment."[33]

Meanwhile, the problem wasn't going away. As Lasker explained in a letter to a friend and major shareholder in the Cincinnati Reds: "What I wanted to talk to you about was arranging a baseball game between Cincinnati and the Cubs at Marion, Ohio . . . Our candidate has been shown in pictures playing golf, and, confidentially, it has drawn a perfectly surprising amount of unfa-vorable reaction from the country. We get hundreds of letters from people, saying it's a rich man's game, a mollycoddle's game, etc."[34]

But the Reds, too, said no. Finally, an exhibition game was arranged between the Cubs and the Kerrigan Tailors, a local minor-league team. Newspapers dutifully parroted Lasker's premise for the game: that one of the "hardships" of the front-porch campaign was that candidate Harding was unable to attend major-league games. On the morning of September 3, accompanied by a brass band hired by the New York filmmakers, the Cubs made their way to the front porch at Marion. There, Cubs president Bill Veeck promised Harding that his team would do their best to play a great game. Following Lasker's script, Harding delivered a windy speech likening President Wilson to a "one-man team."

By the time the Harding party got to the ballpark, seven thousand locals were primed for a ball game. To a rousing round of applause, Harding made his way out onto the field, donned a glove, and played a gentle game of catch with legendary Cubs pitcher Grover Cleveland Alexander. "He caught every ball," the *New York Times* reported dryly, "although Alexander didn't use his wicked twirls, but it was good for the movies."

There was one more stunt planned: "Having 'warmed up,' Senator Harding stood in the pitcher's box and struck out [Max] Flack, the Cubs' right fielder. It was a technical strikeout, for both Flack and the umpire were generous, while the Marion catcher had to reach wide for the last two throws."

What went out to the nation that night were accounts (and shortly thereafter, newsreels) of Harding—no mollycoddle!—playing catch with one of the greatest pitchers in the history of baseball. Soon, audiences in theaters around the country saw moving pictures of the candidate striding out to the mound and striking out the great pitcher's hard-hitting teammate—then enjoying the best year of his career!

Harding and Lasker quickly became close friends. "He was the kindest of men," Lasker said, "and utterly honest." For his part, Harding prized loyalty above all other qualities, and he knew that Lasker was tenaciously loyal.

Despite their very different backgrounds, the candidate and the promoter had a great deal in common. They had both become emotionally unstable at about the same point in their lives. (Through the early years of the twentieth century, Harding had retreated to the Battle Creek Sanitarium on five occasions to cope with his "nervous exhaustion."[35]) Neither drove a car.[36] Both had wives with physical infirmities who lived life at an emotional distance—and at the same exerted powerful influences on their spouses. Lasker shared with Harding a love of baseball, and they frequently stole off to talk baseball. They also played the occasional game of poker at Marion: another of Harding's passions. Soon it was understood that when Lasker was in Marion, he would take his meals with the Hardings without waiting for an invitation.

This, inevitably, brought him closer to Florence "Nell" Harding: "I can't tell you why, but she took an instant liking to me . . . She was a woman who . . . catalogued people, and there they stood. And if she liked you, there you stood for always . . . She made up her mind [that] I was going to be good medicine for Warren G. Harding, and she was good medicine for me right away."[37]

No one outside the Republican power structure appears to have understood Lasker's role in the campaign—or even much noticed his presence. Throughout, Lasker maintained a low profile. "I'd sneak in and out [of Marion] so the newspaper boys couldn't see me," he later explained. "I think they more or less thought I came on paid advertising—paid publicity."[38] In fact, he was carrying—and also inventing—some of the campaign's most important messages.

⸺⸺⸺ ⟨◉⟩ ⸺⸺⸺

In the later weeks of the summer of 1920, candidate Harding came under increasing pressure to begin making appearances around the country. If he did, of course, he would be pressed to clarify his positions on key issues of the day. This presented risks, and neither Hays nor Lasker had any intention of letting Harding off his short leash. Nor was Harding much inclined to slip it. "He listened politely to suggestions," reported the *Times*, "and then vetoed nearly every request for him to leave Marion during the next six weeks." The only concession that the campaign made to the growing demand for statements from the candidate was to move up a League of Nations–related speech ten days: from September 8 to August 28.

This was an event that Lasker was already stage-managing toward another end. His most important job in the campaign was to develop and disseminate a strong core message for the Republicans—one that would motivate, but not necessarily inform. Again, this strategy meshed neatly with the candidate. Harding was by nature a conciliatory man; when challenged, he tended to retreat into generalities. But on the subject of the League of Nations, Lasker wanted unequivocal statements of opposition. Toward that end, he pushed hard to get the candidate and his campaign to adopt a central message: *no more wiggling and wobbling.* Lasker felt that the implied criticisms in the phrase (indecisiveness, evasiveness, even dishonesty) could be applied to both President Wilson and candidate Cox:

> *In the course of the campaign, we want to show how Wilson wobbled from watchful waiting to peaceful penetration in Mexico, and how Mr. Cox is trying to wiggle from the Wilson League to a position where he is for a League with reservations, and he is trying to wiggle from being wet in wet states to dry in dry states, also how the Democrats both in legislature and administration have wiggled and wobbled on all responsibilities, whereas a Republican administration means surety.*[39]

Harding agreed to include the phrase in his League of Nations address on August 28.[40] Lasker told his operatives it was important that they call the attention of reporters and editors to the phrase without making it appear that the "publicity end of the campaign had anything to do with the expression and the thought appearing in the speech."

Lasker had a great deal riding on "wiggle and wobble" gaining currency, since he had to begin exploiting the phrase even before Harding could utter it. He had to order a "wiggle and wobble" billboard campaign in mid-August to allow enough time for an October 2 unveiling of billboards nationwide—an enormous effort. He also wanted to mail the speech to Republican editors in advance of August 28, so that they would have time to "thoroughly digest it and get their bearings."[41] In the last week of August, therefore, he pressed both Will Hays and George Christian to make absolutely sure that Harding would use the slogan—preferably multiple times.

Harding did indeed utter the phrase near the conclusion of his speech, but that was far from the end of Lasker's concerns. Most worrisome, Hays had concerns about whether the message was compelling enough, and whether Lasker could get it to catch fire. Lasker admitted to no such doubts:

> Regarding your phone message on "WIGGLE AND WOBBLE." Don't worry, I will put it over with editorial cooperation and speakers cooperation if I can get it; if I can't I will put it over without, though it will be mid-October until you can notice results, because I shall have to rely entirely on the force of the display advertising in the weekly magazines like the Saturday Evening Post, and the billposting. These two media alone will put it over . . .
>
> It would be better, of course, to get cooperation from speakers, editors, cartoonists, and in booklet work. The trouble is, I guess, that the editors and cartoonists won't take it up until it is already popular, and since I have secured no speakers' cooperation it has been hard to get it to catch on merely from the only speech where the candidate has used it. We will therefore have to rely almost entirely on its catching on through the display advertising which runs in October. But don't you be afraid—I will get it over.[42]

Lasker was frustrated that the Republican National Committee's designated speakers did not seize upon the catchphrase. These speakers were critically important, in part because radio was still in its infancy. (The 1920 election returns were the first ever to be broadcast live, but the campaigns themselves made little use of the new medium.) In the time-honored tradition, the way most Americans heard political messages in the summer and fall of 1920 was through the legions of speakers who fanned out across the country—some five thousand Republicans (and a somewhat smaller number of Democrats)—spreading the word in person.[43] But Lasker didn't control the speakers; all he could do was push his phrase and hope that they picked it up.

"Wiggle and wobble" wasn't the only thing on Lasker's mind in this period. Throughout the relatively short campaign, Lasker performed a host of duties, ranging from the momentous to the offbeat. In the former category, he commissioned and placed ads in the third week of August that would be put in the hands of 22 million women, who in that month had finally won the right to vote, and would be exercising that right in the fall election. He used his considerable clout with newspaper editors to secure favorable editorials.[44] To increase the odds that those editorials might include a picture of Harding, he shipped 15 million pictures of the candidate to papers across the country, at a cost of $200,000.[45] He facilitated the appearances of movie stars, opera signers, and circus magnates on the front porch in Marion, all designed to generate favorable (and tightly controlled) press coverage and newsreel footage.[46]

In the offbeat category, he arranged for the purchase of twenty-five "animated busts" of Harding, at $100 apiece, for use in store windows. ("Mrs. Harding," Lasker explained to Hays, "was very anxious we should give them a try-out.") When the newspaper reporters marooned in Marion demanded that the Republicans supply them with a car to get around in—and perhaps out of—Marion, Lasker bought them a new Marmon with his own money.[47] When the Marion-based press corps threw a banquet for Harding toward the end of September, Lasker arranged the catering.

———

By October, Lasker's work was largely done. The billboards went up: *Let us be done with wiggle and wobble.* The ads were prepared—*Let us be done with wiggle and wobble*—and the necessary magazine and newspaper space was reserved. The October 30, 1920, edition of *Collier's*, for example, contained a full-page ad headlined "Harding and Coolidge," with cameo photos of each that looked as if they belonged on folding money. The copy was standard fare, with unsubtle criticisms of Woodrow Wilson and his League of Nations:

This country will remain American. Its next President will remain in our own country. American affairs will be discussed by American public servants in the City of Washington, not in some foreign capitol . . .

Let's be done with wiggle and wobble.[48]

In the final days running up to the elections, the negotiations with baseball's owners concerning the Black Sox scandal kept Lasker close to home in Chicago. Gradually, he delegated more and more of his responsibilities in the campaign.

Three days before the election, on Halloween night, Nell Harding called Lasker into a room with herself and her husband and closed the door. "Albert," she asked anxiously, "are we going to win?"

Lasker burst out laughing. Everyone who was anyone knew that Harding was a shoo-in. The only question was, how big a landslide would Harding rack up? "I will *guarantee* that you are going to win," he told the worried wife of the future president.[49]

It was a rout of epic proportions. Harding carried thirty-seven of the forty-eight states, racking up a huge electoral margin and garnering more than 60 percent of the popular vote. The Republicans gained more than fifty seats in the House of Representatives. Lasker and other Harding confidantes celebrated the victory at the Mt. Vernon Avenue headquarters; Harding, for his part, sneaked out and enjoyed an election night tryst with Nan Britton in a deserted house down the street.[50]

Given the nation's eagerness to shrug off Woodrow Wilson, Cox and Roosevelt were almost certainly beaten from the start. But the Republicans, with the help of Lasker, adroitly exploited that impulse. They spent extravagantly, more than $6 million, while the Democrats raised only $1.3 million.[51] And much of that $6 million went where Albert Lasker steered it.

By most accounts, Will Hays was the leading political genius of his generation. He found in Albert Lasker a complementary kind of genius, who brought a new dimension to politics. "Lasker jumped into politics like a duck takes to water," Hays said. "He is the super-salesman of the generation."[52]

By the fall of 1920, the Black Sox scandal was exploding on the front pages of papers across the nation. The Hardings invited Lasker to travel with them to Texas and thence to faraway Panama on a mid-November vacation; Lasker begged off, saying that he had to stay in Chicago and fight for his plan to save baseball.[53] He declined to attend the Harding inauguration, and stayed away from the new president. "I figured a president was very busy," he explained, "[and] that you shouldn't see him unless you had something you wanted to take up with him."[54]

One of the more remarkable outcomes of the 1920 presidential race was that Lasker wound up being a personal friend not only of the winner, but also of the loser, James Cox. During the campaign, Cox had come to believe that Lasker was a nearly diabolical figure. The day after the election, though, he phoned Lasker. "I'm Jim Cox," he began. "Remember me?"[55] Cox went on to say that although he held Lasker largely responsible for his crushing electoral defeat, he believed that he and Lasker might overcome their differences, and perhaps even become friends.

Flattered by this unexpected overture, Lasker canceled a meeting with President-elect Harding to meet with Cox. The strange bedfellows did indeed become strong friends. Every year for many years afterward, Lasker threw an elaborate birthday party for Cox at his country estate.

The presidential campaign of 1920 was the last front-porch campaign, the last to rely heavily on legions of political speakers as proxies for the candidate, and the last before radio came into its own as a medium for mass communication. It wasn't, as some have asserted, a revolutionary new approach to American politics.

But the 1920 campaign was all new ground for Albert Lasker. He sized up a new territory, searched out the Big Ideas, spotted the most interesting and talented individuals in the new landscape, and established enduring friendships with those individuals. He genuinely liked and admired people like Will Hays, Ralph Sollitt, Warren Harding, and Jim Cox, and being considered the "super-salesman" of the generation by the likes of Will Hays must have been immensely gratifying.

During the campaign, Lasker realized a number of things about himself. He had been lucky enough to "start at the top" in politics—first through his recruitment by Will Hays in 1918, then in the Johnson campaign, and finally in the Harding campaign. He had found himself in the "high command" almost overnight. But he had never played the role of foot soldier, didn't really understand politics from the inside out, and could never become a master at the game of politics.[56]

He also decided that he didn't have the temperament for politics. "Every little thing worried me to death," he reflected, "and as so many little millions of things happened, a man who worries to death over every little thing hasn't much to contribute."[57]

Lasker knew that he had not personally elected Warren G. Harding; he also knew that the Harding victory was circumscribed by the candidate's serious limitations. At the end of the day, billboards, mysterious slogans, and staged baseball games were inconsequential.

So Lasker remained unfulfilled. He wanted to do something *of consequence*—something that would be a real and lasting contribution to humanity, enabling him finally to step out from behind the long shadows of his uncle and his father. And therefore, the question remained: To what task could he apply his prodigious talents that would be *meaningful?*

Chapter Thirteen

The Damnedest Job in the World

ON JUNE 8, 1921, President Warren G. Harding sent his nominations for the United States Shipping Board to Congress. Six of the seven names stirred no debate. But the seventh—Albert D. Lasker, the proposed chairman of the board—drew partisan jeers from the Democrats. In the House, Representative Joseph W. Byrns of Tennessee rose to speak against Lasker:

> I understand that he is the author of the phrase, "Don't wiggle and wobble," and possibly on account of that great service which he rendered to the last campaign, as well as on account of the distinguished success that he had made in his private business, the gentleman may be qualified . . .
>
> [But] I became pessimistic, indeed, when I read that we are to have as chairman of the board a man who says he knows nothing about ships . . . What qualifications does the management of the Chicago Cubs enable one to bring to the direction of the affairs of the Shipping Board, or Quaker Oats or Van Camp's pork and beans, or Lord & Thomas's advertising agency, when the man begged to be relieved because he knew nothing about ships?
>
> I should have liked to see [U.S. Steel's president] Mr. [James A.] Farrell made chairman of the Shipping Board. It is a great descent from steel to soup and pork and beans. It is a great descent from brains to beans.[1]

Lasker's detractors had a point: he had a lot to learn about ships and shipping. But at the same time, those who assumed he was only a sloganeer—or that he lacked brains, or vision, or determination—had a lot to learn about him.

Following the victorious presidential campaign of 1920, Lasker knew that it was past time to revive his flagging agency. Always in the back of his mind, however, was the urge to *serve*—instilled in him by both his uncle's example and his father's exhortations. Almost immediately after the election, Lasker began trying to land a job in the incoming Harding administration. The job he wanted was Secretary of Commerce: then a relatively low-status cabinet post, but the one most suited to his background and interests. He made his case directly to Will Hays when Hays visited him in Chicago on November 6. But Hays had already told Harding that *he* wanted Commerce for himself.

Harding had announced on November 5 that he was taking a month's vacation in Texas and Panama, and that he wouldn't even start thinking about cabinet appointments before getting back to Marion in December.[2] Upon his return to Ohio, Harding began receiving a parade of job-seekers—*not* including Lasker, who maintained his stance of not bothering the incoming president. The process was choreographed by Hays—which didn't bode well for Lasker's cabinet hopes.

Through the beginning of the New Year, Will Hays continued to covet the Commerce post, and therefore kept fending off Lasker. But on January 17, Harding offered Hays the choice of Postmaster General or the chairmanship of the proposed Commission to Reorganize the Government. Hays settled for the Post Office job, and began encouraging Harding to consider Lasker for Commerce—and also for an alternative post:

> *Having in mind the long talk which we had the day in Marion we took the walk in the snow about your idea as to the importance of the Chairmanship of the Shipping Board.*
>
> *No doubt you have thought of Albert Lasker in this connection. Should you find it impossible to appoint him Secretary of Commerce, he could do a hundred per cent job as Chairman of the Shipping Board. As I have thought over the matter since that time, continually he comes to mind in this connection. As you indicated to me then, I know, of course, that you realize the almost unexcelled business acumen and industry, loyalty and sheer efficiency which Lasker possesses. It is probable that you have considered him in this connection, but I have thought so much about it, I want to send this word.[3]*

Harding, then vacationing in St. Augustine, Florida, wrote back positively about the idea of installing Lasker at the Shipping Board. "I have often thought of him in that connection," the president-elect confirmed. "I have not yet taken the matter up but I will in due time. Frankly, I am just as anxious as you are to call Mr. Lasker to the service of the government, because I have very great respect for his ability and hold him in very high personal esteem."[4]

Lasker—then on one of his rest sojourns to Pasadena, during which his six-year-old daughter, Francie, nearly died of pneumonia—still dreamed of the Commerce position. But there was one compelling reason why Harding might "find it impossible" to give Lasker the job: Herbert Hoover had gotten there first.

Hoover, the future president, had made a fortune as a mining engineer in the first decade of the twentieth century and then distinguished himself in public service, first by supervising Belgian relief efforts from London and subsequently by serving President Wilson as head of the United States Food Administration. At the end of the war, the internationally acclaimed Hoover returned to Europe as head of the American Relief Administration, and—although a lifelong Republican—was briefly considered as a potential presidential candidate by both parties in 1920. Harding, determined to bring the famous and formidable engineer into his cabinet, offered him the Commerce post in early February. His appointment as Secretary of Commerce was announced on February 24.

A scaled-down presidential inauguration, in keeping with the impression of simplicity that Harding hoped to convey, took place on March 4. Harding's inaugural address was the first ever to be amplified, ringing out across the Capitol's broad plaza and reinforcing the new president's image of vigor—a striking contrast to the outgoing Woodrow Wilson, so enfeebled that he couldn't even attend Harding's swearing-in ceremony.

Just over a month later, on April 12, Harding addressed a special session of Congress to outline the policy initiatives of the new administration. Among dozens of other proposed programs, Harding declared himself in favor of building a "great merchant marine."

At first blush, the private shipping industry wasn't an obvious focus for a Midwestern politician. But those who had followed Harding's Senate career weren't surprised. Harding's political mentor, Ohio senator Mark Hanna, had made a fortune in Great Lakes shipping. Harding also had been strongly influenced by Theodore Roosevelt's and naval strategist Alfred Thayer Mahan's advocacy of a powerful navy. Throughout the campaign, he had spoken forcefully in favor of U.S. shipping.[5] "I want to acclaim the day when America is the most eminent of the maritime nations," Harding declared in

December 1920, between his election and his inauguration. "A big navy and a big merchant marine are necessary to the future of the country."[6]

On paper, at least, the solution was already at hand. The Shipping Act of 1916—passed with one eye on the bloody war in Europe—had created a five-member United States Shipping Board charged with fostering a strong U.S. shipping industry, both for transoceanic and coastal trade. The Board was authorized both to build and to operate a government fleet under the auspices of a subsidiary called the Emergency Fleet Corporation (EFC). To placate the operators of private shipping lines, Congress stipulated that the government fleet had to be disposed of within five years of the end of the European war.[7]

President Wilson didn't appoint the Shipping Board's members until March 1917. But the United States' entry into World War I the following month—combined with a congressional appropriation in June of $750 million to buy or build merchant ships—pushed the Board into a higher gear. (The appropriation was quickly increased to $2.9 billion: more than the value of the entire international shipping fleet in 1914.[8]) For the duration of the war, the EFC not only operated existing merchant ships, leased from private operators by the government, but also orchestrated a massive shipbuilding program, whereby private companies built merchant vessels and delivered them to the government.

It was a classic bureaucratic mess, exacerbated by the uncertainties of war. The EFC ordered some 18 million tons of shipping, of which only about 3 million tons were delivered before the Armistice. Another 4.5 million tons were canceled, but the remaining tonnage was delivered to the EFC between November 1919 and May 1922. All told, the EFC received 2,311 ships, the vast majority of which never saw service in World War I, and most of which had been built with taxpayer dollars on a rush basis at staggering expense.[9] Ships that would have cost $75 per ton to build in the United Kingdom cost upward of $145 per ton to build in the United States. As President Wilson's Treasury Secretary, William G. McAdoo, observed: "Appalling prices were paid for everything that had to do with a ship. Engines and other equipment were purchased at such a staggering cost that I fancied more than once that the machinery we were buying must be made of silver instead of iron and steel."[10]

From the outset, the Board was inclined to sell its ships rather than operate them, because it was painfully clear that the government couldn't run ships efficiently. But most of the ships were slow, coal-burning vessels, and a quarter of them were wooden-hulled; few operators wanted to buy ships that were already obsolete.

As the Republicans set out to make good on their campaign promises to cut government waste, the Shipping Board and its nearly useless fleet—then operating at a deficit of $15 million per month—seemed an obvious target. But for a president who wanted the United States to be the "most eminent of the maritime nations," the evisceration of the merchant fleet and the destruction of the domestic shipbuilding industry were appalling prospects.

Sometime in the spring of 1921, Will Hays met with Albert Lasker to talk ships and shipping.[11] Hays told his former subordinate about the sorry state of the Shipping Board and explained that President Harding felt compelled to appoint the Board's seven members as soon as possible.[12] The president planned to make these appointments on a geographic basis, and Harding wanted Lasker to serve as the representative from the Midwest. Lasker, still smarting at being snubbed for Secretary of Commerce, took offense: "I can remember, although I don't think Mr. Hays knows to this day, the hurt I felt at being tendered what I felt to be a very minor position. Shipping was a subject that I wasn't interested in, and which I had never thought about . . . I told Mr. Hays please not to pursue the matter with me."[13]

In fact, Lasker had thought a good deal about shipping. Several months earlier, his friend John Callan O'Laughlin had guessed that Lasker would be offered either a seat on the Shipping Board or its chairmanship. At that time, O'Laughlin had advised Lasker *not* to accept a seat on the Board, but to accept the chairmanship if it was offered. It would be a "wonderful business problem," O'Laughlin noted, and would position Lasker well when the inevitable cabinet reshuffles began.[14]

So Lasker turned Hays down. But toward the end of May 1921, President Harding invited Lasker to Washington.[15] At a White House meeting on a Friday morning, Harding explained the difficult predicament in which he found himself. By law, he had to appoint a new Shipping Board. Rumors of corruption and cronyism at the Board abounded—rumors that Harding had helped fuel during the presidential campaign. Now, the president's advisers were warning him to clean up the Board quickly, before it came to be seen as *his* mess. And to Harding, it went well beyond defensive measures: "It just so happens," he told Lasker, "that the thing that interests me most in being president is the merchant marine."[16]

The *immediate* problem, Harding continued, was that he couldn't find anyone to run the Shipping Board. He had first offered the job to James A. Farrell, president of U.S. Steel, which then operated the largest fleet of tankers in the world. Farrell turned him down.[17] Harding then approached Philip A. S. Franklin. Franklin was the president of International Mercantile Marine—the British-flagged but American-owned shipping combine controlled by J. P. Morgan—and Senate Republicans told Harding that because of the British flagging, Franklin couldn't be confirmed. Harding next tried to recruit William C. Teagle, the president of Standard Oil Company of New Jersey, which owned one of the largest tanker fleets in the world. Teagle also turned the job down, explaining that his Rockefeller connections would make him too controversial.

And so, Harding said to Lasker, *that brings me to my fourth choice: you.*

Lasker immediately declined, citing his complete lack of knowledge of the world of shipping. But he made a creative counterproposal: he would serve as Teagle's assistant on the Shipping Board, and he would work to make the public "enthusiastic about [Teagle's] appointment." Once Teagle was in place and accepted—a selling job that Lasker estimated would take no more than sixty days—Lasker would give up his assistant's post and head back to Chicago.

Harding agreed. Teagle couldn't return to Washington until Sunday night, so the president asked Lasker to stay in town. He could attend a White House garden reception on Saturday, Harding said, and go to church with him and "the Duchess" on Sunday. Lasker consented, although neither activity held much appeal for him. After the church service, the president teased Lasker about putting a five-dollar bill in the collection plate. "Albert," he joked, "you're setting a pretty steep pace."

"I was so glad not to hear that the Jews killed Christ," Lasker later joked, "I wanted to give the minister a reward."[18]

That night, Teagle arrived from New York, and—under heavy pressure from a president and one of the world's great salesmen—he agreed to take the job, on condition that the chairman of his board, Alfred C. Bedford, give his consent. Teagle left on the midnight train for New York, intending to seek an early meeting with Bedford. Lasker boarded the "midnight" to Chicago, delighted with his coup: he would only have to be in Washington for a few months, and then he would be free of the Shipping Board.[19]

But again, things took an unexpected turn: "I didn't get to my home outside Chicago until late the following evening, and when I got there, my wife handed me a telegram from the president. He recounted that he had just talked to Teagle on the telephone, that Teagle had talked it over with Mr. Bedford, and that Mr. Bedford had assented. [But] while Mr. Teagle had the phone call in, Mr. Bedford had a heart attack."[20]

Harding released Teagle from his obligation, and once more needed a chairman, and *quickly*. He sent a telegram to Lasker, insisting that he rescue him from the difficult situation in which he now found himself. "I have every confidence that you can make it go," Harding concluded. "At any rate I know of no one else to whom I may turn with a greater degree of confidence."[21]

At this point, Lasker recalled, Flora had already made up her mind: "My wife handed me the telegram and said, 'I couldn't live happily with a man who would say no to an appeal like that last paragraph.' That's how I came to be chairman of the Shipping Board."

There was more to the story. Flora had been disappointed to learn that Albert had turned the job down in the first place; she thought that a stay in Washington would be a mark of distinction for her husband—perhaps positioning him for future forays into politics—and might also be a good experience for their three children, Mary (then seventeen), Edward (nine), and Francie (five). Now the opportunity had arisen again "You have got to take it," Flora told her husband.[22] He capitulated.

In White House huddles with Harding on June 7 and 8, Lasker put a number of conditions on his service.[23] He would get the job done, he told the president, but he would serve no more than two years. No other department could interfere in his work. If the president didn't like the way Lasker was running the Board, he could fire him. Meanwhile, Harding would support Lasker by paying high salaries to qualified shipping executives, which—Lasker emphasized—was the only way he could lure management talent into short-term government service.

Harding readily agreed to these terms. On June 9, 1921, Lasker and the six other proposed Board members were confirmed by the Senate.[24] Lasker's confirmation represented a quiet milestone: after Louis Brandeis's nomination to the Supreme Court in 1916 and Bernard Baruch's appointment as head of the War Industries Board during World War I, Lasker became only the third Jew ever appointed to a high post in the federal government.

But Harding's congratulatory telegram to Lasker was notable for its bleak overtones. "To be honest about it," Harding wrote, "I have doubts about whether anybody who gets on the Shipping Board is entitled to congratulations, because you have now got tangled up with the 'damnedest' job in the world."

⸻ ⟨◉⟩ ⸻

Lasker told a reporter from *Printer's Ink* that he would cut his ties to Lord & Thomas, turning over day-to-day management of the agency to Herbert Cohn, his long-time general manager in Chicago.

Lasker also talked to a *New York Times* reporter the day after his confirmation, and the story landed on page 1.[25] "It will be the purpose of the new Shipping Board to get the Government out of the shipping business as rapidly as possible," the *Times* reported, in a voice that sounded very much like Lasker's. "There must be nothing that smacks of permanent Government ownership or operation."[26]

From his first day on the job, Lasker found himself taking on water. "I got in Monday morning," he wrote to a friend, "and inherited a great and bitter strike which is pressing for settlement, and is taking all my time."[27] Lasker helped resolve the strike (by the Marine Engineers Beneficial Association) within a few days.[28]

Things would not again be so easy. The Shipping Board was the "most colossal commercial wreck the world ever knew," Lasker told a reporter.[29] It was also a *complex* wreck. On the day Lasker took office, the Shipping Board (through its Emergency Fleet Corporation) owned 1,522 steel ships and 454 wooden-hulled vessels—and that was only the visible tip of the iceberg.[30] The Board also had substantial investments in 200 shipbuilding and industrial plants, 19 drydocks, and 12 marine railways. It had spent $70 million on worker housing during the war; as a result, it had at least a partial stake in 5,555 houses; 72 apartment buildings; 62 dormitories; 20 combined apartment/retail complexes; 11 stores; and hotels, boarding houses, and cafeterias (4 each). In addition, it owned "vast quantities of steel, lumber, engines, boilers, winches, pumps, locomotive cranes, air compressors, and miscellaneous materials."[31]

President Harding assembled the Shipping Board at the White House on June 17 to demonstrate his commitment to a strong merchant marine. In informal remarks to the press after the meeting, Harding praised his relatively youthful chairman. Lasker was not there because he was a shipping expert, Harding said; he was there because he was a "live wire" who would bring energy and ability to the job. In fact, Harding joked, Lasker was the "livest wire" he knew.[32]

In addition to Harding's strong endorsement, Lasker started the job with two other reliable allies. The first was the peripatetic John Callan O'Laughlin, who by 1921 was wearing multiple hats: filing reports as the *Chicago Herald's* Washington correspondent and also working as the Washington lobbyist for a New York export company.[33] Lasker knew that he had to figure out Washington in a hurry and that he needed a skilled writer to help get his messages across to a skeptical Congress and public. O'Laughlin agreed to take a brief leave of absence from his several jobs to serve as Lasker's personal assistant until the post could be filled permanently. Lasker later recalled the deal that they struck (and which he soon reneged on):

> O'Laughlin was tied up with other things, but as a man imbued with a desire for public service, he said, "I'll come with you and give you time to look around and get someone." Which he did. Well, I let one week run into another, and about four weeks had passed, and O'Laughlin said to me, "Where is your other man? I want to get out. I have my work to attend to. I only did this as a favor to you."
>
> [But] he was invaluable. I was really double-crossing him and giving him the runaround. I didn't want anybody else . . . So I just did nothing . . . O'Laughlin got on to that. At the end of six weeks he said, "Well, I have my successor, and I'm quitting."[34]

The successor O'Laughlin had come up with was Ralph Sollitt, by this point a vice president in a Washington bank. Lasker was astonished that someone of Sollitt's caliber could be persuaded to join him at the Shipping Board as his personal assistant. In Washington, as Lasker later observed, a personal assistant to the chairman is the person "on whom they inflict all the humiliations that they would like to put on the board and daren't." So O'Laughlin had pulled off a small miracle.

The second key ally Lasker brought along was his lawyer, Elmer Schlesinger, who was appointed the Board's general counsel. Schlesinger, too, faced daunting tasks. Supervising the Board's seven hundred in-house lawyers—and also bringing in outside help from law firms in New York,

Philadelphia, and Boston—he had to start working off an enormous backlog of claims against the Board: some seventeen hundred admiralty cases involving a total of something like $100 million.[35]

Schlesinger also initiated a review of all the contracts that the Board had signed with private companies to operate government ships. Prepped by Schlesinger, Lasker publicly denounced the worst of the existing contracts as "the most shameful piece of chicane, inefficiency, and of looting of the Public Treasury that the human mind can devise."[36] He had the offending contracts voided, and the Shipping Board took over direct operation of the vessels.

On June 24, Lasker called together the heads of the major shipping companies in New York and asked them each to turn over one of their best managers to Lasker's enterprise. None of these three individuals, once identified, wanted to take the job; it required arm-twisting by President Harding to get them to agree. Lasker made sure that this recruitment process—intended both to infuse the Board with unprecedented talent and inoculate it against his own lack of shipping experience—got plenty of publicity.

During his visit to New York and on many subsequent occasions, Lasker made a point of cultivating the press. He spoke colorfully and with calculated candor, thereby earning friendly treatment even in papers (such as the *New York Times*) that were inclined to be suspicious of a Republican businessman-turned-bureaucrat: "The Chairman spoke of his regret that Mr. Teagle did not take the job, and remarked that the board had been changing chairmen faster than they change pitchers in a losing ball game, said he was going to do his best and if he did not succeed he would just go home very quietly and promise to pose for lots of pictures if, and after, he had made good."[37]

Two months later, when Lasker lost a battle in the House of Representatives and took some personal hits from his congressional adversaries, the *Times* editorialized sympathetically:

> It is no reflection upon Mr. Lasker to say that the Shipping Board has never had such an original character at the head of it. He speaks out in a way that bewilders Congress . . .
>
> Chairman Lasker has a marvelous fluency, and his eyes gleam and sparkle as he talks. 'I have taken a man-killing job, but we will stick until our health breaks,' this human dynamo of a Chairman told the committee. Congress may not believe Lasker, but he believes in himself.[38]

Also in this start-up phase, the "human dynamo" persuaded Robert H. Montgomery—a partner in a large accounting firm—to come to Washington for four months to straighten out the Shipping Board's books. This, too, was a staggering proposition. The Board employed some three thousand accountants when Lasker arrived in Washington, but it had no *books*. "There was no inventory," he recalled. "There was no balance sheet. There was no operations statement. There was just in and out cash."[39]

In some cases, getting a handle on the Board's affairs only made things look worse. "When we finally took an inventory of the ships we owned," Lasker told Columbia's oral historians, "we were one ship short! We couldn't find a ship! Losing a ship is like losing a skyscraper."[40]

Montgomery discovered twenty-eight men who had been put on the Shipping Board payroll on the day before the Armistice—in November 1918, two and a half years earlier—and who had never done anything except collect their salaries. After two weeks on the job, Montgomery came to Lasker with a radical proposal: *Start at the northeast corner of the accounting room, fire every third person, and see if anything bad happens.*

Lasker fumed publicly about the state of the Board's record keeping: "Had the books been kept with a view to cheating and deceiving Congress and the country, they could not have been kept in much different shape than they have been, and I measure the words I am using. It has almost worn me out physically and mentally to get anything from the books that could be considered complete."[41]

While he was recruiting and deploying out-of-town talent, Lasker also had to get to know his fellow commissioners. The only two he had had prior contact with were Frederick I. Thompson, an Alabama newspaper publisher, and Los Angeles political operative Meyer Lissner, who—like Lasker—had been one of California senator Hiram Johnson's prominent supporters. Admiral William S. Benson, the celebrated Naval officer who had headed the Board during part of the Wilson administration and into Harding's tenure, agreed to stay on as a member. George E. Chamberlain was the former Oregon senator and chairman of the Military Affairs Committee who had been defeated in his 1920 reelection bid. T. V. O'Connor, president of the International Longshoremen's Association, had a reputation for being one of the most powerful labor leaders in the country, and had been on Harding's short list for Secretary of Labor. Edward C. Plummer, closely tied to the Hale political machine in Maine—Senator Frederick Hale was one of Harding's closest friends in the Senate—served as the Northeast's representative on the Board.

"I would say, myself included," Lasker observed, "that only a democracy could spew up a board like that."[42] But in fact, it was an able board—mostly "outstanding men," as Lasker later admitted.[43]

<hr />

What Lasker attempted to do in his first few months in Washington, beyond cleaning house, was to map out a plan that would bring together the federal government and the private shipping companies in an informal partnership. One essential piece of this plan, he decided—with ample input from ship operators—was a direct government subsidy of selected routes. In theory, this would increase the sale price of the government ships and pay for the subsidies.

Meanwhile, the Board would attempt to modernize its massive fleet. It would also undertake to build up trade on key routes, which it would eventually sell to private operators. At the same time, it would adopt policies to help strengthen the shippers, so that they would be in a position to buy ships and routes when the international economy recovered. All of these steps, taken together, would ease the federal government out of the shipping business.

But reality didn't conform to the plan. In August, for example, the Board announced its intention to sell 205 of the mothballed wooden ships to a New York company for $430,500, or $2,100 apiece. This was far less than the $700,000 it had cost the taxpayers to build a *single one* of these ships, and a predictable howl went up in the media and among the Democrats in Congress. The sale was voided. "Wooden ships are about as popular with me as yellow fever," Lasker grumbled to a Congressional committee.[44] When New York Yankees owner Jake Ruppert sent the two baseballs autographed by Babe Ruth that Lasker had requested, Lasker ended his thank-you note with a wry offer: "By the way, whenever you want a bunch of wooden ships, be sure to let me know."[45]

Meanwhile, there was a highly visible Shipping Board asset that Lasker had to contend with: the *S.S. Leviathan*, then tied up at Pier 59 in Hoboken, New Jersey.

This fifty-six-thousand-ton passenger liner—one of the largest in the world—had been built in Germany and launched in the spring of 1914 as the

Vaterland. She had made only three transatlantic runs before war broke out in Europe in 1914, at which point she was interned in New York. Seized by Customs officials when the United States entered World War I, the *Vaterland* was rechristened *Leviathan*, stripped of her palatial interiors, painted gray, and pressed into service as a troop transport.[46] Between the spring of 1917 and September 1919, the great ship ferried some 200,000 U.S. troops to and from Europe, along the way acquiring the nicknames "Levi" and "Big Train."

Her decommissioning as a Naval vessel that September kicked off a two-year soap opera centered on the hulk—immobile, tied to her Hoboken pier, rusting, plundered by thieves, and in constant peril of death by fire. Just keeping her mothballed cost the federal government $45,000 a month.[47] In November 1919, the Shipping Board announced that it would sell the *Leviathan* and two other seized German liners to International Mercantile Marine.

But to be put back into transatlantic service, the *Leviathan* would need to be completely rehabilitated—which was impossible because nobody in the United States had a set of plans for the ship. (The German yard that had built the seized ship demanded $1 million for a copy of the missing blueprints.) As a result, IMM's chief designer, William Francis Gibbs, undertook the almost unimaginable task of reverse-engineering the 950-foot liner, drawing up a complete set of plans and bid specifications for rehabbing the ship. It took a hundred draftsmen the better part of a year and a half (and cost approximately $300,000) to produce 1,024 pages of blueprints and specifications.

By October, the Shipping Board was finally in a position to say exactly what it owned: a tally that ran to twenty-five thousand typewritten pages. It could account for assets that had cost just under $308 million to procure. The accountants estimated that these assets were fairly valued at $92.6 million, but that they had a forced-sale value of about $46.6 million.[48] Two departments were set up to oversee the sale of assets: one to sell ships and the other to dispose of the Board's other surplus materials.

In the year before Lasker arrived in Washington, the Board placed approximately $938,000 in advertising, mainly to increase its freight trade, and mostly with little impact. (One problem was that the Board simply paid for ads written, designed, and placed by the ship operators themselves: hardly a Lord & Thomas formula.) This budget stayed fairly constant during Lasker's tenure, but he redirected it for greater impact: first to sell off housing and other surplus materials, and—starting in December 1921—to help build the passenger trade on the Board's liners. He also made the Board prepare its own ads, rather than simply pick up the tab.

When it came to advertising, the Shipping Board now lived by Lord & Thomas's principles. "I do not believe in advertising merely to get general results, just to make your name known, or in advertising that you cannot measure," Lasker testified before a Senate subcommittee in April 1922. He told of the nearly empty passenger liners that his Board had inherited, including a Pacific liner that carried only thirty-four passengers on its last run: a horrendous showing. His accountants had told him that bringing in an additional fifteen hundred passengers would pay for all the advertising and create much-needed momentum for American-flag liners. Within a few months of initiating the ad campaign, the Board had received twelve thousand requests for information and had lured four thousand visitors to its ticket offices around the country.

In effect, Lasker recast his challenge as a *marketing* problem. He and his colleagues at the Shipping Board had to create demand for its goods and services. This, of course, was what Lasker excelled at, but he had never had a "client" as amorphous as the Shipping Board's. (Was he working for the president? For the taxpayer? For the shipping industry? For oceangoing travelers?) Nor had he had ever worked with an inherited staff, or faced hostile legislators, or been so far out from behind his accustomed curtain.

One of the more oppressive realities of life in Washington was the steady onslaught of political favor seekers and patronage hounds. Lasker had extracted a promise from the president that his Board would be spared undue political interference, and Harding mostly kept his pledge—but of course, others weren't bound by it.[49] Throughout Lasker's two-year term, he and his Shipping Board colleagues fielded an almost constant barrage of requests for favors from influential people in and out of Washington. Although politicians on both sides of the aisle publicly professed to despise the gravy train that the Board represented, privately they made sure to dip in their ladles.

In May 1922, for example, the Board got a request from Vice President Calvin Coolidge's office to find summer jobs aboard a U.S. vessel for two college boys who were the sons of one of Coolidge's friends. Lasker reminded the vice president that the Shipping Board didn't actually employ any mariners; all it could do was veto an inappropriate candidate put forward by the private operators of those ships. Nevertheless, members of the House of Representatives sought shore-side jobs for constituents; senators sought raises for

Shipping Board employees from their home states. Lasker had to tread carefully, in all cases; he knew he would need votes when the Merchant Marine bill that was then taking shape finally came before the House and Senate.[50]

Throughout the fall of 1921, Lasker and his Board refined their long-term plan for the American merchant marine. Several junior members of Lasker's staff drafted the bill, while Lasker and his fellow commissioners concentrated on building public support for it.

Finally, the plan was ready and the ground prepared. Harding addressed a joint session of Congress on February 28, 1922, and put the proposed "Merchant Marine Bill" on the table.[51] He reviewed the history of the Shipping Board, including its recent record of trying to sell its ships while still operating many of the ships under its control. Lasker's board had cut its losses, but was still running at a huge deficit. The time had come, Harding declared, to unload the government's ships for whatever they could bring on the open market. After that, the government would subsidize both the construction and operation of private vessels.

In addition, Harding announced, passage of the Merchant Marine Bill would create a merchant marine reserve (of five hundred officers and thirty thousand sailors) for national emergencies, and would favor American-flag shipping in a variety of ways.[52]

Initial reaction was mixed. The shippers who had played a major role in shaping the bill applauded it. More neutral observers offered qualified support, pointing out that the United States' main competitors for ocean trade—especially the United Kingdom—heavily subsidized their fleets. Secretary of Commerce Hoover weighed in with his endorsement, as did the Senate's acknowledged maritime expert, Wesley Jones.

But organized labor quickly voiced objections, viewing the proposed merchant marine reserve as a potential strikebreaking force. Representatives of the interior states expressed suspicions that this was yet another plot on the part of the wealthy coastal states to enrich themselves at the Midwest's expense. Most ominous was the negative response of the agricultural lobby, which was always wary of government subsidies of industry, and soon the "farm bloc" in the Senate—a group of twenty-seven senators who tended to vote together on key agricultural issues—began voicing its skepticism.

Lasker spent three days in front of a joint Senate/House committee in the first week of April 1922, explaining and defending his bill.[53] Lasker stood up under a thorough grilling, occasionally suggesting that skeptical House members save their detailed questions for the Shipping Board experts who would follow him. "I'm not an expert on certain details," he admitted. At one point, he described the Board's overall record at operating ships as "rotten"; he later requested that the adjective be stricken from his testimony.[54]

It was a bravura performance, but it could not overcome the mounting opposition to the plan. By mid-June, Harding and Lasker had to acknowledge that they didn't have the votes they needed. House leaders pointed out that even if the bill passed in their chamber, it would almost certainly fail in the Senate. Harding reluctantly agreed to put the bill on hold during a six-week congressional recess, which started on June 30, 1922, and Lasker spent the summer of 1922 tracking newspaper editorials across the country. From that survey, he knew that he was losing the Midwest, Mountain States, and South, even as the coastal states rallied in support of the bill.[55]

When the House reconvened in August, Republican leaders begged the president to put off action on the bill until more favorable political winds were blowing—and specifically, until after the midterm elections in November. Few in Congress wanted to run for reelection with an unpopular merchant-marine vote on their record.

In particular, in these early years of the nation's uncomfortable embrace of Prohibition, few wanted to be associated with an especially thorny issue: the sale of alcohol aboard Albert Lasker's ships.

The National Prohibition Act of 1919—popularly known as the Volstead Act—enforced the 18th Amendment to the Constitution, which prohibited the manufacture, transportation, import, export, sale, and possession of alcohol in the United States. Prohibition quickly proved unenforceable; illegal domestic production was complemented by the smuggled beverages that flowed across the borders from Canada and Mexico and washed ashore all along the coasts.

In May 1922, August A. Busch, president of St. Louis-based Anheuser-Busch, sailed from New York to Cherbourg aboard the *S.S. George Washington*, a Shipping Board liner. Busch's huge brewery had taken a body blow with the onset of Prohibition; it was forced to diversify into product lines as diverse as truck bodies, ice cream, and baker's yeast.[56] Upon arriving in France, Busch sent a letter to his son Adolphus in St. Louis, complaining that the Shipping Board was violating the Volstead Act by serving liquor aboard its oceangoing vessels. August enclosed a copy of the ship's wine list.

On June 8, Adolphus forwarded his father's letter and the offending wine list ("enumerating intoxicating liquors of every character") to President Harding. He posed an unwelcome question to the president: if American ships were technically American territory no matter where they were in the world, wasn't the government acting as a bootlegger aboard the *Washington* and other Shipping Board vessels?[57]

Someone in St. Louis leaked a copy of the correspondence to a *Chicago Tribune* reporter, who immediately made it public. Harding, wanting nothing to do with this budding controversy, forwarded Busch's letter to Lasker. In his response to Busch, Lasker explained that upon taking office, he had asked the Board's general counsel, Elmer Schlesinger, to determine whether liquor could legally be sold aboard U.S. ships once they were outside U.S. territorial waters. Schlesinger's opinion was that such sales were indeed legal, and Lasker therefore did not put a stop to liquor sales on the high seas.

Lasker then made his first mistake. Rather than simply responding privately to the Busches, Lasker—playing tit for tat—also made his end of the correspondence public. But his letter went beyond making his own case, and impugned the motives and the character of the Busches:

> *I believe you to be thoroughly selfish, and that you are acting in the hope of creating a public revolt against prohibition so that you may again revive the sale of your liquors, utterly regardless of how you might hurt the American merchant marine in your effort to create a situation to benefit your brewery.*
>
> *It is, of course, notorious that the Adolphus Busch who founded your brewery was possibly the Kaiser's closest friend in America, and that your family for many years has maintained a castle in Germany; your action in any event will not displease your German friends, whose greatest hope of a restored German merchant marine is in a hurt to American's new-born merchant marine.*
>
> *I refer to these extraneous facts not in resentment, but that it may be made clear that in my opinion you do not come before the bar of public opinion with clean hands.[58]*

Lasker's accusation that the Busches were seeking to undermine Prohibition was accurate enough. In that effort, they certainly weren't alone: Representative James A. Gallivan—a Boston Democrat, a self-described "wet," and already an established tormentor of Lasker—read the wine list of the *President Pierce* on the floor of the House of Representatives, making the point that this was just a particularly noxious example of how rich people could drink and poor people couldn't.[59] But by pointing to the Busches' alleged German sympathies only four years after the end of a bloody war with Germany, and by invoking the much-despised Kaiser, Lasker went too far.[60]

Lasker committed another, more damaging blunder in his letter to Busch: he argued that as long as foreign ships could serve alcohol on their transatlantic runs, U.S. ships had to do the same to stay competitive. Congressional opponents of the proposed subsidy plan pounced upon this assertion. If U.S. ships could compete only by violating the Constitution, should the taxpayer be asked to subsidize such lawbreaking? Would next year's Congressional appropriation for the Shipping Board include a line item for the purchase of substances that ordinary Americans couldn't legally possess?

Ultimately, the strategy that Lasker's opponents seized upon was delay. First, Republicans persuaded Harding to stall action on the Merchant Marine bill until after Congress's six-week summer recess. Then, upon their return to Washington on August, they demanded that he not bring the bill to a vote until after the November elections. Finally, the Harding administration took the liquor issue off the table. In a sweeping October 6 opinion, Attorney General Harry Daugherty stated that *no* ships could carry intoxicating beverages in U.S. waters. The only exception, spelled out in the Volstead Act itself, was foreign ships transiting the Panama Canal from one foreign port to another.[61]

Lasker was "stunned."[62] Approached by reporters, he said, first, that of course the Shipping Board would comply with the Justice Department's opinion. (Telegrams were dispatched to all Shipping Board vessels, ordering them to immediately stop serving alcohol and to dispose of their liquor in the first foreign port they reached.[63]) He then pointed to some of the practical problems that would grow out of the change. It would take months, or perhaps years, for the implications of applying U.S. law to foreign vessels to be worked out, during which time foreign vessels would gain a clear advantage over U.S. passenger liners.[64] Montreal, he predicted, would enjoy a shipping boom; West Coast cities like Seattle and Portland would suffer a "severe blow." And because "the immigrant . . . uses wine and beer as the American uses butter," the immigrant trade—which represented most of the westbound traffic between Europe and the United States—would shift entirely to foreign ships. "Today's decision," he concluded, "makes immediate passage of the subsidy bill more necessary than ever."[65]

But a vote on Lasker's bill would have to wait until after the November elections.

Chapter Fourteen

A Family Interlude

IME **MAGAZINE,** which over the years kept a skeptical eye trained on Albert Lasker, concluded in the spring of 1923 that the Shipping Board chairman exerted an influence on President Harding that was both "striking" and "mysterious."

Harding had two types of associates, said *Time*: official advisers and "playmates." What was unique about Lasker, the *Time* reporter continued, was that he was both an adviser *and* a playmate. "Able in conversation, brilliant at storytelling, and fond of golf," *Time* concluded. "Little wonder that he became one of the President's best friends."[1]

Although Lasker's friends scoffed at the notion of him exerting a "mysterious" hold on the president, he did indeed enjoy a unique influence at the White House—both with the president and his wife. He was a great storyteller, as *Time* noted, and had a talent for putting people—including the Hardings—at ease amid the intimidating trappings of the presidency. And, of course, he shared with the president three passions: poker, baseball, and golf.

As a senator, Harding had hosted a regular Saturday night poker game; as president, he played twice a week at the White House, with the game starting after dinner and lasting several hours. These were low-stakes games, intended to take Harding's mind off the pressures of the presidency. Regular players included senators, cabinet members, Harding's personal secretary George Christian, and Lasker.

Lasker also golfed with Harding several times a month when the weather permitted. He accompanied the president on a golfing vacation to Florida in March 1923, and for ten days, as the party made its way down the Inland Waterway, Lasker was compelled to play a round at every course they encountered along the way. "I'm glad Harding doesn't skip rope," the exhausted Shipping Board chairman was overheard to remark.[2]

———————

Lasker's two-year stint in Washington also provided an unusual interlude in his personal life. Flora had persuaded him to take the job in the hope that he would distinguish himself in public service. Perhaps she also had a goal of bringing their family together for what might well be the last time, since Mary—the oldest of the three Lasker children—was about to start her senior year in high school. If that was Flora's hope, her experience in Washington both frustrated and satisfied her.

The frustration arose out of her own physical and emotional health, the circumstances of their family, and her relationship with Albert. After the birth of her younger daughter, Francie, in 1916, Flora knew that she would never realize her dream of having six children. She was largely housebound, both before and after Francie's birth. (Albert later commented that Flora "hardly knew a well hour" after Francie's birth.[3]) Albert was on the road much of the time, and while he was away, Flora almost never went out:

> I imagine I was away half the time, and I don't believe in all that time she averaged over one night a year when she wouldn't be home if I wasn't there—just stay[ed] at home alone reading. It was an effort [for her] to go out without me. Whenever we went out, she'd beg me to keep close to her, because her disabilities made her feel particularly sensitive, and she was of a sensitive nature anyhow, so she'd screw up inside of herself. She was very scared about crowds—even to go into a crowd of people she knew.[4]

On her own turf, though, she could be formidable. Among other things, she worried about Albert's *dignity*; left to his own devices, he rarely thought much about that. "You're a very dignified man," she would tell him—and then she'd set about making it so. "I waited until she wasn't around," Lasker later commented, "to let myself go." (He came home drunk once; he never did so again.) Living up to Flora's high expectations sometimes chafed:

> Her standards were those of the 1880s—never changed—which at times was a little difficult for a person who went about as much as I did, to live up to, and it got me so that I had to go through a life of repressions in not being myself.

I think this affected my nervous system quite a good deal, but she was the type of woman you can't be with and disappoint. You just couldn't do it. It was like hurting a dove or a deer, and she was unyielding in her standards.[5]

The Lasker family moved to Washington in stages. Albert arrived first, in June 1921, renting a yellow-brick house at 1706 18th Street N.W., a few blocks from Dupont Circle. The rest of the family followed later that summer. Mary enrolled at Miss Madeira's School for her final year of high school, while Edward enrolled at the St. Albans School in Washington—a relief to Albert, who worried that his son, growing up in the family's Glencoe, Illinois, mansion, was "surrounded only by women."

Briefly, Flora flourished in Washington. For several months, the Laskers were regular guests at formal dinners hosted by the Hardings, including the February 1922 fete in honor of the Supreme Court justices, where Albert and Flora hobnobbed with the likes of tire magnate Harvey Firestone and his wife, Mrs. Marshall Field, and conservationist Gifford Pinchot.[6]

Then something went badly wrong. Toward the middle of that month, Flora suddenly left Washington for three months of near-total seclusion in Atlantic City, New Jersey. Albert visited her on weekends when his schedule permitted, but otherwise, Flora—under doctor's orders—remained completely isolated.

Although Albert regularly reported to family members and close friends about Flora's symptoms, he revealed very little about the *causes* of his wife's illness. In April, for example, he wrote to his in-laws in Buffalo:

She will be in Atlantic City until May 15th. The plan then is for her to come to Washington for a couple of weeks, and from here go June first to Glencoe, where she will be under rigid restrictions until Fall. While she does not know it, she will have to keep a trained nurse all the time so as to insure that she leads the restricted life that she should. Her progress is satisfactory, but she herself realizes that she has no reserve power. If she goes out on the boardwalk for an hour and meets no one, when she comes back everything is normal; but the chart shows that if she meets any one even for five minutes, she has cold feet, fast pulse, and other manifestations. In fact, [son] Edward and [governess] Miss Sachse visited her for two days Saturday and Sunday and she was really glad when they went; she did not see much of them but it excited her . . . With an absence of excitement, she feels better every day.[7]

Clearly, Flora continued to suffer from the physical ailments that had plagued her for more than a decade. Albert's letters suggest that his wife had psychological frailties, as well, evidently including agoraphobia and what would today be called panic attacks. Albert hoped that Flora could build up her physical and emotional strength at Glencoe and then return to Washington in the fall to enjoy the family's remaining months in Washington. As he wrote to her in Illinois toward the end of May: "Remember dear that you can cheat everything else in the world save nature, but you cannot cheat nature. If you will deny yourself everything but an orthodox following out of the doctor's program you can come back this fall and we can have a bully time doing all the things together that have been denied us. But if you feel that you can cheat nature then you may be playing a losing game."

The therapy seems to have worked. Flora began walking and playing a low-key form of golf again during her Glencoe stay, and when she returned to Washington in late October, she was able to enjoy the capital's social scene in a limited way. As Albert later reflected: "I don't mean she was well while we were there, but that she wasn't sick every day, and she could take part in the life, and because of President and Mrs. Harding's very evident prejudice in our favor, why, we were considerably courted. And the President and Mrs. Harding . . . made almost everyone know that we were favorites, [and] made it . . . their business to check up who was nice to us and who wasn't."[8]

The Hardings looked after the Laskers. "Mrs. Harding watched over my wife there as if it was a trusteeship she had undertaken," Lasker remembered.[9] The two couples ate lunch or dinner together at the White House three or four times a week. On several occasions, Lasker remembered, he and Flora were just sitting down to an early dinner at home when the phone rang. Florence Harding would be on the line, asking if the Laskers would like to come over and eat at the White House. "We wouldn't say we were in the middle of [dinner]," Lasker recalled. "We'd just go and start all over again—just the Hardings and ourselves."[10]

Despite this high-level attention, Albert despised the Washington social scene. He later said that he "never heard a worthwhile word spoken the whole time I was there." The events there were on a par with the "dullest evenings anywhere else . . . People didn't open up."[11]

Flora, by contrast, found Washington society intensely interesting, and life in the nation's capital during the last two months of 1922 and the first half of 1923 gave her a rare respite. "With all the people she is meeting," Albert wrote to a family member, "Flora is having a thrilling winter, and one she will remember as long as she lives."[12] The Washington interlude constituted the "two happiest years of her life," he concluded, glossing over the significant difficulties of that first year.[13] Nor was Flora entirely well in those final, happy months in Washington. "Mother has taken a new series of exercises and has been dieting," he wrote to his daughter Mary in May, "with the consequent result that in the last two or three days she has been feeling nervous, tired and depressed, showing that the results is the same as always when she does these things, i.e., her thyroid gland begins acting up . . . She lost ten pounds in ten days, which is too much."[14]

To several family members, Albert admitted that up to this point he had not been a particularly good father, and that he was determined to do better. During this period in Washington, Albert decided to make up for lost time. This resolution came to bear most heavily on the two older children: Mary, then in her late teens, and ten-year-old Edward.

Mary, in particular, lived under her father's watchful eye and bore the brunt of his expectations. Enrolling at Vassar in the fall of 1922—the first child to leave the family nest and also the first in the immediate family to attend college—Mary exhibited an unexpected willful streak. Only a month into the school year, she went dancing in New York City without telling her parents. Albert found out and severely scolded her. Thereafter, Mary was required to ask permission to leave Poughkeepsie for any reason.[15]

Meanwhile, Albert noted pointedly, she had an obligation to write to her parents regularly. "Just because I visited last week with you," he wrote to her, "please don't fail to write us at least three or four times a week. I do not ask more than one long letter a week; on the other occasions a postal card will suffice."[16] Albert knew that he sometimes stepped over the line of parental intrusiveness with his oldest daughter. "Don't get it, dearest, that I am trying to police you," he wrote. "You know that is not the fact; what I want to do is to help you bring out of yourself all there is in you."[17]

Albert also had high hopes for his only son. Perhaps inevitably, young Edward disappointed his father. When Edward finished fifth in his class of twelve at St. Albans, Albert wrote the headmaster, saying he hoped his son could do better the following year. And as Edward's younger sister, Francie, later recalled, Albert's expectations for his son could be unrealistically high: "It was May Day. It was Father's birthday. I was obviously quite little, I remember walking up and down 18th Street with father, before the guests came, and the lights coming on in the house at dusk. Edward was then going to day school at St. Albans. And Father said to me, 'It's my birthday, and your brother didn't remember it.' And at the age of five, I thought, 'Oh my God, what a dreadful burden on Edward!'"[18]

When Edward, Francie, and Flora moved back to Glencoe for the summer of 1922, his father continued in his heavy parenting by mail. The eleven-year-old boy typed a letter to his father on homemade letterhead with the headline "EDWARD A. LASKER," having invented a middle initial for himself. Albert wrote back to protest: "Of course I am greatly complimented that you wanted to use my name; nothing pleases me more than your desire to have my name for your middle name. But when I see you I am going to beg of you not to do this. I believe a name is stronger without a middle name; and while the compliment you pay me is great, I want you to go through life with the strongest possible name."

Then Albert chided his son for using a typewriter when he had asked Edward to write in longhand. He noted that the letter was "carelessly written," and that Edward had neglected to sign it. "Now, while I would rather get a carelessly written letter from you than none," Albert concluded, "do you think it shows the proper interest in your father to address him as covered above?"[19]

Lasker often went overboard in his high ambitions for his son. In September 1922, he wrote a note to Phillips Academy in Andover, Massachusetts, asking what steps should be taken so that Edward could enter the school three years hence. On the same day, he wrote to Yale, inquiring as to what he needed to do to ensure Edward's admission to Yale in the fall of 1929—*seven years in the future.*

Francie, only six years old in the fall of 1922, was largely spared Albert's active parenting. Like many children last in the birth order, Francie was intermittently doted on and overlooked, and the love she got from her parents was relatively unqualified. In addition, her two serious illnesses—in the winters of 1920 and 1921—persuaded her parents to go easy on her. Albert and Flora decided to keep Francie at home (first in Glencoe, and then in Washington) during the 1922–1923 academic year.

"You say you love me," Albert wrote to her, in response to a handwritten letter to him from Glencoe. "Nothing could make me happier. I love you; let's always love each other."[20] On Halloween night of 1922, with the family recently reinstalled in Washington, Lasker left work at the Shipping Board early. "Frances is giving a little party to herself," Albert wrote to Mary at Vassar, "the guests being [governess] Miss Sachse, Edward, and I. I have to hurry home. She is as excited about it as if she had a hundred children."[21]

Lasker's friend W. G. Irwin sometimes stayed with the Laskers on his trips to Washington. Irwin made a wistful confession to Lasker after one of these visits:

> I cannot tell you how great a pleasure it was to me to again see your family and be with them. I was very glad to see Mrs. Lasker looking so much better and apparently in very good health, and then, it was a pleasure to see that intense admiration that Frances showed for Edward and the great interest that she took in the stories that Edward told, but that admiration was no more impressive than was the love that Edward showed for his sister. There is nothing finer than to see that delightful home life and love among all of the family. All old bachelors are not as fortunate as I am in being in touch with it.[22]

In mid-February 1923, Albert wrote to a family member about his satisfaction with Flora's progress, and confessed that he was looking forward to their approaching departure from the nation's capital. "Flora is in better health this winter than she has been," he noted, "and is enjoying her Washington stay exceedingly. She is getting everything out of the winter she can, for, as you undoubtedly know, the middle of June we are returning home for good."[23]

Lasker had made a strong, if belated effort to be a better father and family man. But he was already out of time. Mary was gone, and Edward soon would be off to boarding school. Inevitably, once back in Chicago, Lasker would be drawn back into his business affairs and other pursuits. The Lasker family's interlude of togetherness—brief and interrupted as it was—was coming to an end, and there would not be another.

Chapter Fifteen

A Defeat and Two Victories

*T*HE NOVEMBER 1922 elections proved a disaster for the Republicans, cutting their House majority from 90 to 20 and their Senate majority from 24 to 10. In some cases, Republicans who had left Washington as Shipping Board allies came back as opponents, causing more headaches for Lasker and Harding.[1]

As a result of the election fiasco, the proponents of the Merchant Marine bill faced a new challenge: a lame-duck legislature. Sometimes presidents used the lame-duck session to push through unpopular bills, which could be supported by defeated legislators who had nothing to lose. This was the tactic adopted by Harding when—in November 1922—he convened a special session of Congress. Using all the levers at his disposal, including promises of plum appointments to at least ten members of Congress who had lost their seats, he persuaded the House to pass a much-modified version of the bill by a narrow 24-vote margin.

But the Senate was not so easily manipulated. The battle was joined on December 11, when senator Wesley Jones moved to have the bill introduced for consideration. Four days later, Wisconsin senator Robert La Follette rose to warn his colleagues that passage of the Merchant Marine bill by a lame-duck legislature would run directly counter to the will of the American people as expressed in the recent election. "At least seventy of the votes cast for this bill in the House," La Follette declaimed, "were cast by members who were defeated in the primaries and the elections."

La Follette was especially hard on Albert Lasker, whom he accused of trying to "buy American labor" with special inducements offered in secret meetings eight months earlier.[2] He strongly implied that American shipowners were not losing money, as the Shipping Board had claimed; they were actually making money, and hoped to use the Merchant Marine bill to gouge the public even more deeply. La Follette also used Lasker's own successes at the Shipping Board against him. If within the past eighteen months the Board's monthly deficit had been reduced from $16 million to $4 million, La Follette asked, why should Americans be asked to subsidize private shippers for the indefinite future?[3]

Lasker had less and less use for politicians and their posturings. "Washington makes cowards of most," the frustrated Shipping Board chairman wrote to a friend in December, with the fate of the Merchant Marine bill hanging in the balance.[4] As if to validate Lasker's scornful judgment, the Senate suspended debate on the controversial bill just before the Christmas recess.

Early in 1923, the Harding administration mounted a final push to force the stalled bill through the Senate. But by this point, Senate Democrats were determined to filibuster the bill to death. As the clock wound down on the lame-duck Congress, it became clear that the Merchant Marine bill would not even be brought to a vote in the Senate. Lasker's friends, including W. G. Irwin up in Indianapolis, began wiring their condolences:

I regret that newspaper reports seem to indicate that it will be impossible for the Shipping Bill to pass. I trust that their prediction will not turn out that way. I know it will be a great disappointment to you and to the President. I believe that you have taken the right view of the situation and that there is no better way by which we can get out of the present shipping situation and at the same time, have a possibility of a merchant marine. There is no question but that you have made a wonderful record in the handling of the Shipping Board . . . I am hoping that there is a Cabinet position awaiting you.[5]

The Harding administration formally abandoned the cause on February 28. Lasker was calm in defeat, in part because he saw a way to accomplish his and Harding's goals *without* the dead legislation. He believed that because Congress had defeated a bill that was designed to get the government *out* of the shipping business, the only alternative was to push the government more deeply *into* the shipping business—but along more profitable lines. "Nobody hates government ownership and operation more than I do," he told the *Journal of Commerce*. But now the federal government had to "go more forcibly than it ever has into direct operation."[6]

No doubt the subject of ships and shipping—and the behavior of certain senators—arose frequently during the monthlong vacation that the Hardings and Lasker took together in the wake of the bill's death. On March 5, Lasker left for Florida to join the Hardings on a meandering cruise aboard an eight-person houseboat, while Flora was enjoying rest and recuperation with daughter Mary in Hot Springs, Virginia. She then joined her husband and the presidential party for their final week on the houseboat.

The early months of 1923 presented a range of challenges to Albert Lasker: many related to his chairmanship of the Shipping Board, but others growing out of his complex business affairs. Lasker had resolved to put his business on hold during his Washington service, and for the most part, he honored that resolution. But an episode of client skullduggery made business impossible to ignore completely.

In 1922, Lord & Thomas client Sun-Maid got into financial trouble, and approached Lasker for help. He personally loaned the company $250,000, and—from his temporary perch in the nation's capital—ordered Lord & Thomas in Chicago to kick in an equal amount. Both loans were secured by the raisin crop.

Meanwhile, Lord & Thomas's Los Angeles office—unaware of the half-million dollar loan—agreed to step up Sun-Maid's advertising dramatically, which involved extending more and more credit to Sun-Maid. Before the end of the year, Sun-Maid owed the agency an additional million dollars, and found itself unable both to service its loans and pay for its ads. Having no other choice, Lasker hammered out a new loan repayment schedule with Sun-Maid.

But sometime in late December 1922, talking shop with his banking friends in San Francisco, Lasker made an astounding discovery: the California Associated Raisin Company (CARC), the organization behind the Sun-Maid brand, had pledged its crop as collateral twice—his collateral—once to Lasker, and again to a consortium of California banks. Lasker could no longer remain above the fray.

In fact, as evidenced by a white-hot letter to his associates in Lord & Thomas's Los Angeles office, he could barely contain himself:

Their action simply constitutes a betrayal of the great confidence I imposed in them. Even the hardest Wall Streeter would not do a thing like that to a friend. In their desperation to raise money and keep their enterprise going, they were willing to see me—their trusting friend—possibly stripped of all opportunity to get anything back on the money I had loaned or credited them with . . .

*This is a blow to you boys, but not nearly so much a one as to me; it has lit-
erally made me ill. It is not the possible loss of the money and the prestige to the
business, but the misplaced confidence, that upsets me . . . My confidence was
misplaced in believing they were big men when they were not, for, had they
been big men, they would have realized that for them to take my money in the
way I gave it to them, and then pledge their assets to the bank, was doing an
unthinkable thing.*[7]

Lasker dispatched Elmer Schlesinger—his personal lawyer, and also general counsel to the Shipping Board—to California to negotiate terms with
both the Fresno-based banks and the raisin growers. Schlesinger (whom
Robert Crane in the Los Angeles office described as "the coldest-blooded
man I ever met") played hardball, threatening Sun-Maid with antitrust suits
and other legal actions.

In short order, Schlesinger had extracted $600,000 in cash and another
$600,000 in notes from Sun-Maid, all but some $59,000 of what Lasker and
Lord & Thomas were owed. (On Lasker's orders, Schlesinger insisted that
the raisin company directors offer their personal guarantees on the money
owed to Lasker and Lord & Thomas.) "Delighted you got the money,"
Lasker wired Schlesinger on February 20.[8] Schlesinger then immediately
negotiated a deal whereby San Francisco-based banker Herbert Fleishhacker
bought the notes for 90 cents on the dollar, and Lord & Thomas was out of
the financial woods.[9]

The agency was also out of a job at Sun-Maid, which—after paying off
Lord & Thomas—went with J. Walter Thompson. And there was a very real
risk that Lord & Thomas would now lose the *rest* of its West Coast accounts,
including the treasured Sunkist. As Don Francisco, head of the Los Angeles
office, later recalled:

*Schlesinger made himself very obnoxious about town, and it looked as though
our whole business here was threatened. For example, the banks selected as
their negotiator an attorney named George Farrand, who was the attorney for
two of the clients we had then: the CFGE and the California Walnut Growers
Association. Schlesinger battled with him for days. They would go together on
the train, and Schlesinger would be personally obnoxious, and make Farrand
very mad. As a result, [Farrand] threatened to see that we lost the walnut
account and the Sunkist account . . .*

I remember I dogged [Farrand] around for weeks at board of directors meet-ings . . . One day at the Sunkist board meeting, he made a talk on the raisin sit-uation, in which he said that he had been called in by the banks to settle a very difficult problem, and that basically, the trouble was that their advertising agents had talked them into extravagant expenditure of money . . . because the advertising was handled on the cost-plus-15-percent [basis], giving the agent every incentive to be selfish, and argue for an overexpenditure. Sun-Maid would have been in good shape were it not for the recommendation of Lord & Thomas—the inference being if Lord & Thomas were bad for raisins, they were bad for oranges and lemons.

So I asked Mr. Teague, the president, for the floor, and without reference to what Farrand had said, explained what had happened at Fresno from our standpoint.[10]

These were deep waters, indeed. C. C. Teague was the newly installed head of the CFGE and, as such, was in a position to change advertising agen-cies as he saw fit. George Farrand was not only one of the ablest corporate attorneys on the West Coast; he was also a director of the powerful Security First National Bank, which was a primary financer of the fruit cooperatives. Security's president, Henry Robinson, was so furious with Lord & Thomas that he threatened to "ruin" the agency on the West Coast.

Part of this fury arose, as Francisco later recalled, because Lord & Thomas had been the first player in the game to spotlight Sun-Maid's finan-cial difficulties, and thereby had provoked a literal run on the bank:

One of the interesting and unfortunate things, from our standpoint, was that no one had the slightest knowledge that there was anything wrong with the raisin industry, until they heard that Lord & Thomas had demanded its money [from] the banks and the association. So that we broke the news not only to the industry, but to the banks, and therefore we were blamed for having demanded our pound of flesh in their hour of need, after professing to be their friends for ten years, and having made lots of money off them.

It was even said that Lasker was trying to get control of their industry, which would be impossible unless he bought all the acreage, and would be highly undesirable anyway . . . It was also said that Lasker would "own you or break you." The facts were that he was overly generous and overly confident in dealing with his raisin friends, and trying to help them out.

Ultimately, despite Farrand's threats, Henry Robinson's fury, and the widespread unhappiness with Lasker's allegedly ruthless practices, Teague did not fire Lord & Thomas. The walnut growers, it is true, *did* change agencies, although Francisco later admitted that Lord & Thomas's own shortcomings, rather than any backstabbing by Farrand, led to that particular termination.[11] And in an interesting reversal, Sun-Maid dropped J. Walter Thompson in 1929 and came back to Lord & Thomas. Although the Sun-Maid account by that point was much reduced—down from $1.5 million in 1921 to $220,000 in 1929—Francisco derived great personal satisfaction from the winning back of this account and the burying of the hatchet that it implied.

Meanwhile, there was one more twist to the tale of Albert Lasker's eventful two years in the nation's capital: the rebirth of the mighty *Leviathan*.

In December 1921, in response to the Shipping Board's request for proposals, the Newport News Shipbuilding and Dry Dock Company submitted a bid of $8.2 million to recondition the *Leviathan*—lowest of the eight bids submitted, and substantially less than the previous estimates of around $12 million.[12] The shipbuilding company also promised to have the ship completed in time for the summer 1923 tourist season.[13]

An angry Representative James A. Gallivan of Boston declared in January 1922 that the nation's private ship operators had the Shipping Board "by the throat," and had prevented the Boston Navy Yard from getting the *Leviathan* contract. Gallivan then proposed the elimination of the Board, which in Gallivan's estimation was still a disaster—despite the efforts of Albert Lasker, who had "posed as the man who is going to shake a magic wand."[14]

The aging lion from Massachusetts, Senator Henry Cabot Lodge, took up the cause in February, proposing an amendment to the Shipping Board's annual appropriation which stipulated that without the direct intervention of the president, no money could be spent rehabilitating government ships until the Navy yards around the nation had a chance to bid on the work. His amendment was defeated, the contract was awarded, and the *Leviathan* left for Newport News under her own steam in April 1922, finally escaping her risky internment on the piers of Hoboken.

The refitting and rehabilitation of the *Leviathan* at the Newport News Shipbuilding and Dry Dock Company was supervised by the indefatigable William F. Gibbs, who gradually transferred his professional loyalties from his employer, IMM, to the Shipping Board, which quietly helped Gibbs and his brother (described by Ralph Sollitt as "those tall cadaverous-looking fellows") go into business for themselves.[15]

Some twenty-nine hundred workmen labored on the ship for fourteen months—expending almost 6 million man-hours—gradually transforming it from an outmoded hulk into a showpiece. Its hull above the waterline, totaling three-and-a-quarter acres of steel plating, was scraped and painted with a rust-proofing red paint, making it (in the words of the *New York Tribune*) the "biggest red thing in the world."[16]

Inside the huge vessel, hundreds of miles of German wiring was ripped out and replaced with heavier-gauge wire—along with nine thousand new switches to direct the current. Twenty-five miles of copper tubing were required to restore the system that provided heat to the staterooms. Workmen installed eleven new elevators, five electric dumbwaiters, and an ice-making system capable of producing 6,720 pounds of ice per day. The largest anchor ever made in the U.S., weighing 33,300 pounds, was mounted on the ship's stern. Because the ghost of the *Titanic* was never far from the minds of sailors and potential passengers, the *Leviathan* was fitted with seventy-two lifeboats capable of carrying nearly thirty-four hundred passengers and eleven hundred crew members—the ship's full complement.

Early on, Gibbs made the key decision to put a single design firm—the New York-based architectural firm of Walker & Gillette—in charge of decorations and fittings for the vessel. The New York designers chose all of the fabrics, carpets, furniture, china, silverware, and artworks for the *Leviathan,* creating a cohesive look and feel throughout. Walker & Gillette performed a monumental task, specifying (for example) twenty thousand square yards of broadloom carpet and three thousand square yards of oriental rugs.

Admiral Benson—Shipping Board Commissioner and lifetime Navy man, and the Board's representative to the refitting process—worried aloud that perhaps the ship had been made *too* luxurious.[17] But most of the select few who viewed the ship as it neared completion in Virginia unreservedly hailed its $8.2 million transformation.

On May 16, 1923, the *Leviathan* steamed back out of Newport News. She moved slowly, partly out of respect for the hazardous Hampton Roads crossing, but also because Gibbs didn't want to stress the ship's new oil-fired power plant while her hull was still encrusted with a thick accumulation of barnacles. Two days later, the ship arrived at the Boston Navy Yard, where she would be dry-docked, scraped of her barnacles, repainted, and put to sea. Her first transatlantic crossing was scheduled to begin, not coincidentally, on July 4.

First, though, there was the matter of the shakedown cruise. Gibbs's original specifications for the *Leviathan's* refitting called for "an extended and thorough sea trial to ascertain that everything in connection with it, including the oil fuel installation, is in an entirely satisfactory condition"—a standard procedure for new or rebuilt ocean liners.[18] Clearly, the trial would have to include a full complement of "guests"—to put real-life stresses on the ship's many systems and its crew—and already, requests to take part in the *Leviathan's* maiden cruise were pouring into the Shipping Board's offices.

Albert Lasker now saw an opportunity to reap a publicity windfall. In mid-May, he sent out personalized engraved invitations to hundreds of opinion makers—publishers, politicians, regulators (including the "Prohibition Commissioner" in the Bureau of Internal Revenue), and prominent business figures—offering them the opportunity to participate in the *Leviathan's* first sea trial, scheduled for the third week of June.[19]

Almost immediately, some of those invitees wrote back asking if they could bring their wives along. The answer, according to Lasker, was *no*:

> *We have wanted, in connection with the trial trip, to use that opportunity to acquaint a large number of people with the vessel, to the end that they might, in such good and proper ways as they could, aid in fostering good will toward the ship, and thus help in the development of an American merchant marine. With this in mind, the invitations which have been issued by the Shipping Board have been confined to men only, and no ladies have been invited.*[20]

Starting in the first week of June, voices began to be heard criticizing the proposed "cruise to nowhere," disparaging it as a "million-dollar joy ride" and a "stag party." Rival shipping companies (as well as Democratic-leaning newspapers) helped fuel the opposition to the proposed trip, but at least some of the critics seemed sincere in their outrage. For example, a young House member from Manhattan named Fiorello H. LaGuardia—the future mayor of New York—had traveled twice on the *Leviathan* as a soldier during the war; now, in a letter to Lasker, he condemned the "joy ride," and suggested that the Shipping Board take as its passengers veterans who had been disabled in combat. Quietly, Lasker turned down the proposal.[21]

Lasker refrained from making public statements in support of the trial run until the Democratic National Committee, chaired by an up-and-coming politico named Cordell Hull, blasted it on June 11. Lasker defended himself and his Board. Every responsible owner of a new passenger ship, he noted, tests that ship before putting it into service. The entire cost of the trial run would be approximately $120,000: a pittance when compared with the government's $8.4 million investment to date. The marginal cost of having four hundred to five hundred passengers on board, without whom the trial run would be largely pointless, was $13,000. Lasker implored the Democrats not to "besmirch" the "great shipping enterprise" upon which the United States was now embarking.[22]

Some guests quailed in the face of the controversy. The influential Senator T. H. Caraway, an Arkansas Democrat, initially accepted the invitation and also extorted from Lasker an invitation for Mrs. Caraway—a rare exception to Lasker's men-only policy. "I want her to go," he wrote to Lasker in no uncertain terms. Lasker capitulated. Then the tempest arose, and Caraway sent back his invitations and publicly condemned the trip. "Permit me, my dear Senator," Lasker responded in a frosty note, "to express my further special regret that we could not have both you and Mrs. Caraway with us, as requested in your letter of acceptance of May 21st."[23]

Anxious Republicans approached President Harding directly, begging him to cancel the trip and thereby take the issue away from the Democrats. Harding declined. Rumors began to circulate about a court order to enjoin the trial run. Lasker continued to dismiss his critics, convinced that he was in the right. "I would have been criminal," he wrote to a friend, "if we had not had [the *Leviathan*'s trial run] in just the way we are having it."[24] But there were definitely anxious moments at the Shipping Board. "We had a hard time getting the boat all filled," Ralph Sollitt confessed.[25]

On June 18 and 19, 1923, a steady stream of distinguished-looking people made their way to Boston's Commonwealth Pier. There, a small excursion boat waited to shuttle them to the *Leviathan*, lying at anchor off Boston Light. The 450 or so arriving guests included business leaders like RCA's vice president and general manager David Sarnoff, sportswriter Ring Lardner, cartoonist Rube Goldberg, and W. G. Irwin. Mostly missing from the passenger complement were women, although the White House (and in particular, Florence Harding) had prevailed upon Lasker to allow a small number of spouses on board.

Also missing was Lasker himself. Although he had formally stepped down from the Board a week earlier, his fellow commissioners had named him "special representative to have charge of the *Leviathan*," both on its trial run and its initial transatlantic run.[26] So where was the special representative, who had done so much to make this event possible? Word circulated around the ship that a last-minute emergency had prevented Lasker from joining the cruise.

In fact, writes *Leviathan* historian Frank Braynard, Lasker was hiding aboard ship:

> *Relaxing in one of the former Kaiser's suites, and determined to stay out of sight until the ship passed beyond the three-mile limit, was a cheerful Albert Lasker. He had come aboard on the starboard side opposite from where the excursion boat had unloaded her guests, was admitted through a port quietly opened, and hurried incognito to his suite without anyone noticing his arrival. All of this because he was fearful right up to the final moment that someone would serve him with an injunction ordering him to halt the trial trip.*[27]

According to Ralph Sollitt, *all* of the Shipping Board commissioners aboard, including Lasker, were under lock and key. Sollitt was free to circulate because he wasn't a member of the Board and therefore couldn't be served with an injunction. "And then when the boat started," Sollitt remembered wryly, "we released all of our Shipping Board."[28]

June 19 was a notably hot day in Boston Harbor, and passengers and crew alike were relieved when the great ship got under way promptly at 2:00 p.m. For the first day of the southbound journey, Captain Herbert Hartley held the *Leviathan* to 19 knots, but after a dense fog lifted, he pushed her up to 22 knots.[29]

The trip was intended to be uneventful, and for the most part it was; as a result, the hundred-or-so reporters on board had little to write about. Nevertheless, they documented Captain Hartley's every utterance—as, for example, when he reported that a black cat had slipped aboard in Boston, had been christened "Levi," and was now the ship's mascot. When asked if there were any other stowaways aboard, Hartley replied dryly that he figured that there were "about 500."[30]

The outgoing wireless traffic sent by the reporters was enormous—so much so that the ship's wireless operators soon fell hopelessly behind. Technical problems also arose. RCA's David Sarnoff explained the problem—and his own role in solving it:

> The ship got down into southern waters off the Florida coast on her trip south, and static was very bad, communication therefore slowed up, and the power of the ordinary ship-to-shore stations was not sufficient to be heard easily . . .
>
> I went into the wireless room and saw the operators piled up with press stuff, and the newspapermen clamoring for immediate dispatch with their messages. So I took one of the keys of the transmission and instructed our high-power station at Chatham, Massachusetts—which was normally intended for trans-oceanic operation, and therefore had more power—to establish a circuit with the Leviathan so we could dispatch. They did so, of course, and then I sat down to help the operators get clear of the traffic. Well, there was so much of it I found myself sitting there all night clearing the traffic.[31]

The spectacle of a high-powered guest in a dinner jacket working the wireless key all night generated still more traffic. Sarnoff (who referred to himself and his fellow travelers as the "Unworthy Six Hundred") found this hugely ironic and entertaining. He later pointed out that RCA and the government had split the proceeds from these radio transmissions fifty-fifty. "My impression [is that] the amount accruing to that ship was something like $30,000," he recalled, "which I think paid the whole expense of the ship. I think that the press, which was kicking violently about the trip, paid for it."[32]

Occasionally, Captain Hartley gave the reporters something meatier to report. On the 687-nautical-mile northbound run between Jupiter Light, Florida, and Cape Henry on the southern edge of Chesapeake Bay, despite challenging seas, the Leviathan set a new world record for sustained speed: 27.94 knots per hour. Gibbs told reporters that his ship could generate substantially more than the 85,000 horsepower that she used to break the record. No, he said in response to a question; the Leviathan would not go after the transatlantic speed record when it went into regular service. "Unless the others start some fancy business," he added pointedly. "Then we will use our untouched reserves."[33]

As the *Leviathan* steamed north, the *New York Times* editorialized that although many of the criticisms of the trial run were fair, they were essentially irrelevant. What Albert Lasker had accomplished, the *Times* noted with grudging admiration, was to generate enormous free publicity for his ship, displaying a gift for public relations that put him in a class with Henry Ford and Thomas Edison. Practically the entire nation knew how many millions had been spent making the *Leviathan* one of the most luxurious ships afloat and was well aware that, starting July 4, the great liner would begin offering regular service to and from Europe. "That travelers will be attracted from other lines by this is hardly questionable," the *Times* concluded, "and, as that is what Mr. Lasker wants to do, he can afford to smile at his critics."[34]

Lasker landed in New York on June 25 and immediately departed for Chicago. Although he was still the Shipping Board's "special representative" for the *Leviathan*'s first scheduled run to Europe on July 4, his public service was rapidly drawing to a close.

"It is now rumored," reported *Time* in May 1923, "that when Albert D. Lasker retires from the Chairmanship of the United States Shipping Board, as he plans to do in the next few weeks, he will go into the newspaper business." Supposedly, Lasker planned to buy several papers and set himself up as a "Munsey, Hearst, or Scripps."[35]

These rumors lagged behind reality; Lasker *had* considered going into the newspaper business, but decided against it. He had made another decision, as well—that he was done with Washington. As he wrote to his friend Hiram Johnson: "The lure of public life holds nothing for me; I leave it, delighted that I served the Government, thrilled with my experience, absolutely encouraged in the belief that our dream of an American merchant marine is going to come true, and utterly disgusted with much that I have learned and seen. Now my one thought is to go back and make more money and more money and more money—ain't I an elegant patriot?"[36]

It bears noting that during his two years in Washington, Lasker suffered no known bouts of depression. In fact, he thrived in the political cauldron, gaining new perspectives on his life and summoning up new energy to tackle the continuing challenges of Lord & Thomas. He would later remember the Washington interlude as a happy time for Flora and a miserable time for himself; in fact, the opposite was closer to the truth. By rendering a legitimate service to his president, he escaped from the burden of responsibility imposed by his father and uncle. Because he had served his country, he could afford to joke about being an inelegant patriot.

Looking forward, he was free to do what he wanted, which for the moment meant making money. And when he looked backward, he could do so with humor and relief. "I'm afraid two things will keep me from ever going down into history in any favorable way," he wrote to Walter Teagle in April 1923, "but rather will put me into the dub class, to wit—my golf and my chairmanship of the Shipping Board. I guess I am awful at both."[37]

Against long odds, Albert Lasker escaped from his Shipping Board service with his reputation not only unscathed, but enhanced.

By the spring of 1923, it was clear that Warren G. Harding intended to run for a second term. Lasker pledged to support him if Harding would support Hiram Johnson—California's iconoclastic "bloc of one" senator—in 1928. Harding extracted a major favor in return.

Lasker left for Europe on July 4, 1923, on the *Leviathan*'s first transatlantic crossing since her refitting. He was engaged (he later told his office staff) on a "secret mission" for Harding that had nothing to do with shipping.[38] Lasker's son Edward later revealed that Harding had asked Lasker to persuade Hiram Johnson—then vacationing in Europe, and Harding's only likely opponent in the upcoming primary season—to stay out of the race for the Republican nomination.[39]

On June 20, 1923, Harding left on a fifteen-thousand-mile, two-month "Voyage of Understanding," which was part vacation and part barnstorming. As Harding's train slowly crossed the country, it stopped repeatedly as Harding gave speeches and photo ops—an eerie recreation of the grueling and ill-fated tour that Woodrow Wilson had undertaken three years earlier in support of his doomed League of Nations.

The Harding party boarded a ship in Spokane and sailed northward on a thousand-mile route to Alaska. Just before departing the continental United States, Harding once again clarified his position on the government's role in commercial shipping. "I do not for one moment believe in government ownership and operation as a permanent policy," he told reporters. "But I prefer that hazardous venture to the surrender of our hopes for a merchant marine."[40]

Upon returning to the continental United States, Harding resumed his strenuous schedule of campaigning and speechmaking. While addressing a crowd of sixty thousand in Seattle, he suffered a major heart attack. After being rushed to San Francisco for medical attention and a recuperative stay at the Palace Hotel, Harding died of an apparent cerebral hemorrhage on August 2. The four doctors attending him failed to agree on the exact cause of death, thereby spawning a raft of conspiracy theories centered on murder and suicide. Albert Lasker's son Edward, for one, was skeptical:

> The day before his death, Harding's wife Florence called mother in Glencoe and said that her husband had not heard from father about [Hiram] Johnson's answer. Mother replied that Pop was due back in New York the next day on another American vessel, the George Washington, and she was sure that the first thing he would do would be to phone the President. After Harding's death, there were all kinds of stories that he had killed himself. I have always believed it unthinkable that anyone worrying about his imminent campaign for reelection would commit suicide.[41]

Harding's death created both a political vacuum and some very personal complications for Lasker. Although the newly elevated president, Calvin Coolidge, was Harding's obvious heir apparent in the 1924 presidential sweepstakes, Lasker had little interest in Coolidge, and got involved publicly in Hiram Johnson's short-lived presidential campaign in late 1923. Less publicly, he contributed $5,000 toward a $50,000 fund that was being collected to provide for Harding's mistress, Nan Britton, and Elizabeth Ann, her daughter by Harding.[42]

The coda to Lasker's tenure in Washington: a version of his Merchant Marine bill ultimately passed under President Franklin D. Roosevelt as the Merchant Marine Act of 1936. "It shows how long it takes to educate and agitate Congress on a new idea," Lasker observed two years after the Act's passage. He also noted the irony of a protective tariff originally supported by conservative Republicans finally becoming law during Roosevelt's New Deal.[43]

Almost exactly two years after he promised Warren Harding two years of service, Albert Lasker packed his bags to return to Chicago. There, following more than a decade of substantial disengagement from his business, he intended to pick up the reins again at Lord & Thomas. He explained his thinking to Claude Hopkins in May: "I am delighted beyond all measure that I determined not to go into newspaper work or anything else, but to return home to our firm and our association. The decision took a long time at arriving at. I weighed everything that could be weighed, but I am sure now that my decision was right and will be permanent."[44]

Two days later, he wrote to his brother Edward in a similar vein, although with notably less emphasis on "permanence":

I am of course a little sad at leaving my very interesting work here, hectic though it has been, but I look forward with calm to going back to Chicago, where, for the first time since I have been a boy, I will have no entanglements on my mind, and a comparatively easy job to keep Lord & Thomas in hand. You must remember that heretofore I either was working frantically to build up Lord & Thomas, or I was involved with several other big businesses, or I got mixed up into charitable affairs or political matters; so that altogether I was constantly being driven by a thousand devils. Now I will be disassociated from everything but Lord & Thomas, and I won't have to work frantically to build it up, because it is already built. I mean for a year or two to keep myself free from any other entanglement, no matter how interesting it may appear.[45]

Even though Lasker was returning to a "comparatively easy job," he wasn't returning home alone. He had invited his right hand and alter ego, Ralph Sollitt, to return with him, offering him a post in the senior ranks of Lord & Thomas.

"You have to go home with me," Lasker announced one day to Sollitt.

"What do I know about advertising?" Sollitt asked.

"What does either of us know about shipping?," Lasker replied. "Let's go home."[46]

Chapter Sixteen

Selling the Unmentionable, and More

$\boldsymbol{\mathcal{D}}$ **URING ALBERT** Lasker's two-year tenure at the Shipping Board, Claude C. Hopkins had taken the reins at Lord & Thomas. This added new complexities to their relationship.

Lasker appreciated the flexibility that Hopkins's willingness to lead the firm gave him. "I can only afford to keep on here," he wrote to Hopkins from Washington in May 1922, "because I know that you and Mr. [Herbert] Cohn and others on the job back there are making it possible for me to live."[1] And yet, Lasker returned to Lord & Thomas in September 1923 convinced that his agency urgently needed shaking up—even a rebirth. This sense of urgency came from dramatic changes in both the economy and his industry. A new economic wave was cresting, even bigger than the one that had propelled Lasker and Lord & Thomas to success in the first decade of the new century, and Lasker intended to catch it.

The "Roaring Twenties" ushered in a new era in consumerism. Older companies that had been created to serve mainly business customers—companies like General Electric and Westinghouse—now moved aggressively into the consumer market.[2] The automobile companies founded in the first decade of the new century had gone through wrenching consolidations, and the survivors were now determined to find new customers. These older giants also were joined by a host of new companies in industries that aimed directly at consumers: pharmaceuticals, motion pictures, travel, special-interest publications, and many others. For all of these businesses, it was critical to reach consumers through national magazines and newspapers—and advertising agencies made that all-important connection.

Public policy, too, helped fuel a boom in advertising. During World War I, the Committee on Public Information—an arm of Woodrow Wilson's federal government—had undertaken what journalist George Creel had described as "the world's greatest adventure in advertising" to promote public support for the war. In the immediate aftermath of the war, manufacturers responded to the threat of an excess-profits tax by pouring money into their ad budgets, resulting in a *doubling* of advertising dollars between 1918 and 1920 (from $1.5 billion to nearly $3 billion).[3] In that two-year period, N. W. Ayer's billings increased from $6.5 million to $13.8 million, and Lord & Thomas's increased from $5.7 million to $11.3 million.[4]

———

For the first time in a decade, though, Lord & Thomas was no longer setting the pace for its industry. In each of the first four years after Lasker took control of his agency in 1912, he had beaten out Ayer in terms of billings, establishing his agency as the nation's largest. Beginning in 1916, however, Ayer reclaimed its former top-ranking status, and it continued to top Lord & Thomas until 1923—the year Lasker returned.

Lord & Thomas couldn't claim the top position in 1923. Instead, that distinction went to the New York-based firm of J. Walter Thompson, now led by the dynamic husband-and-wife team of Stanley and Helen Resor. Stanley Resor had bought out founder Thompson in 1916, and—with an eye toward increasing profitability by concentrating on national firms—jettisoned more than two-thirds of the agency's three hundred accounts. A Yale graduate (and the first major agency head with a college degree), Resor was fascinated by psychology and the behavior of populations. Resor loved data, and—in 1922—acted on that passion by hiring marketing professor Paul Cherington away from the Harvard Business School to serve as JWT's director of research. He also recruited John B. Watson, a behavioralist recently fired by Johns Hopkins University for engaging in an affair with one of his graduate students, to serve as Madison Avenue's first resident psychologist.[5]

In only a few years under the Resors, Thompson swept past the competition. The revitalized agency offered an innovative style of copy and other services that most established agencies, including Lord & Thomas, couldn't match. Helen Resor—an accomplished copywriter well before her marriage to Stanley in 1917—wrote an ad for Woodbury's soap ("A skin you love to touch") that Lasker considered one of the landmarks in advertising history, mainly because it opened the door to using sex as part of the sell.

New competitors were on the horizon. One of them, BDO, opened its doors in 1919. It was founded by three young veterans of the World War I propaganda machine: Bruce Barton, Roy Durstine, and Alex Osborn. All graduates of prestigious colleges, and nearly a generation younger than Albert Lasker, the three principals at BDO took for granted some of his innovations—such as "reason-why" advertising—and moved beyond them. Focusing less on the manufacturer's perspective and more on the psychology of the consumer, they met with almost immediate success. Thanks to the prodigious personal connections of Barton, Durstine, and Osborn, BDO had thirty-three corporate accounts the day it went into business, and quickly added more. General Motors and the National Biscuit Company came into the fold in 1922, Macy's and General Electric in 1923, and Union Carbide in 1924. In only a few short years, BDO had surged to fourth on the list of biggest agencies.[6]

The rise of powerhouses and dynamic upstarts in New York must have worried Lasker. The small office that he had put together there in 1910 was foundering. As the industry became increasingly concentrated in New York, Lasker's agency was at risk of becoming marginalized. It had a healthy office in Los Angeles (opened in 1916), a San Francisco office (that had opened in 1919, closed briefly for underperformance, and reopened in 1922), and a small London operation (also opened in 1922). But New York remained problematic.

Lasker acknowledged that Lord & Thomas had lost ground during his absence, although he preferred to put it the other way around: other agencies had caught up. "I was out five years in public service," he told his staff members in 1925, "and during that period . . . advertising began to be so widely understood that we no longer stood out."[7] Lasker claimed that he held the company back from soliciting new accounts during his absence, fearing that Lord & Thomas might spin out of his control: "In all the years I was gone, we were not anxious for new business. I knew I had a machine that could give good service to those I had and that would hold them, but I was afraid of the machine if it took on new business . . . so we were not aggressive."[8]

But by 1923, Lasker had decided it was time to change the formula, especially in terms of shoring up the agency's Chicago base. If this meant starving (or even closing) the New York office, he told Hopkins, then so be it. Reinforcing Chicago's operations would be "profit and glory enough," he wrote to Chicago officer manager Herbert P. Cohn. At the same time, he intended to strengthen his agency's hand at selling, especially to larger national accounts.[9] Within months of returning to Lord & Thomas, he secured two enormously important clients, with whom—over the course of the next decade—he would dramatically change the consumer habits of America.

———————◆———————

It is not clear exactly when Lasker decided that Claude Hopkins had to go. The correspondence between the two men in the early 1920s was mutually respectful, and even warm. But one tiff that erupted in June 1923, just before Lasker left the Shipping Board, suggests that Lasker had to handle the sensitive Hopkins with care.

Hopkins evidently took to heart some passing comments by Lasker to the effect that Hopkins was not one to do "unselfish favors" and didn't place much stock in cultivating friends. In what must have been a blistering letter, Hopkins objected furiously to Lasker's comments. After waiting a few days for passions to cool, Lasker responded in a warmly emotional tone:

> I never in the world could have meant that you did not cultivate friends and that you never do unselfish favors, speaking in the larger sense of intimate friends in a close circle, because no such thought could find lodgment in my mind or in my heart. No one could have ever been the recipient of a finer friendship than I have always had from you, but jealously I aver that I have always reciprocated that friendship in the fullest.[10]

At Lasker's urging, Hopkins in 1922 began work on a manuscript called *Scientific Advertising.* The book, published a year later, is a classic on the fundamentals of the industry in its founding era. Was *Scientific Advertising* an effort to lend even more luster to Hopkins's name and burnish Lord & Thomas's reputation by extension? Or was it, perhaps, Lasker's way to begin easing Hopkins out the door?[11]

By the fall of 1923, with Lasker barely reinstalled in Chicago, he and Hopkins began differing fundamentally on how to recruit clients. Caught up in his entrepreneurial visions, Hopkins wanted to buy companies and mount advertising campaigns for them. But Lasker, who knew the discomforts of doing business with companies in which he was also a major shareholder, opposed this approach. Ultimately, they failed to resolve these differences, and in the spring of 1924, Hopkins left to start his own copywriting service. The two were now competitors, and Lasker took Hopkins's moves as a personal betrayal. He fought Hopkins over the rights to *Scientific Advertising*, and told Hopkins that writing the book was the mistake of his lifetime.[12]

Hopkins's agency was not a resounding success, and it didn't take him long to change his strategy. Although this reversal helped bring about a rapprochement with Lasker, the two never worked together again. Hopkins published the highly readable *My Life in Advertising* in 1927—annoying Lasker once again, who felt that the book underplayed his role in Hopkins's success—and died five years later.

One of the first major clients to come into the Lord & Thomas fold after Lasker's return was the International Cellucotton Products Company, makers of a new women's sanitary product called "Kotex." The product presented major challenges to Lasker and his agency.

Cellucotton was first produced in 1915 by the paper products company Kimberly-Clark, and was a result of the diversification of the pulp and paper industry in the early 'teens. Originally, the company hoped to market the wood-based product as a substitute for cotton surgical dressings, but demand for the substitute cotton remained weak until the American entry into World War I in 1918. Kimberly-Clark—on the defensive because of its founders' German roots—announced that it would provide cellucotton to the War Department and the Red Cross at cost.

But even as cellucotton began to be used to dress wounds, enterprising Army nurses found another use for the product: as the raw material for a homemade sanitary napkin. When the signing of the Armistice led the Army to cancel a 375-ton order for cellucotton, Kimberly-Clark scrambled to find new markets for the product.[13]

The strongest advocate at Kimberly-Clark for the use of cellucotton as a sanitary napkin was a Chicago-based salesman named Walter Luecke. Luecke convinced Kimberly-Clark to start manufacturing sanitary napkins in 1919, and in September of that year, soon after the name "Kotex" was coined, an initial shipment was sent to Woolworth & Company. A full month passed before the first box sold—not surprising, given that the product was unknown, unadvertised, and wasn't even described on its packaging. (The boxes carried only the Kotex name and the Kimberly-Clark logo.) Luecke and his six assistants began visiting retail shops in New York City in October, pushing Kotex hard—but ran up against the enormous challenge of promoting a new product that, for all practical purposes, couldn't be talked about.

This effort was followed in 1920 by a more prolonged campaign, again aimed at retailers rather than consumers. Luecke worked with Kimberly-Clark chemist Ernst Mahler to place ads containing a history of the product and basic technical information in a series of specialized trade journals and magazines. Once again, the response was disappointing. In the same year, Kimberly-Clark established International Cellucotton Products Company (ICPC), a wholly owned subsidiary, in part to distance the parent company from its unmentionable product.

Finally, in 1921, ICPC began advertising Kotex directly to consumers. The first text, written by Nichols Advertising, shied away from describing the actual purpose of the product, citing instead its wartime origins and talking obliquely about a "new use" for the product discovered by nurses. By late November 1921, the ads finally contained the words "sanitary napkins," and throughout the following year, the Nichols agency continued to experiment with different marketing approaches.

ICPC was paying heavily for all of these different marketing attempts—$173,000 in 1921, and a projected $200,000 in 1922—but still, the ads failed to produce results.[14] It was time to look for a new agency.

According to the Lord & Thomas account history, ICPC hired Lasker's agency "because we created a new style of copy, franker, inspiring greater confidence through trained nurses' recommendations."[15] This summary was true enough, but it was by no means the whole story. Lasker acknowledged that the copy that had been generated by Nichols was quite good—even outstanding. A new Lord & Thomas campaign written by Frank Hummert (hired into the New York office in 1920 at a princely $50,000 a year) was better still.[16] But a huge barrier had to be overcome before even the most effective copy could do its job: mainstream magazines had to be persuaded to carry the "franker" advertisements. Edward Bok—publisher of the *Ladies Home Journal* and other leading magazines—had banned the ads from his family of publications.

Bok was then considered the nation's leading authority on women's manners and morals; most advertising executives, upon hearing that his decision not to run an ad was final, would have given up. Not Albert Lasker; instead, he hopped on the Broadway Limited with Hummert's ads in hand and went straight to Philadelphia to meet with Bok. He later recalled the arguments that he made to the publisher:

> *I don't agree with your reservations about the Kotex advertising, Mr. Bok, but I respect them, of course. I know they're based on your vast knowledge of what American women are thinking and what appeals to them. Because of that, I'd like to ask you if you'll let me put that knowledge to the test, right here in your office. Would you be willing to call in your secretary and have her read this first Kotex advertisement that we'd like to place in the* Journal? *If she's embarrassed or repelled by it, I'll accept your judgment. There'll be no further argument.*[17]

Bok summoned his secretary. The door opened to admit a "dignified, white-haired lady, seemingly around sixty"—the very personification of propriety—and Lasker's heart sank. Bok explained the situation and handed her the copy, which she quietly began to read. About halfway through Hopkins's text, the woman looked up. "Why, Mr. Bok, this is a wonderful thing," she exclaimed. "I certainly think we should run this in the *Journal*. Women deserve to be told about it."

In those few short minutes, the biggest obstacle to the distribution of a product vitally important to millions of women vanished.[18]

<hr>

A second formidable hurdle arose: women were reluctant to ask for Kotex at their local druggist. The solution turned out to be the "wrapped box" approach, which (again citing the account history) both reflected and protected the "typical 1923 modesty of women."

At that time, most retail stores still used a full-service model, in which customers would ask clerks for specific items. But asking a male clerk for a sanitary napkin proved too embarrassing for many women. Talking to his staff several years later, Lasker recounted how Lord & Thomas had identified and solved this seemingly intractable problem. "Now, we didn't have to make investigations among millions of women," Lasker said. "Just a few of us talked to our wives and asked them if they used Kotex, and we found out they didn't, and in almost every case it was because they didn't like to ask the druggist for it." The solution, Lasker continued, proved to be relatively simple: "We developed for Kotex the simple idea of putting wrapped packages on the dealer's counter and of advertising in dailies as well as in magazines—diverting part of the appropriation from the perfectly wonderful magazine copy they had been using before and simply saying something in dailies about Kotex and that you could walk into your dealer and walk away with a wrapped package without embarrassment."[19]

In fact, the self-service concept for Kotex had been pioneered several years earlier by a Wisconsin druggist, who had discovered that women would buy more Kotex if the boxes were "wrapped in plain white paper and tied with blue string and then piled on the counter in a pyramid surmounted by a small neat card reading, 'Kotex—Take a Box—65 cents.'"[20] The enterprising Wisconsin druggist had been uncovered by a Nichols Agency copywriter during his travels, and the innovation was promptly reported to ICPC. In 1922, a full year before Lord & Thomas was retained, the wrapped-box model was implemented widely among retailers carrying Kotex.

Lasker's assertion that Lord & Thomas invented the self-service idea is, therefore, fiction. Nevertheless, retail sales didn't jump until 1923, when Lord & Thomas began *advertising* the unorthodox distribution scheme in daily newspapers as well as magazines, so Lasker can claim some of the credit for the wrapped-box approach—and much of the credit for Kotex's subsequent success.

The Kotex ad budget increased from $400,000 in 1923 to more than $1 million in 1925. Soon, "Kotex" was in the enviable position of being synonymous with "sanitary napkin," and although the formidable Johnson & Johnson entered the sanitary napkin market in 1926, ICPC continued to control something like 70 percent of the market through the late 1920s.

Hard on Kotex's heels was another cellucotton product destined to make history. Its origins can also be traced back to World War I, when researchers at Kimberly-Clark began working on an ultrathin form of cellucotton to line gas masks. It never made its way into production gas masks, but in 1923, one of chemist Ernst Mahler's assistants suggested using the material as a makeup remover. Lasker and sales agent Luecke met to brainstorm, and came up with the name "Kleenex."[21]

At first, the advertising strategies for the new product were closely related to that of its sister product, Kotex, but Kleenex soon developed a distinct identity. This was a necessity more than a plan: the amazing success of Kotex conferred almost no "halo effect" on its sister offering. Initial sales of Kleenex fell well below the company's expectations. Lasker's unscientific market research suggested that the tissue's 5-by-6-inch size was hurting the product: "I personally asked half a dozen women who I knew spent a lot of money on cosmetics to use the Kleenex, and these half dozen all said, 'It may be all right, but I can't use it, it is too small; it ought to be the size that is now being put out in paper by Elizabeth Arden and the Dennison Company' . . . So I went to the Cellucotton people and told them, and they changed the size to 9 x 10."[22]

Sales started to grow. In 1930, Lasker and Luecke recommended to ICPC that they make a survey to discover how people were using Kleenex, and the results were surprising. Many more people, it turned out, were using the tissue to wipe noses than to remove makeup. This presented a potential boon to ICPC: the market for the product might well *triple* if it weren't purely a makeup-related purchase. Quickly, the product's name was changed to "Kleenex Disposable Handkerchiefs."

By 1931, Kleenex and Kotex—products that were effectively unknown a decade earlier—were generating nearly half of Kimberly-Clark's profits. At the same time, the habits of American consumers, and especially female consumers, changed dramatically. Thanks to the combined efforts of inventive manufacturers and creative marketers, people's lives—and especially women's lives—became easier, healthier, and happier. Kimberly-Clark's grateful management invited Lasker to become a stockholder in the private company, and he happily accepted the offer.

The year 1923 also witnessed the arrival of another influential client on Lord & Thomas's doorstep: the American Tobacco Company.

American Tobacco was a dominant remnant of the American Tobacco Company owned by James Buchanan Duke, which had enjoyed a near monopoly on tobacco production at the turn of the century. In 1911, at about the same time that Standard Oil was broken up, a Supreme Court decision ruled against the tobacco conglomerate—which then held a 92 percent market share—and broke it up into a number of smaller pieces, including R.J. Reynolds, American Tobacco Company, Liggett & Myers Tobacco Company, and Lorillard. American Tobacco emerged from the breakup with a distinct advantage over its sister companies, with 37 percent of the market, compared with 28 percent for Liggett & Myers and only 15 percent for Lorillard.

R.J. Reynolds retained 20 percent of the then-thriving plug tobacco trade. But it lacked a cigarette line, which it immediately began developing. After a six-month advertising campaign called "The Camels Are Coming"—aimed at building momentum for the new brand—Reynolds introduced Camels: a blend of piedmont bright tobacco, flavored Kentucky burley, and Turkish leaf. The blend proved an immediate hit, capturing a third of the market by 1917.[23] Camels were soon followed by another Turkish blend, Chesterfields, produced by Liggett & Myers.

American Tobacco, headed since 1911 by a mild-mannered Harvard graduate named Percival Hill, remained oddly passive in the new blended cigarette department, concentrating instead on marketing the fifty-odd brands that the company already owned. In 1916, the company finally introduced Lucky Strike, a name previously used by a popular American Tobacco brand of pipe tobacco. The famous Lucky Strike motto, "It's toasted!" appeared on the first package, as the company tried to differentiate Luckies from the other (also toasted) blends. Over the next year, Lucky Strike helped American Tobacco make up some lost ground, but by the time the United States entered World War I, R.J. Reynolds still enjoyed greater market share than either American Tobacco or Liggett & Myers. This proved especially important when the U.S. government used prewar market-share figures to allocate its cigarette purchases for the armed forces fighting in World War I.

The wartime experience (and especially the generous cigarette ration provided to each soldier) turned out to be a boon to all tobacco companies, dramatically increasing consumption among those who served, and—after the doughboys' return—among the entire wartime generation. All cigarette companies benefited, but the market leaders benefited most. In 1922, R.J. Reynolds captured the lead in the industry from American Tobacco for the first time; by 1923, the Camel brand dominated the market with a 45 percent share. A relative newcomer, Philip Morris & Co., incorporated in 1919, also began to capture market share with its popular Marlboro brand.

By 1923, American Tobacco's leaders were anxious. R.J. Reynolds had been pouring money into advertising (notably the 1921 campaign which introduced the slogan, "I'd walk a mile for a Camel").[24] More and more aggressive players were coming on the scene. Meanwhile, American Tobacco's advertising budget was stretched across a wide range of products, leaving only a modest amount to promote Lucky Strikes, the company's top seller.

The advertising accounts were dispersed as well: different brands were handled by different agencies. One of these brands, Blue Boar smoking tobacco, had come to Lord & Thomas by way of Lou Hartman, a Lord & Thomas employee who had previously run his own agency and brought the account with him when he joined Lord & Thomas. Hartman came up with a clever scheme for Blue Boar whereby American Tobacco would reimburse to consumers the price of the government tax on a tin of tobacco. The plan enjoyed immediate success, and American Tobacco head Percival Hill took note. He asked Hartman to arrange a lunch with Lasker, and within weeks, the group was lunching at the Vanderbilt Hotel, along with Percival's son, George Washington Hill, then in charge of advertising for the company.

Percival Hill told Lasker that he was so impressed with the Blue Boar marketing plan that he wanted Lord & Thomas to take over the Lucky Strike account. Lasker—a nonsmoker with little feel for the tobacco trade—hesitated, pondering this unexpected development.[25] He asked Hill with whom Lord & Thomas would be dealing, and Percival told Lasker that his son George would be supervising the account. After further discussion, the group struck a deal. George Washington Hill would come to Chicago for a week and check out Lord & Thomas. If by the end of the week he wanted the agency to take the account, a contract would be signed.

It was a bold stroke on Lasker's part. He may already have sensed the younger Hill's fiery temperament and impulsive nature. He surely was sensitive to the plight of the ambitious son laboring in the shadow of a powerful father. And Lord & Thomas would need George as a strong ally if they were to enjoy long-term success as the company's advertising agents.

The wisdom of Lasker's move became even more evident in 1925, when Percival Hill died, and George Washington Hill prepared to take the reins of the entire company.

※※※ ◄(◐)► ※※※

Percival Hill had been a solid, steady, dependable manager, with a good mind for figures and a strong inclination to delegate. His son, however, was a tobacco baron of another stripe.

George Washington Hill's passion for cigarettes—and especially Lucky Strike cigarettes—knew no bounds. Twenty-one years earlier, during his sophomore year at Williams College, he had dropped out of school and gone to work for American Tobacco.[26] His first job involved hauling recently purchased leaf from the company's warehouse in Wilson, North Carolina, at the unimpressive salary of $5 per week. But he worked his way up through the ranks of the company: making cigarettes in Wilson; going on the road as a "drummer," or salesman; and eventually becoming head of advertising. Unlike his father—who had made his own reputation with the wildly successful Bull Durham plug tobacco—George believed that manufactured cigarettes (as opposed to hand-rolled cigarettes, cigars, or chewing tobacco) were the future of the company. Now he had the chance to prove himself right.

In an era of grey fedoras, Hill showed up for work every day wearing a broad-brimmed Stetson—white or black—which he rarely removed during business hours. He was chauffeured everywhere, and his staff always knew when he was holding court at American Tobacco's Fifth Avenue headquarters because his Cadillac limousine, with its stacked cartons of Lucky Strikes visible through the windows, was waiting for him curbside.

Hill was notoriously brusque, short-tempered, and volatile. He might be speaking calmly about some subject when, "without warning, he would explode in a tirade at his stenographer, advertising executive, or anyone else who happened to be there."[27]

Hill stayed closely involved in every facet of Lucky Strikes, especially its advertising—an approach that created major headaches for Albert Lasker, who tried many times to pull back from his own deep involvement in American Tobacco; only once was he successful, and then only temporarily. The rest of the time, Lasker and Hill alternately fought, made up, and wore each other down. In a 1935 letter to Lasker, George Washington Hill acknowledged his own excesses—"I know I have tried your soul"—but immediately reverted to form, reminding Lasker that "times like these" (i.e., the Depression) imposed an increased burden on all those in positions of responsibility.[28] In other words, Lasker should stop complaining and work harder.

Whatever the psychic costs, Hill and Lasker were extremely successful collaborators, mounting campaign after campaign of innovative advertisements. Lasker claimed that he was the creative sparkplug. "Lasker said to me again and again, in the first years," recalled Sheldon Coons, head of Lord & Thomas's New York office in the early 1930s, "that Hill made no contribution to the advertising, that Lasker did it all."[29] But Hill, like Lasker, possessed a native genius for marketing. He embraced the Lord & Thomas mantra of "salesmanship in print," often expounding its fundamentals in his correspondence and conversations with Lasker. He knew and loved his product and had keen insights about how to talk to consumers who could be persuaded to share that passion.[30]

Lord & Thomas's first piece of advice to American Tobacco must have come as a surprise: *Stop advertising most of your brands.*

Lasker argued that rather than maintaining many modestly successful small brands, the company needed to create one overwhelmingly powerful product that could compete with Camels and Chesterfields. "You can't live unless you have this one brand," Lasker recalled saying, "because 80 or 90 percent of the cigarette business in this country today is on this one type of cigarette. These other cigarettes and other products were a different type of goods . . . Instead of spending a little money and a moderate amount of money on each of these fifty products, milk them all. Take what you spend on them and the milking of their profits and put it in a big push behind Luckies."[31]

Hill agreed. As a result, the money formerly spent advertising Blue Boar—the original Lord & Thomas account—and most of the other minor American Tobacco products was diverted to support Lucky Strike.

The first Lord & Thomas campaign on behalf of the now-favored brand built upon the earlier concept of "toasting," which attempted to differentiate Luckies based on the preparation of the tobacco. The copy stressed the unique benefits of toasting, including improved flavor and reduced acidity, supposedly making it easier on the throat. It was classic Claude Hopkins: true, the tobacco used in Lucky Strikes was heated to somewhere between 260 and 300 degrees during the manufacturing process—but this was common practice in cigarette manufacturing.[32]

The brand still wasn't doing well enough to satisfy the hugely ambitious Hill, so in 1927, Lord & Thomas began complementing the "toasted" theme with a series of advertisements that became known as the "Precious Voice" campaign. This new campaign argued that, in addition to making cigarettes easier on the throat, the vaunted toasting process actually helped *protect* the throat and voice.

One thing that distinguished "Precious Voice" was its target audience. At that time, the social stigma against women smoking was still powerful. Although Philip Morris had introduced the first women's cigarette in 1924 (claiming that it was "mild as May"), few women smoked openly, and most restaurants and other public places prohibited smoking by women. But women were beginning to smoke in the home, and Lasker realized that a vast new market was ready to open up. This was brought home to him one afternoon at the Tip Top Inn, a restaurant near his Chicago home, where he was lunching with his wife. Flora tended toward obesity, and her doctor had suggested that she take up smoking to curb her appetite. But on this particular day, when she attempted to light up after lunch, the restaurant's proprietor rushed over and said that he could not permit a woman to smoke in the main dining room. If Flora wished to smoke, he continued, the Laskers would have to retire to a private room.

"It filled me with indignation," Lasker recalled, "that I had to do surreptitiously something which was perfectly normal in a place where I had gone so much. That determined me to break down the prejudice against women smoking."[33] No doubt the prospect of doubling the potential market for Luckies also influenced his thinking. Lasker took his idea to George Washington Hill, and told him that if American Tobacco acted decisively, the women's market might be theirs for the asking.

Precious Voice—one of the few postwar campaigns that was largely conceived and directed by Lasker—grew directly out of this decision. Lasker decided that testimonials from well-respected foreign women might start to overcome the prejudice against women smokers, and he started with opera singers. "It was very natural that my mind went to the opera stars," he explained, "because at that time there were only one or two American stars, and the rest were foreign. And if I [could] get the women of the opera, it [wouldn't] be long until [I'd] be able to get the women of the stage."[34] The subtext, of course, was that women—sophisticated, worldly, even exotic women—who earned their livelihood by singing were willing to trust their precious voices to Luckies.

Precious Voice was one of the first Lord & Thomas advertising campaigns to rely heavily on testimonials, and very quickly, the campaign expanded to include almost all the stars of New York's Metropolitan Opera.[35] Just as Lasker had anticipated, stage and screen stars (both women and men) also rushed to join the chorus of artists praising Luckies. Incredibly, none of the individuals testifying for Luckies were paid for their contributions; they considered the free publicity compensation enough.

The campaign enjoyed immediate success. "Overnight," Lasker later boasted, "the business of Luckies went up like the land in a boom field where oil has just been found."[36]

But it was another campaign that not only catapulted Luckies to the forefront of the women's market across the United States but also fundamentally revolutionized the cigarette market. There are differing accounts as to which fertile brain conceived this new effort; George Washington Hill claimed that he came up with the idea and pitched it to Lasker, while the Lord & Thomas accounts state that both men came up with the idea independently.

Hill's version of the story begins in his chauffeured limo. As he was being driven down New York's Fifth Avenue, he happened to glance out of his car window and see a heavyset woman on a street corner "munching chocolates" (although alternate versions have her chewing gum). Hill then glanced into a taxicab next to him, where he spied a svelte woman smoking a cigarette. Hill rushed to the office and summoned Lasker.

Lasker—as *he* told the story—was taking a train through Pittsburgh one day when he noticed an article in one of the morning papers reporting that candy manufacturers meeting in the area had appropriated $150,000 to run an advertising campaign against cigarette smoking. "[The candy manufacturers] wanted to stop the growth of cigarettes," Lasker recalled, "so that money could be used for candy."[37] The candy manufacturers' campaign, explained the article, would argue that smoking was bad for the nervous system, and that substituting a piece of candy would help quell the appetite for a cigarette. Reading this account, Lasker remembered that the doctor who was then treating his wife had told her that smoking would suppress her appetite—including her taste for sweets.

Lasker's account suggests that by the time he and Hill next met in New York, they had both hatched more or less the same scheme. Hill said that he didn't want to hear about Lasker's new idea until he had shared his own. He pulled a sheet out of his desk drawer on which was written, "Reach for a Lucky instead of a bon-bon." Lasker was amazed to see his own concept on the page in front of him, but his trained ear caught one mistake. "I think it could be terrific," Lasker admitted, "but as it is, it's no good. One word would have to be changed." He then took a pencil, crossed out "bon-bon," and wrote "sweet."[38]

At the end of 1928, the slogan was added to the Precious Voice campaign, with the women now testifying that they used Luckies to protect both their voices *and* their figures. The surge was immediate, and overwhelming. Lucky Strike sales increased by 8.3 billion units in 1928 to capture second place among cigarette brands, and by an additional 10 billion in 1929. In that same year, Lord & Thomas's billings for Lucky Strike ads totaled $12.3 million, or roughly 30 percent of the agency's entire billings.[39]

The candy manufacturers screamed. A Brooklyn-based candy maker, Wallace & Co., organized the "National Food Products Protective Committee" to mount a vigorous protest against the campaign. Newspaper editorials, particularly in conservative parts of the country, condemned American Tobacco for exploiting women. Competitors piled on, with R.J. Reynolds mounting an opportunistic campaign of its own: "With a cigaret as good as Camels, the truth is enough."[40]

In 1929, the Federal Trade Commission—then investigating American Tobacco for alleged unfair business practices—ordered the tobacco giant to discontinue the mention of "sweets" in its advertisements. The National Better Business Bureau also weighed in, complaining that the Lucky ads had "perverted the judgment and character of the advertising industry."[41] American Tobacco grumbled and backed down, but by then the point had been made many millions of times over. Subsequent campaigns simply stated, "Reach for a Lucky instead." Savvy consumers knew what was implied, and Lucky Strike sales continued to soar.

Albert Lasker's return to Chicago after his stint in Washington reunited him with a large network of friends and business acquaintances. At first, this meant gatherings at his Glencoe mansion, twenty-four miles north of Chicago near Lake Michigan. But in the early 1920s, Lasker—flush with cash and eager to realize a long-standing dream—decided to build a grand estate in the lakeside town of Lake Forest, eight miles north of Glencoe.

The estate, which was eventually named Mill Road Farm, comprised just under five hundred acres of land purchased for about $1,000 an acre from meatpacker Louis Swift, and took three years and uncounted millions to complete.[42] Lasker impishly suggested that the estate should be called "Nonwentsia"—a play on Onwentsia, an exclusive local country club that barred Jews. When completed, the sprawling estate included an impressive residence, a working farm, several greenhouses, a garage and superintendent's residence, a swimming pool, an 18-hole golf course, and—eventually—a movie theater.

The mansion was designed by David Adler, a prominent residential architect known for his exquisite country houses, which combined the French classical, English Tudor, and Italian Renaissance styles, and the Mill Road Farm mansion was completed during Adler's heyday. As the centerpiece of an estate of its size, the residence itself was relatively informal, because Lasker was as much interested in comfort as in grandeur. The mansion was enormous, but many of Adler's architectural touches were chosen to deemphasize its massive scale.

Edward Lasker, who was a teenager when the family first occupied Mill Road Farm, described the stunning estate:

> The drive, which had trees every twenty feet or so on each side, was some three-eighths of a mile curving to the main house, which I would guess was thirty thousand square feet. It contained suites, consisting of bedroom, dressing room, bath, and in mother's case, a boudoir, for each family member, as well as half a dozen guest rooms, about four sitting rooms, an office for father, a wine cellar, pressing room, silver room, and a dozen or so servant's rooms . . .
>
> The exterior was white-washed brick with red awnings. To the east of the house was a swimming pool which was 100 feet by 40 feet, flanked by two commodious bath houses with red tile roofs.
>
> South from the house to the end of the property's end was another drive which bisected the two nines of the golf course, which was generally considered

one of the three or four finest championship courses in the United States. There were two tennis courts, a guest house accommodating eight overnight residents and manned by a full-time couple. Adjoining the guest house was a practice tee and a nursery conducted for the U.S. Golf Association to test different types of grasses.

Bordering Old Mill Farm Road were the Farm's barns, housing seventy Guernsey cattle, my polo ponies, as well as coops for approximately 10,000 white leghorns, and space for ducks and pigeons. The Farm operated a daily route selling milk, chickens, and eggs.[43]

The estate—and especially the 180-acre golf course designed by William S. Flynn—became a sensation among the Chicago elite. John Hertz, the taxicab magnate and intermittently a close friend of Lasker's, lived fifteen miles down Old Mill Road. In a 1938 interview, he described the thrill of being invited to play eighteen holes at the Lasker estate: "Of course everyone wants to play on his course. There isn't anybody in Chicago who doesn't want to play his course . . . There isn't any set-up like it in America. He had two, three hundred people out there to play golf, maybe more. He gives them a card, and he has locker rooms for them, and he furnishes them with food at a dollar a head, and good food."[44]

The "card" deserves a word. According to Edward, Albert devised a scheme to make his friends feel welcome on the course: in the first year that the course was open, Albert sent out "golf membership cards" to his friends. Each card was conspicuously marked "1A," implying to the recipient that he was first in Albert's affections. The one-dollar charge for food was also purposeful; Lasker calculated that his guests would feel free to indulge themselves at his sumptuous table if they had "paid for" their meals.

The movie theater was added in the mid-1930s, when Lasker unexpectedly received repayment on a debt that he had considered bad. It accommodated up to sixty people, was air-cooled, and showed several first-run films a week. "There just isn't a place to compare with it," said Hertz.[45]

Mill Road Farm, Lasker admitted, was his creation. Unlike her husband, Flora was never interested in the trappings of wealth. "She never wanted it," Lasker said of the estate. "She got a great deal of pleasure out of it, but . . . her whole life would have been different and happier if we had just always lived on five or six thousand dollars a year."[46]

Within a few years of returning to Chicago, Lasker could already see the effects of his reinvestment of time and energy in the agency's Chicago headquarters. Billings had increased almost 30 percent between 1924 and 1926, and the agency's stable of clients was steadily being upgraded.

But even this substantial progress wasn't good enough as his agency fell further behind its increasingly potent competitors. In 1926, Lord & Thomas (with billings of $18.8 million) was eclipsed by a resurgent Ayer ($26.1 million) and the steadily expanding J. Walter Thompson ($20.7 million). And although reliable figures aren't available, Lasker's agency was now being challenged by a formidable fourth-place finisher: BDO.[47]

Meanwhile, another young agency, Young & Rubicam, was creating a different kind of stir. It was founded in Philadelphia in 1923 by Ray Rubicam—a refugee from the Ayer agency—and John Orr Young, who had spent two years in Lord & Thomas's Chicago office, where he clashed with the powerful Claude Hopkins. Young & Rubicam won the General Foods account, and—in response to pressure from that key client—relocated their agency to New York, where they built up a respectable book of business ($6 million, by 1927).

But in these early days, the challenge they presented to the industry's status quo owed more to their unorthodox approach than their billings. Unlike the established agencies, Young & Rubicam was a free-spirited shop, full of unconventional characters who kept odd hours and didn't respect protocol. And in explicit contrast to the Hopkins model, which counted on constant reiteration of simple themes until those themes were exhausted, Ray Rubicam pushed his creative talents to constantly develop new directions for his clients.[48] By 1945, Young & Rubicam could boast of $53 million in billings, second only to J. Walter Thompson ($73 million).

Against this turbulent backdrop, Lasker decided to take drastic action. For the first and only time, he brought in a partner, and changed the name of his agency: a step he hadn't taken even when he assumed control of Lord & Thomas decades earlier.

Through his friend David Sarnoff, head of the Radio Corporation of America (RCA), Lasker met a rising advertising star named Thomas F. Logan. Logan had been the Washington correspondent for the *Philadelphia Inquirer* for ten years before starting his own agency in Manhattan in 1919, quickly becaming known as a "wizard of institutional advertising."[49] According to Lasker's aide-de-camp Ralph Sollitt, Logan was deeply involved in the formation of RCA and had helped bring Sarnoff into the company. "Logan was the man more than anybody else," Sollitt said, "who picked out Sarnoff, and who sold Sarnoff on the idea of going into the Radio Corporation."[50] Sarnoff chose Logan's agency to represent RCA, and Logan began polishing Sarnoff's reputation as a major corporate leader.

The relationship between Sarnoff and Logan went well beyond business. Logan once confessed to Sarnoff that it was a "wonderful thing to find in friendship an understanding that permits you to be wholly honest and literally think out loud."[51] Sarnoff's relationship with Lasker (whom he first met during the Leviathan's trial run) was equally close. To an interviewer in 1938, Sarnoff said that he would give "no one a higher rating for character and integrity than Albert Lasker," and asserted that Lasker had a capacity for friendship "given to very few people in the world."[52] For his part, Lasker had enormous respect for Sarnoff, both as an individual and as a businessman, and in the 1930s even offered Sarnoff the presidency of Lord & Thomas at the astounding salary of a million dollars a year. Sarnoff, happy at RCA and well aware of his friend's reputation for burning through chief lieutenants, politely declined.[53]

Sarnoff and Lasker talked often about their respective business challenges, including—in Lasker's case—the struggling New York office. No doubt they also talked about Lasker's newfound determination to groom a successor to take over the agency. With these two themes in the background, Sarnoff decided that Logan and Lasker should meet, and arranged for the two of them to join him at a Gridiron dinner in Washington. Sarnoff subsequently brought Logan with him to Mill Road Farm, where, according to Sarnoff, "those two fellows fell in love and out of it came the merger of Lord & Thomas and Logan."[54]

The news, which broke in the spring of 1926, caught the business community by surprise. In a brief article that was kinder to Logan than to Lasker, Time described the merger as an unlikely marriage of opposites:

> Thomas F. Logan is just the opposite of the aggressive, hammering, obviously successful Lasker. He is slimmer, fairer, quieter—not smoother, for dynamos of the Lasker type are well-oiled—but gentler, more subtly persuasive . . . The effects of his work are felt quite as intimately by the individual consumer [as are Lasker's]—in a comfortable, punctual train; a well-appointed ship; a sound security. But the distinction between the Messrs. Lasker and Logan, in what they do and how they do it, is as marked as their conjunction is notable.[55]

Logan brought in a client list that included Anaconda Copper, the shipping giant International Mercantile Marine, RCA, and—most tantalizing—a General Electric subsidiary. On first glance, the initial benefits of the merger flowed mostly to Logan. The Lord & Thomas client list was many times as long as Logan's, and the Chicago agency's annual billings dwarfed Logan's. (Logan before the merger was doing around $5 million a year, compared with Lord & Thomas's $18.8 million.[56]) But the merger reestablished Lasker's agency as second only to Ayer, and almost overnight created a strong presence in New York. And thinking long term, Lasker believed Logan had the skills and contacts needed to take over the whole agency.

It was not to be. On August 8, 1928, just over two years into the partnership, the forty-six-year-old Logan died at his summer home of a previously undiagnosed heart condition.[57]

Logan's premature death left Albert Lasker with two dilemmas. The first was a financial settlement with Logan's widow; the second was the continuing challenge of the New York office. The anointed miracle worker had been removed from the stage; now what was Lasker going to do about New York?

To tackle the settlement problem, Lasker turned again to Sarnoff. Lasker framed the problem as follows: Lasker and Logan had made a deal whereby Lasker would retire gradually and Logan would take over the company. Now, Logan was dead, and Lasker had yet to gain significant advantage from the partnership. Lasker had to put a value on Logan's share of the merged company, the accumulated goodwill, client list, and other assets of which "belonged" more to Lasker than to Logan.

"I don't know how to deal with [Logan's] widow," Lasker told Sarnoff. "I don't want to do anything that would be inequitable or unfair either to her or to me."[58] Lasker then made an extraordinary request: Sarnoff would have to figure out how to settle the matter. "I hate to put you in this position," Lasker said, "but you simply have got to take the job, being the friend of both parties, and probably the one in which his widow has the most confidence."

Sarnoff didn't like the prospect of being the intermediary "between a dead friend and a living friend." Lasker insisted, however, and the RCA head reluctantly agreed to talk to Mrs. Logan. Sarnoff dreaded the prospect of broaching the subject with Logan's widow, but she spared him that embarrassment by bringing it up herself, and essentially making the same request: could Sarnoff broker a deal with Lasker?

Sarnoff agreed to arbitrate a settlement on two conditions. First, his word would be final; both parties would have to accept whatever he decided. Second, no lawyers would be involved until after he had reached his judgment. Lasker and Mrs. Logan agreed to these conditions.

Sarnoff first developed a complete picture of the net worth of both parties. He was not much surprised by what he had learned. Lasker, as Sarnoff knew full well, was a very wealthy man, and Mrs. Logan was well-off. But there were other factors to weigh, as well. After thinking it through, Sarnoff reached his conclusion, and called for a meeting with Lasker. Before revealing his bottom line, he explained to Lasker how he had reached it:

Albert, there are several things I am taking into consideration. And these are the considerations: (1) That the man who is paying is alive and rich, the person who is to receive this money is a widow, whose husband is dead, and who by comparison certainly has no such wealth as you have. (2) That the man who is paying is a Jew, and the widow and her former husband are not Jews. (3) That whatever mistake is made in this figure, must be a mistake on the side of generosity. Let others criticize you for having paid too much, or her for having accepted too much, or me for having determined too much. But let there be no criticism on the reverse side of the situation.

Based on the purely financial considerations, Sarnoff told Lasker that Logan's stock was probably worth about $240,000. But that wasn't the right figure. Instead, he proposed that Lasker pay Logan's widow $1 million. "You can afford to do it," he told his friend, "and by paying substantially five times what a court of equity might determine, you will more than answer all the specifications I have laid down."

Lasker was stunned; he had expected a buyout figure closer to a quarter of a million dollars, and the price Sarnoff named—a million dollars!—seemed exorbitant. Swallowing hard, he said that he would abide by his friend's judgment. "I think you have decided more than I should be asked to pay, [and] more than she is entitled to," he said, "but when I asked you to take this job of mediator, which was a labor of love more than anything else, I meant it, and I said I would accept your decision, and if you say one million dollars, one million dollars it is."

The story had an ironic postscript. Mrs. Logan—an avid horsewoman—turned over $300,000 of her settlement to the exclusive Sleepy Hollow

Country Club in Scarborough, New York, so that the club could build a well-appointed stable for its members' horses. At the time, Sleepy Hollow rigorously excluded Jews.

This stung both men. "The horse was eligible," Sarnoff grumbled, "but not me."[59]

<hr>

Lasker's second business dilemma involved far higher financial stakes, and took much longer to resolve. The New York office, now largely built around the staff inherited from Logan, was still struggling. Many of Logan's employees had come to him through clients and were not advertising men. Because New York was home to two major accounts—RCA and American Tobacco—the office was in little danger of being shut down. But Lasker was frustrated at the many people working for him in New York who didn't appear to be doing much work. "Lasker not only despised these men who were not advertising men," recalled one associate, "but they were getting dough besides, and *his* dough."[60]

Lasker now had to choose a new director for the New York office almost sight unseen—in part owing to the suddenness of Logan's death, but also to Lasker's increasingly fragile mental state toward the end of 1928. He first installed Logan's longtime colleague, Ames Brown, in the job; but Brown didn't prosper. In the end, Lasker turned to his utility man, Ralph Sollitt.

He took the job reluctantly. "Sollitt never wanted to be head of this business," Coons recalled. "Sollitt didn't consider himself an advertising man; he just wanted to help Lasker."[61] Within several months, however, Sollitt had cleaned house, buying out all of the Logan holdovers—the cost of which reached into the millions of dollars—and bringing in an almost entirely new staff.

<hr>

Albert Lasker's record of accomplishment in the 1920s documents a business genius at the height of his creative powers. The second golden era at Lord & Thomas was powered mainly by an amazing burst of creative energy from him.

By 1928, though, Lasker was drained. In that year, he had yet another serious breakdown—at least his third—and spent several months at the Johns

Hopkins hospital in Baltimore recovering. He ventured out from Hopkins only sporadically, and then only to deal with serious crises.

One of these crises was a proposed summit in Washington with George Washington Hill, called at Hill's urgent request. Everyone understood that when Hill called a meeting with Lord & Thomas, he expected Lasker to attend—a challenge, in this instance, since Lasker was hospitalized and incommunicado. Neither the subject nor the outcome of that meeting was recorded, but one aspect of it remained etched indelibly on the minds of those in attendance.

Sollitt was there. He recalls that against almost incredible odds, considering the depths of his depression, Lasker summoned up his energetic, passionate self. "The part that Mr. Lasker performed," Sollitt later said, "would have been enough to send most anybody to the hospital, because he was so intense and acting and dramatizing everything."[62] After battling his way through a three- or four-hour marathon with the indomitable Hill, Sollitt recalls, Lasker had "fought the thing and got it all shaped around the way he could."

At the end of the slugfest, an exhausted Lasker announced, "I am glad that is over; now I can go back to Johns Hopkins and finish my breakdown."

Unlikely heroics like these compelled people to close ranks behind Lasker in his dark periods. Family, employees, and most clients—with the notable exception of George Washington Hill—learned to live without Lasker, when necessary. The brilliance that shone through his creative periods more than made up for the intermittent darkness.

Chapter Seventeen

Retrenching and Reshaping

N OCTOBER 12, 1927, Lasker's eldest child, Mary, married Gerhard Foreman, the son of Oscar G. Foreman, a director of Chicago's Foreman National Bank. It seemed an eminently suitable match: Mary and Gerhard were in love, and two powerful Chicago Jewish families found themselves united.

The couple was married at the Laskers' Glencoe home, with only members of the two families present.[1] The mansion was lavishly decorated for the occasion, and the young couple was thrilled to learn that it was to be their wedding present: Albert and Flora would live full-time at Mill Road Farm.

Gerhard was named for his grandfather, who had emigrated to the United States from Darmstadt, Germany, in the late 1850s and founded the Foreman Bank in 1862.[2] The bank in the late 1920s was run by Gerhard's father, Oscar, who was chairman of the board, along with a third-generation Foreman, Harold, who served as president. With all of these close family ties, Gerhard seemed assured of a bright future with the bank. Lasker was pleased to see his daughter married to a man with such strong prospects; in addition, Lasker biographer John Gunther reports that Lasker was "enormously fond" of Gerhard and admired his judgment.[3]

As Lasker looked back on the relationship a decade later, he recalled that the young couple was very much in love when they got married, but over the next several years, fissures appeared. There were "a good many private unhappinesses," he said, pointing to the couple's reluctance or inability to have children.[4]

Albert Lasker largely sidestepped the market crash of 1929, thanks to savvy investment decisions by his friend and neighbor, rental-car mogul John

Hertz. Lasker and Hertz had a joint stock market account that was managed by a Chicago investment adviser.[5] Both men were authorized to make changes to the account, and Hertz exercised that authority during the summer of 1929. Early one morning, Hertz called Lasker and told him that he was going to "sell everything," despite the surging market.[6] Lasker protested, but finally accepted his friend's judgment. Several months later, the stock market collapsed.

Lasker's stock in several privately held companies, including Kimberly-Clark, was immune to the wild swings of the public markets and generated a substantial dividend stream. But he kept much of his non–real estate wealth in the cash accounts of Lord & Thomas, so that business had to be managed carefully.

Managing the firm in the Depression took some counterintuitive thinking. Many of the agency's largest clients suffered, and Lasker urged them to cut their advertising budgets—despite public statements by Lord & Thomas president Ames Brown in early 1929 predicting a good year for advertising.[7] Early on, for example, Lasker told American Tobacco's George Washington Hill that he should drastically reduce his advertising budget. The domineering Hill initially responded by threatening to *raise* his advertising budget to $25 million, but Lasker coolly replied, "If you [do], you are not going to spend it through me. I won't place it for you."

Lasker won this topsy-turvy argument; the following year, he talked Hill down again, to $10 million, and the following year to $8 million. Then Lasker called other clients, told them American Tobacco had agreed to cut its advertising budget by 33 percent, and advised them to do the same. "Never mind where the billing of Lord & Thomas falls, never mind anything about that," he told them. "I instinctively believe that we are in for worse times before they are better, and I propose that any clients that are served by me shall survive."

Meanwhile, Lasker did his best to help friends. Several of them lost huge sums on their margin accounts, and Lasker gave them loans to keep them afloat, most of which were never repaid. Lasker grumbled that he was helping his friends do the "very thing that I wouldn't do myself"—i.e., buying on margin and playing a highly volatile market that he had abandoned—and later estimated that he had lost somewhere between $5 million and $7 million in bad loans to friends.[8]

By 1931, the Foreman Bank—which in December 1929 merged with the State Bank of Chicago, and was now the Foreman-State Bank—was on the brink of becoming yet another casualty of the Great Depression. The bank had overextended itself in speculative real estate loans, which quickly went bad in 1929 and 1930 as borrowers' negative leverage caught up with them. Throughout the early months of 1931, the bank became increasingly unstable and by early June the crisis was coming to a head. On Thursday, June 4, whispers of a run on the Foreman-State Bank were in the air in Chicago's Loop district and representatives of the city's leading banks gathered in great secrecy at the home of Melvin Traylor, president of the First National Bank, to head off a crisis.[9] Traylor's solution was simple: a takeover of Foreman by First National.

Foreman's directors, who included Lasker, Hertz, and William Wrigley, were dismayed by Traylor's proposal, which would guarantee the bank's deposits but cost the stockholders dearly. But by Saturday morning, the bank's liquidity was in peril, and Lasker, Hertz, and Wrigley were forced to put up enough money to keep the bank operating through the day.

By this time, the crisis had attracted national attention. Recreating a climactic meeting in the second week of June, *Time* magazine reported that "newspapermen, lolling in the marble lobby of the Foreman Building, grew impatient for definite news of what was taking place on the [thirty-eighth] floor," where members of the Federal Reserve were huddling with the Foreman bank directors and representatives of the other leading Chicago banks.[10]

What took place on that thirty-eighth floor, according to Lasker, was high drama, in which he commanded center stage. "The room was full of the heads of banks and clearing houses on a Sunday afternoon," Lasker recalled, "and I made a talk for about fifteen minutes that made financial history in Chicago; they are never going to forget it."[11] Melvin Traylor demanded that the Foreman directors pay First National to take over the struggling Foreman. Lasker responded that they would never sell Foreman "down the river," and ended by exclaiming to Traylor that he'd never before seen "Shylock performed by a Christian." (In the immediate aftermath, Lasker denied making the inflammatory comment; later, he admitted that he had.[12])

But First National's was the only offer on the table, and in the end, Foreman was indeed sold "down the river," with its directors, Lasker included, compelled to post a $2.6 million indemnity fee. The bank's individual depositors were thus saved, but the directors—as well as the entire Foreman family—lost huge sums on the transaction, and six smaller banks associated with Foreman were forced to close their doors. This led to sixteen additional bank closings in Chicago neighborhoods over the next two days. The Chicago State Bank Examiners rushed to reassure jittery Chicagoans that the merger had "eliminated the only sore spot in the Chicago banking situation," and that additional closings were not imminent.[13]

Lasker, Hertz, and two other non-family-member directors of the bank were named directors of First National a month later.[14] But this episode—along with the unhappy experience of lending money to his stock market-playing friends—sparked a new kind of cynicism in Lasker. "Most of the unhappiness I have had in life," he observed several years later, "has been from people I have helped."[15] Increasingly, he felt detached from business, which he saw as having lost its moorings, with no clear course back to a safe harbor.

Mary and Gerhard's marriage survived the crisis of the Foreman bank failure, but within another couple of years, they had arrived at a crisis of their own, and Mary—an energetic and highly intelligent young woman—needed something to take her mind off her marital difficulties. Flora decided that something should be a job at Lord & Thomas, and she demanded that Albert hire their daughter.

Even though he had entertained ideas a decade earlier of setting Mary up in the newspaper business—perhaps even joining her there—his reaction to this proposal was an emphatic *no*. "Now, look here," he told Flora, "I have given you and Mary and the children everything I have in the world. I have shared it with you. It has been yours first. But the one thing I have kept for myself is my career. Now don't you start on my career; don't you try and bring nepotism in my career. It won't go."[16]

Lasker thought this was only a whim on Mary's part and didn't want to indulge it. It was not that she couldn't do the work, he felt, but that she wouldn't keep it up once she started. Flora believed otherwise—and she told Albert that continually for the following six months. "She'd come into my room every night," Lasker recalled, "and start over again. She was a very determined woman."

Albert approached business manager David Noyes and asked him to get him out of a tight spot by meeting with Mary. "I am going to tell my wife," he said, "that I am going to send my daughter in. Of course it is all nonsense, and you write me a long memorandum why you can't do it. I will take it home and show my wife; I know she won't upset my organization."

After several days, Albert had not yet received the memo from Noyes, so he tracked down his business manager to see what had happened. "Mr. Lasker," a sheepish Noyes said, "I just didn't have the courage to tell you that I hired her. I meant to give her ten minutes, but she stayed four hours, and she is the best prospect we ever had. She has more advertising in her than any human being."

With that, Mary Lasker was on the payroll, at the modest salary of thirty dollars a week. Albert decided that the best tactic was to keep his distance from the firm's newest employee. He did, however, leave a note on her desk on her first day of work (October 29, 1935):

My darling Mary,

Welcome to Lord & Thomas. I hope we have a long business association together—if we do, we will both get much joy from it.

Both as father and employer I give you this advice—try to learn from everyone (high and low), try to be of service to every one (high and low). He finally leads who first learns to serve. And remember—we spend our lives learning. Above all, be yourself—your best self. Always think of the other fellow's viewpoint and try to get him to think of yours. Learn to walk before you run. Believe in yourself—and believing, strive to learn every day and grow creatively every minute so that you will justify your belief.

All my love,

Father[17]

Lasker later concluded that Noyes had been right about Mary's advertising talent. "It's the darnedest story," Lasker told his ghostwriter in 1938. "A little over two years, and I have never known anybody who has been in the business ten years and been [as] successful, and who has gotten as far as she has in proved performance. She is the sensation of the line in Chicago."[18]

As good as Mary was, however, her talent could not salvage her career at Lord & Thomas. Intermittent bouts with alcoholism impaired her performance, as did the bluntness she inherited from her father. The end came in 1941, when Mary fought with one of the agency's managers, and Albert—fearing a charge of favoritism—felt he had to side with the manager. He fired Mary.[19]

Edward, meanwhile, had also launched what appeared to be a promising career at Lord & Thomas. After graduating from Yale, Edward decided to go to work for the family firm because he couldn't come up with a more interesting career.[20] His father believed that before trying to advertise products, Edward needed to learn more about why people bought them, and secured a job for his son in England as a salesman for J. Wix & Sons, a subsidiary of American Tobacco. After several years abroad, Edward returned to work in the New York office, where, upon his request (and with the intercession of American Tobacco's George Washington Hill), he became a mainstay of a growing new department at the agency: radio advertising.[21]

In the late 1920s, Pepsodent toothpaste—which had been on the market for a little more than a decade—was losing ground to its increasingly formidable competition. Its owners, including Albert Lasker, were far from happy about this.

Peposdent had been founded in 1916 by Douglas Smith, the Chicago-based entrepreneur who had already amassed a fortune from the sale of typewriters and patent medicines around the turn of the century. When his cash-cow, Liquozone, was exposed as a fraud, Smith scrambled to find other products to bring to the market.[22]

One of these new products was Pepsodent, which according to Smith was brought to him by a chemist from Lincoln, Nebraska, who told him the formula would make a good toothpaste. The product even came with its own "reason-why" argument: *it removes film on teeth.*[23]

But the company had a poor relationship with both retailers and wholesalers, and sales were almost nonexistent. In fact, toothpaste sales in general were quite low, mainly because very few people practiced—or even knew about—oral hygiene. Although the first toothbrush was patented in the United States in 1857, only a small minority of the population owned a toothbrush until after World War I.

When Smith acquired the toothpaste, therefore, he faced an uphill battle. Hopkins, who had so successfully marketed Liquozone for Smith years earlier, was now a fixture at Lord & Thomas, so Smith decided to hire the agency to see what Hopkins could come up with. Initially, Hopkins tried to turn the account down, saying that the product was overpriced and that (as he later wrote) he did not "see a way to educate the laity in technical tooth-paste theories."[24] Under pressure from Smith, however, Lord & Thomas took the account.

For the first several years of the relationship, the agency's efforts on behalf of Pepsodent were limited, reflecting Smith's modest ad budget. Hopkins focused on the fact that Pepsodent contained pepsin, which allegedly digested the mucin plaques that were the "source of most tooth troubles." Ads placed by Lord & Thomas in dental journals asserted that "the whole object of Pepsodent is to *dissolve* the film," through a somewhat mysterious digestive process. As in the case of Liquozone, Hopkins's claims generated some unwanted attention. As one researcher from Columbia University's College of Physicians and Surgeons icily put it:

> We have found that none of these digestive claims is warranted in any degree. "Pepsodent" is devoid of the digestive power on dental mucin plaques that is commercially ascribed to it. Mucin plaques cannot be digested from teeth by any advertised use of "Pepsodent" . . .
>
> Our results make it evident that "Pepsodent" is put on the market in utter ignorance of the dental and biochemical principles involved, or with intent to mislead the multitude that may usually be deceived by plausible advertisement.[25]

Hopkins shrugged off the complaints, probably because by 1919—with total sales of around $2,000 per week—Pepsodent was still just bumping along.[26] At this point, however, Lasker took a personal interest in the account. In consultation with Hopkins, Lasker made an astounding proposal to Douglas Smith. Smith needed to invest $1 million in advertising, Lasker asserted: an *enormous* sum for a relatively unknown and untested product. Lasker offered to front the money himself and told Smith that if he was satisfied with the results, he could pay Lasker back with company stock. If Smith wasn't completely satisfied, no repayment would be necessary.

No entrepreneur could pass up that offer, and Smith soon gave Lord & Thomas the go-ahead. Hopkins, too, demanded and got stock options, and from that point forward, Lasker and Hopkins were deeply involved in the fate of Pepsodent.

Hopkins already understood the challenges that Pepsodent presented. At the time, all toothpastes were all made from sodium bicarbonate and flavoring. So how could Pepsodent differentiate itself from the growing number of competitors?

Hopkins decided to employ a tactic he later called "altruistic advertising," by which he meant a "test for the good of the parties concerned."[27] In various test cities, Hopkins tried hundreds of "altruistic" ads, and systematically recorded the responses to every ad. Overall, his success was outstanding. In the first test, Pepsodent spent $1,000—and recovered its money before the advertising bills came due. The experiment was repeated in other cities, with similarly successful results. Within a year, Pepsodent had established a demand nationwide, and within four years, a worldwide market.

Part of this success was an accident of timing. The U.S. government began including toothpaste in the ration kits distributed to soldiers on the front lines in World War I, which contributed to a rapidly expanding public awareness of dental hygiene. In addition, nearly 70 percent of all toothpaste advertisements in the early 1920s touted Pepsodent, which certainly built the brand's momentum.

Later in the decade, however, Pepsodent began to falter again. Competitors like Colgate and Forham's increased their share of the advertising market—and also their attacks on the frontrunner. Meanwhile, there was another important contributing factor to what turned out to be a steady downward slide for Pepsodent. Research conducted in the late 1920s confirmed that the product was overly abrasive and could damage teeth. (Colgate capitalized on this research in a series of pointed ads.) Pepsodent's research labs worked furiously to come up with a new formula to reduce abrasiveness; meanwhile, its marketing gurus scrambled to develop a novel marketing angle.

By 1929, Pepsodent sales were down 38 percent from their 1922 peak.[28] The brand was in such a dramatic freefall, in fact, that there was talk of taking it off the market. Just in time, Lord & Thomas hit on a new marketing strategy, involving the fast-evolving medium of radio. This successful gambit reversed the company's fortunes—and in the process, helped change the face of advertising.

***

By the time Lord & Thomas began to investigate advertising Pepsodent on the air, radio was far from a new medium. The earliest wireless broadcasts were transmitted on Christmas Eve in 1906, and regular radio broadcasts by wireless enthusiasts began the following year.[29] But well into the 1920s, radio was still thought of primarily as a means of point-to-point information transmission—for example, communication among ships or between military command centers and the front lines of battle.

After World War I, radio frequencies in the United States were turned over to civilian control, and the number of radio stations mushroomed. Educational institutions, companies, and individuals—all began experimenting with a wide variety of formats, including talk, music, and comedy broadcasts. Over the next decade, as broadcasters learned to use radio to its best effect, programming gradually become more formalized. One especially popular format grew out of a vaudeville model, in which two men would perform a "song and patter" routine that could be shortened or lengthened to fit available broadcast time.

Advertising on radio remained the exception rather than the rule. In part, this was owing to the untested nature of the new medium: nobody, not even the broadcasters, had any idea how many people were listening to their shows. In addition, many radio buffs objected to the idea of bringing advertising "into the home," arguing that radio was a more intimate medium than newspapers. Somehow, advertising on the radio felt more intrusive than advertising in print and therefore should be discouraged.

The first radio advertisements appeared in 1922, when American Telephone and Telegraph offered to sell airtime in a scheme it labeled "toll broadcasting." A real estate company took AT&T up on the offer in August of that year, and many other organizations soon followed suit. These fledgling radio ads rarely mentioned the price of a specific good or service; rather, much like public radio sponsors today, they attempted to promote a positive institutional image.

By the late 1920s, broadcasting had begun to resemble today's industry. National networks (including the National Broadcasting Company, or NBC, formed by David Sarnoff's Radio Corporation of America [RCA]) were established, and the concepts of programming, advertising support, and market research had taken root. In fact, the first books on radio advertising appeared in 1927, although major advertising agencies generally weren't deeply involved in radio advertising until the early 1930s.

Some of Lord & Thomas's earliest experiments with radio came at the behest of the irrepressible George Washington Hill. American Tobacco's first network show debuted in 1928: the *Lucky Strike Radio Hour* (which later became the well-known *Your Hit Parade*). The show consisted of popular songs of the day with minimal orchestration, interspersed with American Tobacco commercials. Hill insisted on the minimal arrangements, believing that they would help listeners relax and leave them more receptive to his commercials.[30]

As far as Lord & Thomas was concerned, the *Lucky Strike Radio Hour* was more of a vanity piece than successful advertising. Lord & Thomas's American Tobacco account history makes no mention of radio campaigns, and Lasker later asserted that radio was not particularly successful for the company.[31] But Hill was driven first by his own convictions. By mid-1936, he was spending about $350,000 a week on radio advertising, and was thoroughly convinced of radio's efficacy.[32]

By that time, Lasker, too, was a convert, owing largely to the results achieved by another client: Pepsodent.

———— ·《◎》· ————

Pepsodent's first forays into radio were initiated by a new recruit: Walter Templin, previously head of the Manhattan Electrical Supply Company, an early manufacturer of radio receiving sets. The Manhattan Electrical Supply Company became a significant client of David Sarnoff's RCA, one of Thomas Logan's key accounts. Logan had been favorably impressed by Templin's work, and after his firm's merger with Lord & Thomas he recruited Templin to join Lord & Thomas in Chicago to work with the Pepsodent Company.

The timing of Templin's arrival at Lord & Thomas couldn't have been worse. He had taken a month off after leaving New York to travel in remote areas of Canada, and during his northern wanderings Logan died. By the time Templin arrived in Chicago, therefore, his champion was buried, and Lasker—the man he would now be dealing with at Lord & Thomas—was confined to Mill Road Farm with yet another serious bout of depression. In addition, Kenneth Smith, who had taken over management of Pepsodent from his father, was largely absent from the company at this time; he left to spend the winter in Palm Beach only weeks after Templin arrived and spent much of the following spring in London.

Lacking any explicit instructions from his absent superiors, Templin decided to tackle the product's biggest failing first. He allocated between $250,000 and $300,000 to reduce the abrasiveness of the toothpaste while still preserving its cleansing ability. He later commented that Lasker's willingness to tackle this kind of problem—even by proxy—was highly unusual in an advertising executive: "We went way further than most companies would go to eliminate this abrasive factor. There are very few men, I think, besides Lasker engaged in the advertising business [who] would have the courage and support such a program . . . Lasker was enthusiastically in favor, always, of making the product the finest it was possible to make it."[33]

Second, Templin—whose background in radio now came into play—pushed both Pepsodent and Lord & Thomas to explore this new advertising medium. "Lasker was cold to the idea of a radio program for Pepsodent," Templin recalled, "because the few clients of his that had tried a radio program up to that time had not, so he said, been able to trace any increase in sales or any benefit from it." In addition, of course, Lasker was a substantial stockholder in Pepsodent, which probably made him more conservative in the management of the account.

At this time, however, Lasker was largely incapacitated, giving Templin far more leeway. In an effort to convince his new colleagues of the benefits of radio, Templin staged a full-dress "audition" in Chicago, complete with a New York announcer reading Pepsodent ads on the air. The studio audience included copywriters for Pepsodent, Lord & Thomas executives, and NBC executives—a "sophisticated and cold" group, in Templin's estimation. Much of what they heard that day was not new, having been lifted out of existing print campaigns. But just as Templin anticipated, the old copy acquired new power and resonance when it landed on the ear, rather than the eye. "As I expected," Templin noted, "when the people in the room for the first time heard, coming over the air, from the loudspeaker these statements about Pepsodent tooth paste, I think every man in that room was impressed tremendously."

Once the decision to pursue radio advertising had been made, the next challenge was to find the right vehicle. At the time, the most common radio advertising model was for a product to sponsor a specific radio program, broadcast every week (or in some cases, every day) at the same time of day. Templin wanted a program "that would be sufficiently interesting to act as a vehicle to carry this series of announcements." Pepsodent conducted a series of auditions, but none of the acts felt "sufficiently fresh or different."

So Templin decided to investigate a local act that had a passionate following in the Chicago area. He first stumbled upon the program while visiting with some friends, who were so engrossed in the broadcast that the whole household stopped what it was doing and gathered around the radio to listen. Even the young children, Templin noted, were allowed to stay up past their bedtimes and listen.

The program, called *Amos 'n' Andy*, was the brainchild of Freeman Gosden and Charles Correll, two bricklayers from Peoria whose on-the-job patter so amused their coworkers that they eventually tried out for radio.[34] The resulting program, *Sam and Henry*, aired briefly in St. Louis before moving to the *Chicago Tribune*'s WGN station in January 1926. Originally a musical production, WGN suggested that the pair add a dramatic element to the show, creating a sort of radio comic strip.[35] When the program's creators later requested a wider distribution of the show, WGN turned them down, and Gosden and Correll left the network. In March 1928, the show found a new home on the *Chicago Daily News*'s radio station, WMAQ, where it was reinvented as *Amos 'n' Andy*.

Amos 'n' Andy was essentially an extension of the traditional minstrel show format: Gosden and Correll, both white, played two black men who move from Atlanta to Chicago in pursuit of opportunity. The two open a taxi company, encounter a number of Chicago characters (all performed by Gosden and Correll), and later relocate to Harlem. An unusual combination of humor and pathos animated the series, and the show quickly became a hit. As broadcast historian Elizabeth McLeod writes:

> *Amos 'n' Andy profoundly influenced the development of dramatic radio. Working alone in a small studio, Correll and Gosden created an intimate, understated acting style that differed sharply from the broad manner of stage actors—a technique requiring careful modulation of the voice, especially in the portrayal of multiple characters. The performers pioneered the technique of varying both the distance and the angle of their approach to the microphone to create the illusion of a group of characters. Listeners could easily imagine that they were actually in the taxicab office, listening in on the conversation of close friends. The result was a uniquely absorbing experience for listeners who in radio's short history had never heard anything quite like Amos 'n' Andy.[36]*

With Smith's backing—and over Lasker's objections—Templin decided to run a thirteen-week test. The program first aired with Pepsodent's sponsorship on August 19, 1929, on the NBC Blue network (one of two radio networks then owned by NBC; it later became the American Broadcasting Company) with the mellow-voiced Bill Hay announcing. This choice was inspired: Hay had been associated with the show since the early WMAQ days and was already a familiar voice to *Amos 'n' Andy* fans. His calm and dignified sign-off, "Use Pepsodent Toothpaste Twice a Day—See Your Dentist at Least Twice a Year," and the earnest and intimate quality of his voice as he read the prebroadcast Pepsodent pitch lent an immediate credibility to the product.

Templin insisted that Hay announce *only* for *Amos 'n' Andy*. This led the public to associate him with Pepsodent instead of with the radio station. As Templin describes it, Hay was able to entrench himself "in the minds of the public as a conservative, sincere, honest representative of the Pepsodent Company, not of the NBC."[37]

The trial failed: after thirteen weeks, sales weren't up, and the area's wholesalers and druggists were grumbling about the huge inventories of Pepsodent they had on hand. But Templin felt in his gut that it was too soon to pull the plug. To test his instinct, he had announcer Hay offer an autographed photograph of *Amos 'n' Andy* to anyone who was interested. More than 150,000 replies poured in from all across Chicago—sufficient to silence his skeptical colleagues at Lord & Thomas and convince the naysayers at Pepsodent to underwrite another thirteen-week trial.

This time, the evidence was unambiguous: a marked increase in Pepsodent sales. Now the toothpaste company and its ad agency decided to plunge, taking the show nationwide. The result was a phenomenon. In 1930 and 1931, at the peak of its popularity, *Amos 'n' Andy* attracted some 40 million people every evening.[38] Phone companies reported that telephone traffic plunged during the show, and movie chains interrupted their features to broadcast the show to patrons in their theaters.[39]

Most important from the advertiser's point of view, Pepsodent sales increased 100 percent between 1929 and 1930.[40] Much of the profit was plowed back into advertising, and by 1932, Pepsodent was the second-largest buyer of radio time in the United States, topped only by George Washington Hill's American Tobacco.[41]

***

Pepsodent's resurgence thanks to *Amos 'n' Andy* was short-lived. While the radio show remained the most popular broadcast on the air, other shows were quickly gaining a national audience, and other brands were capitalizing on the power of the airwaves. By 1934, Lord & Thomas was being outspent on the radio by both J. Walter Thompson and Chicago's pioneering Blackett-Sample-Hummert, and many other agencies were rapidly gaining ground.[42] Blackett-Sample-Hummert was led in part by Lord & Thomas–trained Frank Hummert, a gifted copywriter whom Lasker had hoped would succeed Claude Hopkins, but who had left Lord & Thomas in 1927.[43] Hummert and his wife Anne recognized the enormous potential of serial drama on the radio, and created more than one hundred successful radio series for their clients, including Colgate-Palmolive and General Mills.[44]

Lord & Thomas gave Pepsodent a temporary boost in the early 1930s through a new scheme involving radio promotions. The first of these was an offer of lithographed cut-outs of *Amos 'n' Andy* characters to listeners who sent in a Pepsodent box top. It was a natural extension of Lord & Thomas' long-standing advertising practice of offering samples with strings attached; according to Templin, however, this was the first time that the consumer had to send in a box top in order to receive the product.

This proof-of-purchase scheme eventually became standard practice among advertisers, but Lord & Thomas did it first—and only after overcoming NBC's strong objections. As Templin recalls: "We were the first to include in the specifications that they must send the carton of the product in. The very first. We did that to weed out the professional coupon clippers, as we call them, that never will be customers, that just write in for samples. We had a great battle for it to get the NBC company to permit such an offer to be made on the air."[45]

Like most of Lord & Thomas's best clients, Pepsodent had strong creative talent of its own. In 1935, for example, two up-and-coming vice presidents at Pepsodent, Charles Luckman and Stuart Sherman, came up with a second write-in scheme to boost lagging sales. Luckman, then twenty-seven years old, had been trained as an architect at the University of Illinois and had gone into industry because architectural commissions were few and far between in the Depression; Sherman was a Lord & Thomas alumnus who had recently joined Pepsodent. Sitting together one night over scotches at the Drake Hotel, the two men were brainstorming new merchandising concepts when that evening's *Amos 'n' Andy* broadcast came on. Amos's wife, Ruby, was pregnant at the time in the storyline, and the two characters spent much of the broadcast arguing about the baby's name.

Both Luckman and Sherman slapped the table at the same moment, shouting *"That's it!"*[46]

More or less simultaneously, the two had invented a baby-naming contest. They spent the next few days feverishly working out the details. The contest would run for six weeks, with the company offering a prize of $5,000 to the listener who sent in the winning name. Other prizes totaling $35,000 were also announced. (All entries, of course, had to be accompanied by a Pepsodent box top.)

The success of the contest stunned even its creators. At a meeting with Lasker and Smith on the day following their brainstorm, all four men wrote down their guesses as to the number of entries the contest would generate. The highest guess was Lasker's, at a million entries—but even this proved low. In only six weeks, Pepsodent received more than 2 million box tops. Sales jumped 21 percent.

Wildly successful though it was, the baby-naming contest could only buy time for Pepsodent. As David Noyes later explained, the product's fatal flaw was that it offered nothing special to the consumer: "It seemed that no major product improvement was possible since there were no new ingredients available and that everyone in the dentifrice business was using almost the same ingredients in varying proportions. It was made clear again that advertising could only function when it had a theme that held the consumer . . . because of the advantage to the consumer. There was no advantage at that time in Pepsodent."[47]

The company therefore began a search for a new ingredient that would differentiate Pepsodent from the competition. At a fortuitous juncture, probably some time in 1936, a somewhat shadowy "foreign inventor" showed up in New York City with the "beginning of an answer," according to Noyes. The inventor, who had come up with a foaming detergent substance, apparently contacted every local toothpaste manufacturer on the same day, informing them of his miraculous discovery. Pepsodent cut a deal with him the following day.

The new detergent, though promising, didn't work in combination with any of the known polishing agents on the market, so Pepsodent began a search for a product that would be compatible with the detergent. A new agent called sodium alkyl sulphate was eventually identified, and—in combination with the detergent—showed vastly improved cleansing results in lab tests.

The challenge for Lord & Thomas, once again, was how to market this new ingredient. Lasker decided that it needed a name—one that would spark the public's interest. Ever sensitive to the power of euphony, he told his staff to come up with a name that had five letters: three vowels and two consonants.

From this exercise, the made-up word "irium" was born, and once again, advertising history was made, as "Pepsodent *with irium*" burned itself into the national consciousness. "We didn't go to do it on purpose," Lasker later commented, "but it sounded like irradiated, it sounded like platinum, it sounded like something precious, and it was a success from the [first] second."[48]

The new name worked the magic that Lasker had been hoping for. The American Dental Association had to add a full-time staff member to answer queries about irium from dentists and teachers. Pepsodent received petitions from drugstores asking them to send a detailed explanation of irium so that the druggists could answer their customers' questions.[49] Within a year and a half, Pepsodent had recaptured first place in the toothpaste wars.

Toward the end of 1937, Charles Luckman was summoned into a meeting with Lasker and Noyes. He immediately sensed a strained atmosphere in the room, but before he could ask any questions, Lasker fired one at him: should Lord & Thomas renew the contract with *Amos 'n' Andy*, which expired at the end of the year, or find new radio talent?

Luckman, suspecting that this was a test, took his time weighing his response. Finally, he told Lasker that he would recommend canceling. The program, he explained, had reached a saturation point; listeners by that time were either already sold on Pepsodent, or never would be sold. Luckman passed the test: Lasker agreed with him, and had been arguing the same point with Noyes for the past hour.[50] With that, the eight-year collaboration with *Amos 'n' Andy* came to an end, and Lord & Thomas began looking for a new hit for Pepsodent.

The choice initially came down to two personalities: Fred Allen and Milton Berle. But Edward Lasker, now heading up the radio department in the New York office, had another candidate in mind. He became head of the radio department in early 1938—only weeks after Lord & Thomas made the decision to sever ties with *Amos 'n' Andy*—and therefore was a new voice in these high-stakes discussions. Screwing up his courage, Edward invited Luckman to come to New York to see an obscure comedian named Bob Hope.

Hope wasn't a completely unknown quantity at Lord & Thomas; in December 1937, he had done a thirteen-week stint on American Tobacco's

Your Hit Parade. But George Washington Hill had been unimpressed with Hope, and so far, radio audiences seemed to agree with Hill's assessment.[51] Between 1935 and 1937, Hope had been given guest shots on several radio shows—including the Rudy Vallee show for Fleischmann's yeast and the Woodbury soap show—but had failed to land his own long-term deal.

Luckman, too, had reservations. Although he was impressed with Hope's quicksilver wit, he worried that the brash young comedian might be too sophisticated for a national audience. "Does he have the touch of the common man that you see in Andy's characterization of the Kingfish?" he asked Edward Lasker. "Jack Benny has that touch . . . Fibber McGee and Molly seem to follow the same pattern; so do Edgar Bergen and Charlie McCarthy. Those are three of the top shows on radio."[52]

Edward Lasker transmitted these concerns to Hope's agent. Hope agreed to turn some of his rapier wit on himself, and—thanks to Edward Lasker's lobbying and Luckman's backing—Lord & Thomas agreed to give Hope a trial. The first show aired in October 1938. Critics loved it. "That small speck going over the center field fence," *Variety* raved, "is the four-bagger Bob Hope whammed out his first time at bat for Pepsodent."[53] Audiences loved him, too: after only two months on the air, Hope's was the fourth most-listened-to show nationwide.[54]

Hope's subsequent accomplishments—as a radio, movie, and TV phenomenon and as an entertainer of U.S. troops overseas through the USO—began with that "four-bagger." In 1943, for example, Pepsodent happily paid $225,000 to send Hope on a wildly successful tour of Army camps.

Lasker's involvement in Pepsodent ended unhappily after two odd incidents in which he came into conflict with Charles Luckman, who by the late 1930s was gaining more and more authority at the company. Kenneth Smith continued to be a hands-off, frequently absent figure, and although Luckman continued to get his approval on all major decisions, these consultations increasingly became a formality.

The first incident, which occurred soon after Pepsodent began sponsoring the Bob Hope show, grew out of Luckman's decision to develop a creamier-textured toothpaste. He undertook this experiment on his own initiative, without notifying either Smith or Lasker. Pepsodent's lab produced three samples of varying creaminess, which Luckman distributed to the company's secretaries, executives, tax accountants, lawyers, and so on, asking them to choose their favorite. Almost 95 percent preferred the creamiest formula. Luckman then tested the new formula in Fort Worth, Texas, and Madison, Wisconsin, to equally favorable results. An A.C. Nielsen company survey a month after the new formula was introduced came back with results that Arthur Nielsen himself warned might be "too good to be true," but a second survey two weeks later confirmed the dramatic findings.[55]

Armed with this convincing data, Luckman made a formal presentation to Smith and Lasker, hoping to convince them to adopt the new creamier formula nationwide. According to Luckman, Lasker's response to the presentation was both unreasonable and unwavering. "Let us get one thing straight," he told Luckman. "If the figures say one thing, and I say another, I am right. I say no change."[56]

Lasker's position—if reported accurately by Luckman—bears some exploration. He was a major stockholder in the company and for almost two decades he had been one of its most important guiding forces. It was about this same juncture that Lasker commented to his ghost autobiographer, "I am Pepsodent!"—an attitude that infuriated the company's middle managers.[57] This was one of those occasions. Luckman was incensed—and also convinced that Lasker was dead wrong. He decided to move ahead without his superiors' approval, risking his job to do what he felt was right for the company.

A month later, Luckman found himself summoned by Lasker, who asked him point-blank whether he had in fact changed the formula without approval. Luckman admitted that he had, and Lasker asked if Kenneth Smith knew.

No, Luckman replied, he hadn't told Smith anything.

Lasker picked up the telephone and called Smith in Palm Beach. "Well," he said to Smith, "your young man passed the final test. He didn't let me put him down, but went ahead and ordered the formula changed. Isn't that something?"[58] With that, Smith and Lasker made Luckman vice president and general manager of the company. In 1941, when Smith decided to take another step back from the company, Luckman received another promotion, and was named president and CEO of Pepsodent.

Was this a premeditated test of Luckman's mettle? Or was an increasingly rigid Lasker simply saving face after realizing that Luckman had been right?

A second incident, involving the buyout of Pepsodent, suggests that Lasker may have harbored resentments about Luckman's decision to go around

In May 1922, August Busch, president of St. Louis-based brewer Anheuser-Busch, sailed from New York to Cherbourg aboard one of Lasker's passenger liners—and was surprised to find an extensive bar aboard the government-owned ship when Prohibition had forced his company out of the beer business. His noisy objections occasioned a bitter public fight with Lasker and ultimately led to all U.S.-flagged ships going "dry."

Opposite: Refitting the *Leviathan*, one of the world's largest ships, became one of Lasker's pet projects during in his tenure at the Shipping Board. *Top:* The *Leviathan's* shakedown cruise to the Caribbean and back in June 1923 caused a political uproar, which Lasker (front row, light suit, dark tie, approximately seventh from left) engineered and enjoyed. *Bottom:* Lasker's 480-acre estate in Lake Forest, Illinois, was maintained by a staff of fifty-five and featured a 180-acre, 18-hole, world-class golf course designed by William S. Flynn—and an air-conditioned movie theater that seated sixty. (Lasker house photo courtesy of Chicago History Museum.)

The federal government's promotion of dental health beginning in World War I created a new market for toothpaste and toothbrushes, which the Pepsodent Company (aided by Claude Hopkins and Albert Lasker) adroitly exploited. Advertising campaigns for Kleenex and other personal-hygiene products played on consumers' new awareness of germs and bacteria. Lasker personally engineered the transition of Kleenex from a cold-cream remover to a disposable handkerchief, in part by persuading Kimberly-Clark to make the tissue larger. Lasker became a significant shareholder in both the Pepsodent and the Kimberly-Clark companies; dividends from those holdings produced a significant income stream for Lasker in the 1920s and 1930s, and the appreciation of their stocks vastly increased his net worth. (Use of the trademark PEPSODENT, related trademarks and copyrights is with the written permission of Church & Dwight Co., Inc., Princeton, New Jersey. Kleenex ad © Kimberly-Clark Worldwide, Inc. Reprinted with permission.)

When U.S. Army nurses on the Western Front in World War I discovered a new use for Kimberly-Clark's wood-based cotton substitute—as a sanitary napkin—the company saw a vast new market for its product. Lord & Thomas worked with the company on ways to present Kotex to the world and, at the same time, persuade women to buy the unmentionable product at their local drugstores. Lasker personally convinced Edward Bok—influential editor of the *Ladies Home Journal* and other publications—to allow Kotex advertising in his magazines. (© Kimberly-Clark Worldwide, Inc. Reprinted with permission.)

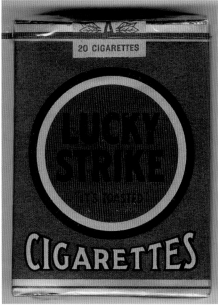

Opposite: The formidable George Washington Hill, president of the American Tobacco Company, who engaged in legendary battles with his favorite ad man—Albert Lasker. (Hill photo © Yousuf Karsh.) *Top:* Lord & Thomas worked closely with American Tobacco to transform "Lucky Strike" from an obscure tobacco sold in tins to one of the world's best-known cigarette brands. *Bottom:* The catchphrase "reach for a Lucky instead of a sweet" achieved instant notoriety and prompted a 1929 injunction from the Federal Trade Commission. (Billboard photo [at Patterson's Mill Country Store near Chapel Hill, North Carolina] © Bruce Henschel.)

Lasker loved movies and the movie business. Here, in a 1927 studio publicity shot, he poses with (from left to right) Jesse L. Lasky, production head of the Famous Players-Lasky (later Paramount) studio; his daughter Mary; actress Esther Ralston; and Dorothy Arzner, then known as "Paramount's girl director." In the early 1930s, Lasker and his friend and business partner John Hertz briefly owned a controlling interest in Paramount.

Top: "Amos 'n' Andy" at work in the NBC studio. Freeman Gosden and Charles Correll were two bricklayers from Peoria whose "blackface" radio program captivated the nation in the late 1920s and 1930s—and sold Pepsodent for Lasker. (Amos 'n' Andy photo reprinted with permission of NBC Universal, Inc.) *Bottom:* Socialist and muckraker Upton Sinclair, whose 1934 California gubernatorial run was thwarted by Lord & Thomas. (Sinclair photograph © Bettmann/CORBIS.)

Top: An anti-Sinclair billboard in Los Angeles, written and paid for by Lord & Thomas. *Bottom:* A pro-Sinclair billboard in Hollywood, September 1934. "I felt pretty sorry for Sinclair," one of Lasker's lieutenants later confessed. "We had been going pretty hard against him." (Both photos © Bettmann/CORBIS.)

Right: Bob Hope was a rising star by the time Edward Lasker proposed him in early 1938 to host *The Pepsodent Hour.* Hope's runaway success in that role further raised his visibility—and sold Pepsodent for Lasker. "That small speck going over the center field fence," *Variety* raved, "is the four-bagger Bob Hope whammed out his first time at bat for Pepsodent." (Hope photo © Getty Images.) *Below:* Lasker landed the Frigidaire account in 1935, and pushed his agency to come up with a memorable "reason-why" slogan: the "Meter-Miser." (Frigidaire ad reprinted with permission of the Electrolux Corporation. All rights reserved.)

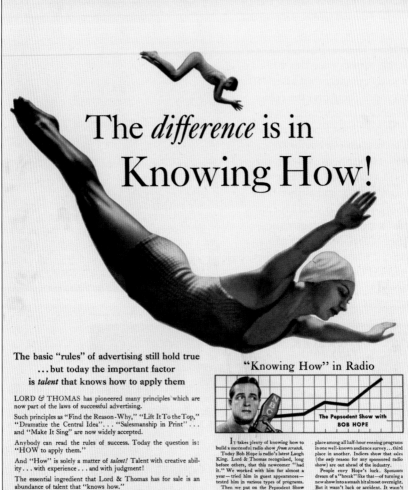

The *difference* is in
Knowing How!

The basic "rules" of advertising still hold true ...but today the important factor is *talent* that knows how to apply them

LORD & THOMAS has pioneered many principles which are now part of the laws of successful advertising.

Such principles as "Find the Reason-Why," "Lift It To the Top," "Dramatize the Central Idea"... "Salesmanship in Print"... and "Make It Sing" are now widely accepted.

Anybody can read the rules of success. Today the question is: "HOW to apply them."

And "How" is solely a matter of *talent!* Talent with creative ability... with experience... and with judgment!

The essential ingredient that Lord & Thomas has for sale is an abundance of talent that "knows how."

Its quality can swiftly be demonstrated by a review of the results that have been achieved for the clients of this agency.

"Knowing How" in Radio

The Pepsodent Show with BOB HOPE

It takes plenty of knowing how to build a successful radio show *from scratch.* Today Bob Hope is radio's latest Laugh King. Lord & Thomas recognized, long before others, that this newcomer "had it." We worked with him for almost a year—tried him in guest appearances—tested him in various types of programs. Then we put on the Pepsodent Show with Bob Hope.

The Pepsodent audience grew and grew. In eight months this show was in fourth place among all half-hour evening programs in one well-known audience survey...third place in another. Indices show that sales (the *only* reason for any sponsored radio show) are out ahead of the industry.

People envy Hope's luck. Sponsors dream of a "break" like that—of turning a new show into a smash hit almost overnight. But it wasn't luck or accident. It wasn't sleight of hand. It was having an organization with *talent* that can recognize ability, and develop it—talent that *knows how.*

LORD & THOMAS *Advertising*

NEW YORK · CHICAGO · LOS ANGELES · SAN FRANCISCO
HOLLYWOOD · DAYTON · TORONTO · MONTREAL · PARIS · LONDON

193

For the most part, Lasker disdained the kind of institutional advertising that competitors like J. Walter Thompson, N. W. Ayer, and BDO (later BBDO) engaged in, believing that ad agencies should be more or less invisible to the public. As competition intensified in the industry in the 1930s, however, Lasker grudgingly approved a series of ads emphasizing his agency's skill at applying the principles that he had helped invent in previous decades—and which were now standard across the industry. Occasionally, he bought space for Lord & Thomas ads in magazines that were "punished" by advertisers for printing articles about family planning and other controversial causes that he supported.

Left: The April 1926 cover of *Motion Picture* magazine featured Doris Kenyon, one of America's most popular and bankable stars from the silent era, who became Lasker's second wife. *Below:* Lasker and Kenyon pose on October 28, 1938, as they board the *Île de France* for their honeymoon trip to Europe. Both the trip and the marriage were a disaster. (Lasker and Kenyon picture courtesy of Acme Newsphotos.)

The inimitable Mary Lasker, Lasker's third wife, who led him into the world of philanthropy. A self-made entrepreneur with progressive—even radical—views on social issues, Mary Lasker is widely credited for steering more public dollars into health-related research than any other individual in U.S. history. This was her favorite portrait, taken at the seven-story Beekman Place townhouse in New York that she and Albert rented (and later purchased) from CBS head William Paley. (Photo courtesy of the Lasker Foundation.)

DON'T FIGHT CANCER ALONE

ASK THESE AGENCIES FOR ADVICE

YOUR STATE OR LOCAL MEDICAL SOCIETY·YOUR STATE OR LOCAL HEALTH DEPARTMENT · CANCER COMMITTEE OR STATE MEDICAL SOCIETIES· THE WOMEN'S FIELD ARMY OF THE AMERICAN SOCIETY FOR THE CONTROL OF CANCER·

U.S. PUBLIC HEALTH SERVICE IN COOPERATION WITH THE AMERICAN SOCIETY FOR CONTROL OF CANCER

Above: Although Mary Lasker spurred Albert (*right*) into active engagement in the battle against cancer, Albert's family had long been interested in the cause, creating the American Society for the Control of Cancer's first endowment in 1922. With an eye toward marketing, the Laskers later persuaded the organization to rename itself the "American Cancer Society." (Lasker photo courtesy of the Lasker Foundation.)

Left: Margaret Sanger headed the Birth Control Federation, and—in the 1920s and 1930s—published books and pamphlets arguing that women had a right to information about family planning and contraception. One of those books caught Mary Lasker's eye in 1937; subsequently, she and Albert became Sanger's largest financial backers—and Albert persuaded the organization to rename itself "Planned Parenthood."

Right: One of Lasker's great disappointments in his later years was that none of his children was both willing and able to carry on the Lord & Thomas agency. His son Edward (shown here with actress Jane Greer, whom he married in 1947) left the agency in 1941 to became a film producer and later a lawyer. Although daughter Mary also worked briefly at the agency in the 1930s, she battled both her supervisor and alcoholism, and was fired by her father. Daughter Frances never involved herself in her father's business. *Below:* Toward the end of Lasker's life, he and Mary assembled an impressive collection of Impressionist works of art, and—although a largely nonobservant Jew—Lasker became an ardent Zionist.

him. In 1944, Luckman was approached by Frederick Peyser, a representative of Lever Brothers, which was then one of the three major players in the soap industry (along with Colgate-Palmolive and Procter & Gamble). Lever Brothers wanted to buy Pepsodent, and was offering $66 per share in cash. Luckman, who by then owned 15 percent of the company, was eager to sell, and when he relayed the offer to Smith, Smith assigned him the voting rights for his 60 percent of the company stock. When Luckman met with Lasker, however, the deal fell apart. Lasker refused to sell and seemed personally affronted by the proposition. "Pepsodent's more my baby than anyone else's," he told Luckman. "I am going to tell Kenneth he cannot sell . . . besides, Peyser should have come to me first!"[59]

As the weeks went by, Lasker refused to budge. Luckman considered a lawsuit, though he dreaded airing the matter in court. Finally, he asked Peyser to make one last effort. He suggested that Peyser and the head of Lever Brothers call on Lasker and apologize for not bringing the offer first to him. Then, Luckman suggested, they should lay on the honey, lauding Lasker's many contributions to the company over the years.

Peyser agreed to try, and the effort was partially successful. Lasker agreed to sell, but he insisted that Lever Brothers pay him a dollar more per share than either Luckman or Smith. What's more, even though Lever Brothers offered to pay him this difference out of their own pocket, Lasker insisted that the difference come from Luckman's and Smith's share of the profits. One last time, Lasker was asserting his dominance at Pepsodent, and Smith and Luckman were forced to accept his terms.

It was not Lasker's finest hour. According to Luckman, neither he nor Smith ever spoke to their former colleague again.[60]

Armed with strong data from the Pepsodent experience, Lord & Thomas began recommending radio campaigns to many other clients.

In 1934, Lord & Thomas approached International Cellucotton Products Company (ICPC) and proposed a broadcast promotion for Kleenex. The vehicle became an on-air soap opera, *The Story of Mary Marlin*, that was fifteen minutes long and aired five times a week.

In November 1935, Lord & Thomas ran a Pepsodent-like promotion on *Mary Marlin*, offering a free packet of Kleenex to listeners who wrote in to the Chicago NBC station to keep the program on the air. The station received 67,300 responses: the largest amount of mail ever received by a station in response to a promotion. In 1936, Lord & Thomas mimicked another successful Pepsodent promotion, offering $10,000 in prizes to listeners who wrote in with naming suggestions for Mary Marlin's baby, as well as the best way to use Kleenex for babies. Again, the response was tremendous: NBC received 168,207 responses, and Lord & Thomas attributed a 13 percent increase in sales to the promotion.[61]

The company saw additional proof of Mary Marlin's success in the case of Quest deodorant, a product launched in 1935 and advertised solely on the radio show. Within months, a consumer survey showed that the product had captured first place in the powder deodorant field, a fact that Lord & Thomas called "conclusive proof" of the success of the show.[62]

But radio advertising was expensive, even for large corporations like ICPC. The Mary Marlin show was so costly, in fact, that ICPC suspended advertising in all other media while the show was on the air. The program clearly earned its keep; according to the account history, sales increases due to the program were "sensational." Nevertheless, The Story of Mary Marlin was dropped in 1937 when Lord & Thomas concluded—as in the case of Amos 'n' Andy—that the show had reached its saturation point. For its subsequent campaign, Kleenex reverted to print media.

With the exception of David Sarnoff's RCA and the General Electric subsidiaries that Thomas Logan had brought to the agency, Lord & Thomas never made significant inroads into the highest reaches of corporate America. (New York upstarts BBDO and Young & Rubicam had far more success on those circles.) For example: Lasker had worked his magic for second-tier automakers—companies like Hudson, Mitchell Motors, and Studebaker—but he had never landed the likes of Ford, General Motors, or Chrysler.

This changed in 1935, when General Motors came into the fold. This time, though, Lord & Thomas wouldn't be advertising cars. Instead, the agency would be advertising refrigerators for General Motors's Frigidaire subsidiary: the leading player in a $300 million industry that was growing dramatically, thanks to the nationwide expansion of the electrical grid and the lower prices that resulted from increased sales volumes.

Frigidaire wasn't Lord & Thomas's first refrigerator account. The short-lived partnership with Thomas Logan brought into the Lord & Thomas fold several General Electric products, including the "Monitor Top" refrigerator, introduced to the public in 1927. Unlike competing models of the day, which concealed their mechanical parts inside their rectangular "boxes," the Monitor Top featured a hatbox-shaped metal box atop its cooling compartment.[63] In the "hatbox" sat the refrigerator's motor and compressor.

One of GE's corporate goals was to increase the overall consumption of electricity, so the Monitor Top favored a relatively inefficient air-cooled system over a water-cooled one.[64] Obviously, Lord & Thomas couldn't promote the Monitor Top as an efficient appliance—it cost about $2.60 more per year to power than competitive models—so the agency focused on "simplified electrical refrigeration" as its campaign theme, and trumpeted the appliance's reliability as its key selling point. *"Not one cent for repairs,"* read the bold headlines in Lord & Thomas's ads.

On the strength of Lord & Thomas's campaign, GE's ungainly new product seized 60 percent of the refrigerator market in 1927. The rest of the industry—Frigidaire, Kelvinator, Westinghouse, and smaller players— howled in protest at the implied warranty inherent in the "not one cent" theme. In response, the powerful home-appliance industry association took a novel tack: it imposed a three-year warranty on *all* home refrigerators, thereby blunting the impact of GE's campaign, and effectively relegating the Monitor Top to its previous status as an industry also-ran. Lord & Thomas and GE's refrigeration unit soon parted company, in part because GE demanded that the agency begin spending a lot of time at individual dealerships—a strategy of which Lasker disapproved.[65]

The real powerhouse in the industry—before and after the anomalous year of 1927—was General Motors' entry into home refrigeration: the Frigidaire, which typically outsold its nearest competitors by nearly two to one. GM first got into the refrigerator business in 1918, when Will Durant applied his auto company's mass-production techniques to refrigerators. The Frigidaire Corporation formally became a GM subsidiary in 1926, with an ambitious young executive named Elmer G. Biechler as its president and general manager. That same year, GM built a huge new Frigidaire factory in Moraine City, Ohio, vastly increasing the subsidiary's output—and necessitating a huge increase in its advertising budget. The combination worked: by 1929, Frigidaire had sold its millionth unit.[66]

In the ensuing half-decade, Frigidaire became nearly synonymous with "refrigerator"—a mixed blessing, in terms of brand awareness. "I heard a woman say, 'I just bought a General Electric Frigidaire,'" Albert Lasker observed pointedly, underscoring the perils inherent in becoming a generic.[67]

In the summer of 1935, Frigidaire went looking for a new agency.

Frigidaire was blessed with considerable marketing expertise, including a network of talented distributors and dealers across the country. At an early meeting, Frigidaire representatives told Lord & Thomas about an interesting experiment then going on in the Dallas-Forth Worth region. In the previous year—1934—the Electrolux refrigerator had successfully invaded that territory, using claims of low operating costs to grab second place behind Frigidaire. Worried about this interloper, the Fort Worth distributor tested the Electrolux, and discovered that, unlike the Frigidaire, it couldn't maintain a constant 50-degree temperature in the scorching Texas summer. In collaboration with Dallas Power & Light, the Frigidaire distributor then handed out three hundred thermometers to randomly selected refrigerator owners, and the results were the same: Frigidaire units performed extremely well and competing models came up short—with Electrolux performing worst of all.

With this information in hand, Frigidaire counterattacked. It shipped ten thousand thermometers to Dallas, handing them out to current and prospective customers through its dealer network and also inviting competing dealers to distribute the thermometers. (The power company did its part by running ads supporting regular checks of refrigerator temperatures for safety's sake.) The result, according to an in-house Lord & Thomas memo, was a near-complete rout:

> *The effect of this campaign on Electrolux was that they dropped from second place to fifth place in one season, lost the power company as a distributor, lost a number of their active dealers, and were flooded with a warehouse full of repossessed jobs. Frigidaire's monthly sales average in the area went from 163 before the campaign started to 298 during July and August, 1934, when the thermometers were being given away. Amazingly enough the campaign resulted in a drop in the Frigidaire service cost because the thermometers led owners to defrost oftener and to take better care of their refrigerators.*[68]

On the strength of this success, Frigidaire wanted to build its 1936 advertising campaign around the concept of "safety-zone temperatures": in other words, the ability of its refrigerators to maintain foods at a safe temperature. In addition, the manufacturer wanted to promote its products' fast-freezing capability, low operating costs, features, and five-year guarantee. These added up to a "five standards of value" story, Frigidaire told Lord & Thomas, and that was what the new ad campaign should push.

But the agency said no. Frigidaire, they contended, was using "product thinking," rather than talking in "consumer words." The standards-of-value story line, Lord & Thomas pointed out, would appeal only to those who had already decided to buy a refrigerator; it wouldn't speak at all to the millions of people who believed that they couldn't afford electric refrigeration in the first place. Many consumers dreaded the idea of a meter spinning away in some dark corner of the house, racking up electric bills that they might not be able to pay.

No, said Lord & Thomas; what was needed was a "potent battle cry" to win over the prospect who worried that he or she couldn't afford an electric refrigerator. And that battle cry had to rescue the Frigidaire brand from its increasingly generic limbo.

Albert Lasker took a personal interest in the Frigidaire account. He maintained a close personal relationship with Frigidaire's president, Elmer Biechler.[69] He also participated actively in the key internal discussions at Lord & Thomas, focusing on the battle-cry challenge. As he later recalled:

> We said, "We have to clothe it with something that makes it seem a new product, so that the name gets a new proportion" . . .
>
> I said, "What is the main working part of it?" And the main working part was a rotary compressor with only two parts—very ingenious—a mechanism which they had had from the beginning. They had never changed it from the first day. I said, "All right, we will name the working part. We will give it a name, and then we will say, 'Frigidaire with the blah-blah,' whatever that is. And then if they go to see a "General Electric Frigidaire," they will ask, 'Is this the General Electric Frigidaire with the blah-blah?' And they won't buy it unless it has the blah-blah . . .
>
> I said, "We can't explain [the compressor] technically. It must be two words where the imagination of the reader will fasten on the fact that nothing is so economical as this . . . And furthermore, don't bring me any two words that aren't alliterative. If you are going to use two words—if you are going to fasten them in the minds of the readers—then they must be alliterative."[70]

Actually, the rotary compressor was brand-new—replacing the far less effective reciprocating model that Frigidaires had used up to this point—but Lasker got the main point of the story right. The entire Lord & Thomas creative staff was asked to submit names for the efficient new compressor (the *blah-blah*), and several dozen people came up with close to two thousand names. At a staff meeting, Lasker reviewed the entries, and rejected all of them. At that point, however, a young copywriter named Ted Little retrieved from a trashcan a crumpled piece of paper that included a name that he had decided wasn't even good enough to submit: *meter miser*.[71] "That's it," Lasker said immediately.

But Lasker wanted to make sure that the phrase worked in the ears of potential consumers. Staffers had "meter miser" printed on five hundred pieces of paper, and then asked pedestrians on the streets of Chicago what the phrase implied to them. An amazing 82 percent said that it had something to do with "saving current."[72]

Clearly, *meter miser* was a winner. Still fighting their client's stated preferences, the agency renamed the product "Frigidaire with the Meter-Miser" and added the phrase "Made only by General Motors." Lasker contributed a tagline: *cuts current costs to the bone.*

The first ads featuring the Meter-Miser appeared on March 6, 1936, and proved a spectacular success. GM had hoped to sell 320,000 units for the 1936 model year; the total came closer to 440,000 units (with those additional 120,000 refrigerators delivering extraordinary profits, thanks to ever-increasing economies of scale). The following year, more than 550,000 Frigidaires were sold.

The growing power of advertising was indisputable: Lord & Thomas had found ways to sell staggering numbers of two distinct kinds of refrigerators, from two different manufacturers, within a decade. The agency, and the old master who still guided its fortunes, at least intermittently, hadn't lost their touch. Inside Lord & Thomas, people were reminded of the importance of listening and being responsive to their clients, but at the same time, sticking to their guns. It also became clear that successful advertising was self-fulfilling: in the wake of the Meter-Miser's astounding success, General Motors's engineers felt compelled to make sure that the Frigidaire *was* stingy with current.

Finally, the wisdom of maintaining a creative tension within the agency, and drawing on the collective talents of a *team*, once again became apparent. Ted Little's inspiration, David Noyes emphasized, almost failed to make it to the table, and that would have been both the agency's and the client's loss:

> That is why [Lasker] has an inviolable rule that no one must sit in criticism over his creative thinking, and no man is privileged to reject his own ideas, no matter how absurd. He must always submit it for final appraisal, where the

decision is made . . . Each man goes to work on the other man, and it is a sort of healthy conflict, where everybody attacks everybody else's work with no quarter given, but no pride at stake with everything you submitted, [and] always with the idea that practically everything is going to be thrown out.[73]

Frigidaire remained a Lord & Thomas account until Lasker closed the agency's doors in 1942, and remained an account of Foote, Cone & Belding (Lord & Thomas's successor agency) until 1955.

In more ways than one, Lasker's triumph at Frigidaire represented the end of an era. It was the last big account that Lord & Thomas won and the last account on which Lasker put his personal stamp.

In addition, it was the last time Albert Lasker developed a close personal rapport with a company's leader—in this case, Frigidaire's president and general manager—and did business on a peer-to-peer level. American business was becoming more stratified, divisionalized, hierarchical, and impersonal, and the kinds of personal relationships that Lasker cultivated and counted upon for his influence were increasingly difficult to establish.

Lasker found hierarchies boring. He relished his head-to-head confrontations with the likes of George Washington Hill and David Sarnoff. He enjoyed being a *player*, especially a player with a significant equity stake. And he believed, with some justification, that injecting bureaucracy into the advertising process only hurt that process.

Eventually, these changes would help drive Lasker out of advertising. First, though, he and his West Coast lieutenants would use the tools of their trade—including their newly acquired skills in radio—to change the course of American politics once again.

Chapter Eighteen

Selling and Unselling California

From 1900 to 1920, Los Angeles was essentially a tourist town. Like most tourist towns, it had its share of freaks, side-shows, novelties, and show-places. Ducks waddled along the streets with advertisements painted on their backs; six-foot-nine pituitary giants with sandwich-board signs stalked the downtown streets; while thousands of people carrying Bibles in their hands and singing hymns marched in evangelical parades . . . During the winter months, Los Angeles was, in fact, a great circus without a tent.[1] —Cary McWilliams

BY 1920, tourism was bringing some 200,000 visitors a year to Southern California.[2] But as McWilliams suggests, this trade was restricted mainly to the December–February period, mainly because people in other parts of the country were convinced that Southern California was unbearably hot during the summer. In 1921, a group of business leaders undertook to change this by organizing the "All-Year Club of Southern California, Ltd." According to a Lord & Thomas account, the stakes were high:

During the summer, no tourists came, and with many residents taking their vacations elsewhere, there was a severe retail business slump every summer, rents went down, resorts and hotels and theaters closed their doors, throwing employees out of work, and every line of trade and industry suffered.

The organizers [of the All-Year Club], most of whom had come here from the east and middle-west, knew that the summer climate was really delightful by contrast with that of their former homes, with cool nights and rainless days. They decided that if the people in the rest of the country knew these things, some of them might be persuaded to come during the summer. Advertising, they believed, might be able to put over this idea.

Prior to World War I, communities, regions, and even nations had mounted advertising campaigns to attract tourists, conventions, industries, or settlers. The Rotary Club of Milwaukee, for example, spent $25,000 in 1916 to create goodwill and attract investment; and the Denver Tourist Bureau allocated $64,000 in 1916 to bring in both conventions and tourists. The following year, the government of Cuba used advertising to attract immigrants from the United States.[3]

The Santa Barbara Chamber of Commerce launched a campaign in the summer of 1919 to bring tourists to "California's wonder play-place," the "Sublimely Beautiful Santa Barbara." It aimed its first newspaper ads at the sweltering populations of Arizona, New Mexico, and Texas. Every Friday during the summer months, a stock ad ran in eighteen newspapers across the Southwest. Only a single line of copy changed from week to week: the mean temperature of Santa Barbara in the preceding week.[4]

Los Angeles, of course, would not be outdone by provincial Santa Barbara. By 1920, Los Angeles had surpassed San Francisco to become California's largest city. The number of building permits issued annually increased sixfold between 1918 (six thousand) and 1921 (thirty-seven thousand).[5] With the creation of the Los Angeles Philharmonic in 1919, the City of Angels had become one of only three cities in American history to support two major orchestras.

The city's biggest cheerleader in the early 1920s was Harry Chandler, then the publisher of the *Los Angeles Times*. Chandler, a native of New Hampshire, had moved to Los Angeles in 1883 to combat a persistent lung ailment. He married the boss's daughter (Marion Otis, daughter of publisher and civic booster Harrison Gray Otis), and took over the paper in 1917. Under Chandler's leadership, the *Times* engaged in fierce circulation wars with William Randolph Hearst's *Examiner*, Los Angeles's other major morning daily, and also promoted Los Angeles relentlessly.

More than a love of community motivated Chandler: along with several prominent colleagues, he was a major land speculator. (His group subdivided and sold house lots adding up to forty-seven thousand acres in the area.) So he was particularly partial to promotional schemes that might enhance property values in his adopted city. One such scheme, recounts journalist and author Carey McWilliams, came into his head sometime in the early months of 1921: "One winter day in 1921, a lady marched into [his] office . . . and complained bitterly that apartment-house owners in Los Angeles prospered in the winter but starved in the summer. Couldn't something be done about it?"[6]

At Chandler's urging, a group of eighteen prominent businesspeople— including representatives from railroad, hotels, banks, newspapers, real estate firms, and other industries—gathered in Los Angeles on May 23, 1921. Their goal was to build on the work of the Southern California Hotel Men's Association's publicity committee, which had been struggling to overcome the seasonality of their trade. Within a month of this gathering, the formation of the "All-Year Club" was announced, and a subscription drive—seeking to raise $300,000 a year for three years—was launched.[7]

Chandler's group made several decisions that proved critical to the subsequent success of the All-Year Club. As one observer later noted:

> The board of directors was made so representative that no interest in the city, or in Southern California, could hold out because it was not represented.
>
> An initial policy was laid down. All funds were to be spent for advertising. None was to be used for patronage. The executive secretary was obliged to be in the position to show at all times that every dollar he was spending would pull the greatest possible load.[8]

The All-Year Club's founders felt some urgency: the national economic recession of 1920–1922 had hit California hard. Well before the hoped-for $300,000 was raised, therefore, they authorized a $50,000 trial campaign, and (in May 1921) hired an agency that by then was well known in Southern California: Lord & Thomas. Lasker's agency had successfully promoted oranges, raisins, and other perishable commodities; now it was being asked to promote California—and *quickly*. As former Sunkist marketer Don Francisco recalled: "When they started to do this, there was a depression throughout the country . . . It was felt that if they could bring in enough tourists to Southern California, we could bring in enough money and activity to [counteract] that depression. So they had to advertise in a great hurry, and we were chosen to handle it without anyone else being considered."[9]

One of the agency's first efforts on behalf of the All-Year Club was an ad entitled "That Vacation Land You've Never Seen," written by "an Easterner." ("Copy was headed 'By an Easterner,'" records the Lord & Thomas account history, "because Southern Californians had a bad reputation for over-enthusiasm.") The Easterner was Robert Crane, recently relocated from Chicago to Lord & Thomas's Los Angeles office. His reason-why copy told of lofty mountains, fertile valleys, trout streams, and sea bathing, "all within a stone's throw of the ninth largest city in size in the United States!" Crane cited U.S. Weather Bureau records from the previous forty-four years to underscore the region's temperate median temperatures: June, 65 degrees; July, 79 degrees; August, 71 degrees, and September, 68 degrees.

The ad appeared in thirty-three newspapers in the "hot belt" states of the Southwest. It included a coupon offer of a free booklet; inquiries resulting from the coupon were turned over to the participating railroads for individual follow-up.

Initial results were positive. One hotel in Los Angeles—a subscriber to the All-Year Club—reported that its head count increased by one hundred people a day during the summer of 1921. Several real estate agencies reported sales to individuals who had been lured to the region by the Lord & Thomas advertising. Despite the recession, the Southern Pacific, Union Pacific, and Santa Fe Railroads sold an unprecedented number of tickets to Southern California in the summer of 1921.[10] When a formal competition for the account finally was held, Lord & Thomas easily retained it.

One of the stronger endorsements of the All-Year Club's efforts came from the supervisors of Los Angeles County, who in 1922 appropriated $50,000 to support the initiative. Only sixteen states nationwide then permitted local tax receipts to be used for community advertising. The fact that California was one of them was a huge boon to the All-Year Club—as well as to "Californians, Inc.," the community advertising group organized in 1922 to promote San Francisco and Northern California.[11] Within two years, six neighboring counties in addition to Los Angeles were also kicking in tax dollars to the All-Year Club's budget. By 1924, something like 40 percent of that $300,000 budget was coming from public sources.[12]

With the influx of public dollars, more systematic assessments began to be made, and again, the results were positive. An astounding 80 percent of the individuals who were contacted by the participating railroads (as a result of having requested the "couponed" informational pamphlet) wound up traveling to Southern California. Before the All-Year Club began its efforts, according to one study, Southern California had 126 winter tourists for every 100 summer tourists. By 1923, it attracted 200 summer visitors for every 126 winter visitors.[13]

———— ◦◦◦ ————

For the rest of the decade, the All-Year Club and Lord & Thomas enjoyed steady success. The agency discovered—perhaps belatedly—that women played a critical role in determining their families' vacation destinations. As a result, ad copy was written with women in mind, and an increasing percentage of the ad budget went into women's magazines. Beginning in 1927, Lord & Thomas began to trade on the increasing allure of Hollywood by including testimonials from Douglas Fairbanks and other celebrities.[14] The All-Year Club's advertising budget exceeded a half-million dollars for the first time in 1929, and there seemed to be no end in sight to the dizzying success of Southern California, shared by Lord & Thomas.

Then came the stock market crash, the Great Depression, and—within a few short years—an extraordinary westward migration of desperate people seeking escape from the Dust Bowl. Californians now had a mixed message to sell. Yes, they badly needed tourist dollars, but they didn't want even greater numbers of poor people to migrate westward.

A typical ad from 1932 included striking imagery of beautiful people playing golf under palm trees, with spectacular mountains rising in the background. The readers of the ad were advised to "bake out their troubles":

Work . . . worry . . . taut nerves . . . fear of the future. They've been a pretty steady diet for the last two or three years. And yet, honestly, what has it all accomplished for you? Forget it for a while. Come on out and have some FUN. Regain your perspective and learn again that life, after all, is meant for LIVING.

In much smaller type, the ad also included a cautionary message:

Come to California for a glorious vacation. Advise anyone not to come seeking employment, lest he be disappointed; but for the tourist, attractions are unlimited.

In other words, the All-Year Club and its advertising agency found themselves in a nearly untenable situation. "Like most promotions of the sort," wrote Carey McWilliams, "the All-Year Club has been too successful. Its seductive advertisements were partially responsible for the great influx of impoverished Okies and Arkies in the 'thirties.'"[15] If too few well-heeled tourists showed up, Lord & Thomas would be in trouble. If too many Okies and Arkies showed up, Lord & Thomas would be in *more* trouble.

On balance, though, the All-Year Club must be counted a great success for Southern California—and an even greater boon to Lord & Thomas. Even before being elevated to the head of Lord & Thomas's Los Angeles office in 1924, Don Francisco had struggled to carve out a distinctive West Coast personality for his office. He had to persuade Californians that Lord & Thomas wasn't simply another carpetbagging firm from the East—that it possessed strong local roots and had California's interests at heart. As he later recalled:

> *After we got the All-Year Club, we would show that we were engaged in helping basic industry, like oranges, lemons, grapefruit, raisins, and the tourist industry. Beyond that, we went into a lot of civic things. We handled the Community Chest publicity and advertising, and we took an active part in the Chamber of Commerce, and [I] served for fifteen years on the Publicity Committee. Our men enrolled in Community Chest drives, and we took an active part in the Advertising Club.*
>
> *I spent an awful lot of time of that, for years, probably too much. Mr. Lasker thought at first it was too much, but I think with the situation the way it was, it was not . . . We had a selling job to do.*[16]

It was against this backdrop that California's power-brokers turned to Lord & Thomas for a higher-stakes kind of help.

Since the later decades of the nineteenth century, California politics had been a volatile mix of radicalism and conservatism. In the late 1870s, for example, California was swept up in a wave of "Kearneyism," named for vigilante and radical labor organizer Dennis Kearney, who seized control of the state's Workingman's Party in 1878. Among other things, the fiery Kearney called for state regulation of railroads and banks, an eight-hour day for laborers (the standard was ten), major tax reform, and the direct election of U.S. senators.

These proposals were radical enough for their day; in addition, Kearney loudly advocated the immediate deportation and exclusion of Chinese immigrants, as well as "a little judicious hanging" among the millionaires clustered atop San Francisco's elite Nob Hill.[17]

Other socialist-leaning political movements followed. In 1901, the Union Labor Party elected a bassoon player named Eugene Schmitz mayor of San Francisco. In 1907, a group of Los Angeles–based reformers founded the Lincoln-Roosevelt League, with their prime target the Southern Pacific Railroad, about which California historian James Bryce observed: "No state has been so much at the mercy of one powerful corporation."[18] The League enjoyed a few years of California glory—culminating in the election of their candidate and Albert Lasker's close friend Hiram Johnson to the U.S. Senate— then wilted and died.[19]

But despite California's tendency to breed radical political movements, it remained a Republican stronghold throughout the early twentieth century. The GOP controlled the governorship, the state senate, and the state assembly for the first third of the twentieth century. Between 1860 and 1932, California registered five Republicans for every Democrat.

So when socialist writer and muckraker Upton Sinclair ran for governor of California in 1934, Republicans at first weren't worried. Some concluded that "Sinclairism was Kearneyism and Johnsonianism all over again."[20] But the Sinclair challenge was different. First, unlike Kearney, Schmitz, and Johnson, Sinclair affiliated with the Democratic Party, and then—to the astonishment of millions—he went on to capture his party's nomination.

The backdrop of the Great Depression, too, mooted traditional political calculations. Desperate people might embrace dramatic change.

Finally, the 1934 governor's race differed from previous socialist uprisings in the state because of the central role played in the contest by modern mass media: radio, motion pictures, newspapers, direct mail, and national fundraising. As the author of an exhaustive study of Sinclair's 1934 election bid put it: "The prospect of a socialist governing the nation's most volatile state sparked nothing less than a revolution in American politics. With an important boost from the image-makers of Hollywood, Sinclair's opponents virtually invented the modern media campaign."[21]

In this drama, Lord & Thomas played a key role. Certainly ad men had been employed in politics before, notably with Lasker's work for Warren Harding in 1920 and Bruce Barton's campaign for Calvin Coolidge four years later.[22] What was different about California in 1934, though, was the degree to which Sinclair's political opponents turned over the development of campaign strategies and tactics to Lord & Thomas and their allied media professionals—and the relentless sophistication with which those new allies plied their trade.

———— ·◈· ————

Born in Baltimore in 1878 and raised in New York, Upton Sinclair earned a bachelor's degree from City College and began churning out "half-dime" novels for a pulp-fiction publisher. A year before joining the Socialist party in 1902, he published the first in a long list of novels, which in the coming decades would flow from his pen at an average rate of about two per year. He toiled mostly in obscurity until the publication of *The Jungle* (1906), which exposed the horrifically unsanitary conditions and ruthless labor exploitation in the Chicago meatpacking industry. Along with the pioneering journalism of Samuel Hopkins Adams and others, Sinclair's impassioned polemics helped lead to the passage of the Food and Drug Act and the Meat Inspection Act.

Sinclair continued to churn out exposés and fictionalized accounts of capitalist scandal and power. Sometimes he highlighted a single social problem (such as venereal disease, in *Damaged Goods*, 1913) or an historic event (the Ludlow Massacre, in *King Coal*, 1917). But his chief delight lay in flaying the nation's most powerful institutions. In domain after domain, he accumulated both impassioned followers and embittered enemies.[23]

In *The Brass Check* (1919), for instance, Sinclair took on American journalism. "What is the Brass Check?" he asked. "The Brass Check is found in your pay-envelope every week—you who write and print and distribute our newspapers and magazines. The Brass Check is the price of your shame—you who take the fair body of truth and sell it in the market-place, who betray the virgin hopes of mankind into the loathsome brothel of Big Business." To make sure no one missed the point, he added: "When I planned this book I had in mind a sub-title: 'A Study of the Whore of Journalism.'"[24]

Sometimes he got personal. In 1905, William Randolph Hearst—whose vast publishing empire included several of California's most influential newspapers—recruited Sinclair and several other prominent muckrakers, leftists, and socialists to write for his newly acquired general-interest magazine, *Cosmopolitan*. Sinclair found Hearst a beguiling figure: his wealth, his political influence, and the salacious rumors that swirled around his personal affairs. So when two years later Sinclair published *The Industrial Republic*, a futuristic social novel, he made Hearst president of a newly socialist United States, depicted the publisher as a "traitor to his class," and wrote of his obsession with Manhattan's "tenderloin" district.[25] Hearst was not one to forgive.

Sinclair also accumulated enemies in Hollywood's film industry, which by the 1930s enjoyed unprecedented popularity, profits, and power. At one point, for example, Sinclair received an overture from William Fox, one of Hollywood's legendary moguls. "He had been robbed of a good part of his fortune during the recent panic," Sinclair recalled, and was willing to pay Sinclair the princely sum of $25,000 to tell his story. After weeks of daily interviews with the deposed studio head, the job was done. But when Sinclair discovered that "Fox was using the threat of publishing my manuscript . . . to get back some of the properties of which he had been deprived"—in other words, as a tool of blackmail—he sent the manuscript to a publisher, who promptly printed twenty-five thousand copies. The book, Sinclair recalled proudly, caused "a bang that might have been heard at the moon if there was anybody there to listen." As a result of these and other adventures, many of the most powerful men in Hollywood—as in so many American establishments—despised Upton Sinclair.[26]

He had gotten a taste of the bully pulpit in 1923 when, after being arrested during a dockworkers' strike in San Pedro, he addressed several large rallies. Once in front of a crowd, he proved himself a skilled orator.[27] A *New York Times* reporter described him as: ". . . a quiet, slight figure, with a pleasant smile constantly on his lips, suggesting inner certainty rather than humor or political winsomeness. Mr. Sinclair avoids emotional appeals and the stage tricks of fighting virility. In an even, bland voice, almost a monotone . . . he talks at once plainly and brilliantly."[28]

He also had dabbled in politics a few times with unimpressive results, running on the Socialist ticket for senator once and for governor twice, never capturing more than sixty thousand votes.

But the Great Depression's devastating effects troubled him enormously. "In the state of California, which had a population of seven million at the time," he later recorded, "there were a million out of work, public-relief funds were exhausted, and people were starving." He began to sketch out a detailed program to "End Poverty in California" (EPIC).

One day at the end of August 1933, as he was in the midst of this work, a letter arrived at his home from a little-known Santa Monica Democrat who urged Sinclair to seek that party's nomination for governor.[29] In his memoir, Sinclair claimed that he agreed to meet with a group of Democrats at a hotel on the beach; that they "argued and pleaded" for him to run; that he refused; and that after much soul-searching, he gave in to his overwhelming sense of social obligation. This account exaggerates the degree of soul-searching that was involved. Less than twenty-four hours after receiving the Santa Monica operative's letter, according to his biographer, Sinclair quietly slipped into Beverly Hills and changed his registration from Socialist to Democrat.[30]

Sinclair and his new Democratic allies moved quickly. The author-turned-politician published his program in a sixty-four-page booklet in which he used the literary device of telling the history of California a few years in the future—one in which, of course, he won the election and governed the state. The awkwardly titled "I, Governor of California—And How I Ended Poverty: A True Story of the Future" described how Governor Sinclair replaced the sales tax with steeply graduated income and property taxes; how he boosted taxes on inheritances and public utilities; and how he paid $50 to every widow, every "needy" person over the age of sixty, and every blind and physically disabled resident in the state. The centerpiece of the EPIC plan, however, was a network of cooperative colonies situated in idle factories and on unused farmland, taken over through eminent domain or punitive taxes and operated by the state. There, workers produced and exchanged the goods they needed to live on a noncash basis, a system that Sinclair dubbed "production for use." The story concludes two years into Governor Sinclair's term, when—with but one poor person remaining in the state of California—he resigns and heads home to write another novel.[31]

Proceeds from *I, Governor*—which sold nearly a million copies—helped fund a grassroots organization that spread like wildfire across the state. There were rallies, bake sales, speakers' bureaus, and an eight-page fold-out magazine, *EPIC News*, which soon boasted a circulation of more than 500,000. Sinclair also offered up his message on the radio, a medium in which his earnest and self-deprecating manner played well.[32]

Sinclair faced six opponents in the Democratic primary, held on August 28, 1934. What they didn't know was that Sinclair's grassroots organizers had registered some 350,000 new Democrats. Despite running in a six-man Democratic field, Sinclair not only came in first, but also attracted more votes than the uncontested Republican nominee, incumbent Governor Frank Merriam.[33]

A collective shudder shook the state's monied interests. California's wealthy elite, Arthur Schlesinger Jr. observed, "saw in EPIC the threat of social revolution by a rabble of crazed bankrupts and paupers . . . [that would] drive all wealth and respectability from the state." Director Billy Wilder, a recent immigrant from Austria, recalled that Sinclair "scared the hell out of the community. They all thought him to be a most dangerous Bolshevik beast." The *New York Times* reported that, "a sense of Armageddon hangs in the bland California air." Even Franklin Roosevelt, in faraway Washington, was uneasy. If he supported EPIC, he risked alienating the Democratic center. If he didn't, he risked losing touch with the electorate's clear drift leftward. Roosevelt could afford neither to embrace nor disown Sinclair.[34]

<hr />

Shortly after Sinclair's victory in the primary, Charles Teague—head of the California Fruit Growers Exchange—approached railroads, utilities, and other major corporations throughout the state to help to defeat the Socialist-turned-Democrat. The group called itself "United for California": a purposefully nonpartisan name, aimed at appealing to disaffected Democrats as well as Republicans. Headquartered in Los Angeles, United for California went public October 3, releasing a statement that the election of Upton Sinclair "would strike at the roots of our most cherished institutions—the home, the church, and the school."[35]

These and subsequent dramatic pronouncements were not Teague's handiwork. As he pondered how best to counter the Sinclair menace, Teague took a bold and unprecedented step. He turned over the campaign to discredit Upton Sinclair and reelect Frank Merriam as governor of California to Albert Lasker's Lord & Thomas.

Still heading the agency's West Coast operations, if only just barely, was Don Francisco. Francisco was then relocating to New York, where he was slated to head up his firm's operations in the East. He had spent several months in New York and had just returned to California in late September 1934—for what he thought was a final two-week visit—when he was summoned by Teague to an emergency meeting.

Teague told Francisco that United for California wanted Lord & Thomas to handle the propaganda side of the anti-Sinclair campaign and that they wanted Francisco to lead the charge. Francisco declined, mindful of his impending departure for New York and probably thinking that the assignment was a risky one for Lord & Thomas. But Teague persisted. In fact, as Francisco recalled, Sunkist's head made it clear that this was not an invitation but a command: "He said, 'Well, Mr. Lasker ought to do it, because if Sinclair wins, why, you haven't any business out here, and neither have most of us. We'll go to the dogs. Mr. Lasker, and Lord & Thomas, ought to be *delighted* to contribute your services to protect their business and their clients' businesses.'"[36]

Francisco placed an urgent call to Lasker in Chicago. If he hoped that Lasker would turn the job down, he was disappointed. Lasker was, Francisco later recalled, "tremendously interested" in the assignment, and instructed his first lieutenant to do Teague's bidding. Reluctantly, Francisco got back in harness. "It's a good cause," he wrote to Lasker toward the end of September, "and because all our California clients are so concerned, it seems a strategic move to take the assignment at this time."[37] He picked one of his most trusted lieutenants, Don Belding, to head up the campaign. He also recruited Don Forker, a former advertising manager for Union Oil who had moved over to Lord & Thomas, to handle the radio broadcasts.

The radio campaign began in mid-October, with "board of strategy" meetings held each night to evaluate the programs. Lord & Thomas spared no expense, with Forker hiring the best writers he could find and retaining a cast of thirty-five actors.[38] The writers produced four shows, some broadcast daily and others three times a week. Overtly or subtly, each series struck anti-Sinclair chords. The family soap-opera format of *The Bennetts*, for example, gave each member of the middle-class family an opportunity to talk about how Sinclairism threatened her or his traditional way of life: Sis feared she wouldn't be able to finish college (because Sinclair opposed higher education) and that church choir practice would end if an atheist governor were elected; Dad fretted he would lose his job because his factory would close; Junior that he wouldn't get to go to the movies anymore. Another series, *Weary Sam and Willie*, followed two hobos as they trekked from the Midwest toward California in pursuit of the handouts promised by EPIC.[39]

Variety, the entertainment industry's weekly bible, was impressed:

> About everything is being adapted to radio in the Beat Sinclair campaign now in progress for the final weeks of the campaign. Every device known to the art of propaganda is being employed. The Lord & Thomas advertising agency is

using four radio programs to undermine the Sinclair argument. The novelty of the presentation is sure-fire, and a check of the listening audience shows that a tremendous wedge is being driven in spots where other agencies of promotion have failed to make more than a superficial dent . . .

It is a cinch that if the Lord & Thomas promotion is successful in keeping Upton Sinclair out of Sacramento, this new textbook on campaigning will gain wide circulation.[40]

Some of Teague's money also went to a pair of press agents based in Sacramento. Clem Whitaker—tall, wiry, and talkative at age thirty-five—was a political reporter who had drifted into public relations. In 1933, his work on a state water referendum brought him into collaboration with a twenty-six-year-old redheaded widow named Leone Baxter, then manager of the Chamber of Commerce of Redding, California. The two (who would marry five years later) founded Campaigns, Inc., one of the nation's first political consulting firms.[41]

They agreed to pitch in against Sinclair, and their method was as ingenious as it was devious. "Upton was beaten," Whitaker recalled, "because he had written books." With the election only two months away, the pair left their office, assembled stacks of Sinclair's writings, and secluded themselves for three days, culling quotations on religion, marriage, sex, the press, communism, patriotism, education, and other topics that might be used against the author. They combined many of the most incendiary quotations with political cartoons to create the "blot of Sinclairism" series, which they then distributed to newspapers throughout the state. More than three thousand were printed. "Sure, those quotations were irrelevant," Baxter later admitted. "But we had one objective: to keep him from becoming governor."[42]

California's newspapers enthusiastically joined the effort to sink Sinclair. William Randolph Hearst wielded the most power: the combined circulation of his five California dailies exceeded the rest of the state's papers combined. And although Hearst went after Sinclair with a vengeance, his treatment of the socialist candidate was muted compared with that of Harry Chandler of the *Los Angeles Times*, which also had been savaged by Sinclair.[43] Chandler made regular use of the Whitaker and Baxter quotations by printing anti-Sinclair "boxes" on the front page: *Sinclair On Marriage, Sinclair On Religion,* and so on.[44]

A *Times* reporter turned a Sinclair jest into a catastrophe. "Suppose your plan goes into effect," he asked the candidate during an interview. "Won't it cause a great many unemployed to come to California from the other states?" According to Sinclair, "I answered with a laugh: 'I told Mr. Hopkins, the Federal Relief Administrator, that if I am elected, half the unemployed of the United States will come to California, and he will have to make plans to take care of them.'"

The headlines in the next day's *Times* read: "*Heavy Rush Of Idle Seen By Sinclair*—Transient Flood Expected—Democratic Candidate Cites Prospect in Event of His Winning Election." In print, Sinclair's words were altered to read: "If I'm elected governor, I expect one-half the unemployed in the United States will hop the first freight to California." The *Times*, pouncing on the grist that the naive Sinclair had provided, estimated the number of indigent job-seekers that would flood into the state at roughly 5 million. The paper also ran follow-up stories with titles like "More Competition for Your Job."[45] For Harry Chandler, it was payback time.

Meanwhile, Don Francisco's stealthy legions were making good use of Whitaker's and Baxter's work. "It was obvious that in five or six weeks, we couldn't possibly kill the EPIC program by economic propaganda," Francisco recalled.[46] Instead, Lord & Thomas began churning out pamphlets that used Sinclair's own words against him in ways designed to inflame particular constituencies. In just over a month, the agency produced almost 8 million such pamphlets. ("We work every night until 12 or 1 o'clock," Francisco wrote to a Chicago colleague, "including Sundays."[47]) They were quick, effective, and dirty, as Francisco later admitted:

We had one pamphlet quoting all he had said against the Catholics, and another against the Jews, and the Seventh-Day Adventists, the Episcopalians, and one against Stanford, and the University of Southern California, and pamphlets of what he said against lawyers, and doctors. He said something against almost every group that there was . . .

And these we wrote very hastily, and put on the cover of each, "By his own words shall ye know him," and just quoted his words without any side comment or explanation, giving the source, of course.

These we sent out to the various organizations. The one on what he said against the Catholics, we sent out to all the Catholic churches, and enclosed a card whereby they could order a big supply, which they usually did. And the next thing that happened was that the priests would preach against him, or the *rabbi, or the minister, and we would see to it that the quotes from their sermons got into the papers . . .*

Pretty soon, all the churches wanted to have a big meeting—which we encouraged—where they had the rabbi, the priest, the minister, and all the other people on the platform talking against Sinclair. We bought time on the air, so that the whole thing went out all over the state. And then we got the excerpts from the talks in the paper the next day . . .

Those pamphlets were the most effective weapon we had. Had Sinclair not said all those things against these different groups, particularly religious groups, he would have won.[48]

In Hollywood, meanwhile, the movie studio heads were also attacking Sinclair. (He had promised that if elected, he would put the state of California into the business of producing and showing movies.) To organize their efforts against Sinclair, the studios turned to Will Hays, Lasker's political mentor and Hollywood's "movie czar" for the past dozen years. Hays raised about $500,000 from the major studios, which assembled this war chest by docking their well-paid stars and directors a day's pay.

Producer and mogul Louis B. Mayer also played a leading role. With his blessing, MGM production chief Irving Thalberg cranked out a series of phony newsreels that portrayed "ordinary" people saying nice things about Merriam, and swarthy indigents with heavy eastern and southern European accents endorsing Sinclair. In one of the most infamous, a scruffy actor asks: *Vell, his system verked vell in Russia, vy can't it verk here?*[49]

Hordes of jobless, hungry, dirty, desperate men streaming into California became a *leitmotif* of the anti-Sinclair campaign. Don Belding later admitted that his agency "hired the scum of the streets to carry placards through the cities, 'Vote for Upton Sinclair.'" More fake newsreels, staged on Hollywood sets, depicted trainloads of out-of-work men heading west for EPIC handouts. Sometimes the newspaper and movie studios worked together. The *Los Angeles Herald and Express* ran a two-column photo of a mob of "hobos," but then someone recognized movie star Frankie Darro as the lead bum; the still had been lifted from the Warner Brothers film *Wild Boys of the Road.*

Don Francisco monitored all this activity with a mixture of satisfaction and anxiety. He knew that only a relentless, all-fronts assault would defeat Sinclair. But such an assault might well create a backlash of sympathy for Sinclair and the EPIC cause. In the final weeks before the election, Francisco wheeled out one final weapon from his arsenal, only to garage it again almost immediately:

> There is a fellow here who had an automobile that looked like a locomotive, which pulled a trailer that looked like a boxcar, and I remembered that thing, and I had him hunted up, and I hired him for the last three weeks of the campaign.
>
> On the side of the boxcar I put a big sign: "If elected Governor, I expect half the unemployed to hop the first train for California." And then I got the fellows out of MGM studios to dress up a lot of hoboes, dummies, and have them sitting up on top of that car, and that was to run around Los Angeles and the suburbs the last three weeks . . .
>
> Well, the night before it was to start . . . I saw this old cheesecloth banner of Sinclair's on the way to Pasadena, and it looked as if a breath on it would blow it down, and I visualized a lot of people tacking that thing up, and compared with our big posters, it looked pretty pathetic. It made quite an impression on me.
>
> The next morning, I came down, and they had this locomotive and freight car pulled up in the parking lot so I could look out the window at it. I looked on this thing, and on top of this pathetic sign I had seen, I felt pretty sorry for Sinclair. We had been going pretty hard against him.
>
> So with that hunch, I had several men and girls from the office go along the sidewalk while this thing was going down the streets, to hear what comments were made. We heard a lot of people were getting a great laugh, but a lot of other people said, "That is a blow below the belt. That is going too far. I feel sorry for Sinclair."
>
> So just on that tip, we canceled it at noon.[50]

Sinclair fought back hard. He quickly penned *The Lie Factory Starts*, a manifesto in which he tried to set twisted quotations straight and reveal the underhanded tactics of his detractors. He held rallies, rodeos, and registration drives. He took to the airwaves. But the dominos continued to fall against him. The newspapers refused to publish EPIC radio program schedules, while running special features on United for California's radio lineup. Sinclair failed to secure a public endorsement from an anxious President Roosevelt. Meanwhile, Raymond Haight, a young attorney and Democrat, joined the race as the Progressive-Commonwealth candidate, aiming for the middle ground between the radical Sinclair and the conservative Merriam.[51]

Don Francisco spent election night—November 6, 1934—at a sumptuous "radio party" at the Midwick Country Club in Pasadena, watching as election returns were posted on a blackboard in the ballroom. The final count pleased him enormously: Merriam won the race with 1,138,620 votes to Sinclair's 879,537. (Sinclair's wife wept with relief at the news; her unwanted ordeal, including death threats against her husband, was over.) Haight polled 302,519 votes; if he hadn't been on the ballot, California probably would have elected its first socialist governor. Timing, too, played a critical role in the outcome. "If the campaign had lasted a little longer," Belding later speculated, "the public might have found out and the whole thing might have backfired."[52]

Francisco agreed: "Had the election been held a month before it was, [Sinclair] would have won, and had it been held a month or a month and a half after it was held, he would have won."[53]

The California gubernatorial campaign of 1934 marked the birth of modern media politics. To that extent, at least, Lasker's agency and its local allies changed history. Upton Sinclair's campaign was scuttled—unfairly and brilliantly—by the stealthy wizards of Lord & Thomas. For better or worse, the democratic process was transformed.

Following his defeat, Sinclair went back to what he knew best: writing books. True to form, his first post-election book was *I, Candidate for Governor—And How I Got Licked*. Although he demonstrated amply his animosity toward the newspaper and the movie moguls, he noted the work of Whitaker and Baxter only briefly, and without naming them ("They had a staff of political chemists at work, preparing poisons to be let loose in the California atmosphere on every one of a hundred mornings"). He wrote nothing about the advertising agency that orchestrated the campaign against him, which begs the question of whether he ever learned about Lord & Thomas's central role.[54]

Sinclair's defeat solidified Lord & Thomas's reputation as a force in California politics, and further raised Don Francisco's profile. As a result, within two years, the agency was recruited to manage yet another major political contest in the land of sunshine, promise, and unconventional politics.

This time, the battleground was the state's retail sector. Millions of independent retailers, supported by powerful wholesalers, sought to use a prohibitive tax to drive chain stores out of their state: a drama that was being played out across the nation, but that erupted in California in a characteristically colorful fashion.

The chains normally went into political battle as prohibitive favorites, but by the time California's chain retailers approached Lord & Thomas to mount their defense, they were fighting for their economic lives. On July 21, 1935, the newly reelected Governor Merriam signed into law a chain store tax steep enough to cripple the state's chain retailers.. At the signing ceremony, Merriam issued an odd challenge: "The chain store operators feel that this legislation will prove discriminatory in its application. If so, the opportunity is theirs to prevent this act from becoming effective by invoking the referendum and submitting the question directly to the people."[55]

That they would do, thanks to a rapidly mobilized Lord & Thomas campaign. Once again, Don Francisco played the leading role. And once again, he was supported by Lasker, who developed a "keen interest" in the fight and authorized a massive marshalling of company resources for the cause.[56] And although Lasker mainly watched the chain store battle unfold from a distance, his behind-the-curtain approach permeated the strategy of this campaign as well. One opponent would deem it—with grudging admiration— "the velvet touch."[57]

Only near the end of the fight did Francisco and his small army take off their velvet gloves and administer their knockout punch. The Lord & Thomas strategy was improbable, counterintuitive, and inspired. It left an indelible imprint on retailing in California, and—by extension—across the nation.

The first stirrings of a retailing revolution came on the eve of the Civil War, when the Great Atlantic & Pacific Tea Company opened its doors in Manhattan in 1858. By 1920, A&P was operating five thousand stores. F. W. Woolworth opened his first discount variety store in 1879; by 1920, his chain had more than eleven hundred stores.[58]

The 1920s brought prosperity to the nation's urban middle class, and the chains expanded rapidly to serve this growing consumer base. By the end of the decade, they controlled 17 percent of the nation's retail stores and 39 percent of total retail sales. A mere half-dozen grocery chains, which collectively operated more than thirty thousand outlets, virtually controlled that sector.

Nine chains dominated the variety-store business, and other chains ruled in shoes, drugs, and apparel.[59]

Chain store success was driven by a combination of modern retailing practices and economies of scale. Whereas the neighborhood independents typically devoted little attention to their public faces, the chain outlets featured large, bold signs—uniform from one store to the next, and thus instantly recognizable—and visually striking window displays. Inside, the differences were even more striking. Independent dry-goods stores tended to be dark and cluttered environments in which customers required the assistance of the clerk to locate goods. In traditional grocery stores, proprietors selected meats and produce for their patrons. Most neighborhood shops were too cold in the winter and too hot in the summer. In sharp contrast, the display of goods inside chain outlets was "scientifically" engineered at the home office and replicated precisely from one outlet to the next. Lighting and climate were carefully considered. Clerks were trained to maximize stock turnover.[60] Goods were placed directly in front of the consumer—not only giving those consumers more control over their purchases, but also minimizing staffing requirements.

Of course, the mom-and-pop stores had some appeal. They were neighborhood institutions, with their owners often living above or behind the shop. The long hours "around the cracker barrel" were filled with socializing and gossip. Customers from the neighborhood usually bought on credit, running tabs that might be settled up every few weeks.

What tipped the balance in favor of the chains was *price*, pure and simple. According to marketing historian Richard Tedlow, the chains charged somewhere between 3 percent and 11 percent less than their independent competitors. They did this by eliminating waste, tracking inventory efficiently, and buying directly from farmers or manufacturers.[61] The chains also leveraged their size in their advertising, buying millions of newspaper and magazine column inches at bulk rates. Gradually, they gobbled up market share in key retail sectors. Contemporary observers wondered how long it would be before "the independent would be crowded out altogether."[62]

Of course, the independents fought back.[63] But when it came to mobilizing for collective action, they faced an acute structural vulnerability. They were, by definition, fragmented into hundreds of thousands of independent proprietorships. They banded together in trade associations—one for grocers, another for druggists, another for hardware stores, and so on—but they remained relatively incoherent as a sector.

The anti–chain store tactic that took hold most firmly was elegant in its simplicity: a prohibitive tax. Most of these tax schemes stipulated an annual levy of one or two dollars for each store under common ownership up to the first five stores, with the tax rate escalating thereafter, until a maximum rate of several hundred dollars per store was reached at about twenty stores.[64] The chains lobbied hard against the bills, but by 1927, thirteen states had enacted anti–chain store tax laws.

Meanwhile, Congress in May 1928 instructed the Federal Trade Commission to launch an investigation of chain store competitive practices. Up to this point, the chains had been poorly organized, especially given their financial resources. In 1928 they transformed a grocery chain store association into the National Chain Store Association (NCSA), which immediately went to work on an ambitious national "educational" campaign.

Initially, it worked: only half a dozen of the 142 anti–chain store bills introduced in the next two years were signed into law.[65] But the anti-chain forces were improving their tactics, as well. One weakness in their approach had been in calling for higher taxes on chains of *five* stores or more, a threshold that raised legal questions about the definition of a chain. New bills proposed higher taxes beginning with the *second* store in a chain.

But was there a legal foundation for this kind of "graduated" tax? The chains took this question all the way to the U.S. Supreme Court in 1931. In a sharply divided opinion, the highest Court found graduated taxes constitutional. In the majority opinion, Justice Louis Brandeis—an established tormenter of big business—argued that chains were, in fact, a fundamentally different kind of business enterprise. In the next two years, eighteen chain store tax bills were enacted into law.[66]

This reenergized anti-chain forces on the state level, and California—with its fast-growing population, a left-leaning streak in its political culture, powerful agricultural interests, and ever-growing numbers of chain outlets—was ripe for battle. A newly formed "Anti-Monopoly League" introduced a chain store tax bill into the 1935 session of the legislature. It included a crippling multiplier: for the first store, an owner would pay $1 for a "license" to operate in California. That would double for the second store, double again (to $8) for the third, and so on until the fee reached $256 for the ninth store. After that—for the tenth store and any more—the "license" was $500 per store.

Heavy majorities of California's lawmakers endorsed the bill. Thirty-four of thirty-eight senators, as well as sixty-eight of seventy-six members of the Assembly, approved it.[67]

All of this put Governor Merriam in a tough spot. The bill enjoyed strong popular support. Only a few months earlier, though, he had held onto his office against the Sinclair onslaught mainly through the intervention of the state's well-heeled business interests, who uniformly opposed the proposed bill. Under heavy pressure from the Anti-Monopoly League, Merriam signed it. But even as he signed, he issued his none-too-subtle challenge to the chains: *If you want to overturn this law, get a petition on the November ballot, and persuade the voters to back you.*[68] Long shot or not, the chains were compelled to take up the challenge. Under the terms of the new law, a five-hundred-store chain would be compelled to contribute more than a quarter-million dollars to the state treasury (versus the $500 paid by 500 independents). Organizing quickly into the "California Chain Stores Association," they collected 150,000 signatures by the end of the summer, far more than needed to put a referendum question on the fall election ballot.[69]

"The next thing, and probably the smartest thing they could have done," recounted *Chain Store Age* editor Godfrey M. Lebhar, "was to recognize their own inability to shape up the kind of campaign the situation called for, or to carry it through. They realized they were in the position of a man who was desperately sick and needed the attention of the best doctor he could get."[70] So they called in a specialized sort of doctor: Lord & Thomas.

Word had spread among leading corporate interests about Lord & Thomas's decisive role in the Sinclair campaign. In addition, an old business connection helped steer the California Chain Stores Association toward Lord & Thomas. W. G. Irwin—Lasker's former partner in the ill-starred Van Camp enterprise—had invested in the Purity Stores chain of West Coast grocery stores. Under the astute direction of Irwin's protégé John Niven, the former general manager of Van Camp, Purity by the mid-1930s had grown to a hundred-store chain.[71] As Irwin later explained: "So when this [chain store] fight came up, [Niven] immediately thought of Albert Lasker's organization to handle the thing—there was a fellow with enough force to present people with the idea. And I think he was in a large measure responsible for selecting Don Francisco."[72]

The California Chain Stores Association vested Lord & Thomas with an extraordinary degree of control, with Francisco being given virtually complete autonomy. The reasons appear to have been twofold. First, discretion was in order; and second, there simply wasn't enough time for the kinds of bureaucratic niceties—organizational meetings, negotiations, and so forth—normally associated with an ambitious campaign.[73]

What happened over the next several months was so unexpected that Francisco had to caution his clients not to judge the campaign by its appearances. (On the face of it, an odd request: after all, what *was* a public relations campaign if not "appearances"?) Francisco knew that as the precious weeks ticked by, little would seem to be happening. During the first phase of the effort, approximately nine months long, advertising would play only a minor role. "Indeed, at the outset," Francisco recalled, "it was seriously questioned whether the plan should include any advertising of this sort at all."

This was because, under Lasker's leadership, Lord & Thomas thought in terms of "advertising in the wider and truer sense of the term." It was a campaign in which Francisco took great pride, and which he later used to illustrate the ways of modern promotion. "It is not enough to be right," Francisco observed, "it is also necessary to seem right." The task at hand was to reengineer the public image of California's chain stores; a frontal assault was unlikely to succeed, and might even backfire—it would not "seem right." Once again, Lord & Thomas had to operate behind the curtain.[74]

A first step involved an honest self-appraisal on the part of the chain stores. Several long years into the Great Depression, the nation had lost its faith in corporate America—which, for millions of struggling Americans, the chains exemplified. California in particular posed "special handicaps to any attempt at interpreting business sympathetically," Francisco observed, in his bland and understated way. "It was a stronghold for all sorts of political doctrines based on discontent."

There were more practical matters to consider, as well. The estimated eighty thousand independent retailers in California had already demonstrated how quickly and effectively they could mobilize. The state was running a huge budget deficit, which made revenue derived from any sort of tax appealing to incumbents. The chain store tax also ran the risk of being lost amid the twenty other referenda on the fall ballot.[75]

In addition, the chains had made mistakes. They had expanded rapidly and, in the process, had defined "success" almost exclusively in terms of profits. As a result, Francisco told his clients, *your customers are not your friends.* "Motorists may buy at your service station," he stated bluntly, "but damn you because they think you are a monopoly. They may go out of their way to save a few pennies at your chain store, and then denounce you for paying low wages." A first and necessary step toward transforming customers into friends was to "eliminate all practices that gave the critics the slightest justification for their attacks."

This applied to dealings with stakeholders of every stripe, but Francisco insisted the chains pay special attention to employees.[76] The number of chain store employees was roughly half that of their independent counterparts—about forty-four thousand—but Francisco saw them as a sizeable army of "natural allies" to be mobilized. But this would require a change in corporate culture. Henceforth, the chain managers had to view workers not as numbers, but as "individuals with personalities, homes, families, birthdays, joys, sorrows, accomplishments, affiliations, interests."

This was a strange new suit of clothes, but the chain store managers—under orders from headquarters—quickly donned it. They sent cards and letters to their employees to mark birthdays, illnesses, deaths, and other personal milestones. They gave out badges and awards. They sponsored "more parties and picnics, more orchestras and glee-clubs, more athletic teams and dances." And, most tangibly, they shortened working hours and awarded more raises and promotions.[77] These weren't just cosmetic changes, Lord & Thomas emphasized; they were "subtler and more important, a revision of manner and spirit."[78]

Chain store managers across the state invited their employees to view "The Spirit of '36"—a Lord & Thomas-produced film that made the antitax case vividly—and then trained them in public speaking techniques so they could carry forth the message more effectively.[79] Two manuals were handed out at these staff meetings: one on public speaking techniques, and the second an eighty-page booklet—produced by Lord & Thomas, and distributed by the California Chain Stores Association—entitled *The Fifty Thousand Percent Chain Store Tax*. This was an ingenious and rhetorically powerful expression of the mathematics involved. Just as $3 is 300 percent more than $1, the proposed $500 tax on the tenth store in a chain was 50,000 percent more than a one-dollar tax on a single independent.

To put the story before the general public, Lord & Thomas once again exploited radio. In April 1936, the agency launched a Monday-evening radio program called *California's Hour*. Although the program mostly featured middle-of-the-road musical selection, it also profiled each week a California community, with locals (recruited by the Boy Scouts) performing in a talent contest. This enormously popular program auditioned ten thousand would-be stars, garnered 170,000 ballots, and ingratiated itself with each week's featured city or town. The program ran no editorials, although the topics of its three essay contests were less than subtle: "Why I trade at chain stores," "How the chains benefit California," and "Why I will vote 'No' on No. 22." Entry forms, conveniently available at chain store outlets, came with background "information" about the chain store tax issue.[80]

California's Hour gave air cover to broadly based community outreach efforts. Chain store managers flocked to join local chambers of commerce, service clubs, and businessmen's associations. Increasingly generous with their donations of cash and merchandise, chain managers repaired their public image, and built new reputations as community benefactors.[81]

California farmers received special attention from Lord & Thomas. They comprised only about half the population of the state's small cities and towns, but they exercised an outsized political influence. In the mid-1930s, California grocery chains sold roughly $230 million in state-grown produce. Advocates of the chain store tax were telling the farmers that the chains' low prices were putting downward pressure on crop prices.

The chains, scripted by Lord & Thomas, retorted that they were of "incalculable value to the California farmer and manufacturer." Their large-scale purchase agreements stabilized the market, they argued, while their efficient operations cut out waste to the benefit of producer and consumer alike. The *real* culprit, they argued, was in the middle layers of the distribution chain. "Lurking in the background are the REAL enemies of the people—the middlemen, who are putting up the money for this vicious campaign against the chain store." The "discriminatory legislation" was their desperate ploy to regain their "monopolistic grip" on the state's agricultural sector.[82] Lord & Thomas recruited one of the state's more prominent growers to serve as the spokesman for its agricultural campaign, and outfitted him with an office and staff.

Quietly, Don Francisco also opened another agricultural front. In late February 1936, the California Canning Peach Association contacted him, distressed about slumping sales. Inspired by a "farmer-consumer merchandising drive" recently orchestrated by one of the state's leading chains, Francisco emulated that model, but on a grander scale. He cajoled leading grocery chains nationwide, with their tens of thousands of retail outlets, to push canned peaches. Soon he convinced drug and restaurant chains statewide to join in as well. The arranged marriage worked beautifully: the California cling peach growers enjoyed surging sales and generous profits, while chains across the continent pitched in against California's chain tax movement.

As the election approached, Francisco launched similar national chain marketing campaigns for California producers of beef and dried fruits. He met with key agricultural and chain interests in New York City and Urbana, Illinois, to explore their mutual interests. The chains agreed to end several long-standing practices that had incensed the farmers—"unreasonable" quantity discounts, loss-leader retailing, unearned advertising allowances, buyer brokerage fees—and the National Co-Operative Council was born.[83]

Lord & Thomas was uniquely positioned to forge this alliance. Through the Sunkist and similar commodities campaigns, the agency had established deep connections throughout California's farming establishment. It combined those connections with strong ties across the country, moving mountains of peaches, beef, and dried fruits, and changing the mechanics of retail commerce nationwide to the advantage of California's growers.

For nine months, Don Francisco's corps had pushed the chains to reform themselves. They had offered Californians a positive image of the chain store— as the exemplar of clean, modern, and efficient business practice; friend to the farmer and local community; creator of jobs; and steward of low prices. For the most part, the message had been positive, delivered in soft tones.[84]

Now, with six weeks remaining before the election, it was time to abandon the velvet touch. Lord & Thomas began to blanket the media with the memorable slogan—"22 is a Tax on You!"—and attacked the other side directly. "We exposed the tax as a scheme engineered by selfish middlemen," recalled Francisco. "We did not hesitate to attack the professional organizers, racketeering money-raisers and self-seeking politicians who worked against us." *California's Hour* went into high gear, putting on scores of farmers, business owners, attorneys, and women to describe how their livelihoods would be damaged if the tax passed.[85]

Chapter Nineteen

The Downward Spiral

*I*N LATE OCTOBER 1936, Flora Lasker left Chicago for an extended stay in New York City. Albert went off for a three-week fishing trip in Florida, planning to join his wife in New York in time for a speech he was scheduled to deliver to the American Association of Advertising Agents on November 19.[1]

Flora was then in her late fifties, and had been an invalid, coping with varying degrees of disability, for three decades. Stout and sallow, she walked with difficulty. Visits to the mineral baths at Watkins Glen, New York, during the summer afforded her some respite and also gave her the chance to visit her family in Buffalo.[2] But she suffered from chronic headaches, often intense enough to send her to bed. In recent years, her son Edward later recalled, she had become obsessed with her own mortality: "She talked constantly about dying . . . If she ever got annoyed about Father, the conversation would never end without her saying, 'Some day you will find me in bed after one of these headaches, and you will find me dead, and then you will realize.'"[3]

There were times when Albert was clearly impatient with his slow-moving wife, and other times when he paid very little attention to her. Because of her physical challenges, and perhaps because she felt outshone, she didn't enjoy socializing as much as her husband. "She was *dull*, compared to him," David Sarnoff observed.[4]

Flora—like so many others—found her husband a challenge. Albert was exhausting, demanding, and difficult—and also endlessly interesting and energizing. Ralph Sollitt, who knew the family as well as any outsider, spoke to the contrasts between Albert and Flora, and the tensions that resulted:

He was aggressive and hard-headed, wanted his house to be 42nd Street and 5th Avenue all the time, from nine o'clock in the morning until midnight, and Mrs. Lasker would have been very delighted to have seen her husband every day and perhaps one other person perhaps every six months . . . She was borne along a little unwillingly on all this Hip Hooray and excitement.

The last years of her life she got to be better physically than she [had been], and I felt that . . . she came to have a tolerance for the exuberance that she felt was quite unnecessary. He had all these animal spirits all the time, and she thought it would be so much better for him and everybody else if he could tone himself down. [But] I had a feeling in the last seven or eight years that she came to see that maybe Albert Lasker wouldn't be nearly so interesting to her, if he didn't have all that.[5]

Lasker's eye may have wandered during the course of his marriage. Edward wrote in his own unpublished memoir that while his father had assured him that he had never been unfaithful to Flora, "I do not take his words too seriously."[6] But through it all, Flora exerted a profound influence over Albert. She was his central point of reference—a stabilizing force. Introspective, conservative, and even from her limited vantage point an acute observer of the world, she provided a strong counterpoint to her husband's own life narrative. "He couldn't get disconnected from her," Sarnoff said. "He had to have an anchor."

On their last night together in Chicago, at the Burton Place mansion, Albert and Flora shared a tender moment. Over the previous several months, Flora had lost a considerable amount of weight, and Albert was proud of her accomplishment. She remained a near-invalid, however; she couldn't walk up a flight of stairs without exhausting herself. Couches had been strategically located on the stair landings so that she could rest and catch her breath, and it was on one of those couches, with Albert attending her, that she made an unusual observation: "You know, we have reached the loveliest time of our married life. All the early, hectic, romantic love is over, and in its place has come a deep and abiding friendship. We love each other not only for our virtues, [but also for] our faults, and we won't change a single virtue or surrender a single fault because then it would be something else."[7]

The Laskers maintained a suite of rooms at the Ritz for their frequent visits to New York. As soon as Flora arrived for her stay in the fall of 1936, friends and members of the extended family began visiting with her.

Edward, then living in Greenwich, Connecticut, and working in Lord & Thomas's New York office, stopped by after work; Albert stayed there when he arrived from Florida. Daughter Mary lived in Chicago, but Francie was at nearby Vassar College and made plans to travel down to New York on December 19 to join her family.

On the evening of December 17—a Thursday night—Flora, Albert, and Edward sat talking quietly at the Ritz. Flora was in her element. "Nothing made her as happy," Edward later commented, "as to be alone with the members of her family, and talking about each other." The conversation meandered, eventually settling on the subject of Albert. "You can't convince me," Flora said at one point, "that you're not the most wonderful man in the world." Albert, embarrassed, told her that she shouldn't say things like that in front of other people—even their own son. After Edward left for the evening, Albert returned to the subject. She shouldn't embarrass him with such grand and sweeping compliments, he insisted.

But Flora held her ground: "I know all your failings, your weaknesses. You are insufferably egotistical on the things you know nothing about, and you are painfully modest about those things about which you know everything." She told her husband that she loved him more than anything or anyone in the world—even more than her children. "You're a wicked woman," a startled Albert replied. "I know," Flora persisted. "I love you more."

The next day was a busy one for Albert, since for the first time, all Lord & Thomas employees making less than $5,000 a year received a surprise Christmas bonus of a half-month's salary. The agency had experimented briefly with bonuses in the 1920s; now—perhaps influenced by the California chain store campaign's successful conclusion a month earlier, which focused in part on creating satisfied employees—Lasker decided to revive the tradition. Most likely the bonus was a topic of discussion at the Ritz that night, as Flora and Albert's suite filled up with guests for an impromptu Friday night soirée. But Flora wasn't feeling well, and she soon excused herself.

On Saturday, Francie arrived, which gave Flora new cause to celebrate. It was to be their last day in New York; tomorrow, the family would decamp for Chicago. (There a surprise awaited Flora: a new $16,000 Lincoln that Albert had had specially modified for her.) But by midday, Flora was complaining of pain in her arms and sweating profusely. "You know," she told Edward, "it is the same way that Blanche Mandel felt just before she died." Edward, annoyed, assured his mother that she wasn't dying. They talked quietly in her bedroom as Albert and Pittsburgh newspaper magnate Paul Block—an old family friend—conversed in the adjoining sitting room. When Block eventually rose to leave, Edward offered to accompany him to the elevator. Some fifty feet down the hallway, he suddenly heard his father crying out his name. He rushed back to the suite and into his mother's bedroom: "Mother was lying there, breathing in a very loud and unnatural way, and I was sure what had happened to her—that she had a stroke—and the maid was being hysterical, and Father was being hysterical, too, saying, 'Do something! Do something!'"

By the time a doctor could be located, Flora was dead of a cerebral thrombosis. The thirty-four-year partnership between Albert and Flora Lasker was over.

According to his biographer, Albert was rendered "completely distraught" by Flora's death. Recuperating with his daughter Mary and son-in-law Gerald Foreman at the Miami Beach estate, he kept Mary awake all night with professions of his undying love for Flora. He obsessed about his shortcomings, as loss and guilt became inextricably bound up in his mind.

Slowly, in the early months of 1937, Albert began patching his life back together. He played poker with the Partridges at Burton Place. He threw elaborate parties at Mill Road Farm, including a June 1937 dinner for 107 guests. Honors came his way: lunch at the White House, membership on the University of Chicago's board of trustees, and others. These distractions were necessary, but insufficient.

Flora left an estate of just over $2.3 million, which after taxes amounted to some $1.4 million. Albert received about half of that amount, with Edward, Mary, and Francie each getting just over $200,000, and the remaining $95,000 going to other family members.[8] The estate was settled almost exactly a year to the day after Flora's death—a coincidence that certainly didn't escape Albert's attention, even though when that unhappy anniversary arrived, he was on the other side of the world.

In the summer of 1937, Albert Lasker took an uncharacteristic step. Finally acceding to a request that Flora had made many times over the years, and ignoring the objections of at least one of his children, he decided to produce an autobiography.[9]

Lasker chose not to write the book himself. His work and family obligations would have made that difficult; his unsettled emotional state also would have interfered. Hiring a ghostwriter, as so many business moguls before him had done, was the natural solution. He settled upon a journeyman writer named Boyden Sparkes, who had been a war correspondent for the *New York Tribune*, had written books for or about several "business celebrities," and had close ties to the editors at the *Saturday Evening Post*, for which he had written inspirational first-person accounts such as White Sox star Eddie Collins's "From Player to Pilot."[10] Walter Chrysler's autobiography, as told to Boyden Sparkes, was serialized in the *Post* in the summer of 1937 and helped bring Sparkes to Lasker's attention.

Lasker and Sparkes settled on a fee of $30,000. But perhaps owing to his distracted state of mind, Lasker failed to define an audience for the project. "I want this book for a circulation of three," Lasker told Sparkes at an early meeting. "Three children, each a copy. That means more to me than all the other circulating, and it is the only purpose of the book."[11] At other points in their conversations, however, Lasker said that the purpose of the book was "to show how to sell," or to explain to readers what kills great companies (their goods becoming commodities, or their owners getting greedy and trying to grow too fast), or to underscore the perils of governmental bureaucracy.

The most grandiose of these schemes held the most appeal for the ambitious Sparkes, who—in addition to getting mixed messages from Lasker—also engaged in some selective hearing. Lasker had been thinking out loud about a sweeping plan to remake the American economy, and it was those visions, rather than a "circulation of three," that Sparkes latched on to.

The project officially began on September 14, 1937, when Sparkes traveled with Lasker aboard the Union Pacific's *Forty-Niner*, a streamliner that ran five times a month from Chicago to San Francisco. Sparkes brought along a stenographer to record the conversations. It must have been a striking scene: Lasker striding around the plush railroad car for hours at a time, gesturing animatedly, punctuating his sentences with his characteristic rapid-fire interjections—*You see? Do you see? D'you see? Do I make myself clear?*—while Sparkes tried to extract from the fire-hose flow of Lasker's hyperactive brain the building blocks of a coherent story. In the corner, a harried stenographer struggled to keep up.

Lasker enjoyed the process. When the *Forty-Niner* reached San Francisco, he invited Sparkes and the stenographer to continue on with him to Honolulu aboard the *S.S. Lurline*. What Sparkes extracted from his subject during those two weeks was a sprawling jumble of anecdotes, insight, emotion, exaggeration, tantalizing leads, red herrings, and dead-ends. "My father [alone] is going to take all morning," Lasker enthused in their opening session aboard the *Forty-Niner*. Then his mind raced off to the Leo Frank case, then to a movie (*They Won't Forget*) that he had just seen, and then to his own policy against self-promotion:

All my life long I felt it was a mistake, I have made up my mind to be in the background of other things, while I was making people and things known. And there is a great reason for that: You can have much more power to make people and things known if you are unknown yourself . . . If you are going to work, and willing to think, and you are nobody, a lot of people will let you do a lot of things they won't if they think you are somebody. Do I make myself clear?[12]

"Quite," was all Sparkes could muster in response.

It must have been a relief for Sparkes to say goodbye to Lasker on the docks of Honolulu and go back east as his hyperactive client plunged into his tour of Hawaii. Sparkes had a suitcase full of gold—Lasker's first round of reminiscences—and a list of contacts to follow up on while his employer circumnavigated the globe. Lasker's candor and magnetism, and the wonderful yarns that he spun—touching an incredible range of subjects, and spanning eras of change and turbulence—probably sent Sparkes home to North Carolina convinced that he had stumbled upon a plum assignment.

Where was Albert Lasker headed, in that unsettled fall of 1937?

The plan, conceived by Albert Lasker's golfing buddy Gene Sarazen—winner of thirty-nine PGA tournaments, and one of only five "Grand Slam" winners in all of golf history—was to get Lasker's mind off Flora's death by sending him on an extended tour around the world in 1937, starting in Hawaii. Of course he would not go alone. The party that ultimately was put together included Lasker, Sarazen and his wife Mary, Flora's maid, Francie Lasker, and a friend of Francie's. Their itinerary included stops in Japan, Manchuria, the Philippines, Bali, Java, Singapore, Cambodia, India, Egypt, Italy, France, and England, with the Sarazens leaving the tour after Singapore.

This was not a typical tour group, including as it did an extremely well-connected businessman and a world-famous golf celebrity. Everywhere they went, they were treated like very important people—even royalty. Old friends, like Lasker's Washington-era buddy Cal O'Laughlin, Standard Oil's Walter Teagle, and newspaper magnate Roy Howard (owner of the Scripps-Howard chain), called ahead to get doors opened, and dinners and cocktail parties in their honor took up many of the evenings over the course of the six-month sojourn. General Motors, grateful for Lord & Thomas's skilled management of the Frigidaire account, had a luxury limousine waiting for them at almost every stop. Traveling for a month in India, Lasker and his entourage enjoyed the use of a private rail car.

Hawaii, their first stop, set the tone, as Lasker recounted in a letter to the card-playing Partridges back in Chicago:

> We have been taken in hand by a very good friend of the Sarazens—Mr. Francis Brown. He is one of the wealthiest men on the Island and, I gather, by far the most popular. He has about fifteen different homes on the different islands—all of which are constantly staffed but many of which he doesn't go to for years at a time. He in turn has arranged that his many friends entertain us in their homes, most of which are feudal estates, so we are really getting a picture of the Islands as seen by few people . . .
>
> The Japanese Premier is one of Mr. Brown's most intimate friends and he has cabled him of our coming and asking him to extend us any courtesies . . .[13]

After spending two weeks in baronial splendor in Hawaii, the group sailed westward to Yokohama. For decades, Lasker had been eager to visit Japan, and now the moment had arrived. Joseph Grew, U.S. ambassador to Japan, took the opportunity to golf with Sarazen, who was a cult figure in Japan. At one public event, some eight thousand people turned out in a drenching rain to watch Sarazen play an exhibition round.

Lasker, recovering from a torn ligament in his leg, skipped this outing. But his interests lay elsewhere, in any case. He viewed his voyage as an opportunity to meet with potentates and pundits around the world and try to get a sense of where global politics and economics were headed. In the fall of 1937—with war clouds gathering in Europe and Asia—that was no easy task. Relations between Japan and the United States were chilly, with murky subcurrents. As one observer wrote in the wake of Lasker's stop in Tokyo:

> He enjoyed very much the Foreign Office spokesmen's conference and got a great kick out of it. After the conference we got together such men as Naghi of

Tass, Cox of Reuter, and Fabius, the Dutch journalist. . . . I think the two hours he had with them gave him all kinds of conflicting opinions. When it was over he said he never in his life had been so confused, and thought he had better give up trying to find out what is going on here.[14]

In Bali, as the first anniversary of Flora's death approached, Lasker contracted a tropical disease—perhaps dengue fever. His temperature soared well above 100 degrees, where it remained for several days, causing him to sweat profusely and lose eleven pounds in less than a week. A local doctor concluded that he was suffering from malaria. Lasker, partly delirious, demanded that a different doctor and two nurses be flown in from nearby Java to attend to him (an extravagance that cost him $2,500).

While in India, Lasker had a chance encounter with John Gunther, journalist and author of *Inside Europe* (1936). Gunther was conducting research in Asia for the second in his series of nine highly successful "inside" books, which surveyed the world continent by continent. Ten years younger than Lasker, Gunther had grown up in Cincinnati and Chicago, attended the University of Chicago—of which Lasker was now a trustee—and knew Lasker by reputation. Remembered today mainly for his compelling account of his son's death from a brain tumor (*Death Be Not Proud*, 1949), Gunther was hired by the Lasker family after Albert's death to write his authorized biography.

From South Asia, the Lasker party made their way to Southern Europe. Here, as elsewhere, Lasker kept his sharp eye trained on social, political, and economic trends. In Italy, he saw Mussolini's fascist regime up close and despised what he saw. He witnessed firsthand a resurgent anti-Semitism and foresaw the coming global war:

Here in Europe, the jitters that they have been feeling for the past several months are quieted for the moment, but to my notion, only quieted. When things are not in turmoil here, it is only because of momentary exhaustion, everyone is giving everyone else a breathing spell. However, it is pleasant to feel that the dynamite fuse is not likely to go off at the moment. For the longer pull, I still feel that war is in the making in Europe, and I hope I am wrong, but I know I am not.[15]

The party's last stop was England, where Albert had a busy schedule, including appointments in London with Sir Josiah Stamp: chairman of the London, Midland and Scottish Railway and one of the richest men in England. Stamp explained how he worked with his unions to run his railroad and told Lasker that the United States was two or three decades behind Europe when it came to labor relations. Reflecting on this conversation and others, Lasker realized that he, too, was an "employer" of consequence—not through Lord & Thomas, but through the boards of the companies he sat on.

He had spent half a year educating himself on the state of the world and the responsibilities of employers, and now he was headed home. He had a vision about how the world of work could be made more humane, and more efficient. What if he could make his newfound awareness—in his word—"contagious"?

The details of his plan mostly have to be inferred.[16] Lasker evidently believed that the strategy that had rescued the California chain store operators—first winning over their own workforce, then bringing in natural external allies such as the peach growers, and finally wooing the public at large—could be applied on a grand scale. Like the chain stores, American capitalism was under attack, and (as Lasker saw it) deservedly so. Only by applying the "velvet touch" across the entire economy could capitalism be rescued from itself.

Equally important, capitalism would be saved from the Democrats, Franklin Roosevelt, and the New Deal. Lasker had met Roosevelt at the White House in the summer of 1937. Although they talked at great length about anti-Semitism and about the state of the American railroads, Lasker—who had no idea why he had been summoned to this private lunch with the president—came away mystified and unimpressed.

Now, not quite a year later, brimming over with impressions from his conversations around the world, his negative opinions about the New Deal had softened somewhat. "I think we would have been through a terrible ferment if there had been no Roosevelt." The New Deal was objectionable not because it was evil, but because it was fundamentally bureaucratic, went too far, and moved too fast.

As Lasker saw it, the time had come for the business community to solve its own problems by rebuilding its foundations. A first and necessary step would be the creation of national labor unions on the European model. A second would be the public embrace by business of federal regulations on wages and hours. Other substantive and symbolic acts would follow, all with an eye toward reshaping the national economic and political debate. "Public relations is the art of private relations," Lasker declared to Sparkes: "In [business leaders'] relations to themselves, they had better position themselves to meet the demands of the day, or they won't have any proper public relations. And I honestly think if they would, the public relations would pretty soon take care of itself. If the people really felt that there was sympathetic leadership, the people would force the politicians to give recognition of that." In other words, business would mend its fences with its various publics. Once that was accomplished, politicians would feel compelled to make sweeping and appropriate changes to the American economy and society.

The scheme was inextricably bound up in Lasker's conception of himself, his stage of life—in his late fifties, recently widowed, and wealthy—and his recurring sense of superficiality and insubstantiality. The grandiosity of the plan, aimed at fundamentally transforming American society, also reflected Lasker's deepening emotional distress.

Upon his return to the United States, Lasker arranged a meeting with Roy Howard and told him of the plan. Howard provided Lasker with letters of introduction to as many as a hundred business leaders, and in the spring of 1938, Lasker set up a series of one-on-one talks with many of those leaders, beginning in Chicago and fanning outward. "Mr. Albert D. Lasker . . . has had a couple of talks with me on a matter in which he is very much interested and has interested me, and to which he has evinced a willingness to devote his time and money," wrote Joseph P. Kennedy to New York banker Thomas W. Lamont in May. "I don't know whether it is anything in which you might be interested, but I told him I would talk it over with you."[17]

Lasker also tried to proselytize on a grander scale. In a rambling conversation with Sparkes, he made reference to a recent meeting in New York—one of a half-dozen such meetings—that included rival advertising magnate (and former Lord & Thomas employee) Bruce Barton, the executive chairman of DuPont, the president of Johns Manville, the senior vice president in charge of labor relations of Standard Oil of New Jersey, a long-time labor-relations expert from the Rockefeller empire, and movie czar Will Hays. Lasker lectured his audience on their opportunities and obligations as business leaders and molders of public opinion. "When I left the room," he recalled, "I heard Bruce say, 'That was the ablest explanation and exploration of the situation in which American business finds itself I have ever heard,' and the other men concurred that they had heard it many times, but the situation had never been made so clear to them."

But that meeting, like Lasker's larger campaign, led only to disappointment. "I had failed," he admitted to his ghostwriter, "because I hadn't inspired them to action." Once again, he had been reduced to the role of mere propagandist, and he found that bitterly disappointing:

I had been so many years with these business leaders that I know how to approach them. I know how to present it, put on an act, not to make an impression but to get them to appraise their situation. But if the purpose to which I had dedicated myself has failed—to get them to do something about it—so to me the thing was a complete failure, and far from being inspired or complimented by what Barton said, I knew somewhere down the line I was lacking at the moment of opportunity, because there certainly is opportunity for someone to be a leader here.

Now, if I had the strength in me, they would follow me. Then I realized what it was. I have been too superficial all my life. I could propagandize them on what was the matter, but I didn't have the strength to take it apart and make them see what was to be done . . . I wasn't a big man.

Albert Lasker usually cared little about his stature. But by the spring of 1938, he was fragile and rudderless, and the perception that he "wasn't a big man" was an outsized blow. He saw himself as a weak and small man, unable to justify his existence.

In July, Lasker announced abruptly that he was moving the headquarters of Lord & Thomas from Chicago to New York, effective immediately, and that he would be retiring from the presidency of Lord & Thomas as of October 1.

To understand the significance of these proposed changes, we need to visit Albert Lasker on a typical day in that tumultuous spring of 1938.[18] The setting is the Palmolive Building, at 919 North Michigan Avenue in Chicago— later the headquarters of *Playboy* magazine, and today a luxury condominium complex.

Lasker's office and conference room were separated from the rest of Lord & Thomas's offices on the eighteenth floor by a hallway and a reception room, with a checkerboard flooring of antique Italian tile that Lasker had picked up on one of his European trips.[19] A visitor had to pass through three sets of doors to get to the inner sanctum. "Lasker walked through these like a man in a trance," his biographer observed, "as if he were totally oblivious of the barriers."[20] But Lasker's visitors were acutely aware of these barriers.

Every day, before Lasker arrived, a secretary checked and adjusted his desk clock. (It tended to lose about two minutes a day.) She filled his fountain pens with ink, and sharpened and put in the tray on his desk a specific array of colored pencils: three green, three brown, and one yellow. She then copied parts of Lasker's "work sheet" from the day before onto a clean sheet of white paper. (Uncompleted tasks were rolled forward day by day until they were completed and crossed off the work sheet.) Appointments for the day were typed out on a piece of small notepaper, a copy of which was also given to Lasker's chauffeur when he arrived in the office. The little green book on his desk was checked for impending birthdays or anniversaries, reminders of which were typed up several days in advance—and left there until Lasker either acted on the reminder or threw it away.

The schedule and the day's mail were placed in a manila folder positioned every day on the same spot on Lasker's desk. The most important correspondence went on top. Letters written in illegible longhand were typed before being put in the folder for his review. Letters written in German were translated. Letters asking for money were culled unless the correspondent showed up in Lasker's address book as a personal friend. A report on the daily sales figures for Kotex and Kleenex were also included in this folder, as were daily newspaper columns by Walter Lippman, Dorothy Thompson, and Mark Sullivan.

A white memo pad was positioned next to the desk blotter. The cigarette box on the desk was topped off—*always* with George Washington Hill's Lucky Strikes—and matches placed nearby. The humidor was stocked with boxes of Antonio y Cleopatra Claras ($13.80 per hundred, purchased at the newsstand in the lobby). Everything was in place for the master's arrival.

That generally happened around 9:00 a.m., although punctuality was not one of Lasker's strong suits. One of the first things he did upon arrival was to sit for a shave in the barber's chair in the washroom that adjoined his office. While he was being attended to by George Andrews, who had been his barber for a quarter-century, he was not to be disturbed, unless for a long-distance call or a call he had already said that he wanted to take. In those cases, a secretary ventured into the impromptu barbershop, announced who was on the line, and gave Lasker the opportunity to take the call. On rare occasions, senior Lord & Thomas managers would approach the open doorway and make quick reports. ("That is one of the best chances to talk to him," confided Los Angeles office head Don Francisco, "because he can't talk back."[21]) Meanwhile, the office staff was placing the flowers that his chauffeur brought in from the Mill Farm Road estate in vases—fresh water daily—set in prominent places, including the conference room's fourteen-foot eighteenth-century Sheraton dining table.[22]

Next came an hour or more devoted to the daily correspondence file, with Lasker scribbling comments in pencil on the various letters and reports. During this ritual—and in fact, throughout most of the day—the secretaries were under strict orders to refrain from speaking to him if a typed message would suffice.

Correspondence was typically followed by a dictation session, when Lasker strode around his office giving oral responses to his letters, issuing directives to his subordinates in Chicago, New York, San Francisco, Los Angeles, Toronto, London, or Paris, or perhaps nudging family members in one direction or another. (Letters to one member of the immediate family were automatically copied and sent to all others.)

Outgoing phone calls were placed in the order that Lasker specified. When phone calls came in, the secretaries checked Lasker's "black book" to see if he knew the caller. If he did, the secretary typed out the name and put it in front of him, and he either took the call or shook his head *no*. When someone was relegated to the "no" list often enough, they stayed there; Lasker was henceforth "either out of the city" or "tied up" when that person called. One woman in particular achieved a special deep-banishment status: "Mrs. Mina Shakman will send letters to Mr. Lasker and seldom is her name signed. The handwriting is large and unmistakable. Never show them to Mr. Lasker but discard them. Should she call on the telephone she will say it is a personal friend but he is not to be told that she has called. Treat with kindness always so that she cannot take offense."

Of course, no one who wasn't known to Lasker could hope to walk in off the street, pass through those three sets of doors, and secure an audience with the master. Even if they carried an impressive letter of introduction, they were asked to leave the letter with the receptionist, who would get back to the visitor as soon as possible.

This was the highly structured life that Lasker, in his July 1938 announcement, now proposed to give up.

He named the forty-six-year-old Don Francisco, spearhead of the California campaigns, as his successor, and also promoted David Noyes and Sheldon

Coons to the posts of executive vice president. According to *Time,* the scuttlebutt within the industry was that Lasker had grown "more interested in cruises than in clients," and had long planned to quit the agency.[23] For his part, Lasker informed his clients that he had always intended to "withdraw from active service" as president of Lord & Thomas when he completed his fortieth year of service with the agency—a milestone that he had reached on May 31. "I shall retain financial interest in Lord & Thomas," he said, "and shall contribute to the agency's policies as may be required."[24]

This decision was soon reversed. Francisco did not thrive in his new job, in large part because Lasker never really left the stage. In October 1940, Francisco took a leave of absence from Lord & Thomas to work in Washington with Nelson A. Rockefeller on relations between the United States and Latin American countries; the leave turned out to be permanent.

That fall, Lasker—still grieving over the loss of Flora and afflicted by the ever-present specter of depression—left Chicago for what he thought would be an extended recuperation in California. (Just before departing, he made another precipitous and perhaps symbolic decision: selling off the herd of prize-winning Guernsey cattle at Mill Road Farm.) By that point, his friend and long-ago political mentor, Will Hays, had been serving as the moral policeman of Hollywood for a dozen years. Hays, convinced that what the grieving and disoriented Lasker needed was a new wife, arranged a series of dinners with eligible Hollywood starlets.

At one of those dinners, probably in September, Lasker re-encountered Doris Kenyon, an accomplished actor and singer who had achieved national celebrity during the silent-film era—signing a movie contract in 1916 while still a teenager for an astounding $50,000 per year, and starring in one of Paramount's first all-talking pictures (*Interference,* 1929)—but whose acting career had been trailing off for a decade.[25] Over the course of that career, she had run afoul of censors both in New York and Hollywood, owing in equal parts to her assertive personality and her smoldering screen persona.[26] One of those censors was Will Hays—who in 1931 had objected strongly to a Warner Bros. film, *The Road to Singapore,* which starred Kenyon and William Powell as a pair of hot-blooded and unrepentant adulterers—but Hays and Kenyon nevertheless became friends.[27]

Kenyon divorced her second husband in 1933, and was evidently open to finding a new partner. Then forty years old, she was still striking, with wide-set eyes, a broad and ready smile, and wavy blond hair. Lasker had met her briefly in California the previous fall, just before embarking on his world tour. On this second encounter, the ad man and the actress became infatuated with each other, and decided to marry immediately.

The couple signed a prenuptial agreement on October 14, 1938. Lasker's net worth was then in excess of $10 million—mainly in the form of securities and his Florida and Illinois properties—whereas Kenyon (who had an eleven-year-old son from her first marriage) had almost no assets. The agreement stipulated that if Kenyon was still living with Lasker as his wife when he died, she would be entitled to a lump-sum payment of $200,000 and could keep any properties that they acquired together. In the case of a divorce or separation, the prenuptial agreement would become null and void.[28]

The wedding was scheduled to take place in Lasker's apartment at New York's Waldorf-Astoria Hotel on October 28. Francie Lasker agreed to stay with Kenyon during the two days of festivities. She remembered Kenyon as naive but charming—"a lovely woman"—and recalled that October interlude as a jarring combination of drama and farce:

The whole thing was really heartbreaking. It was too ridiculous. I mean, he was a man in his fifties. Father had this dinner with 50 people two nights before he was married. I remember looking at everybody. I was in the middle of the table, and he was at the end of it. I didn't know whether to laugh or cry.

It was so strange. The night before he was married, he had a bachelor's dinner. Doris and I were having dinner in the rooms, and she turned to me and said, "Frances, is your father always like this?"

Oh, my god! That's no marriage, right?[29]

After exchanging vows—and after Lasker gave his new bride a magnificent sable coat as a wedding gift—the couple set sail on the *Île de France* for a honeymoon in England.[30] Almost immediately, it became clear that the marriage had been a terrible mistake. Lasker found that in the company of a movie star, he was no longer the center of attention. He badgered and bullied her in small ways, insisting—for example—that she eat foods that she disliked.[31] He experienced problems with impotence, no doubt a devastating blow to a man whose new wife had been, for millions, the embodiment of sex appeal.[32] Well before the monthlong honeymoon was over, the union had collapsed. Lasker sent an urgent cable to his son-in-law, Gerhard Foreman, begging for help in dissolving the marriage. Upon the Laskers' return to the

United States on December 1, they immediately split up. Lasker moved in with Gerhard and Mary at their North State Street home in Chicago; he lived there for several months, his emotional health in peril.

Kenyon behaved admirably throughout the humiliating episode. Although Lasker paid her $375,000 as a full settlement on December 21, 1938—very generous, in light of the terms of their prenuptial agreement—no public word of the couple's troubles leaked out until the following year. On February 6, a distraught Lasker, unraveling quickly, checked himself into the Mayo Clinic in Rochester, Minnesota.[33] Two weeks later, Kenyon admitted to reporters that she and Lasker had split. "Mr. Lasker and I found our hasty marriage incompatible," she said. "We have decided to end it, and thus maintain our valued friendship, for we hold only the highest regard for each other."[34]

In June, Kenyon traveled to Reno, where the divorce was finalized on June 8, 1939.[35] By that time, Lasker was already obsessed with the woman who would become his third wife, and he tried hard—and successfully—to erase the painful memory of this disastrous marital interlude. Some years later, Lasker saw an attractive woman in a theater. "I know that pretty woman," he said to his new wife. "I *know* her. What's her name? Who is she?"

That pretty woman was Doris Kenyon.[36]

Concurrent with the disastrous Kenyon affair was Lasker's involvement in a series of legal proceedings, collectively known as the "Manton case," which also caused Lasker much misery.

The case grew out of a $250,000 loan that he had made in 1932 at the request of his friend Paul H. Hahn, legal adviser and vice president of the American Tobacco Company, and an assistant to George Washington Hill.[37] Lasker believed that the loan was intended to cover stock losses suffered by executives at American Tobacco, perhaps even Hill himself. He had good reason for thinking so: a year earlier, he had loaned $150,000 to Louis Levy—another of his friends, and a partner in the New York law firm of Stanchfield & Levy, which represented American Tobacco—for this same purpose.[38]

Lasker made the loan personally, rather than through the business, although his decision certainly was influenced by the fact that American Tobacco was then a $19 million Lord & Thomas account, with commissions running around $2.8 million a year. Ralph Sollitt signed the check for Lasker and delivered it—in May 1932—to a shady intermediary named James J. Sullivan.[39] This time, though, the funds never reached American Tobacco executives. Instead, they were funneled into several firms controlled by U.S. Second Circuit Court of Appeals judge Martin T. Manton.

Manton, senior judge on the three-judge court in New York City, had no qualms about engaging in business as a sitting judge; in fact, he owned or controlled a dozen corporations and used his judicial position to benefit those companies. (Manton's abuse of his position was well known in the underworld, and had earned him the nickname of "Preying Manton.") Sullivan was one of his many partners. A month after receiving Lasker's money, however indirectly, Manton provided the tie-breaking vote on a verdict in favor of American Tobacco in a $10 million stockholder lawsuit.[40]

Lasker soon realized that the loan had the potential to be embarrassing to him, and he tried for several years to collect from Sullivan, who died in 1935.[41] Another three years passed, at which point the headline-hungry New York district attorney, Thomas Dewey, began investigating Manton's affairs. In September 1938, that investigation led Dewey's staff to Albert Lasker, who told them everything he knew about the loan.

On January 30, 1939, on the front page of the *New York Times*, Dewey accused Manton of accepting bribes from at least six litigants in return for favorable verdicts. Lasker's role in the drama appeared on page 3—mortifying publicity for a man who rarely sought it.[42]

Manton resigned from the federal bench and was indicted by a federal grand jury in April. At his trial in May, the prosecution called Lasker as a witness. Because the statute of limitations on the incidents involving Lasker had expired, the case against Manton did not include any criminal charges pertaining to the Lasker loan. But the details of that loan were introduced as evidence, and Lasker was called upon to explain himself.

Lasker believed that his good name was at stake. He was closely connected to several of the principals in the case, and his money had lined the pockets of a corrupt federal judge. He became increasingly agitated, convinced that the case would ruin him.

Those worries turned out to be misplaced. The evidence showed unequivocally that he had known nothing about the scheme. In fact, as his testimony and that of others amply demonstrated, Lasker was a victim, rather than a perpetrator. Manton was convicted on corruption charges, and spent seventeen months in federal prison.[43]

While Lasker's friends Hahn and Levy faced no criminal charges, disbarment proceedings were initiated against both men in the summer of 1939.

Late that summer, Lasker returned to court to testify against them. Again, he proved a strong witness, with the judge in the case noting that Lasker had been "shamefully treated" by his friends. United States Attorney John Cahill even extended compliments to Lasker: "The only person whose conduct is consistent with his testimony of what took place is Albert D. Lasker of the firm of Lord & Thomas, who, it seems to us, has been grossly misused in the situation, and in fairness to them I think it should publicly be said that we find absolutely no ground for criticism of the conduct of Lord & Thomas."[44]

Levy—who was deeply involved in Manton's many schemes—was disbarred.[45] Hahn, although scolded by the presiding judge for his poor judgment, was exonerated, and later became president of American Tobacco. To Lasker, these were secondary concerns; what mattered to him was his own good name. "A. D. Lasker wholly blameless," read the welcome subhead on the front page of the *Times*.[46]

During this bizarre interlude in Albert Lasker's life—rife with both private and public turmoil—Boyden Sparkes continued to labor away on the autobiography. He conducted interviews with people who had known Lasker at all stages of his life, ranging from family members and high school friends to potentates at the highest reaches of corporate America. When possible, he met on a monthly basis with Lasker. By March 1938, he had generated 378 pages of personal interviews with Lasker and 761 pages of interviews with others.

By this time, too, he probably had inklings that the project was in trouble. It had taken Sparkes only a week to do the background interviews in and around Detroit for his Alfred Sloan biography; now, given the turmoil in Lasker's professional and personal lives, this new book threatened to drag on indefinitely.

In March 1939, shortly after checking out of the Mayo Clinic, a beleaguered Lasker stunned Sparkes by telling him that throughout all of their interviews to date, he had been "a man practically in a state of amnesia," and couldn't be held responsible for his words. As Sparkes noted in a memo to himself:

What does this mean? If I accept his statement—and he said it so many times as to leave me no choice—it means that none of the material he gave me previously can be regarded as valid. It means that I have to start from the beginning.

Now, I expect to rewrite where I have failed to capture the spirit of a story or for some other failure of my own, but I can't be held accountable for such a thing as this. A study of my conversations with Mr. Lasker shows many other conflicts, conflicts in instructions. I have no desire to take the slightest advantage of him. I do believe that if he had not burdened me with so many instructions, I would have been through with his story, that it would have been published in the Saturday Evening Post *months before several embarrassing circumstances had arisen to plague this undertaking.*[47]

Lasker continued to offer Sparkes intermittent encouragement—as in the spring of 1940, when he wrote that he hoped the manuscript that Sparkes had started writing "after the first of the year is nearing, or has reached completion."[48] But, conflicted, he also sabotaged Sparkes's efforts to get the story serialized in the *Post*.

The project stalled. Client and author had reached an impasse over money, scope, and distribution of the work, but that wasn't the real problem. Lasker had moved on to new realms, with a new partner. For Lasker, then at the end of one phase of his life and the beginning of another, looking back simply proved too painful.

Chapter Twenty

Changing a Life

ALBERT LASKER'S failed marriage to Doris Kenyon might have seemed ample reason to avoid yet another intense personal relationship. But Lasker believed that he needed the stability of married life—an anchor to keep him from drifting into dangerous waters—and so he once again set out to find the right match. He would discover the right woman, he told a friend, even if it meant marrying ten times over.[1]

When the right woman did come along, Lasker almost failed to notice her. On the afternoon of April 1, 1939, Lasker was taking a long lunch with William Donovan—lawyer, former New York gubernatorial candidate, and future "father" of the Central Intelligence Agency—at New York's storied Twenty-One. Donovan introduced him to a friend, Mary Woodard Reinhardt, who was seated at a nearby table. Although the thirty-eight-year-old Reinhardt was a striking woman—with piercing eyes set deeply into a wide face, a dramatic head of wavy brown hair, and a broad grin—Lasker acknowledged the introduction with little more than a vague smile. A few minutes later, he passed Mary's table on his way to use the telephone without giving her a glance.

Mary thought to herself, "That man is making a great mistake not to pay any attention to me."[2]

After lunch, still in the restaurant, Lasker got another chance: he and Mary were introduced a second time by their mutual friend Lewis Strauss. Minutes later, they were introduced a *third* time by art collector Max Epstein. This time, finally, something clicked. After Mary left, Lasker began quizzing Donovan about this elegant woman who seemed to know everyone who mattered. He was intrigued to learn, among other things, that Mary was divorced, much admired in the right circles, and an entrepreneur and businesswoman of no small reputation.

———— ·《●》· ————

Mary got a phone call the following afternoon from Mrs. Bernard Gimbel, who was hosting Lasker the following weekend at her country house and was anxious to have Mary join them. The next day, she got another phone call, this time from Max Epstein, inviting her for cocktails at 5:00 the next day. Mary, preoccupied with her mother's health, missed some of the details, but agreed to stop by.

The following day, she arrived at Epstein's residence at 6:00, assuming that she was fashionably late for a cocktail party. To her surprise, she found only her host—and an irate Albert Lasker, aggrieved at being kept waiting for a *full hour*! Mary, amused, managed to calm Lasker down. As the two talked, she was surprised by his informed opinions on many of her favorite subjects. When she mentioned her love of flowers, he airily observed that he had the best garden border in the country. When she raised the subject of boats and sailing, he offered to take her on a cruise of Lake Michigan on his yacht. "I was impressed with anyone who was so downright about what he knew and what he did and what he had, and factual and entertaining at the same time," Mary recalled. "He had an extraordinary quality of vitality, and this business of being amusing at the same time. He was so down to earth that it was almost funny, and he often said very funny things."[3]

Albert and Mary met again at the Gimbels' for lunch on the following Sunday, where they took a long walk before lunch and talked of more serious topics, including the prospect of global war, then weighing heavily on Albert's mind. Mary decided that Lasker was the most brilliant man that she had ever met. But there was a cloud over that brilliance. "He was very agitated and nervous," Mary later recalled, "and I realized that he was terribly distressed, but he was at the same time extremely interesting and entertaining."[4]

Mary and Albert got together several more times that spring—once for dinner on May 1 (Lasker's birthday), after Lasker returned from a visit to Mill Road Farm, and again at a party on June 21, the day that the Manton verdict was brought in. That party was thrown by Mary and her close friend Kay Swift, the Broadway composer, on the terrace of Mary's penthouse apartment on East 52nd Street—a soirée that brought together many of Mary's closest friends, including Margaret Sanger, the head of the Birth Control Federation of America; Lasker's friend David Sarnoff; and famed analysts Karl and William Menninger. Also in attendance was utility executive and prominent New Deal foe Wendell Willkie, whom Mary thought would be a good candidate to run against Franklin Roosevelt in the upcoming presidential election. (Albert told Mary that this was the craziest idea he had ever heard; within the year, he would be helping Willkie secure the Republican nomination.)

Lasker was struck by Mary's business sense, her self-confidence, and the rarified social circles in which she traveled—in many ways loftier than his own—and her sense of *style*. When he first visited her penthouse apartment, he was staggered that Mary managed to live so well on what he guessed to be a small income. Lasker later told Mary, in jest, that he had decided to marry her for her money; but he was clearly taken with the idea, and the reality, of a self-made woman.

By the time Mary Woodard Reinhardt met Albert Lasker, she had been divorced for three years from Paul E. Reinhardt, a New York art dealer. Mary met Reinhardt in the 1920s, after completing postgraduate work in art history at Oxford. She moved to New York City and took a job in Reinhardt's gallery; the two married in 1926 and emerged as a strong force in the New York art scene. The marriage—under constant pressure because of his alcoholism—was less successful than the gallery, and in 1934, Mary filed for divorce.

Mary's resolve to be financially independent was forged early, resulting at least in part from to her parents' complicated relationship with each other and with money. Her father precipitated wrenching emotional scenes whenever his wife purchased items that he considered to be luxuries, infuriating the young Mary. "I decided," she later recalled, "that never would I let any man speak to me like that, and that I would earn my own money."[5] When she divorced, therefore, Mary founded a company called Hollywood Patterns, which used Hollywood starlets to advertise dress patterns. The patterns were designed by *Vogue*, and Mary received a third-of-a-cent commission on every sale.[6] Arriving on the fashion scene at the start of the Great Depression—just as women across the country were returning to their sewing machines to save money on their wardrobes—the patterns became hugely popular (and are still highly collectible today).

Mary augmented her income by steering customers to Raymond Loewy, then emerging as one of America's most significant industrial designers. She became familiar with Loewy's work in the early 1930s; with her art and business connections, she was able to open doors for him, for which he paid her commissions. In 1934, for example, she helped Loewy get a commission from Sears, Roebuck and Co. to redesign the Coldspot refrigerator, the success of which catapulted Loewy into the top ranks of industrial designers.[7]

A month into the courtship between Albert and Mary—in May 1939—his mental state was worsening. The Manton affair was still unfolding; his divorce was not yet finalized. He wanted to get closer to Mary, but he was paralyzed by the raw memories of his unhappy months with Doris Kenyon. He also wondered if he should be pursuing a woman who was twenty-one years his junior.

Mary left for London in June, on a business trip that had been planned months earlier. While she was in Europe, Lasker sent her orchids "by the bushel," dispatched telegrams warning her that the outbreak of war in Europe was imminent—and even overcame his distaste for transatlantic telephone communication to call her once in England. And yet, when she returned to New York, Lasker failed to meet her at the pier. Mary was confused and put off by the mixed signals; but when she saw Lasker that night, she realized that he was in "profound distress."

Shortly thereafter, she left for California on another business trip. While at the Golden Gate Fair in San Francisco, she received an urgent call from Lasker. He was in a state of "nervous exhaustion," he told her, and his friend Merrill ("Babe") Meigs had sent a plane and a private nurse to take him to a ranch in Arizona for rest and recuperation.

He remained there for more than two months, in almost complete isolation. (The nearest phone was ninety miles away; once a week, he was driven to the phone so that he could call Mary in New York.) A doctor who examined Lasker concluded that his patient's adrenal glands were malfunctioning. The diagnosis may have given Lasker some satisfaction—perhaps his problems weren't "in his head," after all—but it was misguided. When Lasker returned to New York in November, Mary convinced him to go see a world-renowned internist, Dr. Robert Loeb, at the Presbyterian Medical Center.

Loeb, immediately charmed by Lasker, turned his new patient over to colleagues who were specialists in endocrine problems. All the tests came back negative: they could find nothing physically wrong with Lasker.

Increasingly worried, Mary demanded that Loeb refer Lasker to a psychotherapist. Loeb was a deep skeptic of the psychoanalytic method and responded with scorn: "What! Send that wonderful man to a psychoanalyst?" But Mary—who had undergone some analysis several years earlier—insisted, and Loeb reluctantly came up with the name of a colleague, George Daniels, who (he told Mary) "would at least do [Lasker] no harm," and was strong enough to stand up to Lasker's overwhelming personality.

Mary had far greater ambitions for the treatment. Her experience with psychotherapy had given her insight into her patterns of behavior and, she said, built up her "stamina, persistence, and patience." Now, she desperately hoped that Lasker could find similar relief.

First, though, she had to sell psychoanalysis to Lasker. She found her opening in *Bacchanale*, a Metropolitan Opera production—based on the life of the mad king of Bavaria, Ludwig II—which she and Albert attended. Surrealist artist Salvador Dalí designed the scenery and costumes for the opera, based on a Freudian concept of the subconscious. Mary, who had been interested in Freud for years and had tried unsuccessfully to meet with him during her recent trip to London, explained the concept to Lasker. "It had a profound and dramatic effect on him," she later recalled: "He hadn't realized that one's subconscious played such an enormous part in one's life. He had been one of these people of action who had really not dared to take the time to look under the surface, under his own surface or anybody else's, a great deal. He was very intuitive, but he didn't really know that there was a whole world of the unconscious that you could explore."[8]

Mary built on this interest and eventually broached the idea of Albert going to an analyst.[9] (According to Lasker's daughter Francie, Mary probably made it a precondition to their marriage.[10]) In December 1940, Lasker paid his first visit to Dr. Daniels. Weary of the emotional rollercoaster of his illness, he was willing to try anything.

Lasker's discussions with Daniels touched on his parents, his feelings of guilt about his frustrating relationship with Flora, and how he had treated his children. His father had given him a strong sense of responsibility but had also overshadowed him, which ultimately compelled him to leave home. His mother he remembered as beautiful, passionately neat, and devoted to her children—and yet somehow indistinct, especially in contrast to Morris. Not wanting to re-create the emotional barrenness of his own childhood, Albert had *"overwhelmed* his kids with love" (as Mary told John Gunther).[11] He talked a great deal about his children, regretting that he had made them financially independent by conferring large trusts on them—$5 million each, in those Depression days—and worrying that he had unfairly favored Edward over his sisters.

The treatment was intensive: four or five sessions a week for six months. Therapist and patient forged a strong bond, and Lasker came to enjoy his meetings with Daniels. Cutting short a lunch with publisher Richard Simon, for example, Lasker explained that he was late for an appointment with his analyst. "I'm not being analyzed for what you probably think," he told Simon. "I'm doing it to get rid of all the *hate* the advertising business put into me." He was learning to think about himself in new ways. "You know what it did for me?" he later said of analysis. "It taught me to forgive myself."[12]

It also helped him begin to cut ties to his troubled past. On January 2, 1940, he donated his beloved Mill Road Farm to the University of Chicago, expressing the hope that the university could find an appropriate educational use for the property.[13] Lasker's biographer John Gunther noted the precipitous nature of this decision; the hurried disposal of the grand estate may well have reflected Lasker's continuing emotional distress—or it may have reflected progress in his therapy.[14] Explaining the move to his children, Lasker joked: "Mill Road is the kind of place that's going to be surrounded by an angry mob someday. They'll say, 'Let's get the so-and-so who built this place!' When that happens, I intend to be a member of the mob."[15]

Lasker ended his treatments far short of a complete psychoanalysis, which would have required many years.[16] Even so, therapy gave him tremendous relief. He "got relaxed," according to Mary. His impotence also became less of a problem.

"By this time," Mary reported, "I realized that I was in love with him, and around this time he realized that he was in love with me."[17] They wed on June 21 at New York's City Hall, only a little more than a year after their first meeting. The marriage was performed in "great secret" by their friend, Judge Samuel Rosenman; Mary recalled that it was a "very unimportant looking ceremony, with a judge who had left the court and brought his robes down in a newspaper, and he had two very bedraggled clerks who stood up [as witnesses]."[18] The newlyweds left on a yacht for a honeymoon on Long Island

Sound, ultimately winding up in Philadelphia at the Republican Convention, to which Lasker was an Illinois delegate. In that role, he helped swing his delegation to Wendell Willkie, the long-shot candidate Mary had begun pushing a year earlier.

The Willkie story can be seen as an early tracing of the pattern of the rest of Lasker's life. Already, Mary had begun to exert a profound influence on Albert. With her at his side—and more often, several steps ahead of him—Lasker was able to deploy his prodigious talents in the service of new causes. For most of his adult life, he had been searching for a way to make a significant, enduring contribution. Public service had proved a dead-end. Business seemed superficial and was increasingly unsatisfying. The world had responded with indifference to his grand scheme for remaking the American economy. But now, with Mary, he moved forward. Those close to him noticed a profound change. "He was a whole different man," recalled his daughter Francie, a half-century later. "He became mellow . . . he found a purpose."[19]

Mary initially hoped to retain her financial independence after her marriage to Lasker. "I don't want to hear anything about money from you or anybody else, and I have my money and you have your money," she told him. "I'll go and live with you wherever you want to live, but I'll take care of all my expenses and you take care of your expenses, and you can buy the food."[20] Lasker relished Mary's fierce resolve—deeming it "cute"—and this state of affairs lasted through the first year and a half of their marriage. Eventually, though, Mary found the arrangement awkward when worthy causes came asking for money: opulent as her new lifestyle was, she had no money to give them. Lasker's son Edward weighed in, strongly objecting to his stepmother having no access to substantial funds. Ultimately, Lasker resolved the matter by writing Mary a check for $1 million.

Albert and Mary supported many causes. They actively embraced birth control, cancer research, mental health research, a national heart institute and a national dental institute, the Arthritis and Rheumatism Foundation, and national health care—to cite only a few.

The first of these causes was birth control, to which Mary had been drawn before their marriage, and in which she soon enlisted Lasker's help. She first became interested in the movement in 1937 when she read a biography of birth-control activist and crusader Margaret Sanger. She was impressed by

Sanger's courage; she also felt a profound sympathy with "anybody, male or female, any family that didn't have the right to control the size of their families."[21] Mary made a small donation to Sanger's organization, the Birth Control Federation, and was soon asked to join the Federation's board.

Several months after becoming a director, Mary met Margaret Sanger for the first time at Sanger's country home near Fishkill, New York, and the two became friends. After Mary grew closer to Albert, she brought him into Sanger's orbit, as well.

This was a delicate juncture in the history of reproductive rights. In response to pressure from Sanger and others, the courts had legalized discussion of birth control methods by physicians in 1936. Nevertheless, the topic was still largely taboo, and Mary was considered extremely eccentric for her public support of birth control. So she was thrilled to discover that Albert shared her passion: "Imagine my pleasure and joy when after I met Albert Lasker and told him of my interest in the Birth Control Federation he said that he, too, felt it was one of the most important human and health problems in the United States and in the world. I was really deeply moved by his interest in the area and also by the fact that he was willing to contribute."[22]

In fact, Albert was not the first of the Laskers to get involved with the work of the Birth Control Federation. In the 1920s, his sisters Loula and Florina served as executors of a bequest made by their mother to "help women"—a broad mandate that the Lasker sisters decided to carry out by making a gift in support of Sanger's work.[23]

Albert carried this family tradition forward in the fall of 1939, when (through Lord & Thomas) he gave $10,000 to support the so-called "Negro Project," which focused on providing family-planning advice to black families in South Carolina, one of the first states in the nation to incorporate contraception in its formal public health program. Although the project was criticized in some quarters as racist—one of its aims being a reduction in the number of babies born to black families on relief—Albert saw it as a high-minded pilot program with important implications for the larger society.[24] As he wrote in a July 1942 letter to Sanger: "With you I thoroughly agree 'that the Negro question is coming to the fore in America.' For my part, I do not see how we can have the secure democracy for which our men are fighting and dying until we find a place of security and dignity for the Negro in our national life. If one minority is degraded, we are all affected, for we all belong to some minority."[25]

By the time Albert made his 1939 gift, Sanger had reduced her role to honorary chair of the organization and was spending much of her time in Arizona with her ailing husband. As Albert's growing knowledge about the subject began to overlap with his own business experience, he developed strong opinions about how the federation should present itself to the world. He saw a Big Idea that was being undersold, and he set out to change that. "The main reaction I got from the [1940 annual] meeting," Lasker wrote to Sanger, "was . . . that the Birth Control movement is something far beyond the implications of its name."[26] In that spirit, Lasker suggested a new name for the organization—*Planned Parenthood*—arguing that it "sounded more constructive and would meet with less public opposition."[27] Sanger resented what she perceived as a semantic retreat from the fray and made her displeasure known to the Laskers and the board.[28]

But the name change stuck. No doubt the board was predisposed to side with Lasker because of his growing financial support of the organization: In February 1940, he made a commitment of $25,000 a year for three years, and at the same time, convinced several friends to contribute similar sums. Ever the pragmatist, Lasker knew that his financial support would mean far more if the organization broadened its base of support—and if that happened, he would be even more helpful. "I shall be glad," he promised Sanger, "if the movement is financed for a larger operation, to give such of my time and experience in the carrying out of the plan as I might be called on to give."[29]

Mary, too, was doing her part to steer and strengthen Planned Parenthood. She raised funds for the organization and began using her political connections on its behalf. In 1941, for example, she asked Eleanor Roosevelt—whom she had met through her close friend, Anna Rosenberg (later to be named assistant Secretary of Defense)—to arrange a meeting with Surgeon General Thomas Parran Jr. Although Parran pushed her off on his assistant, Warren Draper, Mary was able to win a critical concession from Draper. While the Public Health Service (PHS) did not feel it could initiate or promote Planned Parenthood programs, Draper told Mary that the PHS would look favorably on states that asked for money for this purpose. Mary asked him to confirm this statement in a letter, which he did. It was the first time the PHS committed itself in writing to the concept of "child spacing"—that is, having children several years apart, according to a family plan—and this constituted a major step on the part of the federal government.

That night, Mary went to dinner at the White House, where she mentioned the day's activities to President Roosevelt. Roosevelt replied that the subject was a political "hot potato," and admitted that he had done little on the subject except in Puerto Rico, where he had convinced local Catholic authorities to accept the practice under the bland banner of "adult sex hygiene."[30] Eleanor Roosevelt arranged another White House lunch for Mary, allowing her to invite anyone she wanted to come talk about birth control. Unfortunately, the lunch took place on December 8, 1941—the day after the Japanese attack on Pearl Harbor—and the participants were too distracted to focus on anything but war.

Mary also found ways to manipulate the media for her purposes. She established an annual dinner for Planned Parenthood, and gave citations to those who had contributed to the movement. She arranged to have a radio broadcast about Planned Parenthood on the same night as the first awards ceremony—a coup that she owed mainly to the behind-the-scenes interventions of her husband. "It was [done] with great trepidation on the part of [David] Sarnoff and Niles [Trammell] of the NBC," she later explained, "and really only the enormous influence that Albert Lasker had on them made them do this."[31]

In the fall of 1940, when *Look* magazine agreed to run an article on birth control, leading companies to cancel three full pages of advertisements, Albert agreed to buy the canceled space for Lord & Thomas house ads, thereby helping *Look* avoid a financial drubbing.

Planned Parenthood gave Mary her first sustained exposure to a nonprofit organization. She found the experience of working with an all-volunteer group—many of whom took their responsibilities lightly—difficult and frustrating. "The people interested in [Planned Parenthood]," she later admitted, "were not used to organization or to thinking on any large scale about fundraising or of action of any kind."[32]

These organizational shortcomings eventually convinced Mary to look for another context in which to exert her growing influence. Before leaving the family-planning fray, however, Albert and Mary made a final gift of $50,000 to Planned Parenthood. It was the largest donation the organization had ever received up to that point.

The next few years of Albert's and Mary's marriage coincided with World War II, and the war necessarily took precedence over all other causes.

Early in 1942, Mary came across a copy of a best-selling book called *Victory Through Air Power*, written by Major Alexander de Seversky. The author—a colorful Russian immigrant who had served in Czar Nicholas II's naval air service and later invented the first gyroscopically stabilized bomb-sight—contended that control of the air had become all-important in modern warfare, and argued that the United States was woefully underequipped along a number of critical dimensions: the number of planes as well as their range, speed, weaponry, and altitude capability. Nothing in the U.S. arsenal, Seversky argued, remotely compared with the sophisticated fighter planes then being manufactured by the nation's enemies.[33]

Mary became a convert, but when she tried to convince Albert of the book's thesis, the two had what Mary later described as a "knock-down, drag-out discussion about the whole matter," with Albert refusing even to read *Victory Through Air Power*. Mary persisted, however, and when Albert finally read the book, he also was won over, and set up a meeting with the author. Seversky turned out to be even more persuasive in person, and the Laskers resolved to do whatever they could to advance his cause.

First they took him to meet Secretary of the Navy William Franklin "Frank" Knox, and subsequently introduced him to the influential Rear Admiral Forrest Sherman. Mary distributed some two thousand copies of *Victory Through Air Power* to members of Congress and other major opinion makers in the United States. The Laskers tried to get Seversky an audience with President Roosevelt but, as Mary recalled, the president was very "Navy-minded," and thought of air power only as an adjunct to naval power.

In this particular battle, the Laskers joined forces with another private citizen: Walt Disney. When the influential Hollywood mogul decided to make a film version of *Victory Through Air Power*, he asked Albert to serve as a "consultant" on the picture. In that vaguely defined capacity, Lasker hosted an elaborate dinner in the Grand Ballroom of New York's Waldorf Hotel on February 14, 1943, for the first semipublic screening of the film. Mary described the evening as "a large and astonishing private party of about 1,000 people at which Albert made one of his rare public speeches."[34]

The movie was an awkward combination of animation and on-camera exposition by Seversky, aimed at persuading Americans to demand that their government build up its air power. "If *Victory Through Air Power* is propaganda," the *New York Times* wrote in a generally positive review, "it is at least the most encouraging and inspiring propaganda that the screen has afforded us in a long time."[35] Disney's distributor, RKO, declined to release the odd film, and he was compelled to use United Artists to get it into theaters. According to one account, Winston Churchill insisted that Franklin Roosevelt view *Victory Through Air Power*—after which, allegedly, Roosevelt embraced the concept of long-range bombing.[36] At the end of the war, the Disney studio removed the film from circulation, and it wasn't released again for more than half a century.

Seversky later received the prestigious Harmon Aviator Trophy for his stubborn personal crusade.

Albert Lasker had a hard time letting go of Lord & Thomas. But after the false start of 1938, he dissolved the agency once and for all in December 1942.

This was in part a decision driven by other people's decisions. Lasker knew, finally, that there were no family members in line to succeed him at Lord & Thomas. His son Edward, increasingly immersed in Hollywood and film production, had no interest in taking over the business. Daughter Mary had been fired. At the same time, the agency's senior ranks were thinning. Ralph Sollitt had retired in the mid-1930s. Don Francisco—once the heir apparent—had departed in 1940 for government service. Sheldon Coons had launched his own business. David Noyes had left advertising to run a ranch out West. If Lord & Thomas *were* to go forward, it would require a substantial rebuilding on Lasker's part, and now, at sixty-two, Lasker was feeling his age. "I am tired," he told Fairfax Cone, head of the Chicago office. "I go to bed tired, and when I wake up I wake up more tired than when I went to sleep."[37]

One reason, he told Cone, was that he was *bored*. For many years, changes in the industry had been making the job less fun for him, and the strange new world of advertising—now dominated by marketing vice presidents and account reps—no longer played to his strengths. The pioneering days of advertising, he believed, were over. In an eloquent letter to the head of Lord & Thomas's London office, Leonard "Mike" Masius, Lasker looked back on his career, and on the state of the industry:

I was connected with the first advertising ever done on canned pork and beans, canned soup, canned spaghetti. When I with my associates conceived and financed the first advertising of tires; when I was of that group who first advertised automobiles; when with associates I defined advertising so that it became a force of social good to introduce to the people new and better ways of life, I could work inspired, because I was fulfilling myself. But now the social frontiers that advertising could open have been crossed, and advertising is merely an instrument for competitive expression. As such it becomes only a money-making device, and since one cannot keep the money, there is nothing left in advertising itself which is inspiring to me.[38]

In addition, the business model that had served Lasker and Lord & Thomas so well over the years was now a hindrance to growth. When Don Francisco first considered moving to New York in 1933 to take over that office and thereby position himself to succeed Lasker as head of the overall agency, he wrote a powerful letter to Ralph Sollitt explaining why he thought the agency was in trouble:

My impression is that Lord & Thomas heretofore has wanted to be an agency with a few big accounts controlled by two or three men at the head of the agency; accounts held largely through the personal contribution of those top executives to the success of those advertisers, plus perhaps a personal investment in the business, close personal relations with the heads of those advertisers, etc. With such accounts held at the top this way, there is no need for a lot of special service, window dressing, or wasted motion. A fine job can be done and the maximum profit per million of billing yielded to the agency.

However, there comes a point where the capacity of this kind of an organization is reached. Then it either stops growing or expands too far and the business starts to break up. This type of business finds it difficult to grow when the capacity of the top men is reached because up to that point it has not really been on a competitive basis. Its accounts are held at the top as above referred to. The agency has not found it necessary to add or hold the number of strong men that other agencies have or to do some of the things that other agencies have found it necessary or worthwhile to do. Therefore, for the most part, its business-getters come home empty handed.

If they do bring home accounts, they are not likely to be kept very long because the major effort of the organization is directed to serving those clients in whom the heads of the business feel the most personal interest. Other clients suffer because the energies of the staff are commandeered for the principals' clients.

That, I think, is, roughly, the kind of an agency that Lord & Thomas is. The heart of our business has been . . . accounts secured very largely through

Mr. Lasker's extraordinary influence and amazing capacity . . . But when you get beyond his influence . . . the record is quite appalling.[39]

Nothing much had changed in the ensuing nine years. Lasker still remained the essential ingredient in the agency's success—but now he was tired and bored and had no allies.

The final compelling reason to shut down Lord & Thomas was financial.[40] By 1942, as a result of his opulent lifestyle, his real estate purchases, his philanthropic efforts, his settlement with Doris Kenyon, and his generous gifts to his children and Mary, Lasker was running low on cash. His taxable income—mainly consisting of his Lord & Thomas salary and dividends—amounted to just under $200,000, down from nearly $900,000 in 1936.[41] He still owned about $1.5 million in marketable equities, principally Pepsodent and Cellucotton stock. But most of his wealth was tied up in Lord & Thomas's cash reserves.[42]

For much of the previous year, Mary and his son Edward had been encouraging Lasker to begin taking capital out of Lord & Thomas, but Lasker couldn't bring himself to cut the cord. If the payout came in the form of dividends, moreover, it would be subject to a tax rate of close to 80 percent.

There was a loophole, however: the federal tax code specified a flat tax rate for businesses in liquidation. That rate had been 12.5 percent until 1941, when it was raised to 15 percent. Then, in the fall of 1942, the tax rate went up again—to 25 percent—and the liquidation that would have cost Lasker something like $800,000 in taxes in 1941 would now cost between $1.2 million and $1.3 million. Lasker's legal and financial advisers warned him that the rate was likely to be raised again in 1943, perhaps to a level that would make liquidation unfeasible.

Lasker returned from lunch one day and told his wife that he had decided to give up the company.[43] Surprised at this sudden turnaround, Mary asked him to think the matter over for forty-eight hours, but Lasker had made his decision, and now he would not look back.

Word went out to the senior executives in New York, Chicago, and Los Angeles: Emerson Foote, Fairfax Cone, and Don Belding, respectively. These three met intensively with Lasker during the third week of December 1942, and worked out a plan to dissolve Lord & Thomas. At the same time, the group laid plans to create a new agency—Foote, Cone & Belding—with three equal partners. For legal and tax purposes, it would be a complete break.[44] Nevertheless, Foote, Cone & Belding would open its doors with some significant competitive advantages. It would have some one hundred employees in five floors in Chicago's Palmolive Building, about sixty at 437 Park Avenue in New York, about forty in two floors of Los Angeles's signature Electric Building, and a slightly smaller number in San Francisco. It would not have international branches; Lasker decided to "give" the Toronto, London, and Paris offices to his managers in those cities.[45]

For turning over his preferred and common stock in the agency's liquidation, Lasker would gross some $3.7 million. After setting aside $1.2 million for taxes and contingencies, he would net $2.3 million.[46]

Lasker took several steps to get the new agency off on the right foot. First, by assigning the January 1943 profits of $260,000 to the new firm, he gave it sufficient cash flow to get going. Second, he turned over the old agency's furniture and equipment (including its two engraving and typographic plants in New York and Chicago) to the new one for the token sum of $68,000. Most important, he convinced all but two of Lord & Thomas's clients—the two exceptions being relatively unimportant accounts in California—to stick with the new company.

Public reaction was generally disapproving. *Time*, not always friendly to Lasker, lamented the death of a legendary agency. "To the advertising world," its writer sniffed, "it was almost as if Tiffany had announced that from now on it would be known as Jones, Smith & Johnson."[47] But Fairfax Cone understood Lasker's motivations: "He had turned full circle from hectic business to a calm and consoling life filled with endless unexpected wonders, and he was using his large fortune to seed a growing list of projects in the public interest. He had traded what he saw as a life of repetition for one of new exploration and discovery, and he wanted to make the closing of the first so complete and so unequivocal that it could never impinge upon the second."[48]

Lasker granted one of his rare interviews in mid January 1943. The timing was not accidental; he sought to dispel any notion that he had lost faith in the economy in general, or in advertising in particular. "With the tremendous backlog of new products waiting to be marketed, the period after the war may well be the golden age of marketing," he told a reporter. He talked enthusiastically of plastics and planes. "There will be new products, new impetus to stimulate advertising in the post-war world, as new industries and new firms offer new wares to the people."[49]

Lasker saw into the future, contradicting those who already were predicting a postwar economic collapse. But from that day on—although he and Mary maintained close ties with all three of the new agency's principals—Albert Lasker no longer had any direct say in the business he had spun off, or in the industry he had helped to reinvent.

Chapter Twenty-One

Finding Peace

WITH LORD & THOMAS gone, where would Albert direct his still-formidable energy and invest his newly liquid financial resources? One answer was the Lasker Foundation, which Albert and Mary established with the goal of supporting medical research. Lasker put only half the proceeds from the sale of Lord & Thomas into the Foundation, but he added money from time to time and through his will provided the Foundation with another large infusion of cash.

One of the initial activities of the Foundation was to establish awards to recognize outstanding contributions in the field of medical research. The first recipient was William Menninger, who received the award from the National Committee for Mental Hygiene in 1944. The awards were Mary's inspiration; she was drawing up a will at about this time, and this spurred her to think about her legacy: "When thinking aloud with a lawyer about how I wanted to dispose of my funds, I thought that I would like to establish awards, similar to the Nobel Prizes, in medical research only or in the field of health and medicine. And when the idea struck me, I was so emotionally moved by the idea that I might be able to do this after I died, that I thought, 'Well, why don't I do it while I'm alive, if this is all so exciting to me?'"[1]

Albert was less enthusiastic. He didn't relish the idea of having his name attached to so public a gesture. Mary understood his reticence—acknowledging her husband's "absolute passion for anonymity in anything he did"—but strong-armed him into going along with her.[2]

The fields of medicine and health had preoccupied Mary since she was a child. She vividly recalled her own sickly childhood, as well as a deeply upsetting childhood visit to the sickroom where the family's laundress lay dying. When Mary's mother told her that the woman had cancer and her breasts had been removed, Mary was shocked. "I thought this shouldn't happen to anybody," she recalled. "I was absolutely infuriated, indignant, that this woman should suffer so and that there should be no help for her."[3]

Cancer seemed to lurk on the periphery of Mary's life. The mother of her close friend, Kay Swift, died of breast cancer. In 1943, the Laskers' cook was diagnosed with cancer. Mary arranged for the woman to be seen by a doctor and receive radium treatments, but the disease had progressed too far. Mary was shocked to find that almost no progress had been made in the field in the previous two decades, especially when she came across a pamphlet published by the New York City Cancer Committee, which asserted that if a hospital or research group was given $500,000 a year for a few years for cancer research, great progress could be made. Mary was "infuriated" that nobody had come up with this kind of money, especially in light of the "vast economic resources of the people of the United States."[4]

At about this same time, the Laskers were vacationing with their friends Dan and Florence Mahoney in Palm Beach, and Mary discussed her outrage with Florence. Florence jumped into the cause, taking over the annual fundraising drive for the Cancer Society in Miami. That year, instead of the typical total of between $800 and $900, the Mahoneys managed to raise $35,000 for cancer-related work in Miami. Mary was thrilled, and the two women became staunch allies in the fight to support cancer research.

Albert Lasker initially steered clear of direct involvement in this cause. Although willing to help financially, he didn't want to become deeply engaged in the details of the work. "He wasn't interested in health," Mary later explained. "Medical problems and illnesses frightened him, and he knew absolutely nothing about them and didn't want to learn."[5]

Her summary wasn't entirely accurate. In 1922, in memory of Albert's younger brother, who had died of cancer a year earlier, the Laskers had established the Harry M. Lasker Memorial Fund as a permanent endowment of the American Society for the Control of Cancer. Albert added $25,000 to this fund the following year; together, these two gifts represented almost the entire endowment of the Society in its first decade of operations.[6] Then, in 1928, Albert and Flora made a $1 million gift to the University of Chicago to establish the "Lasker Foundation for Medical Research" to support research into the "causes, nature, prevention, and cure" of degenerative diseases.[7]

So Albert had a history of supporting medical research. He also fully understood the importance of seed money, and leverage, to pursue Big Ideas. It was Albert, for example, who gave Mary the crucial suggestion to seek public funds for her crusade. "You need federal money," he said, "and I will show you how to get it."[8]

Lasker was constitutionally inclined to think big. From his stint on the Shipping Board, moreover, he understood both the "mechanics of legislation, and the psychology of politicians" (as Mary later phrased it). His broad vision and insider know-how, coupled with Mary's tenacity, proved a formidable combination.

Their first target in Washington was Senator Claude Pepper, Democrat from Florida. Pepper was Chair of the Senate Subcommittee on Wartime Health and Education, which funded the Office of Medical Research (OMR): the only federal organization that then controlled significant medical research funds. By this time, OMR had spent between $10 and $15 million on diseases related to military service, and had made great strides in the fight against typhus. But in the summer of 1944, the war appeared to be nearing its end, and there was no impetus in Washington to transfer these funds to research into civilian-oriented health issues.

Pepper could exert considerable influence in this area, and the Laskers could exert considerable influence on Pepper, who was up for reelection in the fall of 1944. During the summer of 1944, therefore, Pepper sent two aides to call on the Laskers to discuss hearings on national health issues. At this time, the Public Health Service contained both the National Institutes of Health and the National Cancer Institute, which between them controlled about $2 million for research. The National Cancer Institute, founded in 1937, was limited by law to an overall budget of only $700,000, and—amazingly—had only $70,000 to distribute for outside research grants in 1944.[9] Mary convinced Pepper's aides that research should be a much bigger priority in the landscape of federal spending on disease, citing the notably successful wartime OMR campaigns as a case in point.

After this meeting, Pepper arranged subcommittee hearings for September 17 and 18, which Albert and Mary attended. These hearings generated compelling testimony. Selective Service representatives, for example, revealed that

40 percent of all individuals drafted for service in World War II had been rejected because of poor health resulting from inadequate medical care—an astounding and disgraceful state of affairs in a relatively wealthy country. The subcommittee agreed to pursue the matter more fully, and Congressional hearings were set for December 13 and 14. These hearings ultimately led Pepper to agree to support a draft "National Medical Research Bill."

⸺⸺◦((◉))◦⸺⸺

Concurrently, the Laskers were pushing the American Society for the Control of Cancer (ASCC) to raise money for research. During the fall of 1943, Mary and Florence Mahoney paid a visit to Dr. Clarence Cook Little, then director of the Society, and were shocked to discover that the ASCC was spending *no* money on cancer research.[10]

The main role of the Society at that time was educational; it published thousands of pamphlets yearly detailing the "danger signs" of cancer. As noted, the Lasker family had created an endowment for this purpose in the 1920s. Unfortunately, as Mary dryly observed, Lasker had never actually reviewed the pamphlets he had funded, "or some dynamite could have been put in the organization much earlier."[11]

Upon hearing the concerns raised by Mary and Florence about research, Little asked Mary if Albert could be persuaded to join the Society's board of directors. Mary guessed that Albert would refuse, so she steered Little toward Emerson Foote—partner in the newly established Foote, Cone & Belding—whose parents had died of cancer, and seemed more likely to respond positively to the invitation.

Foote joined the board early in 1944. He had only limited impact in that first year, although donations more than doubled (to $832,000). But in that seemingly quiet period, Foote and Mary Lasker were laying the groundwork for a full-fledged fund-raising campaign. When presented with the far-reaching plan, Little overcame his reluctance and agreed—largely because the Laskers agreed to fund the entire cost of the campaign. But the Laskers imposed one condition: the Society would have to agree to put 25 percent of the proceeds of the campaign directly into cancer research.

The first substantial donation to the campaign came on December 1, 1944, from the Lever Brothers Company. This was a result of Albert Lasker's behind-the-scenes maneuvering growing out of the July sale of Pepsodent.

Lasker agreed to relinquish his Pepsodent holdings on condition that Lever Brothers make a $50,000 corporate contribution to the Society for each of the succeeding five years.[12]

Mary, meanwhile, was pushing for changes of her own. The organization's name—the American Society for the Control of Cancer—had always struck her as weak. (The "control" of cancer, she thought, implied that the Society wasn't interested in a pursuing a *cure* for the disease.) With Emerson Foote's strong backing, therefore, she persuaded the Society to change its name. Thus was today's American Cancer Society (ACS) born.[13]

By May 1945, the money was pouring in—to the extent that the treasurer of the ACS complained to Mary that he wasn't prepared to deal with the unprecedented flood of contributions. These successes brought with them an unanticipated benefit: when Albert Lasker realized that the revamped Society had an opportunity to make a real difference in the medical field, he became passionately interested in its affairs. He joined the ACS board, and began exerting his influence in the broadcasting community to get several groundbreaking cancer-related programs on the air.

One of these was the popular nationally syndicated radio show *Fibber McGee and Molly*, which—on April 28, 1945—aired a precedent-shattering show with an explicit cancer theme. The program focused on Fibber's concerns about his friend Charley, who feared that he might have cancer but was afraid to bring up the subject. Bluntly, the show delivered messages that had never before been heard on the radio: *Cancer isn't a thing that will go away if you close your eyes. Cancer isn't a disgrace; it's a disgrace to think it's a disgrace.* The broadcast ended with an appeal to send money to the American Cancer Society to fight the disease, asserting that "the more money you give, the fewer lives cancer will take."[14]

This first campaign ended in the summer of 1945, having raised just under $4.3 million in donations, of which $960,000 went directly into research. The Laskers understood that this was only a start—but they also knew that such an outpouring of support would put pressure on Congress to begin funding cancer research, and medical research more generally.

In 1946, Mary learned that veteran West Virginia congressman Matthew Mansfield Neely was introducing a bill calling for $100 million for cancer research. She immediately pushed Albert to convince the ACS to support the bill, which by almost any measure seemed a huge leap. Up to this point, the ACS had raised a total of $10 million in new money, of which $2 million was targeted for research, so the prospect of $100 million for research seemed almost fantastical.

The bill got through the House of Representatives, and Claude Pepper brought it to the Senate floor in the summer of 1946. It died there, stymied by a series of parliamentary blocking maneuvers, but its near success convinced the Public Health Service (PHS) that Congress might be willing to fund medical research at a significant level. This led the PHS to request $14 million for cancer research in fiscal 1948. The approval of this PHS budget, although little heralded at the time, represented the first sizeable federal government commitment to the fight against cancer.

Another of the Laskers' medical interests was mental health.

Mary's passion for this field stemmed in part from friendships with legendary psychoanalyst Franz Alexander and famed American psychiatrists (and brothers) Karl and William Menninger. In the late 1930s, Alexander asked her to join the board of the Chicago Institute for Psychoanalysis, which he had founded in 1932. After her marriage to Albert, she convinced him to help support a study in 1941 and 1942 on how psychoanalytic techniques might be applied more widely; the couple also supported three psychotherapy council meetings organized by the Institute for Psychoanalysis. These proved a disillusioning experience for Mary, who was appalled when the doctors involved fought bitterly among themselves about controversial new ideas in the field. "These men," she later lamented, "who were expected by lay persons to have such great understanding of themselves and others, didn't always seem to me to have been thoroughly analyzed."[15]

Disillusioned but not discouraged, Mary readily agreed when longtime mental-health activist Blanche Ittleson asked her in 1942 to become a member of the National Committee for Mental Hygiene (NCMH). At the time, this was the only nationwide voluntary mental-health organization, and—like its counterpart in the field of cancer—its members lacked basic organizational and fundraising skills.

In early 1945, Mary convinced Dr. George Stevenson, head of the NCMH, to suggest the idea of a "National Mental Health Institute" to the PHS. Meanwhile, she also manipulated the media adroitly. She fed information on the sorry state of the nation's mental health to Pulitzer Prize–winning reporter and columnist Thomas L. Stokes, who published a powerful article that was syndicated in newspapers across the nation. Representative Percy Priest, Democrat from Tennessee, publicly demanded that the PHS draft a proposal to remedy the situation. The National Mental Health Act, authorizing a National Mental Health Institute, was passed in June 1946, and signed into law by President Harry Truman on July 7. It was the first major piece of federal mental-health legislation in almost one hundred years.

The NCMH provided only minimal support to Mary Lasker and her fellow activists during the congressional campaign; at that time, the organization's mission (like the early mission of the American Cancer Society) focused principally on publicizing mental-health issues rather than advocating for research in the field. In frustration, Mary resigned in 1949 and founded a new organization, the National Committee Against Mental Illness (NCAMI).

NCAMI began life with little more than the Laskers' money behind it (and a total budget of less than $80,000 per year). But it soon began exerting an influence far beyond its size—a process that intensified in 1953, when nationally celebrated writer and mental-health activist Thomas "Mike" Gorman signed on as executive director of the organization. Working as a team, he and Mary began demanding that more federal dollars be spent researching mental illness. "It is probably safe to say," wrote one observer in 1970, "that no comparable expenditure of funds has ever resulted in as much research-fund allocation [as the Laskers' investment in NCAMI]."[16]

Mary and Gorman soon encountered a dismaying lack of interest among health professionals in mental-health research, especially in the area of new drug development. Some of that skepticism could be found even within the volunteer ranks of NCAMI. "Too often," Mary later recalled, "the people who were on the Council, the professionals, were interested only in the psychiatric aspects of mental illness, and didn't conceive of the idea that it could be based on any chemical disorganization within a person."[17] Mary herself became so convinced of the potential of drug therapies that she attended a conference on drug use in 1953, where she heard the first reports about the effect of Serpazil and Thorazine on schizophrenic patients. She immediately phoned Dr. Nathan Kline, research director of the Rockland State Hospital in New York. Kline agreed to run some experiments with Thorazine among his eight thousand patients, and the results led to a revolution in the management of mental illness.[18]

Even in the face of new evidence, however, many analysts remained extremely skeptical. In fact, one member of the NCAMI resigned from the Committee because he felt that the NCAMI was advocating drugs too strongly. Dr. Robert Felix—head of the National Mental Health Institute— at first weighed in against the use of drugs in the treatment of mental illness. At Mary's and Gorman's insistence, however, he established a psychopharmacology testing center within the National Mental Health Institute. Over the next several years, as the evidence of the effectiveness of drug therapies mounted, Felix himself became a convert to the use of psychoactive drugs.

By 1963, the funds for the National Mental Health Institute had increased to more than $143 million, thanks in large part to Gorman's and Mary's efforts.

Better than most philanthropists, the Laskers understood how to use their wealth and influence to fight for social causes. But they also drew on Albert's fortune to enrich their life together and to pursue hobbies not open to ordinary people.

Soon after their marriage, Albert rented (and later purchased) CBS founder William Paley's spectacular seven-and-a-half-story New York City townhouse at 29 Beekman Place, overlooking the East River. Later, at Mary's insistence, he also acquired a farm near Millbrook, New York, comprising 410 acres of rolling green hills, fields, and forests. "I enjoy the quiet," Lasker wrote of the Millbrook estate. "I have now reached the grand old age where I like to be away from excitement."[19] Typically, Lasker (with prodding from Mary) made his own local excitement:

> We are building two houses at our farm, one a gardener's cottage and the other a guest house, and supervising these operations has really kept me occupied. These architects, contractors, and workmen can think up more double talk than anyone could imagine, and the net of all this double talk is that there is a double delay on whatever they are doing, and a double price for their not doing. By the time our houses will be finished, I think I will have lost the capacity to enjoy them, but it is going to be very lovely.[20]

Mary also gradually interested Lasker in the world of fine art. She knew that her husband was not interested in paintings, but some months after their marriage, Mary attended an auction in the hopes of buying a Renoir, and convinced Lasker to go with her. What ensued surprised them both:

> I went to the door of the sale with Albert and he said, "Well, I'll wait for you out here," and I said, "Oh, why don't you come in?" "Well," he said, "It will take too long." I said, "No, come in, sit with me."
>
> Well, then, there were no chairs, so he sat behind me, and I bid for the picture and when I stopped bidding at $10,000, I heard two other people bidding and I looked around and one of them was Albert. He bid up to $25,000 against [prominent New York art dealer] Paul Rosenberg. He didn't know who he was bidding against, and then he got frightened because he had never bid for a picture in his life before and he thought maybe he had gone mad, so he stopped bidding at $25,000. And we didn't get the picture; Mr. Rosenberg got it.[21]

Rosenberg won that skirmish, but Albert was hooked, and he started to visit Rosenberg's gallery. "How long has this been going on?" he asked Rosenberg on that first visit.[22] Eventually, Albert bought the Renoir ("Young Girl in a Boat") that he had been bidding on at the auction, as well as a second ("Flowers and Cats") that Rosenberg had, for the then-staggering price of $105,000.

Over the years, Albert became more and more interested in art and also increasingly knowledgeable. Although his collecting started on the relatively conservative ground of Renoir, he soon became more adventurous, building up an extensive but discerning collection of works by Degas, Monet, Cezanne, Van Gogh, Chagall, Dalí, and many other notable contemporary painters.

Mary continued to buy paintings as well, supplementing Lasker's collection with her own more eclectic tastes. On one occasion, their aesthetics clashed: Mary bought a Picasso—"Still-Life with Fishes," a Cubist work depicting three dead fish on a table—to which Lasker took a violent dislike. The painting wound up being hung in an out of-the-way corridor in the upper reaches of Beekman Place, with a sign prepared by Albert affixed to the back: *This picture belongs to Mary Lasker and is not to be thought of as part of the Albert Lasker collection.*[23] Albert occasionally would make his way up to the sixth-floor hallway, study the work closely, grunt with disapproval, and then turn it over to make sure that his disclaimer was still attached.

And yet he bought other Picasso works, and understood and admired them. When the wife of a Hollywood studio head challenged him to say exactly what he saw in Picasso's strange shapes and colors, he had a ready answer: "Don't you understand that after the camera was invented and there was no more need to paint with fidelity to nature, artists began to paint how they felt about nature—really the *color* of their feelings about it?"[24]

Increasingly, Albert's favorite was Henri Matisse, whom he saw as the successor to Renoir and as the artist to "bet on." Matisse favored the kinds of bright colors, sharp contrasts, and dazzling depictions of daylight that appealed to Albert's eye and on a deeper level probably helped combat Albert's depressive tendencies. As Matisse himself wrote: "What I dream of is an art of balance, of purity and serenity devoid of troubling or depressing subject matter, an art which might be for every mental worker, be he businessman or writer, like an appeasing influence, like a mental soother, something like a good armchair in which to rest from physical fatigue."[25]

Albert considered his visit with Matisse—at the artist's studio in Nice, in 1949—one of the highlights of his life.[26] Youth and aging were a dominant subtext of the visit. Albert, then sixty-nine years old, told the artist that he wished he were a little younger; Matisse, then eighty, assured Lasker that he was "still a child." And when Albert asked him who the greatest young artist of the day was, Matisse replied, *"Moi."* After Lasker died, Matisse did preliminary sketches for a memorial window for him, but died before finishing it.

The "Lasker Collection" of almost two hundred oils, watercolors, and etchings, sketches, and sculpture remained intact until 1971, at which point Mary sold several of the Renoirs and Mirós when she moved from Beekman Place to a smaller apartment. "They didn't look good here," she told the *New York Times*, "and I wanted to be able to give away the money."[27] The rest of the collection—including the forever-offending Picasso—was left by Mary to the Lasker Foundation.

In the last decade of his life, Albert Lasker had two experiences that reminded him of a lesson he had learned a quarter-century earlier: that although a relatively secular Jew, he nevertheless had a Jewish identity.

The first episode caused him to sever his relationship with the University of Chicago. Lasker, himself only a high-school graduate, believed strongly in education, and was a strong proponent of the University, dating back to his gift in support of medical research in the 1920s. In 1929, the University recruited the thirty-year-old dean of Yale Law School, Robert M. Hutchins, to serve as its president. Early in the Depression, Hutchins made common cause with Lasker in raising money for the relief of Chicago's destitute. The young president came to enjoy the company of the seasoned ad man—likening him to Yellowstone Park's geyser, Old Faithful: a "bizarre and overwhelming, but predictable, force of nature"—and in August 1937 asked Lasker to join the University's board of trustees.[28] Lasker, flattered to be invited into this exclusive bastion of Chicago's overwhelmingly Gentile power elite, happily accepted.

Although this new formal connection complicated their warm relationship, it didn't tie either Lasker's or Hutchins's tongue. In 1939, for example, Hutchins approached his board with a radical proposal: to do away with football. Lasker disapproved. "Football is what unifies a university," he declared at one board meeting. "What will take its place?"

"Education," Hutchins replied, and the board voted its approval.[29]

Lasker gave his beloved Mill Road Farm to the University in the early months of 1940, but by that time the bonds between Lasker and Hutchins already were weakening. The first reason was Hutchins's strongly isolationist stance toward the war in Europe, which was then heating up. Lasker—once an outspoken isolationist—now believed that U.S. involvement in World War II was inevitable. But the proximate cause of the rupture between Lasker and his friend was an article published in the March 1942 edition of the *Saturday Evening Post,* entitled "The Case Against the Jew." Its author was Hutchins's close friend and sometime ghostwriter, Milton Mayer. Although Mayer was a half-time employee in the University's public relations office, he also freelanced for the *Post* and other publications. No one at the University—certainly including Hutchins—had anything to do with "The Case Against the Jew."

Lasker, who didn't get past the article's incendiary title, was furious at Mayer's seemingly anti-Semitic stance. The fact that Mayer was himself Jewish, and that the article (upon closer scrutiny) actually "made a case" *for* Jews, failed to calm Lasker. He decided to resign as a University trustee, and in an April 16 phone call, he informed Hutchins of his intent. In that conversation and in subsequent talks and correspondence, Hutchins tried to persuade his angry friend and ally to change his mind, but Lasker was adamant. Although the two men parted company on amicable terms—with Lasker joking that Hutchins could still count on being the "tenant of his furniture" at Mill Road Farm in the coming summer—their close friendship was over.[30]

Years later, when Lasker and Hutchins met by chance at a social gathering, Lasker confessed that he finally had read "The Case Against the Jew," and decided that it was a good piece of work. "It wasn't a bad article," Lasker admitted. "But the title was unfortunate."

"Wasn't it," Hutchins replied coolly.[31]

<hr />

The second episode that sparked Lasker's renewed awareness of his Jewish identity during these last years of his life was a sixteen-day trip to Israel in May 1950, immediately after his seventieth birthday. A year earlier, Lasker had donated $50,000 to help establish a children's health clinic in Jerusalem, and this trip was scheduled to allow him to attend its dedication. He and Mary sailed to France together on the *Queen Mary*, and—while Mary stayed in Paris with her close friend Anna Rosenberg, scouting up available works of art—Lasker went on to Israel with his two sisters and his friend Emery Reves, a well-known writer and literary agent.[32]

"I went there with an open mind," Lasker later said. "I had never been a Zionist, but I had never been an anti-Zionist. I had been a non-Zionist."[33]

In fact, Lasker had been a close observer of the process that led to the creation of the Jewish state in May 1948. Early in that year, for example, he indirectly lobbied President Truman to intervene in the fighting then raging between the Jewish and Arab residents of Palestine. "Unless the President gets this Palestine matter settled pretty soon," he warned one of Truman's closest advisers, "the Jews will clobber him in the election this fall."[34]

Now, two years later, the Lasker party was criss-crossing the young country and meeting with its leaders. (Lasker had long conversations with Prime Minister David Ben-Gurion and President Chaim Weizmann, among others.) But he also met and mingled with less-exalted Israelis, encountering Jews from a startling range of nationalities: Afghans, Turks, Rumanians, Bulgarians, Yemenis, Algerians, Moroccans, Russians, and Germans, many dressed in their native garb and speaking their own languages.

Reminiscing with Columbia's oral historians shortly after his return, Lasker's mind was still full of the sights and sounds of the infant Jewish state. Always the marketer, he declared that Israel faced unique marketing challenges. It had to present its most dire problems to the international Jewish community, because it was dependent on their "charity money." At the same time, it had to present its *best* face, so that potential donors would have cause for hope.

Lasker had been struck by the outstanding quality of Israel's leaders—"realists but idealists"—and likened them to America's founding fathers. This was no coincidence, he asserted:"When a *great* revolution that is going to affect the world for decades and maybe a century or more takes place, it gives opportunity for men who would have remained hidden, to rise. It's because the times call, that these men of ability get chosen for leadership."

Israel was a "miracle," Lasker concluded—a tiny Jewish state of 800,000 people that had beaten back Arab forces representing more than 30 million people. It was a place where Jewish immigrants were never refused, where Jews didn't have to keep looking back over their shoulders, and where they could finally *belong*.[35] He was struck by the life on the kibbutzes he visited, marveling that at the end of the workday, farmers of both genders traded their blue jeans for khakis or dresses and spent the next several hours in various cultural pursuits. Again, he was reminded of a long-ago home: "Here in this ancient [biblical] country you have a strange feeling. It is a pioneer country. I had the same feeling there that I had as a boy in the '80s and '90s in Texas. It is a pioneer people, with all the released energy of pioneer people who are going to open up a new country against that Biblical background of worn land."

"For the first time in my life," Lasker later observed, "I know what the expression, 'the Jewish people' means. These are my people, and I am part of them."[36] For Lasker, then nearing the end of his life, traveling to Israel was a journey home.

Shortly after Lasker returned from Israel, he began experiencing severe abdominal pains. He first thought that he was suffering from liver trouble caused by a rich Continental diet on his trip. Soon, though, it became clear that his condition was serious, and on July 5, he underwent an exploratory operation. The surgeons found a tumor, and—within a few weeks—the lab results pointed to a malignant cancer. Mary, well aware of Lasker's intense fear of the disease that had claimed his brother Harry's life, kept the diagnosis from him. Lasker never learned, even during his terminal battle against the illness, that he was fighting colon cancer.

Lasker recovered from this first surgery, returning home in mid-August. Because his lymph nodes had been removed, there seemed to be some chance that he would make a full recovery. He regained most of his strength, and in November, he and Mary once again began their intensive lobbying in support of medical research. They met with the Director of the Bureau of the Budget on November 9, but were able to extract only small increases in funding. The following month, Mary met face-to-face with President Harry Truman, who agreed to appoint one of his executive assistants as the White House liaison for health issues.

The Laskers visited Europe one last time in the spring of 1951, during which Albert experienced an ominous spike in his blood pressure. ("I overdid [it] in Paris," he explained to a friend, "having too much fun."[37]) When an executive at International Cellulose retired in December, Lasker wrote him a tongue-in-cheek note of reassurance:

> A hearty welcome to the Retired Men's Club, of which I have been an active member for almost ten years now. I understand that during the coming year you are going to quit your business activities, and I want to be among the first to give you a hearty welcome into the charmed circle of which I found myself a member when I retired.
>
> I did so with much trepidation, only to learn to my amazement that the richest years of my life lay before me, for in the almost ten years since I have retired, I have found interests and usefulness that I never knew before which have given me cause for great satisfaction. I am sure that in full measure the same kind fate awaits you.[38]

By February 1952, Albert's colon cancer had returned. Mary moved into the hospital to be able to spend most of her time at his side. Once again—now from a hospital room—the two campaigners followed the progress of appropriations bills through the House and Senate. This time, the results were far more positive. Mary later recalled that the positive reports coming in from Washington were "one of the few things that gave Albert pleasure in the last few weeks of his life."[39]

As May drew to a close, Lasker quietly slipped into a coma. On May 30, a month past his seventy-second birthday, he died at 8:00 a.m., with Mary at his side.

In his will, Lasker made it clear that he had already provided for his children and grandchildren, and that they were not expecting anything from his estate. He made a number of $50,000 and $100,000 bequests to individuals—including $50,000 to his psychiatrist—and bequeathed his art collection and half of his remaining estate to Mary, with the balance going to the Lasker Foundation. He also requested (but did not require) that the directors of the foundation spend its resources down within twenty years.[40]

In the years to come, Mary continued the battles that the two had begun, especially her campaign against the disease that took her husband's life. The Lasker Foundation carries forward its charitable work, and the Lasker Awards—which Mary renamed the "Albert Lasker Awards" in 1954 in his honor, and are today known as the Lasker Prizes—continue to keep Albert Lasker's name and memory alive.

Chapter Twenty-Two

The Lasker Legacy

*I*N THE CLIMACTIC SCENE of the *Wizard of Oz,* Dorothy, the Tin Man, the Scarecrow, and the Cowardly Lion are quaking in the great hall of the wizard's palace. A huge, disembodied head looms over them, bellowing at them, ordering them to go away: *Do not arouse the wrath of the Great and Powerful Oz!* Peals of thunder accompany his bellicose threats.

But Dorothy's intrepid terrier Toto scampers over to a corner of the hall, grabs a hanging curtain in his teeth, and pulls. The parting fabric reveals a thoroughly ordinary-looking man shouting into an oversized microphone as he shakes a sheet of metal to simulate the sound of thunder. He sees the four travelers at the same instant that they see him.

"Pay no attention to that man behind the curtain!" he blusters into his microphone. But it's too late: His cover is blown.

"You *humbug,*" the Scarecrow shouts angrily.

"Yes, that's exactly so," the Wizard says, instantly deflated. "I'm a humbug."

Albert Lasker shared some traits with the Great Oz. Both hawked patent medicines early in their lives. Both built astounding careers based in part on substance, and in part on humbug. Both counted on appearing larger than life, and neither wanted the curtain that separated them from their publics to be parted. But behind their respective curtains, both were warm and generous. They enjoyed people. They would have enjoyed each other.

There is a second connotation to our "man behind the curtain" description of Lasker. He believed, strongly, that his business benefited from his relative invisibility. He didn't need the limelight; his clients and their products did. His business goal, he declared, was "to always put the client's interest before my own."[1] And although Lasker's ego could best be described as privately boundless, he only once sought to establish himself as a public figure—during his stint in Washington—and quickly retreated from that role, thus thwarting his wife Flora's dream of a run for the U.S. Senate.

"I was never made for public life," he concluded. "Never. Never could have been a success at it."[2]

Lasker's periodic depressions pushed him out of the spotlight. So did his growing disenchantment with the advertising world, and so did his increasingly cynical estimation of his own accomplishments. "I have been too superficial all my life," he concluded in the spring of 1938.[3] *Yes*, the wizard admitted; *I am a humbug*.

And yet he wasn't. "The settling of the country," he wrote, "the machine age, the coming of the automobile, telephone, movies, radio, the advances in fine arts and all the sciences, demanded that our capacity to accept and use new ideas be developed to a point never before seen on the pages of history."[4]

In an almost bewildering variety of contexts, Lasker made that happen. He helped people accept and use new ideas.

Who was the man behind the curtain, and what was his legacy?

David Sarnoff, Albert Lasker's closest friend among the prominent business leaders of the twentieth century, likened Lasker to an orchestra in which things sometimes drifted out of balance. *At times the brasses get a little too loud*, he observed. And sometimes there are sounds that are "not always as musical as they really are, or would be, when taken as part of a symphony."

But Lasker had a deeper capacity for friendship, Sarnoff observed, than anyone else he had ever met. In character and integrity, Sarnoff continued, no one ranked higher. And yes, Sarnoff volunteered—anticipating a question that successful Jews of the day sooner or later faced—Lasker loved to make money. "I know no one who will fight harder than Lasker to make money," he said. Then he added, "But I know of no one who will fight less to keep money after he has made it. He is, without doubt, the most generous man I know."

Ralph Sollitt, Lasker's closest business confidante, said that although Lasker made "oodles of money all his life," his friend and boss was "never interested in making the money."[5] Money, said Sollitt, was Lasker's way of keeping score in business. When business lost its appeal, so did the score-keeping.

Was the man behind the curtain a genius? Yes, said rental car magnate John Hertz: "There isn't any question about him being a genius."[6]

Was Lasker a genius? David Sarnoff equivocated:

I should say that I do not regard Albert Lasker—this is hard to say—a profound thinker. I never have. I don't regard Albert Lasker a philosopher. I don't regard Albert Lasker a fellow who meditates or contemplates over things. But I regard him as a genius impelled by his emotions. He has that facility of putting his finger on the meat of the cocoanut. . . .

He does not waste any time in contemplation, or asking himself whether he is right or wrong. That he knows, he assumes, and he knows, and he is generally right about it . . . He belongs to the vocal aggressive type, confident in their own judgment, [who] use their energy and their time either to shout or impose their views upon somebody else.[7]

Coming from a friend, it sounds like a harsh verdict. But Sarnoff went on to explain that after the shouting stopped, he always understood his own business challenges far better than he had previously. Give Lasker all the facts, and sufficient time to assimilate them, and he'd rather have Lasker's judgment than anyone else's.

Was Lasker a genius? Mary Woodard Reinhardt, who became his third wife, had another suitor when she and Lasker first met. Frustrated by Lasker's arrival on the scene, this other suitor approached Roy Durstine—cofounder of the archrival agency Batten, Barton, Durstine & Osborn—in search of dirt on Lasker. Durstine's response was not helpful. *Lasker is a business genius*, he told his visitor. *He not only knows how to tell a client how to do advertising, but he knows how to advise him about changing his business and how to make money out of his business.* "My friend," Mary Lasker observed dryly, "found no comfort at all from this."[8]

Lasker had a unique capacity to *get to the kernel of the nut,* as Frank Hummert (who worked at Lord & Thomas between 1920 and 1927) put it.[9] And certainly, his mind moved faster than most people's. "He thinks so fast himself," observed longtime associate Elmer Bullis, "that he just feels everybody ought to think as fast as he does, and reply as rapidly, and people are not built that way . . . He thinks like a shot."[10]

Lasker was a great salesman, who learned early how to sell *himself.* When he chose to set out and win people, he was intensely seductive. People who began a meeting hostile to Lasker soon found themselves eating out of his hand. As Frank Hummert observed:

> *He has that marvelous control over people. You can put twenty people in this room who are antagonistic to Lasker, and probably with good reason, and at the end of [a half an hour], why, Lasker will walk out of there the friend of everybody in the place, and they will think he is wonderful, because he will pull one rabbit out of the hat after another. You have never seen him operate. It is hard to explain. I have seen that sometimes. He knows just when to charge, and when to retreat, and when to stand still. That is a wonderful exhibition, his control of men.*[11]

But ultimately, he remained elusive, even to those whom he pursued. Sollitt, who understood him better than most, cautioned ghostwriter Boyden Sparkes against becoming attached to Lasker. "You will be sick when the book is ended," he said, "because you are just going to find him more engaging all the time, and the queerest combination of qualities and personalities in all your experiences that you ever went in." The energy and excitement might *feel* directed at you, Sollitt warned, but it wasn't: "He has to go through this, all of which makes this certain theater that he lives in all the time, for himself."[12]

Lasker was both actor and audience, judge and jury. "Everything is drama with me," he said. "It is all a play."[13] And the character who was most interesting to him, by far, was Albert Lasker. He was the only character in the play, he told his autobiographer, whose motives he could thoroughly explore and understand.

So he was self-absorbed. At the same time, he was enormously generous. To his friends, he was selfless to a fault—giving without demanding anything in return. "Albert Lasker," Warren G. Harding said to him with admiration, "you are the only, single, solitary man I have around me that doesn't want something."[14]

His generosity was not simply passive. When the preferred stock in Van Camp Packing that he had sold to friends and family members began to look shaky, Lasker bought all that stock back at its original price. He supported his wife Flora's family surreptitiously for many years. Throughout his life, he was one of the biggest contributors to the Associated Jewish Philanthropies of Chicago, with a rough rule of thumb of giving as much as he spent to live. ("If I spent $10,000 to live," he explained, "I gave $10,000. If I spent several hundred thousand, I gave several hundred thousand."[15]) He gave George Andrews, his barber of twenty-five years, the necessary funds to set up a three-store chain, and also paid off the mortgage on Andrews's house. He made huge loans to his speculator friends in the wake of the Crash of 1929 with almost no hope of getting any of that money back. He gave each of his children $5 million while they were still young adults. He paid well more than necessary to wriggle out of his marriage to Doris Kenyon (although in this case, guilt may have played as large a role as generosity). At the urging of his son Edward, he gave his third wife, Mary, $1 million to make her financially independent—a gift on which he paid an additional $350,000 in taxes.[16]

He saw himself as greedy: "One key to my character is greed. Not greed for money, but greed for experiences. I sip of them, and go on to something else." This was not a trait he was proud of: "I have destroyed myself with greed."[17] And yet it was a philosophy of life that he prescribed for young people just starting out in their professional lives: *Never mind about saving your money; save your experiences.*

Dating back to 1907, and perhaps earlier, Albert Lasker battled a severe emotional illness that at irregular intervals immobilized him. Lacking any effective help from the outside, Lasker developed a number of tactics to stave off his attacks as long as possible. He understood that he was particularly sensitive to changes of weather and season, and structured his life in ways that minimized their negative effects on him. His four-month winter sojourns— first to Southern California, and later to Miami—weren't simply vacations; they were emotional vaccinations against the gray reality of Chicago.

His succession of increasingly grand country homes outside Chicago also served as a barricade against emotional upset, whose signs he had long since learned to recognize. "I am staying out in my country place for a few weeks' rest," he wrote to his friend W. G. Irwin in the summer of 1917. "I found I had been going at a pretty stiff pace, and was accelerated beyond the safety point. It was the first time I ever felt that way, and I thought I had better take warning of the signs."[18]

Lasker mounted a heroic struggle; but when the barricades fell, so did Lasker. We know almost nothing about his stays at spas, hospitals, and therapeutic communities—in Germany, Illinois, Mexico, Maryland, Minnesota, and Arizona, probably among others—but they must have been searing interludes.

He sought out creative genius in many walks of life. He hoped to understand it, affiliate with it, and perhaps to derive comfort from consorting with like minds—people who could *put their finger on the meat of the cocoanut* and *get to the kernel of the nut.* Over the years, his taste in genius evolved. Early in his life, for example, he embraced baseball stars, sportswriters, business magnates, and master politicians. Later he embraced painters and painting, including Henri Matisse, Salvador Dalí, and Raoul Dufy, to name only a few.

The lives of Hamilton, Jefferson, Lincoln, and Churchill argue for a more complete understanding of the intersection of manic depression and politics. The life of Albert Lasker—and of others in his industry—argues for a more complete understanding of affective illness in advertising. Bruce Barton, founder of the formidable Barton, Durstine & Osborn, suffered from a chronic insomnia that forced him to take frequent "rest cures" (and led some of his colleagues to consider him lazy).[19] At least one of Lasker's three chosen successors, Emerson Foote, suffered from debilitating psychological problems and was compelled to leave Foote, Cone & Belding in 1950 because of his deep depressions. Fairfax Cone, another of Lasker's three agency "heirs," suffered from a mysterious malady in the 1930s—an affliction that he asserted was physical rather than emotional. Yet his autobiographical musings raise questions about whether his self-diagnosis should have been so straightforward:

> *Advertising people were supposed to live under just the kind of pressure that results in mental breakdown . . .*
>
> *Agency people are continuously perched on the edge of anxiety . . .*
>
> *The advertising agency man and the media salesman live much of the time under a tight wire that stretches thinly between hope and despair . . .*
>
> *I had moments of fear and hours of depression because I never knew when the fatigue would become overpowering. Fortunately, no one among my business associates knew that it still existed; I had learned to cover up.*[20]

The other side of bipolar illness, of course, is mania—or in Lasker's case, hypomania.[21] Lasker was nothing if not intense. He was "radium," by his own accounting. He was brilliant and exhausting. "I don't remember ever seeing him yawn," his longtime colleague Robert Crane reflected.[22] He possessed what columnist Mark Sullivan called a "furious energy."[23] *He wears people out*, said Ralph Sollitt. "He wears everybody down," said rental car magnate John Hertz.[24] "If he gets close to you," David Noyes observed, "he overwhelms you."[25] Hearst editor Arthur Brisbane, Lasker's ally in the doomed campaign to save Leo Frank, coined the phrase "human dynamo" to describe his friend. The phrase stuck.

This tidal wave of energy could be a burden on friends and subordinates, but it had its clear upsides. Clients often told him that he "revitalized" them, and that the effect sometimes persisted for weeks after one of his visits. This wasn't something that he did consciously. "All that I can figure out that I have is this tremendous energy, [and that] I can energize other people," he said. "And that makes me a sham, because that isn't a very high talent."[26]

But he wasn't a sham, or a humbug. Lasker put his energy and creativity to extraordinary uses, across an amazing range of contexts.

Lasker presented many faces of leadership, not all of them pleasant or consistent.

To his subordinates, he could be alternately inspirational, baffling, and demoralizing. He could be cheerful, playful, irascible, generous, or petty—and he could shift from mood to mood with bewildering speed. He had a powerful work ethic, and within the bounds of his sometimes fragile emotional state, drove himself hard. Equally, he drove the people around him, including Lord & Thomas personnel and his subordinates at the Shipping Board.

Part of Lasker's success in managing creative talent grew out of the sheer range of opportunities he put in front of them, and—at least in the lower ranks of the organization—a purposeful prohibition against office politics. As copywriter Mark O'Dea later commented: "There was no great interference [with the copywriters]. There was a brilliant creative organization, so much going on all the time, so many interesting jobs, and there seemed to be no resistance toward anyone going ahead. In fact, I went right ahead—my salary went up amazingly, and I was given every opportunity. Other men had the same opportunity. A grand organization, [which] seemed to be particularly free of politics."[27]

Lasker was far less successful at managing his managers, which guaranteed that he was fated to burn through a series of leaders at Lord & Thomas. William Benton, who later emerged as a major figure in the advertising industry in his own right, once was asked by Lasker how Lord & Thomas was different from the Batten agency, where Benton had worked previously. Benton had a ready (and courageous!) answer for his boss: "There's a big difference. In the other agency, my boss hired second-rate men, and then gave them every opportunity to become first-rate. Here you hire first-rate men, browbeat them, humiliate them, refuse to give them parity, and drive them so hard they become second-rate."[28]

But the underlying dynamic was far more complicated than that. Lasker was drawn to excellence, and according to Sollitt, this presented its own problems: "When he finds anybody that has any type of excellence, he is so delighted with it that he has a great tendency to magnify it far beyond its desserts." Inevitably, though, the time would come when Lasker would allow himself to see people as they actually were:

> Nearly all of the people with whom he has been associating to my knowledge, in the business, he has striven harder than they could possibly strive to make them bigger and better than they were, and then has had this heartbreak when he found out that they weren't as fine . . .
>
> You will hear it said by people that he has a tendency to take these young men—or not necessarily young men—but these men of talent and he just squeezes them dry, like an orange, and then after he squeezes them dry, he throws them aside.
>
> Well, that isn't true. Some of those people think that for a while, and that is simply because of their reaction to his reaction when he finds out that they are not as great as he thought they were, and as he so deeply hoped that they would be.[29]

This is a constant refrain in the history of Lord & Thomas: gifted managers comparing themselves with Lasker and despairing of their own inadequacies. David Noyes told the story of a Lord & Thomas directors' meeting at Mill Road Farm sometime in the middle 1930s. During lunch on the second day, with Lasker seated at the head of the table, New York office manager Sheldon Coons rose to address the group. Awkwardly, he confessed that he and West Coast head Don Francisco had stayed up almost until dawn discussing their complex relationship with Lasker. Coons said that he and Francisco viewed themselves as accomplished and effective professionals—right up until the moment that they returned to Chicago and encountered Lasker. "We come into your office," Coons said, now addressing Lasker directly, "and feel so damned inferior, and it hurts so much, that when we get back to the office, it takes a month to recover."

Lasker rose to his feet—slowly, and with a grim look on his face, according to Noyes. He began by correcting Coons's choice of adjective: "What you mean is that in my presence, you feel *inadequate*, not inferior. That is part of my desire, part of my management [style]. I want you to feel inadequate. All the great men of the world have felt inadequate—the greatest writers, the greatest poets. It is this constant striving that has made them great, and it has always been my policy to make my associates, especially the best of them, feel inadequate."

So Lasker (who so often felt inadequate himself) deliberately fostered insecurities and anxieties in his top lieutenants. Toward that end, he played favorites and didn't hesitate to use one Lord & Thomas executive to throw another off balance. Edward Lasker said that his father manipulated his subordinates the same way he raised his children: "When he was displeased with one of the children, he very definitely let that child feel that the other two were the favorites. This was also true in business. When Coons was in the doghouse, Noyes was one of the greatest advertising men who ever lived, and vice versa."[30]

Despite his willingness to knock people off balance, Lasker hated confrontation. He was loath to fire people, generally leaving the dirty work to others. In the case of people to whom he owed a special debt, he simply declined to pull the trigger. Longtime colleague Elmer Bullis, for example, had been an underperformer for years, and then got into some sort of unspecified trouble at Lord & Thomas in the later 1920s. But Lasker—who remembered that Bullis had given him his first break in advertising, decades earlier—couldn't bring himself to dismiss his former mentor.[31]

All in all, this is not a picture of a flexible, empathetic, decisive manager of people, at least in conventional terms. But Lasker didn't care. He resolutely declined to define himself as a conventional business leader. "I was always a poor executive," he readily admitted. Unlike the heads of Ayer and J. Walter Thompson, who in Lasker's eyes were good business leaders, he lacked the right motivation to build a great business. "I have always been a poor executive," he reiterated, "because what I was after was neither volume, money, nor organization."[32]

Learning from Albert Lasker and defining his legacy, present many challenges.

For one thing, he exaggerated, embroidered, and sometimes fabricated his life's narrative. You will find it "intensely interesting," Sollitt observed with dry understatement, "to discover what is the actual truth about a lot of things."[33] Lasker generated so much electricity—and static—around himself that the reality of his life tended to be hidden from its observers. Finally, Lasker tried consciously to obscure his own role in almost all that he did—to remain the man behind the curtain and let others command the limelight.

At the same time, Lasker was intensely proud of his contributions to advertising. So what were those contributions, and how durable have they been?

Lord & Thomas was already a pioneer before Lasker arrived on the agency's doorstep in 1898. Earlier in that decade, the agency had become one of the first in the United States to analyze and plan *campaigns* for its clients, rather than simply taking orders for ad placements.

Lasker took Lord & Thomas in new and profitable directions. He realized that by persuading clients to increase the creative content of their ads, and then by preparing those ads in-house, Lord & Thomas could earn its full 15 percent commission. Working with John Kennedy, he puzzled out the fundamentals of "reason-why" advertising—one of his two major contributions to the field. If advertising was "salesmanship in print," then ads had to *sell*. They had to give people a compelling reason to buy this particular product or service.

The second of Lasker's great contributions to the field was his use of research to test and validate various advertising approaches. Working first with Kennedy and later with Claude Hopkins, Lasker systematically tracked the impact of his ads, tweaked and revised them, and then tested their impact again. The mail-order business, in particular, sharpened these instincts. "There is no better training in the advertising business than mail order," observed one-time colleague Herbert Field, "and he had it in the *nth* degree. He finally became the best judge of copy of any man I knew."[34]

With the other advertising greats of the early twentieth century—and of course, with the manufacturing geniuses and publishing magnates of that era—Lasker deserves enormous credit for building markets enough to achieve economies of scale, and thereby bringing an incredible range of goods within the reach of ordinary consumers. The refrigerator that cost $150 in the 1920s cost under $100 a decade later, and at the same time was a significantly better product. Advertising campaigns like the "Meter-Miser" (for Frigidaire) may have begun as flights of marketing fancy, but they actually compelled manufacturers to perform better. Even in the realm of commodities, consumers derived indirect benefits from advertising. If a brand was worth investing in, then it was worth defending. If you are paying a penny a case to advertise Sunkist oranges as the *very best*—with the ultimate goal of commanding a premium for your product—then you would be a fool to dump frost-damaged goods on the market and damage the Sunkist brand.

Perhaps inevitably, Lasker the marketer went from being a revolutionary to a conservative. He was a "fundamentalist," in the eyes of his final first lieutenant, David Noyes: a leader who resisted departures from the tried-and-true formulas that he himself had helped invent decades earlier. As a result, credit for the move into radio belongs mainly to others. But even in this strange new context, Lasker asked good questions of his staff and demanded good answers—including, first and foremost, proof of radio's efficacy in selling products. When that evidence became irresistible, he embraced the new medium, and pushed his clients toward it.

Many of the products that Lasker helped introduce, and most of the companies that made them, have long since vanished. Sunkist, Sun-Maid, Kotex, Kleenex, Palmolive, and Puffed Rice are enduring exceptions; the Hupp, Mitchell, and Studebaker car companies, Van Camp's pork and beans, and Pepsodent are the rule.

On a more fundamental level, though, it doesn't much matter whether individual brands or manufacturers have survived. Lord & Thomas taught us to drink orange juice, use sanitary napkins and Kleenex, and brush our teeth. Lasker's agency also trained us to tune in to the radio for soap operas and variety hours, and persuaded us to tolerate the ads that supported those entertainments. Accepting the bargain served up by Lasker and his competitors—commercials in return for "free" entertainment—preconditioned us to accept the same deal with technologies that emerged years or decades after Lasker's departure from the scene, including television and the internet.

On the public relations side, Lasker's legacy is clear and profound. He learned politics at the knee of Will Hays, the grand master of Republican politics in the World War I era. The techniques he refined in the congressional elections of 1918 and the presidential race of 1920 stuck with him; more than a decade later, his West Coast office kept socialist Upton Sinclair out of the California governorship and shortly thereafter persuaded Californians to repeal a punitive tax on chain stores. "A few simple ideas were hammered home steadily, steadily, steadily," said W. G. Irwin.[35] Again, this formula sounds self-evident to the modern ear, but it was far from obvious in the day when it was invented.

But in Lasker's mind, all of these general contributions to the advertising industry, and specific contributions to individual companies, products, and politicians, didn't amount to a legacy. Throughout his life, Lasker wanted to do something of *significance*, and feared he hadn't. His whole life, said Sollitt, was aimed at doing something good—and business wasn't a big enough stage: "Business didn't really justify his existence."[36]

This fear was the wellspring of his involvement in advocacy—for example, in the Leo Frank case—in politics, and in philanthropy. His philanthropic activities, shaped and advanced by Mary Lasker, were enormously influential. The Laskers took on causes, such as national health insurance and birth control, that politicians didn't dare embrace. They helped advance the concept of leverage in philanthropy—"seeding" worthy causes with their own money, and counting on larger infusions of private and public dollars to carry the cause forward. These were Big Ideas, which Albert loved to shape, manipulate, and disseminate.

Albert also exerted his considerable personal influence with the media to persuade broadcasters to tackle taboo subjects. *Cancer isn't a disgrace*, the wildly popular radio character Fibber McGee told his friend Charley, with an astonished national audience hanging on every shocking word. *It's a disgrace to think it's a disgrace*. Lasker changed the way people understood the world—and thereby set the world on a better course.

Albert Lasker loved a wager. At the same time, he cheerfully and unabashedly hedged his bets.

W. G. Irwin told the story of walking down the streets of Chicago with Lasker one day in search of confirmation of the rumor that an armistice had been signed ending World War I. "Well," Lasker fretted aloud, "I am going to lose some money. I made a bet last week on this thing, that it wouldn't end this year."

A half a block later, he brightened up, and announced with a smile, "But I'm all right. I made a bet before that it *would*."[37]

So he was hedger of bets—someone who enjoyed the game, but at the same time, remained outside the game. This was true in almost all of his endeavors: He retained the eye of the outsider.

This was in part because he was a German (of sorts), a southerner, a westerner, and a Jew: all perspectives that placed him outside of the mainstream. His mental and emotional problems also contributed to his outsider status, and all these differentiating factors, it seems, combined to help him see things objectively and dispassionately. Notably, when he became an insider— as at Mitchell Motor, Van Camp's, and Pepsodent, and arguably during his government service—his genius declined precipitously. He lost his ability to put his finger *on the meat of the cocoanut*, to *get to the kernel of the nut*. He became merely another stakeholder.

So he succeeded most notably as an outsider. But he was also, paradoxically, the quintessential *insider*. Impish, funny, breezy, flamboyant, exuberant, exaggerated, generous—and dark—he embodied something at the very heart of America.

And this made him the perfect person to sell America.

A Note on Sources

One Lasker biography already exists: John Gunther's *Taken At the Flood*, published by Harper & Brothers in 1960, eight years after Lasker's death. Gunther was an internationally renowned travel writer who achieved literary significance in 1949 with the publication of *Death Be Not Proud*, a moving account of his son's death from a brain tumor. He had known Lasker socially and undertook his biography at the request of Lasker's widow, Mary.

Taken At the Flood is an engaging piece of work by a skilled journalist who had the great advantage of being able to talk to many of the people who played important roles in Lasker's life. We have drawn on Gunther's work extensively and have also dug through his Lasker-related papers at the University of Chicago. Citations in the notes are "John Gunther papers." Gunther's original manuscript was closely edited not only by Mary Lasker, but also by all three of Lasker's children: Mary, Edward, and Francie. Another half century has passed, and all of the principals are now dead, so we have reinstated details that the Lasker family removed from Gunther's manuscript. But for readers interested in seeing another side of Albert Lasker, *Taken At the Flood* remains an indispensable resource.

In addition, we have drawn extensively upon a very special resource in coauthor Schultz's collection: hundreds of pages of verbatim transcripts generated in the late 1930s for a Lasker autobiography that was never completed. From the biographer's standpoint, having uncensored access to a long-dead subject's mind is a windfall—almost literally, a gift from the beyond—and we have taken full advantage of it. Much of the material in the following pages, especially Lasker's first-person observations about his own life, has never before seen the light of day. The ghostwriter's name was Boyden Sparkes; we abbreviate these citations as "Sparkes" (denoting a Lasker interview) or "Sparkes interview with _____." Where dates and page numbers are available, we have provided them.

Both Albert and Mary Lasker gave interviews to Columbia University's oral historians. By historical coincidence, Mary Lasker's reminiscences take up almost exactly where Albert's conversations with Boyden Sparkes left off, and are therefore invaluable. We have drawn heavily on these interviews, and thank Columbia for their permission to do so.

Also interesting, and not entirely fact-based, is *The Lasker Story: As He Told It,* a little volume published in 1963 by *Advertising Age.* It is an edited transcript of a marathon lecture that Lasker delivered extemporaneously to his Lord & Thomas colleagues in April 1925.

As with most unstructured oral histories, these various first-person accounts raised almost as many questions as they answered. To sort out Lasker fact from Lasker fiction, we consulted a number of archives that provided additional perspectives on Albert Lasker and his times, including W. G. Irwin's extensive correspondence, repositories in Texas, the Harding presidential collection in Ohio, the Will Hays papers in Indianapolis, Margaret Sanger's papers at Smith College, the American Jewish Archives, the Don Francisco papers at the Syracuse University Library, the Joseph P. Kennedy collection at the Kennedy Library, the Roosevelt archives at Hyde Park, and the official records of the Shipping Board in Washington. This latter collection contains a wealth of personal and family materials; we are fortunate that no one ever bothered to cull out these personal papers from the government's official record. In fact, to our knowledge, no one has looked at this material since Albert Lasker happily fled the nation's capital in the late summer of 1923.

Notes

INTRODUCTION

1. William Hard, "Who Wants to Be a Rich Man's Son?" *Collier's*, March 10, 1923, 13. Lasker's authorized biographer, John Gunther, notes that Hard was a friend of Lasker's, and that they sometimes dreamed up *Collier's* articles together, probably including this one. See John Gunther, *Taken at the Flood: The Story of Albert D. Lasker* (New York: Harper & Brothers, 1960); and "A Note on Sources."

2. Albert Lasker letter to William Wrigley, February 6, 1923, Box 29, United States Shipping Board (USSB) records.

3. In 1986, the Georgia State Board of Pardons and Paroles granted a posthumous pardon to Frank without addressing the issue of his innocence or guilt.

4. Albert Lasker letter to Arthur Brisbane, February 14, 1923, Box 29, USSB records.

5. See, for example, Albert Lasker, letter to William Randolph Hearst, March 5, 1923, Box 29, USSB records: "There are only four or five men in the United States who are really deeply interested in the future of the American Merchant Marine. You are one of those men."

6. Albert Lasker letter to Edward Lasker, June 1, 1923, Box 30, USSB records.

7. "Business: Coalition," *Time*, June 14, 1926, www.time.com/time/magazine/article/0,9171,751559-1,00.html.

8. Sparkes, 390–391.

9. Sparkes, 346.

10. Sparkes, interview with Herbert Field, March 16, 1938, 15–18. Field's original surname was Cohn, which he changed for business purposes.

11. Sparkes interview with "Hackett" (otherwise unidentified).

12. From Robert Eck, "A Face of Character," typewritten collection of reminiscences about Lasker, March 30, 1994, 7.

13. Ibid., 5.

14. Sparkes interview with Sarnoff, January 11, 1938. See "A Note on Sources."

15. Sparkes, 40.

16. Sparkes, 249.

17. Reminiscences of Mary Lasker, Columbia University Oral History Research Office Collection, 612. See "A Note on Sources."

CHAPTER ONE

1. "For the Young People," *Galveston Daily News*, May 2, 1889, 3.

2. James F. Harris, *A Study in Theory and Practice of German Liberalism: Eduard Lasker, 1829–1884.* (New York: University Press of America, 1984), 3.

3. Harris, *A Study in the Theory and Practice of German Liberalism*, 3.

4. Louis L. Snyder, "Bismarck and the Lasker Resolution, 1884," *Review of Politics*, 29, no. 1 (1967): 42.

5. More accurately, Lasker was on the left end of the centrist political spectrum. To the left of him and his fellow progressives were the Socialists, Marxists, and others. See Carlton J. H. Hayes, "The History of German Socialism Reconsidered," *American Historical Review* 23, no. 1 (1917): 62–101.

6. Snyder, "Bismarck and the Lasker Resolution, 1884," 43.

7. A severe episode evidently occurred in 1875. See James F. Harris, *A Study in the Theory and Practice of German Liberalism* (Lanham, MD: University Press of America, 1984) 14.

8. Most of these dates are approximate. Many are contradicted in *East Texas: Its History and Its Makers*, by T. C. Richardson, published in 1940 by the Lewis Historical Publishing Company of New York.

9. See the *Handbook of Texas* online entries for Weatherford (http://www.tshaonline.org/handbook/online/articles/WW/hew3.html) and Isaac Sanger (www.tshaonline.org/handbook/online/articles/SS/fsa66.html). The latter indicates that the Sangers "encountered anti-Semitic prejudice" in Weatherford.

10. Morris tells this story in "A Letter from a Texas Pioneer" in *The Menorah Journal* 24, no. 2, (Spring 1936): 197.

11. The date comes from ibid., 201. The "letter" is notably short on dates.

12. David G. McComb, *Galveston: A History* (Austin, TX: University of Texas Press, 1986), 92–94.

13. See www.genforum.familytreemaker.com/cgi-bin/print.cgi?baum::746.html.

14. "A Letter from a Texas Pioneer," 203.

15. Again, much in this sequence is approximate. See T. C. Richardson, *East Texas: Its History and Its Makers* (New York: Lewis Historical Publishing Company, 1940), 418–420.

16. The timing is confusing. Morris Lasker recalls that his letter reached Eduard on the very day that Eduard was acquitted of the charge of lèse-majesté. But Eduard was never tried for this crime. Perhaps Morris was confusing Eduard's story with that of German socialist Ferdinand Lasalle, who was jailed for that alleged crime in 1874 and released in 1875. That timing is close for Morris's story. See Hayes, "The History of German Socialism Reconsidered," 73.

17. Box 99, Folder 2, John Gunther papers, University of Chicago.

18. Snyder, "Bismarck and the Lasker Resolution, 1884," 54.

19. In 1880, Galveston had 22,248 residents, more than any other Texas city. From *The Texas Almanac* online, www.texasalmanac.com/history/highlights/html, accessed Feb. 17, 2005.

20. McComb, *Galveston: A History*, 47.

21. See Eric Larsen, *Isaac's Storm: The Drowning of Galveston* (London: Fourth Estate, 1999), 13.

22. Ibid., 49.

23. Ibid., 63–64.

24. "A Letter from a Texas Pioneer," 194.

25. Box 99, Folder 2, Gunther papers.

26. Elizabeth Hayes Turner, *Women, Culture, and Community: Religion and Reform in Galveston, 1880–1920* (New York: Oxford University Press. 1997), 143.

27. Herman D. Allman, *A Unique Institution: The Story of the National Farm School* (Philadelphia: The Jewish Publication Society of America, 1935). http://campus.devalcol.edu/library/archives/uniqueinstitution/chapter8.htm.

28. Morris Lasker, letter to Albert Lasker, December 23, 1914.

29. Sparkes interview with Ralph Sollitt, November 5, 1937, 17.

30. Ibid., 18.

CHAPTER TWO

1. See "John H. Reagan and Early Regulation," Texas State Library & Archives Commission, www.tsl.state.tx.us/exhibits/railroad/early/page1.html.

2. John Gunther's *Taken at the Flood: The Story of Albert D. Lasker* (New York: Harper, 1960), 30.

3. Ibid., 18.

4. John Gunther interview with Loula Lasker, Box 104, Folder 20, John Gunther papers, University of Chicago.

5. Sparkes, 50.

6. Gunther interview with Loula Lasker.

7. Sparkes interview with Mrs. Charles Haynes (formerly Miss Ann Austin), May 12, 1938, 5.

8. Albert Lasker and Boyden Sparkes, *My Interest in You*, unpublished manuscript, 15. The "sheenie" reference comes from a recollection by Lasker that Sparkes chose not to include in his Galveston chapter.

9. Sparkes, 192.

10. Gunther, *Taken at the Flood*, 28. Given that Lasker's children reviewed this biography, the charges seem to have had merit.

11. If this building project came hard on the heels of the great Galveston fire of November 1885—in which 568 buildings, including Morris Lasker's first mansion, were destroyed—then Albert Lasker must have been closer to six years old than nine. See Gary Cartwright, *Galveston: A History of the Island* (New York: Atheneum, 1991), 149–150.

12. Sparkes, 21.

13. Sparkes, 178.

14. Lasker and Sparkes, *My Interest in You*, 28

15. Ibid., 30.

16. See "Ball High School," http://en.wikipedia.org/wiki/Ball_High_School.

17. Sparkes interview with Haynes, 4.

18. Sparkes, 57.

19. Sparkes interview with Haynes, 8.

20. Sparkes, 59.

21. Nathan Miller, *New World Coming: The 1920s and the Making of Modern America* (New York: Scribner, 2003), 99.

22. This is Ralph Sollitt's version, as told to Sparkes (pp. 6–7). Sollitt was simply relating the story that Lasker had told him, although with obvious skepticism.

23. Philippe Lorin, *Five Giants of Advertising* (New York: Assouline Publishing, 2001), 8–9. John Gunther was taken in by this story as well (*Taken at the Flood*, 34–35).

24. Geoffrey C. Ward, *Unforgivable Blackness: The Rise and Fall of Jack Johnson* (New York: Alfred A. Knopf, 2004), 13–14.

25. Lasker and Sparkes, *My Interest in You*, 32.

26. Reminiscences of Albert Lasker, in the Columbia University Oral History Research Office Collection (hereafter "Albert Lasker oral history, CUOHROC"), 22.

27. Lasker later told Boyden Sparkes that he received his high school diploma only because the geometry teacher, a Mr. Underwood, agreed to give Lasker an individual "examination." The interview took place at Underwood's home. Underwood was smoking his pipe, and Lasker asked if he could try the pipe. Underwood agreed, Lasker became "deathly ill," and the examination was abruptly canceled. Underwood gave Lasker a passing grade, and he was able to graduate.

28. In subsequent years, Debs would mount five campaigns for president of the United States as an avowed Socialist, the last—in 1920—from a federal jail cell in Atlanta.

29. See "The Debs Matter," *Galveston Daily News*, September 16, 1896; and "Debs Is Exonerated," *Galveston Daily News*, September 22, 1896.

30. This story also shows up in Lorin, *Five Giants of Advertising*, 7.

31. Gunther, *Taken at the Flood*, 3.

32. Albert Lasker oral history, CUOHROC, 5.

33. Gunther, *Taken at the Flood*, 35.

34. Mark Muhich, "Link to Isle Culture's Origin Rediscovered," reprinted with permission from the *Galveston County Daily News*, http://mgaia.com/images/ESLevy/LevyNews.htm.

35. J. S. Gallegly, *Footlights on the Border: The Galveston and Houston Stage Before 1900* (The Hague: Mouton & Co., 1962), 219 and 228. Gallegly's remarkable book lists every theatrical performance in Galveston and Houston from 1838 through 1900.

36. Sparkes, 234.

37. Albert Lasker oral history, CUOHROC, 10.

38. Ibid., 6. Certainly, the Galveston reporters—like their counterparts almost everywhere else in the world—were a hard-drinking, hard-partying bunch, and Albert seems to have fallen under their spell.

39. Sparkes interview with Sollitt, April 22, 1938, 4.

40. Albert Lasker oral history, CUOHROC, 10.

41. Ibid., 11.

CHAPTER THREE

1. John Gunther, *Taken at the Flood: The Story of Albert D. Lasker* (New York: Harper & Brothers, 1960), 39. Gunther's account of Lasker's early years in Chicago is full of interesting details, mostly from unattributed sources.

2. Sparkes, 98.

3. Much of this description of Chicago in the second half of the nineteenth century is from Emmett Dedmon's colorful *Fabulous Chicago* (New York: Random House, 1953); and Timothy B. Spears's *Chicago Dreaming: Midwesterners and the City, 1871–1919* (Chicago: University of Chicago Press, 2005). Dedmon describes the Chicago Fire in great detail (95–109).

4. Spears, *Chicago Dreaming*, xvi.

5. Rob Paral, "Chicago's Immigrants Break Old Patterns," www.migrationinformation.org/usfocus/display.cfm?ID=160.

6. "Hold your heads up," Debs wrote to his parents from prison. "Don't be in the least anxious. I am only to be envied." See *Letter of Eugene Debs*, vol. 1, J. Robert Constantine, ed. (Chicago: University of Illinois Press, 1990), 82.

7. Quoted in Dedmon, *Fabulous Chicago*, 186.

8. Ibid, 203.

9. Ibid, 221–225.

10. See "The Wizard of Oz, An American Fairy Tale," at http://www.loc.gov/exhibits/oz/ozsect1.html.

11. Spears, *Chicago Dreaming*, 16–17.

12. See the entire poem online at http://risa.stanford.edu/chicago.php.

13. "Rotten to the Core," *Chicago Daily Tribune*, March 5, 1896, 12.

14. "Chicago Is Enveloped in Smoke," *Chicago Daily Tribune*, December 2, 1898, 3.

15. "Chicago Real Estate," *Chicago Daily Tribune*, May 29, 1898, 26. Schlesinger & Mayer hired architect Louis Sullivan to produce an ornate building; unfortunately, by the time it was completed in 1904, the company couldn't afford it, and it was taken over by rival Carson, Pirie, Scott—a setting that was soon to serve as the backdrop for a dramatic episode in Albert Lasker's life.

16. "Wheat Outlook Is Fine," *Chicago Daily Tribune*, May 31, 1898, 10.

17. This was certainly a living wage. At this same time, Theodore Dreiser's fictional Caroline Meeber (*Sister Carrie*) found employment at a cap factory, where she was paid $3.50 a week.

18. Description of the office based on Albert Lasker and Boyden Sparkes, *Hammered Brass*, unpublished collaboration, Installment 2, 2.

19. Reminiscences of Albert Lasker, in the Columbia University Oral History Research Office Collection (hereafter "Albert Lasker oral history, CUOHROC"), 46.

20. Sparkes, 102.

21. Lasker and Sparkes, *Hammered Brass*, 5.

22. Sparkes interview with Elmer Bullis, October 27, 1937, 102.

23. *Historical Statistics of the United States*, U.S. Department of Commerce, 1970 edition, 259–271.

24. Ibid., Q 518–523.

25. Ibid., Q 329–345, Q 331–345.

26. Ibid., Q 530–547.

27. Ibid., R 1–12, R 1–16.

28. Dedmon, *Fabulous Chicago*, 189.

29. *Historical Statistics of the United States*, R 232–257.

30. John Morrish, *Magazine Editing* (New York: Routledge, 1996), 7.

31. George P. Rowell, *Forty Years an Advertising Agent* (New York: Printers' Ink Publishing, 1906). Of one highly successful competitor, Rowell wrote (on p. 446), "If he had any office I never knew where it was. For his correspondence he commonly used the stationery of his clients. He doubtless did have a billhead."

32. Mark Tungate, *Adland: A Global History of Advertising* (Philadelphia: Kogan Page, 2007), 14.

33. Ralph M. Hower, *The History of an Advertising Agency: N. W. Ayer & Son at Work, 1869–1949* (Cambridge, MA: Harvard University Press, 1939), 638–639.

34. Stephen Fox, *The Mirror Makers: A History of American Advertising and Its Creators* (New York: William Morrow and Company, 1984), 39.

35. Daniel Pope, *The Making of Modern Advertising* (New York: Basic Books, 1983), 121.

36. Albert Lasker oral history, CUOHROC, 21–22. But patent medicines, as we will see, were about to undergo a steep decline. For example: they represented 15 percent of Ayers's billings in 1900, but only 3.4 percent of its billings in 1901, according to Hower, *The History of an Advertising Agency*, 639.

37. Lord & Thomas, "Pocket Directory, 1892–93," 658.

38. From an advertisement in *Printers' Ink*, August 1895. Quoted in Pamela Walker Laird, "The Business of Progress: The Transformation of American Advertising, 1870–1920." *Business and Economic History* 22, no. 1 (Fall 1993).

39. Fox, *The Mirror Makers*, 14.

40. Albert D. Lasker, "A Call for Dedication to Fundamentals in Advertising," undated speech, probably from the late 1920s.

41. Hower, *The History of an Advertising Agency*, 96–97.

42. From "A.D. Lasker Traces Advertising Agency's Development," *Printers' Ink*, October 13, 1927, 142. Lasker also recounted this story in "Salesmanship in Print," *Printers' Ink*, July 29, 1926, 1.

43. Sparkes interview with Ralph Sollitt, 9.

44. Lasker and Sparkes, *Hammered Brass*, 8.

45. Sparkes interviews, 115.

46. Lasker and Sparkes, *Hammered Brass*, 8.

47. Albert Lasker oral history, CUOHROC, 39.

48. Sparkes, 119.

49. Ibid., 120.

50. Lasker and Sparkes, *Hammered Brass*, 17.

51. Sparkes, 354.

52. Lasker and Sparkes, *Hammered Brass*, 19.

53. Sparkes, 113.

54. Ibid., 130.

55. Lasker told Columbia's oral historians that Thomas went with him to pay off the debt. If so, that underscores the affection that Thomas felt for his young protégé.

56. Albert Lasker, *The Lasker Story: As He Told It* (Chicago: Advertising Publications, 1963), 16.

57. Ibid., 20.

58. Sparkes, 135.

59. Albert Lasker oral history, CUOHROC, 34.

60. Sparkes, 132.

61. Albert Lasker oral history, CUOHROC, 37.

62. "A. D. Lasker Traces Advertising Agency's Development," 142.

63. These numbers changed with each retelling of the story. John Gunther's numbers were substantially higher; he had Wilson's monthly ad budget at $20,000—an implausibly large figure. See Gunther, *Taken at the Flood*, 46.

64. Sparkes, 225.

65. According to Don Belding's 1952 recollections upon the occasion of Lasker's death, these six copywriters were Robert P. Crane, Walker Evans Jr. (father of the celebrated photographer), Carl Johnson, William Merriam, Arthur Palmer, and George Spencer. In addition, the fledgling creative department included a "merchandising man," Paul Faust, and an artist named Charles Church. From Don Belding's papers in the Southwest Collection at Texas Tech University.

66. Albert Lasker oral history, CUOHROC, 39.

CHAPTER FOUR

1. Quoted in Albert Lasker, "Salesmanship in Print," *Printers' Ink*, July 29, 1926, 1.

2. Albert Lasker, *The Lasker Story: As He Told It* (Chicago: Advertising Publications, 1963), 13.

3. Ibid., 14.

4. Ibid., 25. Since Armour was then a valued Lord & Thomas client, Lasker probably kept this particular opinion to himself.

5. Ibid., 19; and Sparkes, 227.

6. Sparkes, 230.

7. Albert Lasker, "A Call for Dedication to Fundamentals in Advertising," undated speech, probably from the late 1920s, 4.

8. Sparkes, 228.

9. Tommy Smith, "John E. Kennedy," in *The Ad Men and Women: A Biographical Dictionary of Advertising*, ed. Edd Applegate (Westport, CT: Greenwood Press, 1994), 200–204.

10. According to an internal Foote, Cone & Belding memorandum dated November 8, 1977, the fiftieth anniversary issue of *Printers' Ink* (1938) records that "in 1903 John E. Kennedy joined the Postum Cereal Company." Since this is the same period that he was living in Wisconsin and working for Dr. Shoop's Family Medicine, it seems unlikely that he could have joined the Post payroll fulltime.

11. This version of this key moment is from Lasker, *The Lasker Story*, 21.

12. Sparkes, 230.

13. Almost every recorded version of this proposed deal uses much higher figures. Lasker's 1925 oral history (later published as *The Lasker Story*) sets Kennedy's annual salary at $28,000, of which Shoop proposed to pay half of half, or $7,000. But the contract extension that Lord & Thomas offered to Kennedy on September 15, 1904, states that the firm was paying Kennedy "$16,000 per year for [his] full time service" in 1904. This lower figure is confirmed by a feature about the recently hired Kennedy in the July 1904 issue of *Judicious Advertising*. We infer that Shoop proposed to pay half of half of $16,000, or $4,000.

14. Sparkes, 231.

15. Lasker, *The Lasker Story*, 25.

16. Ibid.

17. Alternatively, Kennedy stated this principle as "salesmanship on paper."

18. Adelaide Hechtlinger, *The Great Patent Medicine Era: or, Without Benefit of Doctor* (New York: Galahad Books, 1970), 208.

19. The quote belongs to Claude C. Hopkins, another Shoop alumnus, to whom we will return shortly. From Claude C. Hopkins, *My Life in Advertising* (Lincolnwood, IL: NTC Business Books, 1991), 76.

20. The description of Thompson is from a Lasker autographical excerpt regarding Kennedy, ghost-written by Boyden Sparkes in 1938–1939.

21. Sparkes, 229. See note 13 regarding Kennedy's salary. We have adjusted the figures attributed to Thompson in this quote (from $28,000 to $16,000) to reflect the numbers actually reported in *Judicious Advertising*, which is most likely where Thompson would have read the offending salary figures.

22. Sparkes, 229.

23. The Nineteen Hundred Washer Co. went through a series of mergers in subsequent decades. It acquired the Whirlpool brand name in 1922—a brand that became so powerful that in 1950, Nineteen Hundred renamed itself the Whirlpool Corporation.

24. Lasker, *The Lasker Story*, 29.

25. Sparkes, 231.

26. Sparkes, 411.

27. Lasker, *The Lasker Story*, 31. Emphasis added.

28. From Article III in *The Book of Advertising Tests*, from typescript copy dated 1912, 8.

29. Sparkes interview with Noyes. Noyes didn't join Lord & Thomas until long after Kennedy had departed, so this was office hearsay.

30. Lasker, *The Lasker Story*, 34.

31. The 300 figure comes from Don Belding's 1952 recollections upon the occasion of Lasker's death. From Don Belding's papers in the Southwest Collection at Texas Tech University.

32. Lasker, *The Lasker Story*, 34.

33. From the January 1905 issue of *Judicious Advertising*.

34. John Gunther, *Taken at the Flood: The Story of Albert D. Lasker* (New York: Harper & Brothers, 1960), 62.

35. Lasker, *The Lasker Story*, 34–35.

36. There appear to be two episodes compressed into one, in many of Lasker's retellings of this phase—as, for example, in a confused passage from Sparkes, p. 232. Apparently, the original staff of six recruited by Lasker was expanded to nine after Kennedy's hiring. According to Don Belding's subsequent recollections (see above), the new recruits included George Daugherty, Hugo Levin, and Lucius Crowell.

37. Ralph M. Hower, *The History of an Advertising Agency: N. W. Ayer & Son at Work, 1869–1949* (Cambridge, MA: Harvard University Press, 1939), 97.

38. Daniel Pope, *The Making of Modern Advertising* (New York: Basic Books, 1983), 139.

39. Ibid., 143.

40. Albert Lasker, "Salesmanship in Print," *Printers' Ink*, July 29, 1926, 166.

41. Sparkes, 236.

42. Sparkes, 233.

43. Sparkes, 240.

44. Sparkes, 227.

45. Sparkes, 253.

46. Sparkes, 411 and 254.

47. Sparkes, 232.

48. Sparkes, 230.

49. Sparkes, 253.

CHAPTER FIVE

1. Unless otherwise noted, the account of Lasker meeting and marrying Flora Warner is from Sparkes, 160 ff.

2. Sparkes, 75.

3. Flora Warner frequently understated her age.

4. John Gunther, *Taken at the Flood: The Story of Albert D. Lasker* (New York: Harper & Brothers, 1960), 54.

5. Albert Lasker and Boyden Sparkes, *My Interest in You*, unpublished manuscript, second installment, 36.

6. Lasker biographer John Gunther reports that the Warner family had some misgivings about Lasker, in part related to his drinking (*Taken at the Flood*, 53). Perhaps Arthur had brought home stories about Grand Rapids.

7. Lasker later said that the woman who befriended Flora in the Chicago Beach Hotel also contracted typhoid fever.

8. Chicago statistics from "Historical Information for the Chicago Metropolitan Area," http://landcover.usgs.gov/urban/chicago/hist_ch.html; national statistics from "Achievements in Public Health, 1900–1999: Safer and Healthier Foods," *Boston Medical and Surgical Journal*, Volume 126, January–June, 1892, 128.

9. Gunther, *Taken at the Flood*, 54.

10. "I can't go through this," a distraught Lasker told his ghostwriter at this point in his retelling of the story. "Why should I live that over? I put that out of my mind." Sparkes, 207.

11. Gunther, who had access to other family members, tells a different story. He says that Flora was encouraged to have a child to "improve her circulation," and then was forbidden to have more (*Taken at the Flood*, 54).

12. This story, through the departure of Daniel Lord and the partnership agreement with Lasker and Erwin, is from Sparkes, 210–215.

13. One of the first policy changes that Lasker made when he gained complete control of Lord & Thomas in 1912 was to do away with these contracts, on the theory that his agency would provide better service without them. The business "grew tremendously under that policy," Lasker asserted, and most other agencies soon adopted it.

14. This chronology may be somewhat compressed, but Lasker later said the whole episode transpired over the course of only a few days. John Gunther gives a sanitized account of this momentous episode (*Taken at the Flood*, 57).

15. Lasker later said that his father "never forgave [him]" for not asking him for the money. At that point, Morris's businesses—especially his flour mills—were profitable, and he had ample cash to make the loan. But Albert wanted to prove that he could "do it without [him]." Sparkes, 217.

16. The quotations in this section are all from Sparkes, 233–238.

17. "Ambrose L. Thomas Dead," *Chicago Tribune*, November 11, 1906, 4.

18. Sparkes, 240. The December 1906 issue of *Judicious Advertising* says that Thomas and Lasker had just gotten out of the elevator on the seventh floor when Thomas, "without a word or a cry, collapsed and sank to the floor near a pile of rugs which he intended to inspect."

19. Albert Lasker, *The Lasker Story: As He Told It* (Chicago: Advertising Publications, 1963), 48.

20. Sparkes, 249.

21. All after-the-fact psychological interpretation is risky. We are indebted to Kay Redfield Jamison's books, especially *Touched with Fire: Manic-Depressive Illness and the Artistic Temperament* (New York: Free Press, 1993), for a clear delineation of the spectrum of manic-depressive disorders.

22. See Joshua Wolf Shenk, *Lincoln's Melancholy: How Depression Challenged a President and Fueled His Greatness* (Boston: Houghton Mifflin, 2005) for an account of Lincoln's affective disorder. The first breakdown is described on pages 19–22. Curiously, just before Lincoln had his breakdown, he was caring for a typhoid fever victim, Ann Rutledge, for whom he had deep feelings.

23. Jamison, *Touched with Fire*, 5.

24. Ibid., 6.

CHAPTER SIX

1. The Van Camp brand ultimately was acquired by ConAgra Foods in 1995. These details are from http://conagrafoods.com/consumer/brands/getBrand.do?page=van_camps.

2. Bert Van Camp letter to R. W. Bullis, January 11, 1938, Schultz collection.

3. *Printers' Ink*, July 28, 1938, 97–98.

4. Ibid.

5. Reprinted in Albert Lasker, *The Lasker Story: As He Told It* (Chicago: Advertising Publications, 1963), 42.

6. Albert D. Lasker and Boyden Sparkes, *Hammered Brass*, unpublished collaboration, 54.

7. This description of the evaporated milk production process, as well as the account details that follow, are from the Van Camp client account notes. These accounts were written mainly to help Lord &

Thomas representatives sell business. While generally boosterish, they provide invaluable detail about how the agency actually did its work.

8. Sparkes, 246.

9. Lord & Thomas, Van Camp client account notes.

10. Ibid.

11. Sparkes interview with W. G. Irwin, 7.

12. J. George Frederick, "Advertising Canned Goods," *Judicious Advertising*, November 1905.

13. Sparkes, 107.

14. From an AdAge.com biography of Curtis (www.adage.com/century/people/people088.html, accessed April 10, 2005), and a summary of his publishing ventures at www.scripophily.net/curpubcom .html.

15. Lasker, *The Lasker Story*, 39.

16. Hopkins provides this detail in his memoir. He also writes that Curtis told him this story himself; see Claude C. Hopkins, *My Life in Advertising* (Lincolnwood IL: NTC Business Book, 1991), 85.

17. Reprinted in John Gunther, *Taken at the Flood: The Story of Albert D. Lasker* (New York: Harper & Brothers, 1960), 69.

18. Hopkins, *My Life in Advertising*, 8–9.

19. Many of the facts in this section about Hopkins's life are from Rob Schorman, "Claude Hopkins, Earnest Calkins, Bissell Carpet Sweepers and the Birth of Modern Advertising," *Journal of the Gilded Age and Progressive Era* 7, no. 2 (April 2008), www.historycooperative.org/journals/jga/7.2/schorman .html. To track down the elusive Hopkins, Schorman scoured city directories, courthouse records, and local newspaper files in southern and western Michigan and cross-referenced his discoveries with clues in early trade publications and Hopkins's own writings. We are grateful to Schorman for his assistance.

20. Hopkins, *My Life in Advertising*, 7.

21. Ibid., 35.

22. Ibid., 46.

23. Ibid., 58.

24. Ibid., 63.

25. Given the fuzziness of the dates involved, it is possible that Hopkins and Kennedy met in Racine, or even overlapped. Alternatively, Kennedy may have been hired to replace Hopkins when Hopkins left Racine in 1902.

26. Hopkins, *My Life in Advertising*, 76.

27. Ibid., 95.

28. Lasker remembered Stack as "the biggest man" at Lord & Thomas when Lasker arrived in Chicago—presumably excepting Ambrose Thomas and Daniel Lord.

29. Hopkins, *My Life in Advertising*, 84.

30. Ibid., 100. The "milk" reference may be a reference to the all-milk diet then in vogue because of Thomas A. Edison's endorsement of it. Alternatively, it may be Hopkins's way of signaling that he had temporarily given up alcohol.

31. Samuel Hopkins Adams, "The Great American Fraud," *Collier's*, October 7, 1905, http://www .museumofquackery.com/ephemera/oct7-01.htm, accessed October 7, 2001.

32. Ibid.

33. www.bottlebooks.com/LIQUOZONE/LIQUOZONE%20EXPOSED.htm.

34. Ibid.

35. Lasker and Sparkes, *Hammered Brass*, 23.

36. Lasker, *The Lasker Story*, 41.

37. Ibid., 41.

38. This was an interesting replay of the discovery of John E. Kennedy, who also had written several campaigns that Lasker had noticed and admired.

39. This version of the story is from the Sparkes interview, 260–261.

40. Two years later, in a rare speech (before the Sphinx Club of New York, on January 14, 1909, as reported in the January 1909 issue of *Judicious Advertising*), Hopkins admitted that he had "longed to be a Jack London."

41. Hopkins, *My Life in Advertising*, 100–101.

42. Although this is a story from *Hammered Brass*, and doesn't ring true as Lasker's speaking voice, it certainly sounds like the way Lasker would have chosen to introduce Hopkins to the Lord & Thomas staff. By way of corroboration, the same scene is remembered by the anonymous author of "A Midwestern Ad Man Remembers," *Advertising & Selling*, May 20, 1937, 42.

43. The direct quotations are from *My Life in Advertising*, 82.

44. Hopkins, *My Life in Advertising*, 101–102.

45. Ibid., 105.

46. Ibid., 105–106.

47. Another family that came into the business at the founding was the Stuarts, who ultimately led the company for three generations. After Robert D. Stuart Jr. retired in 1983, the succeeding management sold the company to PepsiCo.

48. See J. George Frederick, "Selling Quaker Oats, Pettijohn's, Apitezo, Quaker Rice, etc.," *Judicious Advertising*, September 1906. This account implies strongly that Quaker was a small Lord & Thomas account that the agency hoped might grow.

49. Except where noted, this story comes from Hopkins, *My Life in Advertising*, 146–153.

50. According to Lasker and Sparkes, *Hammered Brass*, Quaker was already embarrassed that a dime would purchase 22 ounces of oats, but only 8 ounces of puffed rice. Lord & Thomas pointed out that this made the puffed product a luxury item, and that raising the price only recognized that reality. Copywriter Bob Crane, however, remembers that Quaker was eager to raise the price, and that "if we maintained the volume that they had at ten cents, after raising the price three cents a package, they would give us their entire business."

51. Lord & Thomas, Quaker Oats client account notes.

52. Hopkins, *My Life in Advertising*, 148. Hopkins's ads referred to Anderson as a "famous dietician"— which soon enough became true.

53. Ibid., 148.

54. The oats campaign, Hopkins later admitted, was far less successful, because his strategy of creating new oatmeal-eaters proved too expensive.

55. Hopkins, *My Life in Advertising*, 149.

56. Ibid., 150.

57. *Safe Advertising*, written by (but not attributed to) Claude C. Hopkins, and published in 1909 by Lord & Thomas, 33.

58. Hopkins (on page 135) may have gotten Johnson's first name wrong; the head of the company in this period was Caleb Johnson.

59. From the Palmolive client account notes.

60. Hopkins, *My Life in Advertising*, 137.

61. Ibid., 138.

62. Lord & Thomas, Palmolive client account notes.

63. Where discrepancies arise, we have corrected Hopkins's numbers to conform to those in the client account.

64. Palmolive client account notes.

65. Sparkes interview with David Noyes.

66. From "Our History," on the Colgate-Palmolive Web site, http://www.colgate.com/app/Colgate/US/Corp/History/1806.cvsp.

67. Hugh Allen, *The House of Goodyear: Fifty Years of Men and Industry* (Cleveland, OH: Corday & Gross, 1943), 340–341. Much of this story comes from Hopkins, *My Life in Advertising*, 126–133. *The House of Goodyear*, however, contains some specifics that contradict or complement Hopkins's rather loose account; we have favored Allen where those discrepancies arise.

68. Sparkes interview with Robert Crane.

69. "Corporate History by Year," at the Goodyear corporate Web site, www.goodyear.com/corporate/yhistory.html.

70. Hopkins, *My Life in Advertising*, 128.

71. Allen, *The House of Goodyear*, 341. The Goodyear client account notes give very different growth numbers, and don't correlate them with specific years. Car production figures are from the U.S. Census (www.census.gov/Press-Release/www/releases/archives/facts_for_features_special_editions/012439.html).

72. "Corporate History by Year."

73. Hopkins, *My Life in Advertising*, 130.

74. Sparkes interview, 262.

75. "We arranged to absorb the business of the George B. Van Cleve Agency," Lasker later wrote, "[and] Van Cleve and some of his men came with us." Quoted in Lasker and Sparkes, *Hammered Brass*.

76. Sparkes, 280.

77. Ibid., 281.

78. Sparkes interview with Mark O'Dea. Seiberling didn't like being contradicted, and the fact that Seiberling and Hopkins were very similar in appearance may have further complicated their relationship.

79. Sparkes, 282.

80. Ibid., 231.

81. Ibid., 261.

82. Mark Leland O'Dea, "An Ad Man Remembers," eulogy following Hopkins's death, 1932.

83. Sparkes, 256.

84. Ibid., 121.

85. Lasker, *The Lasker Story*, 44.

CHAPTER SEVEN

1. In 1934, Lasker said that he "vividly remembered" his first encounter with the growers, at a meeting that included a representative of the Southern Pacific Railway. That meeting didn't occur until 1907, as explained in subsequent pages. Either Lasker wasn't at the ill-fated 1904 meeting, or his memory failed him after three decades—or he chose in 1934 not to make reference to the false start in 1904.

2. Kevin Starr, *Inventing the Dream: California Through the Progressive Era* (New York: Oxford University Press, 1986), 162.

3. Much of this historical background is derived from two books: Rahno Mabel MacCurdy, *The History of the California Fruit Growers Exchange* (Los Angeles: CFGE, 1925; and *Heritage of Gold: The First 100 Years of Sunkist Growers, Inc., 1893–1993* (Van Nuys, CA: Sunkist Growers, Inc., 1993). *Heritage of Gold* was based, in part, on the previous book.

4. From Claude C. Hopkins, *Real Salesmanship in Print*, first published by Lord & Thomas in 1911, 81. The publication was updated periodically; in this account, we draw on the revised printer's galleys.

5. Don Francisco, "The Cooperative Advertising of Farm Products," address delivered at the 57th Annual Convention of the CFGE, Sacramento, CA, December 10, 1924.

6. Albert D. Lasker, "The Relationship of the Freedom of Advertising to a Free Press," address delivered at the Boston Conference on Retail Distribution, September 25, 1934.

7. In Brandon's obituary in the *Fargo* (North Dakota) *Forum*, he is described as an "expert in fruit marketing" (*Fargo Forum*, November 29, 1937). His career with Lord & Thomas apparently spanned the two decades between 1904 and 1924.

8. The ad is reproduced in full (and in full color) in *Heritage of Gold*, 43. The cartoon is reproduced in *The History of the California Fruit Growers Exchange*, 60.

9. The California girl, incidentally, has long blond hair; the Iowa girl appears to have short brown hair under her winter hat.

10. *Heritage of Gold*, 44.

11. *The History of the California Fruit Growers Exchange*, 62.

12. It was not until 1952 that the CFGE officially changed its name to "Sunkist Growers, Inc."

13. *The History of the California Fruit Growers Exchange*, 63.

14. Hopkins, *Real Salesmanship in Print*, 84.

15. *Heritage of Gold*, 45.

16. Hopkins, *Real Salesmanship in Print*, 88.

17. Ibid.; and *Heritage of Gold*, 46

18. Sparkes interview with Don Francisco, October 6, 1937.

19. Hopkins, *Real Salesmanship in Print*, 90.

20. Ibid.

21. *Heritage of Gold*, 48.

22. Starr, *Inventing the Dream*, 162.

23. *Heritage of Gold*, 50.

24. John Gunther, *Taken at the Flood: The Story of Albert D. Lasker* (New York: Harper & Brothers, 1960), 160.

25. Sparkes interview with Don Francisco, October 6, 1937.

26. Ibid.

27. The ad is reproduced in full in *Heritage of Gold*, 50.

28. Extractor sales figures are from the Francisco interview; consumption figures are from *Heritage of Gold*, 55.

29. Lord & Thomas art director Charles Everett Johnson deserved the credit for the new, more sophisticated look, according to Don Francisco.

30. Francisco, "The Cooperative Advertising of Farm Products," 27.

31. Ibid., 23.

32. The unsuccessful exception was the olive industry, which suffered from an unworkable exchange that combined growers and packers, which Francisco likened to "trying to drive a horse and a cow together." A spate of olive-related poisonings in Detroit in 1921 also crippled the industry.

33. Francisco, "The Cooperative Advertising of Farm Products," 44.

34. The History of the California Fruit Growers Exchange, 70.

35. Don Francisco, "The Marketing of Commodities," in Associated Advertising, August 1920, 11, quoted in Daniel Starch, Principles of Advertising:A Systematic Syllabus of the Fundamental Principles of Advertising (Madison, WI: The University Cooperative Co., 1910), 105.

36. "Annual Report of the Federal Trade Commission for the Fiscal Year Ended June 30, 1920," www.ftc.gov/os/annualreports/.

37. The best source on the California Associated Raisin Company (CARC) is Victoria Saker Woeste, The Farmer's Benevolent Trust: Law and Agricultural Cooperation in Industrial America, 1865–1945 (Chapel Hill, NC: University of North Carolina Press, 1998).

38. Sparkes interview with Don Francisco, October 11, 1937.

39. Reproduced in Woeste, The Farmer's Benevolent Trust, 122.

40. Ibid., 128.

CHAPTER EIGHT

1. "Trial of Leo M. Frank on Charge of Murder Begins," Atlanta Constitution, July, 29, 1913, 2.

2. "Girl Is Assaulted and Then Murdered in Heart of Town," Atlanta Constitution, April 28, 1913, 1–2. Much of our account is taken from Leonard Dinnerstein, The Leo Frank Case (New York: Columbia University Press, 1968); and Steve Oney's And the Dead Shall Rise: The Murder of Mary Phagan and the Lynching of Leo Frank (New York: Pantheon, 2003).

3. Dinnerstein, The Leo Frank Case, 3; Oney, And the Dead Shall Rise, 20–21.

4. Oney, And the Dead Shall Rise, 11, 27, 35, 37, and 60.

5. "Trial of Leo M. Frank on Charge of Murder Begins," 2–3; Dinnerstein, The Leo Frank Case, 3; Oney, And the Dead Shall Rise, 48.

6. Oney, And the Dead Shall Rise, 22, 32, 35, and 37.

7. Sparkes, 42.

8. Dinnerstein, The Leo Frank Case, 13.

9. Ibid., 4.

10. "Frank and Lee," Atlanta Constitution, May 2, 1913, 1.

11. Oney, And the Dead Shall Rise, 74, 75, and 97.

12. "Conley Says He Helped Frank," Atlanta Constitution, May 30, 1913, 2; "Mary Phagan's Murder Was Work of a Negro, Declares Frank," Atlanta Constitution, May 31, 1913, 1–2.

13. Oney, And the Dead Shall Rise, 88.

14. "Frank Convicted, Asserts Innocence," Atlanta Constitution, August 26, 1913, 1.

15. "Frank Sentenced on Murder Charge to Hang Oct. 10," Atlanta Constitution, August, 27, 1913, 1.

16. "Troops on Alert for Mob," New York Times, May 2, 1913, 5; "Politics Enmeshes a Murder Mystery," New York Times, May 24, 1913, 6; "Indicted for Girl's Murder," New York Times, May 25, 1913, 4; "Says Employer Slew Girl," New York Times, August 5, 1913, 2; "Frank Sentenced to Die," New York Times, August 27, 1913, 3; "Says Frank Is Innocent," New York Times, October 20, 1913, 1; "Frank Seeks New Trial," New York Times, December 17, 1913, 6.

17. Dinnerstein, The Leo Frank Case, 95–98.

18. Sparkes, 286.

19. David Marx to Louis Marshall, August 30, 1913, in Oney, And the Dead Shall Rise, 346.

20. Ibid., 346 and 348.

21. Sparkes, 284.

22. The quotes in this section are from Sparkes, 43.

23. Sparkes, 286–287. John Gunther also credits Lasker's sister Etta, who had friends in Atlanta, with getting her brother involved in the case (John Gunther, Taken at the Flood: The Story of Albert D. Lasker [New York: Harper & Brothers, 1960], 88).

24. Interview, Francie Lasker Brody, March 22, 2004.

25. Sparkes, 31.

26. Sparkes, 287.

27. From pamphlet entitled *Morris Lasker, Pioneer, 1840–1916*, New York Public Library, 1940 *PWZ (Lasker, M).

28. Oney, *And the Dead Shall Rise*, 367.

29. Sparkes, 43–45.

30. "Split Court Denies New Trial to Frank," *New York Times*, February 18, 1914, 3.

31. Sparkes, 290.

32. Sparkes interview with Mark Sullivan, November 30, 1937.

33. Oney, *And the Dead Shall Rise*, 374–375.

34. *New York Times*, February 19, 1914, 1.

35. "Frank Alibi Upheld by New Witnesses," *New York Times*, March 6, 1914, 2.

36. Sparkes, 290.

37. Dinnerstein, *The Leo Frank Case*, 94.

38. Sparkes, 49.

39. Dinnerstein, *The Leo Frank Case*, 95.

40. Albert D. Lasker to Herbert Haas, April 20, 1914, Leo Frank Collection, American Jewish Archives.

41. Albert Lasker to Louis Wiley, April 22, 1914, Leo Frank Collection.

42. Herbert Haas to Albert Lasker, April 30, 1914, Leo Frank Collection.

43. *New York Times*, March 19, 1914, 1; March 22, 1914, 3; March 25, 1914, 5; and April 27, 1914, 9.

44. Eugene Levy, "'Is the Jew a White Man?': Press Reaction to the Leo Frank Case," 1913–1915, *Phylon* 35, no. 2 (1974): 212–222.

45. Albert Lasker to Herbert Haas, April 20, 1914, Leo Frank Collection.

46. "Burns Attacked by Mob," *New York Times*, May 2, 1914, 1.

47. Quoted in Oney, *And the Dead Shall Rise*, 393.

48. Ibid., 421–423.

49. For a summary of Connolly's career, see Dennis Swibold, "The Education of a Muckraker," *Montana: The Magazine of Western History*, 53 (Summer 2003), 2–19, visitmt.com/history/Montana_the_Magazine_of_Western_History/summer2003/swibold.htm.

50. Oney, *And the Dead Shall Rise*, 444–445.

51. "Justice to Frank Doubted by Holmes," *New York Times*, November 27, 1914, 1.

52. Oney, *And the Dead Shall Rise*, 451.

53. "Finds Mob Frenzy Convicted Frank," *New York Times*, December 14, 1914, 4.

54. Albert Lasker to Jacob Billikopf, December 28, 1914, in Oney, *And the Dead Shall Rise*, 456.

55. Oney, *And the Dead Shall Rise*, 460.

56. Ibid., 451.

57. Ibid., 467.

58. Gunther, *Taken at the Flood*, 88.

59. Oney, *And the Dead Shall Rise*, 472, 476, and 477.

60. Sparkes, 49.

61. Oney, *And the Dead Shall Rise*, 502–503.

62. Ibid., 1.

63. "Soldiers Now Guard Him," *New York Times*, June 22, 1915, 1 and 6.

64. Oney, *And the Dead Shall Rise*, 535.

65. Ibid., 557.

66. "Leo Frank's Throat Cut by Convict; Famous Prisoner Near Death," *New York Times*, July 18, 1915, 1; "The Hideous Mob Spirit," *New York Times*, July 25, 1915, 14.

67. "Warden Is Overpowered," *New York Times*, August 17, 1915, 1 and 4.

68. "Took Frank's Life in 'Resentment,'" *New York Times*, August 18, 1915, 3

69. "Grim Tragedy in Woods," *New York Times*, August 19, 1915, 3.

70. Steve Oney, "Murder Trials and Media Sensationalism: The Press Frenzy of a Century Ago Echoes in the Coverage of Trials Today," *Nieman Reports* (Spring 2004): 63–67, www.nieman.harvard.edu/reports/04-1NRSpring/63-67V58N1.pdf.

71. Gunther, *Taken at the Flood*, 90. Gunther dates this letter as December 26, 1915, but this would be over four months after the lynching of Frank, and therefore Lasker would not be spending time on the case. Most likely the letter should be dated December 26, 1914.

72. Albert Lasker letter to Morris Lasker, January 5, 1915.

73. Sparkes, 288.

74. Sparkes, 45–46.

75. Sparkes, 288.

76. Dinnerstein, *The Leo Frank Case*, 162.

77. Albert Lasker letter to (brother) Edward Lasker, October 17, 1922, Box 28, Shipping Board records.

CHAPTER NINE

1. Sparkes interview with W. G. Irwin, 6.

2. Sparkes, 290.

3. Sparkes, 291.

4. Lasker told this story twice to Sparkes (291–292; 432–433). This version combines those two stories.

5. Sparkes, 432.

6. Sparkes, 291.

7. Cortland Van Camp's hardware business was a substantial local enterprise. According to surviving financial records, Van Camp Hardware & Iron Co. in 1912 had a capitalization of $1.6 million.

8. Sparkes, 291.

9. In fact, Frank Van Camp continued to ask Lasker for financial favors. After selling out in 1914, he moved to San Pedro, California, where he founded the Van Camp Sea Food Company. In July of that year, he asked Lasker for help in getting through a cash crunch. "When I had my last talk with you," he wrote, "I remember your saying you would do me a favor if I gave you the opportunity and you were in position to do so. Well, here is the opportunity, and I hope you have a fat bank account." (From a July 21, 1914, letter, a copy of which is in the Irwin papers.) Van Camp and his son, Gilbert, made a notable success of their tuna enterprise, inventing the purse seine method of tuna-fishing that helped transform tuna into an affordable food. In the 1950s, the company adopted the "Chicken of the Sea" brand name.

10. Sparkes, 433.

11. For more on Irwin and Cummins, see Jeffrey L. Cruikshank and David B. Sicilia, *The Engine That Could: Seventy-Five Years of Values-Driven Change at Cummins Engine Company* (Boston: Harvard Business School Press, 1997).

12. Letter from Merchants National Bank, October 10, 1912, to W. G. Irwin.

13. W. G. Irwin letter to G. W. Mann, March 4, 1914.

14. From W. M. Wilkes's May 1914 "Salesmen's Bulletin."

15. W. G. Irwin letter to Frank Van Camp, January 6, 1916.

16. Albert Lasker letter to W. G. Irwin, July 16, 1917.

17. Albert Lasker letter to W. G. Irwin, July 25, 1917.

18. W. G. Irwin letter to Albert Lasker, October 13, 1917.

19. Albert Lasker letter to W. G. Irwin, October 17, 1917.

20. Albert Lasker letter to W. M. Wilkes, July 8, 1914.

21. See, for example, the write-up of Freda Ehmann in "California Olive Oil News" at www.oliveoil source.com/olivenews4-8.htm (accessed September 19, 2005). Lord & Thomas recommended a three-year moratorium on advertising, which the olive industry accepted.

22. W. G. Irwin to Albert Lasker, November 13, 1917.

23. Albert Lasker letter to W. G. Irwin, December 20, 1916.

24. W. G. Irwin letter to Albert Lasker, December 12, 1917.

25. "TEB" letter to W. G. Irwin, April 6, 1918.

26. Albert Lasker letter to W. G. Irwin, July 16, 1917.

27. W. M. Wilkes letter to Albert Lasker, September 22, 1917.

28. Albert Lasker letter to W. G. Irwin, April 25, 1918.

29. Albert Lasker letter to W. G. Irwin, February 10, 1919.

30. *The Lasker Story: As He Told It*, 51. The exact timing of these various breakdowns and sabbaticals is fuzzy.

31. Albert Lasker letter to H. F. Vorhies, February 5, 1918.

32. Albert Lasker letter to W. G. Irwin, January 6, 1919.

33. Albert Lasker letter to W. G. Irwin, February 10, 1920.

34. Albert Lasker letter to W. G. Irwin, April 16, 1920.

35. Albert Lasker letter to W. G. Irwin, August 18, 1917.

36. W. G. Irwin letter to Albert Lasker, March 28, 1921.

37. W. G. Irwin to Albert Lasker, December 6, 1919.

38. Albert Lasker letter to W. G. Irwin, December 8, 1919.

39. W. G. Irwin letter to Albert Lasker, May 13, 1920.

40. Albert Lasker letter to W. G. Irwin, May 15, 1920.

41. Albert Lasker letter to W. G. Irwin, January 27, 1922.

42. Sparkes, 293.

43. Sparkes interview with W. G. Irwin, 8.

44. Sparkes, 292.

45. There is very little mention of Mitchell in the various Lasker collections. John Gunther says Lasker lost $1 million in a single year on his Mitchell investment, but this seems unlikely. In a conversation with Boyden Sparkes, Lasker said that he signed the papers to terminate his investment in Mitchell on the day his daughter Francie was born in 1916—a memorable day, because the negotiations were more complicated than he expected, and he didn't arrive at the hospital until after Flora had delivered Francie. "Though my wife never mentioned it to me," Lasker told Sparkes, "I think it is one thing I did that she never forgave me." (Sparkes, 328) To his brother-in-law Arthur Warner, he wrote in 1923 that the Mitchell interlude was "one of the saddest experiences of my business career. I put in a fortune in money I loaned them, in addition to the stock I owned, in an attempt to extend the time, but it was impossible." See Albert Lasker letter to Arthur Warner, February 15, 1923, Box 29, Shipping Board records.

46. Sparkes, 294.

47. Albert Lasker letter to H. F. Vorhies, February 15, 1918.

48. Albert Lasker letter to W. G. Irwin, February 5, 1921.

CHAPTER TEN

1. The Cubs did not become the Cubs until early in the twentieth century; before that, the Chicago Nationals were known variously as the Orphans, Spuds, and Colts. We'll refer to them as the "Cubs."

2. Reminiscences of Albert Lasker, in the Columbia University Oral History Research Office Collection (hereafter "Albert Lasker oral history, CUOHROC"), 69.

3. Peter Golenbock, *Wrigleyville: A Magical History Tour of the Chicago Cubs* (New York: St. Martin's Press, 1999), 111; and Sparkes, 110.

4. David Pietrusza, *Judge and Jury: The Life and Times of Judge Kenesaw Mountain Landis* (South Bend, IN: Diamond Communications, Inc., 1998), 157.

5. Ibid, 156.

6. Steven A. Riess, "The Baseball Magnates and Urban Politics in the Progressive Era: 1895–1920," 41, http://www.la84foundation.org/SportsLibrary/JSH/JSH1974/JSH0101/jsh0101d.pdf.

7. Albert Lasker oral history, CUOHROC, 71. The "year" is an inference based on the date of the out-of-court settlement and Lasker's recollection of when a desperate Weeghman approached him.

8. Lasker remembered that not only Weeghman attended this meeting, but also seafood wholesaler Walker. Sparkes, 284.

9. As Lasker later told the story to Boyden Sparkes, Weeghman's option was expiring at ten o'clock the next morning. Given the intervening steps that had yet to occur, either Lasker compressed the timeframe in the retelling of the story, or the option was extended.

10. Albert Lasker oral history, CUOHROC, 72.

11. Eliot Asinof, *Eight Men Out* (New York: Holt, Rinehart and Winston, 1963), 127. This is the best reference on the 1919 World Series; it was made into a successful movie by director John Sayles.

12. Albert Lasker oral history, CUOHROC, 91. The description applies equally to Lasker himself.

13. Ibid., 74.

14. Ibid., 75.

15. Ibid., 76.

16. According to Jerome Holtzman and George Vass, *The Chicago Cubs Encyclopedia* (Philadelphia: Temple University Press, 1997), 301, Wrigley invited the Chicago baseball writers to a dinner at his home in Pasadena, California, in the spring of 1918. At that function, he met and was greatly impressed by Veeck, who—writing under the pen name "Bill Bailey"—had regularly criticized the Cubs' management in ways that struck Wrigley as both thoughtful and fair.

17. Albert Lasker oral history, CUOHROC, 78. Lasker also told Boyden Sparkes a story about giving Grover Cleveland Alexander a ride home the day after a game that "Alex" had lost in the ninth inning on a hit by a "third-rater." Alexander admitted that he had made a mistake: "I forgot that any man with a bat in his hand can hit once in a while!" Sparkes, 415.

18. Lasker misremembered many of the details of this story. The authors are indebted to baseball historian Jacob Pomrenke, who directed us toward the Magee story online at www.baseballlibrary.com/baseballlibrary/ballplayers/M/Magee_Lee.stm (accessed February 8, 2005).

19. Sparkes, 317.

20. Wrigley, according to Lasker, had not yet "come that far along in baseball" to be involved in these discussions.

21. Albert Lasker oral history, CUOHROC, 79.

22. Sparkes, 317.

23. Albert Lasker oral history, CUOHROC, 80–81.

24. From   www.baseballlibrary.com/baseballlibrary/ballplayers/M/Magee_Lee.stm   (accessed February 8, 2005).

25. There was an interesting precedent to this episode in August 1919, when Bill Veeck learned that Cub pitcher Claude Hendrix might be involved in a plot to throw a game to the Phillies. Veeck took Hendrix out of the lineup, and went with star Grover Cleveland Alexander instead. (Alexander still lost, despite Veeck's offer of a $500 bonus if he won.) Hendrix was released at the end of the 1919 season and never played professional ball again. See the Holtzman and Vass, *Chicago Cubs Encyclopedia*, 302.

26. See, for example, Robert I. Goler, "Black Sox," *Chicago History*, 17, no. 3 and 4 (Fall/Winter 1988–189): 42, and http://www.chicagohistory.org/static_media/pdf/historyfair/chm-chicagoblack sox.pdf. The authors are indebted to the Chicago Historical Society for supplying copies of this and other relevant articles.

27. Albert Lasker oral history, CUOHROC, 81–82. Only a few years later, of course, America would learn that a member of President Harding's Cabinet had been bribed.

28. Albert Lasker letter to W. G. Irwin, September 19, 1919.

29. Asinof, *Eight Men Out*, 199.

30. Ibid., 199.

31. Albert Lasker oral history, CUOHROC, 83.

32. The authorship of the "Lasker Plan" has been attributed to various people over the years. Stung by these allegations, Lasker maintained (in 1938) that he "thought [it] up single-handed, with nobody else present when I thought it up, and reduced it to paper before I showed it to another soul." Sparkes, 414.

33. Sparkes, 318.

34. Shortly after Landis handed down his staggering judgment against Standard Oil, Lasker and his good friend Moritz Rosenthal—a member of the oil giant's defense team—were lunching together at Rector's, a Chicago restaurant. Landis happened to come into the restaurant. He sat down with Rosenthal and Lasker, introduced himself to Lasker, and then apologized to Rosenthal for having brought in the judgment against Rosenthal's client. He congratulated Rosenthal for having done a fine job for his clients—Standard Oil directly, and the Rockefellers indirectly—and suggested that even though Rosenthal had lost, he should get at least $25,000 for his efforts. After Landis departed, Lasker later recalled, Rosenthal "laughed hysterically" at Landis's naïveté: Rosenthal's actual compensation from Standard Oil ran well into the hundreds of thousands of dollars. Sparkes, 320.

35. Pietrusza, *Judge and Jury*, 76.

36. Ibid., 153–154.

37. Sparkes, 318.

38. "Owners of Five Clubs Talk Over Lasker Plan," *New York Times*, October 5, 1920.

39. Sparkes, 317.

40. Ibid., 320.

41. "Owners to Discuss Baseball Changes," *New York Times*, October 18, 1920.

42. Albert Lasker oral history, CUOHROC, 86.

43. Sparkes, 317.

44. Albert Lasker oral history, CUOHROC, 86.

45. Ibid., 88.

46. See, for example, "Reichow, the Original Landis Man, Pays Tribute to His Choice," *Sporting News*, November 11, 1920, 1.

47. Austrian's role in the unraveling of the Black Sox scandal was, like the ballplayers' trial, murky at best. As attorney for the Chicago White Sox, Austrian elicited the confessions that ultimately got the offending ballplayers banned from baseball. But serving simultaneously as a member of New York gambler Arnold Rothstein's defense team, Austrian not only got Rothstein off his legal hook, but also indirectly helped bring in a not-guilty verdict for the ballplayers. See Pietrusza, *Judge and Jury*, 187. See also Leo Katcher, *The Big Bankroll: The Life and Times of Arnold Rothstein* (New York: Harper, 1959), 145.

48. Albert Lasker oral history, CUOHROC, 91.

49. Sparkes, 319. When he told this story to Columbia, Lasker omitted the expletive.

50. "Baseball Conflict Shifts to Minors," *New York Times*, November 10, 1920.

51. "No Backing Down, Says Lasker," *New York Times*, November 11, 1920.

52. Albert Lasker oral history, CUOHROC, 89. The Sparkes interview (p. 419) makes the same point.

53. "Major Moguls Get Together and Cancel Their War Plans," *Sporting News*, November 18, 1920, 1.

54. Albert Lasker oral history, CUOHROC, 95.

55. Pietrusza, *Judge and Jury*, 170.

56. Another reason the Black Sox were found not guilty is that Alfred Austrian conveniently "lost" their confessions and waivers of immunity, which didn't turn up again for several years—thereby helping two of his clients at once: Charles Comiskey and Arnold Rothstein. See Riess, "The Baseball Magnates and Urban Politics," 52.

57. Pietrusza, *Judge and Jury*, 187.

58. Ibid., 188.

59. Arthur R. Ahrens, "Chicago's City Series: Cubs vs. White Sox," *Chicago History* 5, no. 4 (Winter 1976–1977): 248.

60. There is confusion about the date of this overture. Most sources, including John Gunther (*Taken at the Flood: The Story of Albert D. Lasker* [New York: Harper & Brothers, 1960, 123), cite June 1925; but Golenbock cites 1921 (*Wrigleyville*, 175).

61. Sparkes, 415.

62. Gunther, *Taken at the Flood*, 121.

63. "Jewish Degradation of American Baseball," *Dearborn Independent*, September 10, 1921.

64. Sparkes, 321.

65. Sparkes, 318.

CHAPTER ELEVEN

1. Reminiscences of Albert Lasker, in the Columbia University Oral History Research Office Collection (hereafter "Albert Lasker oral history, CUOHROC"), 117.

2. Sparkes, 71.

3. Sparkes interview with Will H.Hays, 14.

4. Albert Lasker oral history, CUOHROC, 120.

5. Albert Lasker, *The Lasker Story: As He Told It* (Chicago: Advertising Publications, 1963), 55.

6. "Unofficial but Authoritative," *Time*, January 22, 1946.

7. Elmer Schlesinger letter to John C. O'Laughlin, May 26, 1916, "Schlesinger" folder, Box 11, John Callan O'Laughlin papers, Manuscript Division, Library of Congress, Washington, D.C.

8. John C. O'Laughlin letter to W. Murray Crane, July 11, 1916, "Lasker" folder, Box 8, O'Laughlin papers.

9. Elmer Schlesinger letter to John C. O'Laughlin, August 3, 1916, "Schlesinger" folder, Box 11, O'Laughlin papers.

10. Sparkes, 297–298.

11. Sparkes, 299.

12. Albert Lasker letter to John C. O'Laughlin, July 2, 1917, "Lasker" folder, Box 8, O'Laughlin papers.

13. Albert Lasker letter to John C. O'Laughlin, September 27, 1917, "Lasker" folder, Box 8, O'Laughlin papers.

14. Sparkes interview with Hays.

15. Albert Lasker oral history, CUOHROC, 120.

16. In a 1938 interview with his ghostwriter, Lasker also hinted at another motivation: "I felt if I could get to the Colonel, I could put to him my plight about myself. I had reached the point where I just felt I had to go to war, if for no other way than to enlist." Sparkes, 301.

17. There is confusion about the date of this meeting. Lasker remembered it clearly as taking place just before his wedding anniversary—June 9—but also remembered discussion at the lunch table about Roosevelt's son Quentin, who had just been killed in action in Europe, which happened in mid-July.

18. This version is from Lasker, *The Lasker Story*, 57. It sounds more authentic than the stilted version that Lasker later recounted for Columbia's oral historians: "In your presence, Colonel, who would have the temerity to claim that distinction?" Albert Lasker oral history, CUOHROC, 121.

19. This version is from a September 27, 1918, letter from Lasker to John C. O'Laughlin, "Lasker" folder, Box 8, O'Laughlin papers. It provides the only reliable date for the September meeting, which Lasker later variously placed in June, July, and August. The book Roosevelt shared with the group was William S. Howe's *War and Progress: The Growth of the World Influence of the Anglo-Saxon* (Boston: L. Phillips, 1918).

20. Lasker, *The Lasker Story*, 57.

21. Albert Lasker oral history, CUOHROC, 132.

22. Sparkes, 305.

23. Albert Lasker oral history, CUOHROC, 119

24. Sparkes, 309. In *Taken at the Flood* (New York: Harper & Brothers, 1960), John Gunther adds that the pamphlet was aimed primarily at swaying opinion within the ranks of Republican operatives (p. 103).

25. According to Warren G. Harding's biographer, such a deal probably was cut, at least informally. See Francis Russell, *The Shadow of Blooming Grove: Warren G. Harding in His Times* (New York: McGraw-Hill, 1968), 301.

26. Will H. Hays, *The Memoirs of Will H. Hays* (Garden City, NY: Doubleday and Company, Inc., 1955), 176.

27. Sparkes, 304. Hays makes no mention of this episode in his own memoirs, although he briefly recounts the reconciliation between Taft and Roosevelt in March 1918 (*Memoirs*, 155).

28. For a description of this speech, which apparently contributed to Roosevelt's rapid decline and death in January 1919, see Nathan Miller, *Theodore Roosevelt: A Life* (New York: William Morrow and Co., 1992), 563.

29. "I am not a member of any organized political party," Rogers once quipped. "I am a Democrat."

30. This passage, including all quotes, is from Sparkes, 305–307.

31. O'Laughlin, traveling along the Western Front that day, claimed to have heard the last shot fired in World War I. Letter to Albert Lasker, November 19, 1918, "Lasker" folder, Box 8, O'Laughlin papers.

32. Sparkes, 301.

33. Unlike Lasker, Hays was not one to share credit with his subordinates. In addition to nearly leaving Lasker out of his *Memoirs*, Hays completely omits Sollitt.

34. Sparkes, 303.

35. Lasker, *The Lasker Story*, 57.

CHAPTER TWELVE

1. He also accepted a place—alongside the ubiquitous John Callan O'Laughlin—on Hays's platform committee. When Lasker succumbed to an unnamed illness in August 1919—possibly depression—and tried to resign from the committee, O'Laughlin talked him out of it: "Hays and I are agreed that it would be in the interest not only of the party but of the nation for you to serve on the committee, and I sincerely trust that through the shifting of other matters you can give the time to this most important duty . . . Certainly, I shall feel like a ship without a rudder if I haven't your keen brain to rely upon." From John C. O'Laughlin letter to Albert Lasker, August 28, 1919, "Lasker" folder, Box 23, John Callan O'Laughlin papers, Manuscript Division, Library of Congress, Washington, D.C.

2. Reminiscences of Albert Lasker, in the Columbia University Oral History Research Office Collection (hereafter "Albert Lasker oral history, CUOHROC"), 127. Lasker was nearly forty at the time; Lodge was approaching seventy.

3. Francis Russell, *The Shadow of Blooming Grove: Warren G. Harding in His Times* (New York: McGraw-Hill, 1968), 323–324.

4. John Gunther, *Taken at the Flood: The Story of Albert D. Lasker* (New York: Harper & Brothers, 1960), 63. The first ad for the pageant appeared in the January 6, 1907, issue of the paper.

5. Richard Coke Lower, *A Bloc of One: The Political Career of Hiram W. Johnson* (Stanford, CA: Stanford University Press, 1993), viii.

6. Albert Lasker oral history, CUOHROC, 125.

7. The subcommittee is mentioned in a John Callan O'Laughlin letter to Albert Lasker, February 2, 1920, "Lasker" folder, Box 23, O'Laughlin papers.

8. One reason why Hays didn't accept Lasker's resignation is that by February 1920, Lasker had agreed to organize the "popular subscription work"—that is, Republican fundraising—for Hays. See Albert Lasker letter to O'Laughlin, February 3, 1920, "Lasker" folder, Box 23, O'Laughlin papers.

9. Albert Lasker oral history, CUOHROC, 125–126.

10. Sparkes, 311.

11. Lower, *A Bloc of One*, 147–152.

12. Albert Lasker oral history, CUOHROC, 129.

13. Sparkes, 312.

14. Albert Lasker oral history, CUOHROC, 130–131.

15. Ibid.

16. Albert Lasker, *The Lasker Story: As He Told It* (Chicago: Advertising Publications, 1963), 58.

17. MIC 3 Warren G. Harding Papers [microform], letter from Will Hays, June 1920: Ohio Historical Society.

18. MIC 3 Warren G. Harding Papers [microform], letter to John D. Works, 2 July 1920: Ohio Historical Society.

19. Albert Lasker oral history, CUOHROC, 133.

20. Sparkes, 314.

21. Albert Lasker oral history, CUOHROC, 133a. Lasker was correct in this belief. Herbert Hoover recalled that Harding "carried water on both shoulders" during the campaign—meaning that he both supported and opposed the League, as political circumstances demanded. When a group of Republican dignitaries signed a statement in support of the League, according to Hoover, they did so "in consequence of personal assurances from Mr. Harding." See *The Memoirs of Herbert Hoover, 1920–1933* (New York: Macmillan Co., 1952), 13.

22. "The only thing that worries me," Wrigley wrote to Ralph Sollitt on August 24, "is that we don't appear to have any money to advertise this wonderful man to the voters. We received about as much so far as I spend every week advertising a penny stick of [c]hewing gum." From Box 6, Folder 5, Will H. Hays Collection, Manuscript Section, Indiana State Library.

23. Will H. Hays letter to John T. Adams, September 3, 1920, Box 7, Folder 1, Hays Collection.

24. "Will Boom Harding by Big Advertising," *New York Times*, July 28, 1920.

25. The rumor had dogged previous generations of Hardings. See Russell, *The Shadow of Blooming Grove*, 26.

26. Ibid., 40. Francis Russell notes that even in the later years of the 1960s, Harding's Ohio-based descendents remained sensitive about allegations of black ancestry.

27. Ibid., 405.

28. This story is derived from ibid., 402–403. Lasker did not mention this episode in any of his oral histories, and it was omitted from his authorized biography.

29. See, for example, Stephen Vaughan, "The Devil's Advocate: Will H. Hays and the Campaign to Make Movies Respectable," *Indiana Magazine of History* 101 (June 2005): 131–132.

30. John A. Morello, *Selling the President, 1920: Albert D. Lasker, Advertising, and the Election of Warren G. Harding* (Westport, CT: Praeger, 2001), 56. According to an Albert Lasker letter to George Christian, August 30, 1920, the filmmaking impresario was a New Yorker named Grant.

31. The results from a Syracuse, New York, theater are described in "Will Boom Harding by Big Advertising."

32. MIC 3 Warren G. Harding Papers [microform], letter from Albert D. Lasker to George B. Christian, 28 July 1920: Ohio Historical Society.

33. MIC 3 Warren G. Harding Papers [microform], letter from Albert D. Lasker to George B. Christian, August 7, 1920: Ohio Historical Society.

34. MIC 3 Warren G. Harding Papers [microform], letter from Albert D. Lasker to Walter Friedlander, August 7, 1920: Ohio Historical Society.

35. Russell, *The Shadow of Blooming Grove*, 156.

36. But there is evidence that Lasker learned to drive in his twenties. According to the August 15, 1908, edition of the *Chicago Tribune*, he was caught in a speed trap in Glencoe, Illinois, and fined $10 for exceeding the twenty-mile-per-hour speed limit. Lasker refused to drive the police officer who wrote the ticket to the station, "as is the usual custom," so the officer had to drive himself. "While he was gone to be fined," the *Tribune* noted, "three young women of his party took positions at each end of the course and warned autoists of the existence of the trap."

37. Sparkes, 316.

38. Sparkes, 316.

39. Albert Lasker letter to J. Wellover, August 20, 1920, Hays Collection.

40. Harding evidently felt that the phrase wasn't appropriate as a closing note for the speech, and added his own favorites—"Steady, America!", and "Let's assure good fortune to all"—after "wiggle and wobble." Albert Lasker letter to Scott Bone, August 18, 1920, Hays Collection.

41. Ibid.

42. Albert Lasker letter to Will H. Hays, September 3, 1920, Hays Collection.

43. Will H. Hays, *The Memoirs of Will H. Hays* (Garden City, NY: Doubleday and Company, Inc., 1955), 265. John Morello notes that fully two thousand of these Republican speakers were women. See *Selling the President, 1920*, 65.

44. Albert Lasker letter to Arthur Brisbane, August 18, 1920, Box 6, Folder 10, Hays Collection.

45. Richard M. Fried, *The Man Everybody Knew: Bruce Barton and the Making of Modern America* (Chicago: Ivan R. Dee, 2005), 120.

46. In *Selling the President, 1920*, John Morello gives Lasker credit for the work of the "Harding-Coolidge Theatrical League," which put some of the most famous stars of the silver screen in harness for the Harding campaign. This credit may be misplaced. Lasker seems to have been at least partly responsible for bringing circus master John Ringling, tenor Enrico Caruso, and others to the front porch, and for securing testimonials from World War I flying ace Eddie Rickenbacker and others. But Lord & Thomas and Lasker didn't embrace the testimonial approach to advertising until the later 1920s, so this was not part of the agency's stock-in-trade. See, for example, Albert Lasker letter to Will Hays, August 21, 1920, Box 6, Folder 11, Hays Collection.

47. Albert Lasker letter to Will Hays, August 18, 1920, Box 6, Folder 10, Hays Collection.

48. *Collier's*, October 30, 1920, 25.

49. Sparkes, 316–317.

50. Russell, *The Shadow of Blooming Grove*, 418–419.

51. Ibid., 409.

52. Sparkes interview with Hays, 22.

53. "Had Harding's Good Wishes," *New York Times*, November 13, 1920, 16.

54. Albert Lasker oral history, CUOHROC, 135–136.

55. Gunther, *Taken at the Flood*, 113–114.

56. Sparkes, 315.

57. Ibid.

CHAPTER THIRTEEN

1. "Picks Ship Board Headed by Lasker," *New York Times*, June 9, 1921, 13.

2. Robert K. Murray, *The Harding Era: Warren G. Harding and His Administration* (Minneapolis: University of Minnesota Press, 1969), 92. This is the trip that Lasker declined to take with the Hardings and a small group of friends, as described in the previous chapter; had he gone, he might well have secured the Commerce position for himself.

3. Will Hays letter to Warren G. Harding, January 29, 1921, Box 8, Folder 13, Will H. Hays Collection, Manuscript Section, Indiana State Library.

4. MIC 3 Warren G. Harding Papers [microform], letter to Will Hays, 14 February 1921: Ohio Historical Society.

5. Mahan, an officer at the Naval War College in Newport, Rhode Island, was the author of the classic *The Influence of Sea Power upon History, 1660–1783* (Boston: Little, Brown and Company, 1890).

6. Murray, *The Harding Era*, 280.

7. Andrew Gibson and Arthur Donovan, *The Abandoned Ocean: A History of United States Maritime Policy* (Columbia, SC: University of South Carolina Press, 2000), 110.

8. Ibid., 113.

9. Murray, *The Harding Era*, 280.

10. Gibson and Donovan, *The Abandoned Ocean*, 114. "We built extravagantly," Albert Lasker later wrote, "but war is the mother of extravagance." MIC 3 Warren G. Harding Papers [microform], letter from Albert D. Lasker to Henry W. Elliott, August 2, 1921: Ohio Historical Society.

11. This meeting was presumably colored by an episode in mid-March when Harding—at the behest of Hays—sent a telegram to Lasker offering him one of four Assistant Postmaster Generalships "while other things are developing." Lasker turned down the job. See Albert Lasker letter to John Callan O'Laughlin, March 25, 1921, from "Lasker" folder, Box 23, John Callan O'Laughlin Papers, Manuscript Division, Library of Congress, Washington, D.C.

12. Under the pressures of wartime, the board was expanded from five to seven members.

13. Reminiscences of Albert Lasker, in the Columbia University Oral History Research Office Collection (hereafter "Albert Lasker oral history, CUOHROC"), 138.

14. John Callan O'Laughlin letter to Albert Lasker, December 27, 1920, from "Lasker" folder, Box 23, O'Laughlin papers.

15. Unless otherwise noted, this whole account comes from the Albert Lasker oral history, CUOHROC, 138–144. The details, most of which can't be corroborated, should be taken with a grain of salt.

16. Lasker told this story to Boyden Sparkes. An audiotape of this interview was provided to the author by the Lasker Foundation.

17. "Schwab Wants Piez Ship Board's Head," *New York Times*, May 27, 1921, 8.

18. Sparkes, 352.

19. By this time, Lasker's name was being bandied about publicly for the Shipping Board post. See "A.D. Lasker Is Mentioned," *New York Times*, June 4, 1921, 3.

20. Bedford, then only in his mid-fifties, recovered from this attack, but died of heart disease in 1925. When Lasker finally met Bedford at a White House function in 1922—a year into his tenure at the Shipping Board—Lasker joked that Bedford had done him "more hurt than any living man." Albert Lasker letter to W. C. Teagle, June 17, 1922, Box 27, Shipping Board (USSB) records.

21. This is from the actual text of Harding's telegram. MIC 3 Warren G. Harding Papers [microform], telegram to Albert D. Lasker, June 2, 1921: Ohio Historical Society. The telegram makes no mention of the heart attack, but otherwise conforms to Lasker's account.

22. Teagle refers to this telegram in a June 6, 1921, letter to Harding. MIC 3 Warren G. Harding Papers [microform], letter from Walter Teagle, June 6, 1921: Ohio Historical Society. Harding evidently encouraged Teagle to pressure Lasker to accept.

23. The date comes from "Lasker Sees President," *New York Times*, June 8, 1921, 3. The conditions come from the Albert Lasker oral history, CUOHROC, 149.

24. "New Shipping Board Confirmed," *New York Times*, June 10, 1921, 3.

25. Unnamed sources presented the course of action agreed privately by Harding and Lasker. Since Harding certainly didn't speak to the *Times* on this subject, Lasker must have been the source.

26. "Board to Wipe Off $2,000,000 Loss on Merchant Ships," *New York Times*, June 11, 1921, 1.

27. Albert Lasker letter to W. G. Irwin, June 16, 1921.

28. "Ship Strike at End; Sign Peace Today," *New York Times*, June 14, 1921, 19.

29. "Ship Board Faces 'Colossal Wreck,'" *New York Times*, June 25, 1921, 1.

30. James True, "The Shipping Board—A Selling Problem as Lasker Sees It," *Printers' Ink*, June 21, 1926. Note that in the previous five months, the Shipping Board's inventory of vessels had gone *up* by almost 350.

31. Ibid.

32. "President Confers with Shipping Board," *New York Times*, June 17, 1921, 18.

33. "Picks Ship Board Headed by Lasker," *New York Times*, June 9, 1921, 13.

34. Sparkes, 424. According to an August 19, 1921, article in the *New York Times*, O'Laughlin resigned in mid-August 1921.

35. "Ship Board Gets Counsel," *New York Times*, June 24, 1921, 3; "Ship Board Faces 'Colossal Wreck.'"

36. Murray, *The Harding Era*, 284.

37. "Ship Board Faces 'Colossal Wreck.'"

38. "The Shipping Board Job," *New York Times*, August 15, 1921, 10.

39. Albert Lasker oral history, CUOHROC, 151.

40. Ibid., 152. Again, these accounting-related assertions and the related numbers should be taken with a grain of salt.

41. "Lasker Finds Fleet Squandering Money in Morass of Debt," *New York Times*, July 19, 1921, 1.

42. Albert Lasker oral history, CUOHROC, 146.

43. Sparkes, 354.

44. "Ship Policy Fails, Lasker Declares," *New York Times*, April 5, 1922, 11.

45. Albert Lasker letter to Jacob Ruppert, June 13, 1922, Box 27, USSB records.

46. Readers interested in the unabridged story of the *Leviathan* should start with Frank O. Braynard's astounding six-volume set: *World's Greatest Ship: The Story of the Leviathan* (New York: South Street Seaport Museum, 1974). Volume 1 details the birth, launching, and brief pre-war career of the ship; Volume 2 spans the years relevant to our story.

47. Much of the expense grew out of the need to keep a fifty-seven-man fire guard on duty at all times to protect the uninsured vessel against accidental fires and vandalism.

48. "The Shipping Board—A Selling Problem as Lasker Sees It," 26.

49. One of those exceptions is alluded to in a cryptic letter from Harding to Albert Lasker. MIC 3 Warren G. Harding Papers [microform], letter to Albert D. Lasker, 14 June 1921: Ohio Historical Society.

50. The USSB records are full of such requests. See, for example, the Coolidge correspondence (May, 4, 1922), Box 5; the correspondence with Representative George Scott Graham (October 18, 1922), Box 26; and the correspondence with Senators James W. Wadsworth Jr. (November 21, 1922) and Charles Curtis (December 2, 1922), Box 24.

51. The proposed legislation was also known as the "Ship Subsidy Bill," after its most controversial feature. We use "Merchant Marine" throughout.

52. "Harding Presents His Plan to Help American Shipping," *New York Times*, March 1, 1922, 1.

53. Lasker's fifty-nine-page opening statement is a masterful summary of the highly complex situation facing his Board, Congress, and the nation, touching on many subtleties omitted from this chapter owing to space constraints. MIC 3 Warren G. Harding Papers [microform], Merchant Marine Act of 1922, testimony of Albert D. Lasker, April 1922: Ohio Historical Society.

54. "Ship Policy Fails, Lasker Declares."

55. See, for example, the tally sent to George B. Christian. MIC 3 Warren G. Harding Papers [microform], letter from Albert D. Lasker to George B. Christian, 13 June 1922: Ohio Historical Society.

56. See the Anheuser-Busch Web site at www.anheuser-busch.com/press_room/73rdAnn_Repeal_040606.html, accessed January 4, 2007.

57. "Busch Protest to Harding," *New York Times*, June 14, 1922, 18.

58. Ibid.

59. "Pokes Fun at 'Wet' Regime on Liners," *New York Times*, June 14, 1922, 18.

60. Busch shot back at Lasker in a letter dated June 14, 1922: "The temperature in my office is well above 90, and the law prohibits me from making here in America a glass of wholesome beer such as my grandfather, Adolphus Busch, made famous over the world as an American product. Yet as I write, I contemplate the Shipping Board approving vouchers for the disbursement of American government money from the Treasury in payment for German and British beers and wines to be sold by our government at a profit. The prospect does not, I assure you, tend to lower the temperature." Box 4, USSB records.

61. "Harding Prohibits Liquor on Our Ships and on Foreign Craft in American Ports; Backs Sweeping Ruling by Daugherty," *New York Times*, October 7, 1922, 1.

62. Albert Lasker letter to R. P. Crane, October 14, 1922, Box 28, USSB records.

63. MIC 3 Warren G. Harding Papers [microform], letter from Albert D. Lasker, October 9, 1922: Ohio Historical Society.

64. Lasker was right in this regard. Foreign governments immediately began talking about reprisals against American interests, and a myriad of knotty legal problems began to present themselves. If Spanish ships carrying liquor were prevented from stopping in Puerto Rico, for example, Puerto Rican coffee exports to Spain most likely would be destroyed.

65. "Lasker Sees Blow to Our Shipping," *New York Times*, October 7, 1922, 2. Lasker immediately began casting about for ways to make U.S. liners competitive without alcohol. "I want to put fine jazz bands, and generally arrange to give entertainment on our ships such as was never given before," he wrote to a friend several weeks after Daugherty's opinion came down. See Albert Lasker letter to Paul Block, November 4, 1922, Box 28, USSB records. See also Lasker's speech to a gathering of Chicago publishers two weeks after Daugherty's action. "Until two weeks ago last Friday," Lasker said straight-faced, "Moses was thought to be the greatest law-giver of all times. Oh no, it is Daugherty, for Moses only made the Red Sea dry."

CHAPTER FOURTEEN

1. "The Presidency: The Kitchen Cabinet," *Time*, May 12, 1923.

2. Mark Sullivan, *Our Times: Volume VI, The Twenties* (New York: Charles Scribner's Sons, 1935, 100). The date is from "Harding's Florida Trip to Be a Golfing Cruise; Gillett and Lasker Among Houseboat Guests," *New York Times*, February 28, 1923, 1.

3. Sparkes, 323.

4. Sparkes, 325.

5. Sparkes, 326.

6. "President Host to Chief Justice Taft," *New York Times*, February 3, 1922, 14.

7. Albert Lasker letter to Dr. Julius Y. Cohen, April 10, 1922, Box 26, Shipping Board (USSB) records.

8. Sparkes, 324.

9. Sparkes, 328.

10. Sparkes, 327.

11. Sparkes, 327.

12. Albert Lasker letter to John R. Warner, February 24, 1923, Box 29, USSB records.

13. Sparkes, 323.

14. Albert Lasker letter to Mary Lasker, May, 11, 1923, Box 30, USSB records.

15. Albert Lasker letter to Mary Lasker, October 17, 1922, Box 28, USSB records.

16. Albert Lasker letter to Mary Lasker, May 7, 1923, Box 30, USSB records.

17. Albert Lasker letter to Mary Lasker, April 27, 1923, Box 29, USSB records.

18. Authors' interview with Frances Lasker Brody, March 22, 2004.

19. Albert Lasker letter to (son) Edward Lasker, September 11, 1922, Box 27, USSB records.

20. Albert Lasker letter to Frances Lasker, September 20, 1922, Box 27, USSB records.

21. Albert Lasker letter to Mary Lasker, October 21, 1922, Box 28, USSB records.

22. W. G. Irwin letter to Albert Lasker, December 16, 1922, W. G. Irwin Collection.

23. Albert Lasker letter to Elsa Cohen, February 15, 1923, Box 29, USSB records.

CHAPTER FIFTEEN

1. See, for example, Albert Lasker's November 16, 1922, letter to Harding regarding the influential Kansas Representative Jasper N. Tincher, Box 28, Shipping Board (USSB) records.

2. Although La Follette gave few details about the proposed deal, this apparently referred to the Merchant Marine reserve, which Harding and Lasker eliminated in April 1922 in an effort to placate organized labor.

3. "La Follette Opens Subsidy Fight with Warning to Harding," *New York Times*, December 16, 1922, 1.

4. Albert Lasker letter to Douglas Smith, December 7, 1922, Box 28, USSB records.

5. W. G. Irwin letter to Albert Lasker, February 24, 1923.

6. Transcript of an interview with the *Journal of Commerce*, April 18, 1923, Box 10, USSB records.

7. Albert Lasker letter to Robert Crane and Don Francisco, January 29, 1923, Box 29, USSB records.

8. Telegram, Albert Lasker to Schlesinger, February 20, 1923, Box 29, USSB records.

9. In February, Fleishhacker asked Lasker if he wanted to keep doing business with the raisin company. "I told him no," Lasker wrote in a telegram to Schlesinger. "They had deceived me once, and I would not want to take another risk." See Albert Lasker letter to Herbert P. Cohn, February 14, 1923, Box 29, USSB records.

10. Sparkes interview with Don Francisco, October 11, 1937.

11. In one of his 1937 interviews with Boyden Sparkes, Francisco said that Lord & Thomas had originally split the walnut account with McCann Erickson, with the rival agency handling the outdoor advertising and Lord & Thomas running the magazine advertising—an inherently awkward situation that was eventually resolved in McCann's favor. But the real problem, Francisco suggested, was that his organization was undergunned, and couldn't cater adequately to the general manager of the walnut growers: "We gave them fine advertising and good service, but we lacked manpower to give him the extra ten percent of contact and service that would have made him delighted."

12. "Predicts *Leviathan*, Refitted, Will Pay," *New York Times*, January 19, 1922, 15.

13. MIC 3 Warren G. Harding Papers [microform], letter from Albert D. Lasker and W. H. Benson, May 8, 1923: Ohio Historical Society.

14. "Assails Publicity of Shipping Board," *New York Times*, January 21, 19, 3.

15. Sparkes interview with Ralph Sollitt, 49.

16. This headline, and all of the statistics in this section, are from Frank O. Braynard, *World's Greatest Ship: The Story of the Leviathan*, Vol. 1 (New York: South Street Seaport Museum, 1974).

17. "Calls Leviathan Biggest of Ships," *New York Times*, April 12, 1923, 20.

18. Braynard, *World's Greatest Ship*, Vol. 2, 48.

19. A copy of George Christian's invitation—which looks like an invitation to a society wedding—is in the Harding papers. MIC 3 Warren G. Harding Papers [microform], invitation from Albert D. Lasker to George B. Christian, May 1923: Ohio Historical Society.

20. Albert Lasker letter to Frank W. Mondell (Director, War Finance Corporation), May 22, 1923, Box 15, USSB records. But Lasker made exceptions—as, for example, when he invited C. C. Hopkins to bring along his wife. See Albert Lasker letter to Hopkins, May 29, 1923, Box 30, USSB records.

21. Albert Lasker letter to Fiorello H. La Guardia, June 7, 1923, Box 25, USSB records.

22. "Lasker Answers 'Junket' Critics," *New York Times*, June 15, 1923, 1

23. Albert Lasker letter to T. H. Caraway, June 16, 1923, Box 30, USSB records.

24. Albert Lasker letter to Douglas Smith, June 14, 1923, Box 30, USSB records.

25. Sparkes interview with Sollitt. Sollitt recalled that Lasker turned the chore of picking the passengers over to him, and "didn't have a thing to do with it," but the guest list—dominated by Lasker's business acquaintances and political cronies—would seem to undercut this assertion.

26. MIC 3 Warren G. Harding Papers [microform], Edward P. Farley biography: Ohio Historical Society.

27. Braynard, *World's Greatest Ship*, Volume 2, 261.

28. Sparkes interview with Sollitt.

29. Ralph Sollitt later told Boyden Sparkes that Lasker had asked the Gibbs brothers to recommend the best captain they could find, and Hartley was their choice.

30. "Aboard the Steamship *Leviathan*," *New York Times*, June 20, 1923, 1.

31. Sparkes interview with Sarnoff.

32. Ibid.

33. "*Leviathan* Breaks World Speed Record in 25-Hour Spurt," *New York Times*, June 24, 1923, 1.

34. "Expensive and Yet Profitable," *New York Times*, June 23, 1923, 10.

35. "The Presidency: The Kitchen Cabinet," *Time*, May 12, 1923.

36. Albert Lasker letter to Hiram Johnson, May 22, 1923, Box 30, USSB records.

37. Albert Lasker letter to W. C. Teagle, April 12, 1923, Box 29, USSB records.

38. Albert Lasker, *The Lasker Story: As He Told It* (Chicago: Advertising Publications, 1963), 62.

39. From Edward Lasker's unpublished autobiography, 28.

40. Robert K. Murray, *The Harding Era: Warren G. Harding and His Administration* (Minneapolis: University of Minnesota Press, 1969), 444.

41. From Edward Lasker's unpublished autobiography, 28–29.

42. Francis Russell, *The Shadow of Blooming Grove: Warren G. Harding in His Times* (New York: McGraw-Hill, 1968), 626

43. Reminiscences of Albert Lasker, in the Columbia University Oral History Research Office Collection, 139.

44. Albert Lasker letter to C. C. Hopkins, May, 29, 1923, Box 30, USSB records.

45. Albert Lasker letter to (brother) Edward Lasker, June 1, 1923, Box 30, USSB records.

46. Lasker, *The Lasker Story*, 63.

CHAPTER SIXTEEN

1. Albert Lasker letter to C. C. Hopkins, May 22, 1922, Box 26, Shipping Board (USSB) records.

2. Roland Marchand, *Advertising the American Dream: Making Way for Modernity, 1920–1940* (Berkeley: University of California Press, 1985), 2.

3. Stephen Fox, *The Mirror Makers: A History Of American Advertising and Its Creators* (New York: William Morrow and Company, 1984), 75–77.

4. Ayer billings figures are from Ralph M. Hower's *The History of an Advertising Agency*, 577; Lord & Thomas figures are from exhibits in the Schultz collection. Additional agency billing totals (all partial) are available online.

5. Fox, *The Mirror Makers*, 84–86.

6. Richard M. Fried, *The Man Everybody Knew: Bruce Barton and the Making of Modern America* (Chicago: Ivan R. Dee, 2005), 55–56.

7. Albert Lasker, *The Lasker Story: As He Told It* (Chicago: Advertising Publications, 1963), 63.

8. Ibid., 89.

9. Albert Lasker letter to Herbert P. Cohn, February 12, 1923, Box 29, USSB records. Certainly, Lasker once again had large ambitions for his agency. A January 3, 1924, letter from W. G. Irwin to Lasker indicates that Lasker recently had told Irwin that his goal was to double Lord & Thomas's business.

10. Albert Lasker letter to Claude C. Hopkins, June 4, 1923, Box 30, USSB records.

11. A February 23, 1923, letter from Lasker to Hopkins (Box 29, USSB records) makes passing reference to Lasker's dream of someday being Hopkins's "manager"—probably in the sense of a newspaper's managing editor—so that Hopkins could "win as outstanding a place in the editorial field as you did in advertising."

12. Fox, *The Mirror Makers*, 113.

13. Heinrich Thomas and Bob Batchelor, *Kotex, Kleenex, Huggies: Kimberly-Clark and the Consumer Revolution in American Business* (Columbus: Ohio State University Press, 2004).

14. Ibid., 56.

15. Lord & Thomas, International Cellucotton Products Company (Kotex Division) account notes.

16. Marchand, *Advertising the American Dream*, 311.

17. Taylor Adams, "How Lasker Maneuvered for Kotex Ad Acceptance in 'Ladies' Home Journal,'" *Advertising Age*, June 17, 1974.

18. Ibid.

19. Lasker, *The Lasker Story*, 104–105.

20. Wallace Meyer statement, September 21, 1960, Meyer Collection, State Historical Society of Wisconsin. From the Museum of Menstruation and Women's Health Web site, www.mum.org/kotdispl.htm.

21. Thomas and Batchelor, *Kotex, Kleenex, Huggies*.

22. Sparkes, 223.

23. Tobacco timeline Web site, http://www.tobacco.org/resources/history/Tobacco_Historynotes .html#aacamel.

24. Ibid.

25. New York office–based Mark O'Dea sent a package of Blue Boar cigarettes to Lasker in the spring of 1923. "I don't think I have smoked half a dozen cigarettes since I was born," Lasker wrote in response, "therefore, I am no judge of the quality of cigarettes." See Albert Lasker letter to Mark O'Dea, May 7, 1923, Box 30, USSB records.

26. From *Sold American*, American Tobacco's official corporate history (no author listed), printed in 1954, 35.

27. Larry Tye, *The Father of Spin: Edward Bernays and the Birth of Public Relations* (New York: Henry Holt & Co, 1998), 27–28.

28. George Washington Hill letter to Albert Lasker, February 21, 1935, Schultz collection.

29. Sparkes interview with Coons, 23.

30. Or, in contemporary terms, that "addiction."

31. Reminiscences of Albert Lasker, in the Columbia University Oral History Research Office Collection (hereafter "Albert Lasker oral history, CUOHROC"), 105.

32. Richard Kluger, *Ashes to Ashes: America's Hundred-Year Cigarette War, the Public Health, and the Unabashed Triumph of Philip Morris* (New York: Vintage Books, 1996), 76.

33. Albert Lasker oral history, CUOHROC, 108.

34. Ibid., 108–109.

35. Ibid., 108. Although Lasker sometimes took credit for refining the testimonial, that technique was more often associated with J. Walter Thompson, which used celebrity-testimonial campaigns to promote Pond's cold cream (1924) and Lux soap (1927), among many other products.

36. Ibid., 109.

37. Ibid., 110.

38. Ibid., 111.

39. Fox, *The Mirror Makers*, 115.

40. "Babies' Blood," *Time*, May 6, 1929, www.time.com/time/magazine/article/0,9171,732326,00.html.

41. Fox, *The Mirror Makers*, 116.

42. Some of these statistics are from the minutes of the Committee on Finance and Investment of the University of Chicago, July 7, 1943.

43. Edward Lasker, autobiographical manuscript, 40.

44. Sparkes interview with Hertz, 8.

45. Ibid.

46. Sparkes, 199.

47. BDO at this point was only two years away from its merger with the Batten agency, which created a powerhouse—BBDO—that was briefly the largest agency in the country.

48. This Young & Rubicam summary is drawn from Fox, *The Mirror Makers*, 132–137.

49. "Coalition," *Time*, June 14, 1926, www.time.com/time/magazine/printout/0,8816,751559,00.html.

50. Sparkes interview with Sollitt, 10.

51. Thomas F. Logan letter to David Sarnoff, December 26, year unknown, Sarnoff collection.

52. Sparkes interview with Sarnoff, 4.

53. Kenneth Bilby, *The General: David Sarnoff and the Rise of the Communications Industry* (New York: Harper & Row, 1986), 268.

54. Sparkes interview with Sarnoff, 6.

55. "Coalition."

56. The Logan billings are from Elmer Bullis, interviewed by Sparkes, 12.

57. From the August 10, 1928, edition of the *Brooklyn Standard Union*, www.bklyn-genealogy-info.com/Newspaper/BSU/1928.Death.August.html.

58. This and following Sarnoff quotes are from Sarnoff's interview with Sparkes, 7.

59. From John Gunther's notes on an interview with Sarnoff, Box 105, Folder 12, John Gunther papers, University of Chicago.

60. Sparkes interview with Coons, 14.

61. Ibid., 19

62. Sparkes interview with Sollitt, 43.

CHAPTER SEVENTEEN

1. "Foreman-Lasker," *New York Times*, October 13, 1927.
2. Walter Roth, "Demise of the Foreman-State Bank: Was It 'Shylock in Reverse'?" *Chicago Jewish History* 27, no. 3 (Fall 2003).
3. John Gunther, *Taken at the Flood: The Story of Albert D. Lasker* (New York: Harper & Brothers, 1960), 184.
4. Sparkes, 277.
5. Letter from Edward Lasker to John Gunther, December 17, 1959, Schultz Collection.
6. John Gunther papers, University of Chicago; Box 104, Folder 15, notes on Hertz intervew.
7. "Advertising Forecasts Better Business in '29," *Wall Street Journal*, January 4, 1929.
8. Sparkes, 41.
9. "Week-End in the Loop," *Fortune*, September 1931.
10. "In Chicago," *Time*, June 15, 1931.
11. Sparkes, 276.
12. Ibid.
13. "Chicago Bank Status Clears," *Wall Street Journal*, June 10, 1931; and "3 More Chicago Banks Closed," *Wall Street Journal*, June 11, 1931.
14. "Chicago First National," *Wall Street Journal*, July 17, 1931.
15. Sparkes, 395.
16. Sparkes, 278.
17. Albert Lasker letter to Mary Lasker, October 29, 1935, Schultz Collection.
18. Sparkes, 128.
19. Very little is known about the specifics of Mary's departure.
20. Edward Lasker's unpublished memoirs, 69.
21. Letter from George Washington Hill to Albert Lasker, March 9, 1938, Schultz Collection.
22. Sparkes interview with Templin, 40.
23. Claude Hopkins claims in *My Life in Advertising* that he came up with this slogan, but Lord & Thomas's account history contradicts this (Claude C. Hopkins, *My Life in Advertising* [Lincolnwood IL: NTC Business Book, 1991]).
24. Hopkins, *My Life in Advertising*, 154.
25. William J. Gies, "Pepsodent: Ancient History That Commercial Dental Journals Continue to Ignore," *Journal of the American Medical Association* 68 (April 28, 1917): 1278.
26. "Irium-Plated Alger," *Time*, April 10, 1944, www.time.com/time/magazine/article/0,9171,796571-1,00.html.
27. Hopkins, *My Life in Advertising*, 157.
28. Lord & Thomas, Pepsodent client account notes, January 1939.
29. This brief history comes largely from *The Museum of Broadcast Communication Encyclopedia of Radio*, Volume III, ed. Christopher H. Sterling (Michael C. Keith, consulting editor), 1424–1427.
30. "*Sold American!*" *The First Fifty Years*, copyright 1954 by the American Tobacco Company, 85.
31. "The American Tobacco Co.," *Fortune*, December 1936, 154.
32. Ibid., 97.
33. All Templin comments are from the Sparkes interview with Templin, 45–47.
34. Charles Luckman, *Twice in a Lifetime: From Soap to Skyscrapers* (New York: W. W. Norton & Company, 1988), 123.
35. Michele Hilmes, *Radio Voices: American Broadcasting, 1922–1952* (Minneapolis: University of Minnesota Press, 1997), 85.
36. Elizabeth McLeod, *The Original Amos 'n' Andy: Freeman Gosden, Charles Correll and the 1928–1943 Radio Serial* (Jefferson, NC: McFarland, 2005), quoted on Wikipedia, http://en.wikipedia.org/wiki/Amos_N_Andy#_note-0.
37. Sparkes interview with Templin, 50.
38. Hilmes, *Radio Voices*, 86.
39. Ibid., 86.
40. Lord & Thomas, Pepsodent client account notes, January 1939.
41. From the "Stray Facts" column in the *Wall Street Journal*, June 5, 1933, 3.
42. "Radio Spenders," *Time*, March 18, 1935.

43. Hummert is considered by many to be the third of the three great copywriters whom Lasker discovered, along with John Kennedy and Claude Hopkins. Hill Blackett was also trained at Lord & Thomas; he took the Ovaltine account with him when he left Lasker's agency.

44. See Jim Cox, *Frank and Anne Hummert's Radio Factory: The Programs and Personalities of Broadcasting's Most Prolific Producers* (Jefferson, NC: McFarland and Company, 2003).

45. Sparkes interview with Templin, 55.

46. Luckman, *Twice in a Lifetime*, 131.

47. Sparkes interview with Noyes, 27.

48. Sparkes, 339.

49. Sparkes interview with Noyes, 28.

50. Luckman, *Twice in a Lifetime*, 136.

51. Bob Hope, as told to Pete Martin, *Bob Hope's Own Story: Have Tux, Will Travel* (New York: Simon and Schuster, 1954), 233.

52. Luckman, *Twice in a Lifetime*, 140.

53. William Robert Faith, *Bob Hope, a Life in Comedy* (Cambridge, MA: Da Capo Press, Perseus Books Group, 1982), 104.

54. Ibid., 105.

55. Luckman, *Twice in a Lifetime*, 148.

56. Ibid.

57. Sparkes interview with Templin, 40.

58. Luckman, *Twice in a Lifetime*, 151.

59. Ibid., 172.

60. Ibid., 174.

61. Ibid.

62. Lord & Thomas, Kleenex client account history, January 1939.

63. The celebrated Union ironclad warship, the *U.S.S. Monitor*—often described as a "hatbox on a raft"—may have loaned its name to the Monitor Top.

64. See the history of General Electric's products at www.otal.umd.edu/~vg/amst205.F97/vj11/project5.html.

65. Sparkes interview with Francisco, 41–42. Francisco said that Lasker told GE's president, Gerald Swope, that Lord & Thomas couldn't do its best work if it wasn't happy, and that the agency wasn't happy because "you fellows are picking on us all the time."

66. This story is from the finding aid to the Frigidaire Historical Collection, MS-262, at the Paul Laurence Dunbar Library at Wright State University. The finding aid is on line at www.libraries.wright.edu/special/manuscripts/ms262.html.

67. Sparkes, 337.

68. From "Memorandum on Copy Meeting with Frigidaire Division of General Motors Corporation," documenting meetings on September 26 and 27, 1935. The power companies also approved of frequent defrosting, which consumed more power.

69. In his autobiography, *With All Its Faults* (Boston: Little, Brown & Co., 1969), Fairfax M. Cone makes an obscure reference to Lasker and Biechler "running the [Frigidaire] advertising as an adjunct to some other aspects of the business in which the two men were deeply engaged." See p. 129.

70. Sparkes, 337.

71. Henry Guy "Ted" Little later became chairman of the Detroit-based Campbell-Ewald agency, where he oversaw the $60 million Chevrolet account: at the time, the single biggest account in the world. See *Time*, October 12, 1962, "The Men on the Cover," www.time.com/time/magazine/article/0,9171,829288-5,00.html.

72. Sparkes interview with Noyes, 24.

73. All Noyes comments are from the Sparkes interview.

CHAPTER EIGHTEEN

1. Carey McWilliams, *Southern California: An Island on the Land* (Salt Lake City: Gibbs Smith, 1995), 132–133.

2. This story comes from the All-Year Club's "Account History," written in September 1937 by Lord & Thomas's C. W. Tarr.

3. R. Germain, "The Early Years of Community Advertising," *Journal of Nonprofit and Public Sector Marketing*, 1 (1), 85–106. See Exhibit 1 (domestic U.S. examples) and page 95 (Cuba).

4. H. A. Stebbins, "Getting Away from the Commonplace in Resort Advertising," *Printers' Ink*, August 7, 1919, 31–32.

5. From the introduction to Rob Leicester Wagner, *Red Ink, White Lies: The Rise and Fall of Los Angeles Newspapers, 1920–1962* (Upland, CA: Dragonflyer Press, 2000).

6. McWilliams, *Southern California*, 136.

7. E. B. Weiss, "Advertising a Misadvertised Community," *Printers' Ink*, July 6, 1922, 117–122.

8. William C. Garner, "Leaves from a Community Advertiser's Experience Book," *Printers' Ink*, July 23, 1925, 77–80.

9. Sparkes interview with Francisco and Crane.

10. Weiss, "Advertising a Misadvertised Community," 117–122.

11. "The Early Years of Community Advertising," Exhibit 3. "Californians, Inc." is described in "A National Advertising Campaign for One of the Best-Advertised States," *Printers' Ink*, January 4, 1923, 17–18.

12. John Allen Murphy, "How to Raise the Money for Community Advertising," *Printers' Ink*, May 15, 1924, 105–114.

13. Garner, "Leaves from a Community Advertiser's Experience Book."

14. This campaign was written by Frank Hummert, then copy chief in the Chicago office.

15. McWilliams, *Southern California*, 137.

16. Sparkes interview with Francisco and Crane.

17. Carey McWilliams, *California: The Great Exception* (New York: A.A. Wyn, 1949), 174.

18. See James Bryce, *The American Commonwealth*, vol. II (London: Macmillan and Co., 1891), 403.

19. McWilliams, *California*, 176–180; Bryce, *American Commonwealth*, 387.

20. McWilliams, *California*, 182.

21. Greg Mitchell, *The Campaign of the Century: Upton Sinclair's Race for Governor of California and the Birth of Media Politics* (New York: Random House, 1992), xii.

22. See, for example, Richard M. Fried's *The Man Everybody Knew: Bruce Barton and the Making of Modern America* (Chicago: Ivan R. Dee, 2005), 116–127.

23. See Leon Harris, *Upton Sinclair: American Rebel* (New York: Thomas Y. Crowell Company, 1975).

24. Upton Sinclair, *The Brass Check: A Study of American Journalism* (Pasadena, CA: self-published, 1919), 436–437.

25. David Nasaw, *The Chief: The Life of William Randolph Hearst* (Boston: Houghton Mifflin Company, 2000), 115–116.

26. Upton Sinclair, *The Autobiography of Upton Sinclair* (New York: Harcourt, Brace & World, Inc., 1962), 260–261.

27. James N. Gregory, "Introduction" to Upton Sinclair, *I, Candidate for Governor: And How I Got Licked* (Berkeley, CA: University of California Press, 1994), vii; Kevin Starr, *Endangered Dreams: The Great Depression in California* (New York: Oxford University Press, 1996), 126–128.

28. Quoted in Harris, *Upton Sinclair*, 311.

29. Arthur M. Schlesinger Jr., *The Politics of Upheaval, 1935–1936* (Boston: Houghton Mifflin, 2003), 112; Sinclair, *Autobiography*, 268.

30. Sinclair, *Autobiography*, 269; Harris, *Upton Sinclair*, 297.

31. Upton Sinclair, "I, Governor of California—And How I Ended Poverty; A True Story of the Future," pamphlet, 1933.

32. Mitchell, *Campaign of the Century*, 6; McWilliams, *Southern California*, 298; Gregory, "Introduction," viii.

33. Mitchell, *Campaign of the Century*, 7; Starr, *Endangered Dreams*, 138–139.

34. Schlesinger, *Politics of Upheaval*, 114–118; Harris, *Upton Sinclair*, 307; Starr, *Endangered Dreams*, 150.

35. Mitchell, *Campaign of the Century*, 189 and 291.

36. Sparkes interview with Francisco and Crane, 14.

37. Don Francisco letter to Albert Lasker, September 21, 1934, "Correspondence, Lord & Thomas" file, Don Francisco papers, Syracuse University.

38. Mitchell, *Campaign of the Century*, 202 and 344.

39. Ibid., 344.

40. *Variety*, October 29, 1934, as quoted by Don Francisco in his October 13, 1937, interview with Sparkes.

41. Irwin Ross, "The Supersalesmen of California Politics: Whitaker and Baxter," *Harper's*, July 1959, 55–61.

42. Ibid.

43. In *The Brass Check*, Sinclair had written of the *Times*: "This paper, founded by Harrison Gary Otis, one of the most corrupt and most violent old men that ever appeared in American public life, has continued for thirty years to rave at every conceivable social reform, with complete disregard for truth, and with abusiveness which seems almost insane." See, for example, David M. Fine's *Imagining Los Angeles: A City in Fiction* (Reno, NV: University of Nevada Press, 2000), 62.

44. Mitchell, *Campaign of the Century*, 5; Nasaw, *The Chief*, 501; Starr, *Endangered Dreams*, 143; Sinclair, *Brass Check*, 202; Sinclair, *I, Candidate*, 144–148.

45. Sinclair, *I, Candidate*, 139–140.

46. Sparkes interview with Francisco and Crane, 4.

47. Francisco letter to Ralph Sollitt, October 1, 1934, "Correspondence, Lord & Thomas" file, Francisco papers.

48. Sparkes interview with Francisco and Crane, 4–5.

49. Sinclair, "I, Governor"; Mitchell, *Campaign of the Century*, 295–297; Schlesinger, *Politics of Upheaval*, 118; Starr, *Endangered Dreams*, 148.

50. Sparkes interview with Francisco and Crane, 8–9.

51. Gregory, "Introduction," viii; x; Starr, *Endangered Dreams*, 152.

52. Mitchell, *Campaign of the Century*, 530 and 574.

53. Sparkes interview with Francisco and Crane, 9.

54. *I, Candidate*; quotation from 144.

55. Godfrey M. Lebhar, *Chain Stores in America, 1859–1969* (New York: Chain Store Publishing Corporation, 1952), 231.

56. Sparkes interview with Francisco and Crane, 16.

57. Lord & Thomas, "Discrimination vs. Business," 27.

58. Lebhar, *Chain Stores in America*, 28–38.

59. Ibid., 53 and 66.

60. Ralph M. Hower, "Urban Retailing 100 Years Ago," *Bulletin of the Business Historical Society* 12 (December 1938): 91–101; Richard S. Tedlow, *New and Improved: The Story of Mass Marketing in America* (New York: Basic Books), 186–199.

61. Tedlow, *New and Improved*, 198.

62. Lebhar, *Chain Stores in America*, 66.

63. Joseph Schumpeter, "The Creative Response in Economic History," *Journal of Economic History* 7 (November 1947): 149–159.

64. Lebhar, *Chain Stores in America*, 129 and 159–162.

65. Ibid., 154–169.

66. Ibid., 129–147.

67. Ibid., 230.

68. "Discrimination vs. Business," 4.

69. Ibid., 5.

70. Lebhar, *Chain Stores in America*, 233.

71. Jeffrey L. Cruikshank and David B. Sicilia, *The Engine That Could: Seventy-Five Years of Values-Driven Change at Cummins Engine Company* (Boston: Harvard Business School Press, 1997), 88.

72. Sparkes interview with W. G. Irwin, 10.

73. Lebhar, *Chain Stores in America*, 234; "Discrimination vs. Business," 8.

74. "Discrimination vs. Business," 8 and 15.

75. Ibid., 7.

76. Ibid., 6 and 9; Lebhar, *Chain Stores in America*, 235.

77. "Discrimination vs. Business," 16–17.

78. California Chain Stores Association, "The Fifty Thousand Percent Chain Store Tax"; "Discrimination vs. Business," 17–18.

79. "Discrimination vs. Business," 18.

80. Ibid., 27–28.

81. Ibid., 23–24.

82. "The Fifty Thousand Percent Chain Store Tax."

83. Lebhar, *Chain Stores in America*, 237–238; "Discrimination vs. Business," 22.

84. "The Fifty Thousand Percent Chain Store Tax."

85. Lebhar, *Chain Stores in America*, 240.

86. Sparkes interview with Noyes, June 23, 1938, 8.

1. Mark O'Dea, who worked for Lasker from 1914 to 1930 and then went into competition with him, set up the speaking engagement for him. It was, O'Dea told Boyden Sparkes, the largest group of his peers that Lasker had ever addressed. Sparkes interview with O'Dea.

2. In the summer of 1935, Lasker wrote several letters to his children, then touring Europe, and mentioned Flora's impending stay at Watkins Glen.

3. Sparkes interview with Edward Lasker (undated). Unless otherwise noted, the quotes in this section are from Sparkes's conversations with Albert and Edward about Flora's death.

4. From the Gunther papers at the Chicago Historical Society, Box 105, folder 12, notes on Sarnoff conversation.

5. Sparkes interview with Sollitt, 24.

6. Edward Lasker's unpublished memoirs, *Of Me I Sing*, 17.

7. Sparkes, 200.

8. "Flora Lasker's Heirs to Divide $1,359,000 Estate," *Chicago Tribune*, December 16, 1937.

9. In his interview with Ralph Sollitt, Boyden Sparkes recounts Mary Lasker Foreman's objections to the project.

10. *Saturday Evening Post*, June 9, 1934, 8

11. This and the following descriptions are from various conversations between Sparkes and Lasker.

12. Sparkes, 5.

13. Albert Lasker letter to "Partridges," October 1, 1937.

14. Letter to Paul Patterson from his nephew, October 29, 1937, from the Arthur Schultz collection.

15. Albert Lasker letter to "D. L." and "A. K." (Partridges), April 14, 1938.

16. Except as noted, these details and quotes come from a rambling conversation with Sparkes, which most likely took place on either June 22 or June 24, 1938.

17. Letter, Joseph P. Kennedy to Thomas W. Lamont, May 4, 1938, from the Joseph P. Kennedy Papers Collection, John F. Kennedy Presidential Library.

18. Unless otherwise noted, all office details are from an undated six-page "Memorandum," prepared by the Lord & Thomas administrative staff in 1938.

19. From Robert Eck's "A Face of Character," March 30, 1994, typewritten collection of reminiscences about Lasker, 6.

20. John Gunther, *Taken at the Flood: The Story of Albert D. Lasker* (New York: Harper & Brothers, 1960), 205.

21. Sparkes interview with Crane and Francisco, October 11, 1937, 54.

22. Eck, "A Face of Character," 6.

23. "Francisco to Manhattan," *Time*, August, 1, 1938.

24. See, for example, Lasker's July, 25, 1938, letter to Pepsodent's Kenneth G. Smith.

25. "I like Doris Kenyon very much," playwright Mary P. Hamlin wrote in 1931. "She is blond but she can act." See the summary of Hamlin's memoir and letters in the *University of Rochester Library Bulletin* 30, no. 1 (Autumn 1977), www.lib.rochester.edu/index.cfm?PAGE=3570.

26. "To Fight Movie Censors," *New York Times*, April 24, 1916, 11.

27. Mick LaSalle, *Dangerous Men. Pre-Code Hollywood and the Birth of the Modern Man* (New York: Thomas Dunne Books/St. Martin's Press, 2002), 139–140.

28. See 138 F.2d 989, *Lasker v. Commissioner of Internal Revenue*, No. 8322, Circuit Court of Appeals, Seventh Circuit, December 4, 1943.

29. Authors' interview with Frances Brody, March 22, 2004.

30. The sable coat reference is from Eck, "A Face of Character," 6.

31. From John Gunther's first draft of *Taken at the Flood*, Box 99, Folder 13, John Gunther papers, University of Chicago.

32. Kenyon's stepdaughter gives a colorful rendition of Lasker's relationship with Kenyon, including the impotence reference. See the Doris Kenyon Web site at www.lind.org.zw/people/doriskenyon/doriskenyon.htm. Third wife Mary Lasker later also mentioned Lasker's problems with impotence.

33. From Leonard Lyons's February 2, 1939, syndicated column, The Lyons Den.

34. "Doris Kenyon to Sue," *New York Times*, February 21, 1938, 21.

35. "Doris Kenyon Given Divorce," *Los Angeles Times*, June 9, 1939, 22. The stated reason—cruelty—was either a legal convenience or it accurately reflected how Kenyon felt she had been treated during her brief marriage to Lasker.

36. Gunther, *Taken at the Flood*, 278.

37. Lasker first ran across Manton many years earlier, when Manton—as U. S. Second Circuit Judge in New York—issued a ruling regarding a 1921 Shipping Board case. See "U.S. Mail Line Fleet Regained by Lasker," *New York Times*, August 28, 1921, 1.

38. John Gunther devotes a chapter to the Manton affair, and provides substantially more detail than we include here. See *Taken at the Flood*, 244–256.

39. "Letter Is Offered in Levy-Hahn Case," *New York Times*, July 26, 1939, 3.

40. "Borrowing Judge," *Time*, February 8, 1939, www.time.com/time/magazine/article/0,9171,771417,00.html?promoid=googlep. See also "Not a Pretty Story," *Time*, June 5, 1939, www.time.com/time/magazine/article/0,9171,761412,00.html.

41. Manton appears to have had a notion of using Lasker's influence to merge National Cellulose—the bottom-feeding firm in which Manton and Sullivan had an interest—with the far more reputable International Cellulose, with which Lasker had been associated for almost two decades. Lasker wanted nothing to do with any such deal. See "Hahn, as Witness, Backs Loan Deal," *New York Times*, July 29, 1939, 10.

42. For the particulars of Dewey's charges against Manton, including those involving Lasker, see "Dewey Letter on Manton," and "Dewey Says Judge Manton got $400,000 from Litigants; Sends Charges to Congress," *New York Times*, January 30, 1939, 1.

43. In his own defense, Manton argued that he took bribes from *both* sides in cases before his court, listened to the arguments, made up his mind, and returned the losing side's bribe. This argument prompted Justice Learned Hand—Manton's former colleague on the Circuit Court of Appeals, and his successor as chief judge—to refer to Manton as a "moral moron."

44. "Lasker Held Dupe in Manton Deal," *New York Times*, July, 25, 1939.

45. "Not a Pretty Story."

46. "L. S. Levy Is Barred from U.S. Courts over Manton Loan," *New York Times*, November 15, 1939, 1.

47. Sparkes memo to himself, August 30, 1939.

48. Albert Lasker letter to Sparkes, May 14, 1940.

CHAPTER TWENTY

1. John Gunther, *Taken at the Flood: The Story of Albert D. Lasker* (New York: Harper & Brothers, 1960), 234.

2. Reminiscences of Mary Lasker, in the Columbia University Oral History Research Office Collection (hereafter "Mary Lasker oral history, CUOHROC"), 57.

3. Ibid., 59.

4. Ibid., 60.

5. Ibid., 47.

6. "Hollywood Is Redoing All the Hey-Hey Girls," *New York Post*, March 6, 1935.

7. Paul Jodard, *Raymond Loewy* (New York: Taplinger Publishing Company, 1992), 37. The details of the commission are from Mary Lasker oral history.

8. Mary Lasker oral history, CUOHROC, 72.

9. In her Columbia oral history, Mary recalled that she had made the same request of her first husband, Paul Reinhardt. Reinhardt went to one session, declared ironically, "I have been analyzed," and never went back. Mary Lasker oral history, CUOHROC, 530

10. Authors' interview with Frances Brody, March 22, 2004.

11. Box 99, Folder 14, John Gunther papers, University of Chicago. Gunther also talked to George Daniels, who provided additional details (Box 104, Folder 10).

12. Gunther, *Taken at the Flood*, 260.

13. Parker Hall letter to William Benton, January 7, 1954, University of Chicago Library.

14. The University sold the estate (which was thirty-two miles from the main campus, as the crow flies) in seven transactions beginning in 1943 and ending in 1947—the year that Lasker's fabulous golf course fell victim to a developer. University officials put the proceeds from these sales into a special account and later used them to build a new administration building and purchase a thirteen-story apartment building adjacent to the campus.

15. Gunther, *Taken at the Flood*, 262.

16. According to Gunther's original manuscript, Lasker continued to see Daniels at irregular intervals in subsequent years.

17. Mary Lasker oral history, CUOHROC, 73.

18. Ibid., 80.

19. Authors' interview with Frances Brody, March 22, 2004.

20. Mary Lasker oral history, CUOHROC, 49.

21. Ibid., 440.

22. Ibid., 449.

23. Sanger made reference to this influential early gift in an address delivered on October 25, 1950, at the thirtieth annual meeting of the Planned Parenthood Federation. Margaret Sanger Papers, Sophia Smith Collection, Smith College Library.

24. See Woodbridge E. Morris, MD, letter to Albert Lasker, November 21, 1939, Margaret Sanger papers.

25. Albert Lasker letter to Margaret Sanger, July 14, 1942, Margaret Sanger papers.

26. Albert Lasker letter to Margaret Sanger, February 9, 1940, Margaret Sanger papers.

27. Mary Lasker oral history, CUOHROC, 87.

28. See Madeline Gray, *Margaret Sanger: A Biography of the Champion of Birth Control* (New York: Richard Marek Publishers, 1979), 399.

29. Albert Lasker letter to Margaret Sanger, February 9, 1940.

30. Mary Lasker oral history, CUOHROC, 88.

31. Ibid., 467.

32. Ibid., 449.

33. See the Seversky biography on the "AcePilots" Web site, at www.acepilots.com/wwi/pio_seversky .html.

34. Mary Lasker oral history, CUOHROC, 99.

35. Review, *New York Times*, July 19, 1943, movies.nytimes.com/movie/review?res= 9404EFDF1738E33 BBC4152DFB1668388659EDE (accessed January 3, 2008).

36. See Leonard Maltin's introduction to *Victory Through Air Power* on *Walt Disney on the Front Lines*, a DVD collection of Disney wartime propaganda, 2004.

37. Fairfax Cone, *With All Its Faults: A Candid Account of Forty Years in Advertising* (Boston: Little, Brown & Co., 1969), 140–141. Cone gives a fascinating account of Lasker's decision to shut down Lord & Thomas.

38. Albert Lasker letter to Leonard Masius, December 19, 1942.

39. Don Francisco letter to Ralph Sollitt, December 15, 1933, "Correspondence, Lord & Thomas" file, Box 2, Don Francisco papers, Syracuse University Special Collections.

40. Unless otherwise noted, this financial analysis comes from Lasker letter to Masius, December 19, 1942.

41. From a June 3, 1943, accounting from A. E. Rood to the firm of Appel & Brach. It is worth noting in this context that Lasker paid between half and two-thirds of his income in taxes.

42. From the Arthur Andersen auditors' report dated December 31, 1942.

43. Gunther, *Taken at the Flood*, 269.

44. This complete break between old and new was necessitated by Lasker's inability to get a reading from the Treasury Department—then swamped by tens of thousands of such inquiries, owing to the dramatic spike in the liquidation tax—as to the taxability of goodwill. Lasker simply couldn't afford to risk a tax liability of unknown size.

45. With his Foote, Cone & Belding colleagues, coauthor Schultz spent years trying to rebuild this "lost" international network.

46. Andersen auditors' report.

47. "End of a Name," *Time*, January 4, 1943, www.time.com/time/magazine/article/ 0,9171,790682,00.html. The article concluded on an interesting note: "Dopesters figured that he took his identification with the name too personally to leave it to someone else."

48. Cone, *With All Its Faults*, 142.

49. "Advertising Will Play Major Post-War Role, Lasker Says," *Columbus (Ohio) Dispatch*, January 17, 1943.

CHAPTER TWENTY-ONE

1. Reminiscences of Mary Lasker, in the Columbia University Oral History Research Office Collection (hereafter "Mary Lasker oral history, CUOHROC"), 612.

2. Ibid., 612.

3. Ibid., 105.

4. Ibid., 476.

5. Ibid., 128.

6. See *The American Society for the Control of Cancer: Its Objects and Methods and Some of the Visible Results of Its Work*, published by the Society in 1925, 65–67.

7. For details on the Smith gift, see "Appropriate," *Time*, June 15, 1925; for details on the Lasker Foundation, see the University's "Developing the Medical Center" historical summary at www.lib.uchicago.edu/e/spcl/excat/donors5.html. The medical context of the gift is described in great detail in "Donate $1,000,000 to Prolong Life," *New York Times*, Jaunary 9, 1928, 1.

8. Mary Lasker oral history, CUOHROC, 77.

9. See "Important Events in NCI history" on the National Institutes of Health Web site at www.nih.gov/about/almanac/archive/2002/organization/NCI.htm.

10. Mary Lasker oral history, CUOHROC, 136.

11. Ibid., 479.

12. Ultimately, according to Mary, this gentlemen's agreement wasn't honored. Although Lever Bros. contributed $50,000 in 1944, the company gave only $25,000 for each of the next two years, and then stopped its contributions altogether. Mary Lasker oral history, CUOHROC, 484–485.

13. Another version of this story has Emerson Foote as the prime mover behind the name change. See Walter S. Ross, *Crusade: The Official History of the American Cancer Society* (New York: Arbor House, 1987), 37.

14. "Wartime Cancer Show," *Fibber McGee and Molly*, April 28 1945.

15. Mary Lasker oral history, CUOHROC, 534.

16. Louis Lasagna, *The Doctors' Dilemmas* (1962; rpt. Ayer Co. Publishing, 1970), 69.

17. Mary Lasker oral history, CUOHROC, 170.

18. Kline later became celebrated as the author of the best-selling *From Sad to Glad* (New York: Putnam, 1974).

19. Alfred Lasker letter to Ernst Mahler, August 2, 1951, from the Arthur Schultz collection.

20. Alfred Lasker letter to Charles Mendl, October 4, 1951, from the Arthur Schultz collection.

21. Mary Lasker oral history, CUOHROC, 710.

22. See Alfred Frankfurter's introduction to *The Albert D. Lasker Collection: Renoir to Matisse*, published in 1957 by Chanticleer Press with a subsidy from Mary Lasker, xiv.

23. Mary Lasker oral history, CUOHROC, 714.

24. *The Albert D. Lasker Collection*, xvi.

25. Ibid., 109.

26. John Gunther, *Taken at the Flood: The Story of Albert D. Lasker* (New York: Harper & Brothers, 1960), 312.

27. Nadine Brozan, "Woman in the News: Mary Lasker; Lobbyist on a National Scale," *New York Times*, November 21, 1985.

28. Gunther, *Taken at the Flood*, 181.

29. Ibid., 225.

30. Transcript of a telephone conversation between Alfred Lasker and Robert Hutchins, May 14, 1942, University of Chicago Library.

31. Milton Mayer, *Robert Maynard Hutchins: A Memoir* (Berkeley: University of California Press, 1993), 229. Mayer provides a remarkably dispassionate—even sympathetic—view of Lasker in this episode.

32. One of Lasker's sisters became ill en route to Israel and had to return home for emergency surgery.

33. Unless otherwise noted, Lasker's quotes regarding Israel are from the reminiscences of Albert Lasker, in the Columbia University Oral History Research Office Collection, 153–180.

34. J. R. Fuchs's oral history interview with Oscar R. Ewing, Harry S. Truman Library & Museum, www.trumanlibrary.org/oralhist/ewing4.htm.

35. Gunther, *Taken at the Flood*, 336.

36. Ibid., 335.

37. Alfred Lasker letter to Charles Mendl, June 20, 1951.

38. Alfred Lasker letter to Harry Meyer, December 26, 1951.

39. Mary Lasker oral history, CUOHROC, 274.

40. Alfred Lasker, *Last Will and Testament*, February 1952.

CHAPTER TWENTY-TWO

1. Sparkes, 341.

2. Sparkes, 345.

3. Sparkes, 39.

4. From "Advertising and Its Contribution to the General Welfare," an undated speech (or perhaps article) from the 1930s.

5. Sparkes interview with Sollitt, November 5, 1937, 18.

6. Sparkes interview with Hertz, May 29, 1938, 7.

7. Sparkes interview with Sarnoff, January 11, 1938, 4–11.

8. Reminiscences of Mary Lasker, in the Columbia University Oral History Research Office Collection (hereafter "Mary Lasker oral history, CUOHROC"), 76.

9. Sparkes interview with Hummert, 32.

10. Sparkes interview with Bullis, October 27, 1937, 17.

11. Sparkes interview with Hummert, 37.

12. Sparkes interview with Sollitt, November 3, 1937, 14.

13. Sparkes, 209.

14. Sparkes interview with Sollitt, April 22, 1938, 10.

15. Sparkes, 3.

16. Mary Lasker oral history, CUOHROC, 50.

17. Sparkes, 252.

18. Alfred Lasker letter to W. G. Irwin, August 18, 1917, from the W. G. Irwin papers.

19. Richard M. Fried, *The Man Everybody Knew: Bruce Barton and the Making of Modern America* (Chicago: Ivan R. Dee, 2005), 82–83. Barton visited rest-cure camps in upstate New York for a decade, took long "vacations" with his brother in Wyoming, and also sought relief at a clinic in Canada.

20. Fairfax Cone, *With All Its Faults: A Candid Account of Forty Years in Advertising* (Boston: Little, Brown & Company, 1969), 70–80.

21. The few documented "manic" episodes that Lasker had—such as the wild night in Grand Rapids in 1900 with Arthur Warner that culminated in a youthful Lasker attempting to drive a carriage into a bar—seem to have been the result of drink, rather than mania. The three-day lecture that Lasker delivered to his associates in April 1925, apparently at a fever pitch, makes a stronger case for mania.

22. Sparkes interview with Crane and Francisco, 32.

23. Sparkes interview with Sullivan, November 30, 1937, 2.

24. Sparkes interview with Hertz, May 29, 1938, 3.

25. Sparkes interview with Noyes, June 23, 1938, 14.

26. Sparkes, 99–100.

27. Sparkes interview with O'Dea, December 3, 1937, 9.

28. John Gunther, *Taken at the Flood: The Story of Albert D. Lasker* (New York: Harper & Brothers, 1960), 207.

29. Sparkes interview with Sollitt, November 16, 1937, 8–9.

30. Edward Lasker letter to John Gunther, December 16, 1959, 9.

31. Sparkes interview with Sollitt, November 5, 1937, 8.

32. Sparkes, 146.

33. Sparkes interview with Sollitt, November 16, 1937, 18.

34. Sparkes interview with Field, March 16, 1938, 9.

35. Sparkes interview with Irwin, 11.

36. Sparkes interview with Sollitt, November 5, 1937, 18.

37. Sparkes interview with Irwin, 1.

Index

Irwin, William Glanton (W. G.) (*continued*)
Van Camp management and, 146–147, 148,
149, 150, 151, 152, 153
Island City Savings Bank of Galveston, 18
Israel, trip to, 362–363
Ittleson, Blanche, 356

J. L. Stack Advertising Agency, 97
J. Walter Thompson agency, 43, 44, 58, 228,
240–241, 257, 276, 375
J. Wix & Sons, 268
Jackson, "Shoeless Joe," 162
Jamison, Kay Redfield, 87
Jefferson, W. T., 109–110
Jeffersonian, The (newspaper), 129, 137
Jefferson & Wasey agency, 110
Jewish community
father Morris Lasker's connection to, 18, 132
Flora Lasker and, 74
Frank case and reactions among, 2–3, 127,
129–130, 133, 134, 141
Frank's position in, 125, 127, 129, 133, 142
Hearst newspapers and, 2–3, 127
Lasker family in Chicago and, 263, 370
Lasker family's Prussian background in, 10, 11
Lasker's early business dealings and, 47, 69
Lasker's Shipping Board appointment and, 202
Lasker's social life among, 69, 70, 131
philanthropy in, 16, 131, 132, 370–371
proposed Ford presidential run and, 2–3
relationship of state of Israel to, 362–363
Sinclair's California gubernatorial campaign
and, 302
uncle Eduard Lasker's reputation in, 16,
19, 132
Jewish identity of Lasker
anti-Semitism experiences and, 3, 23, 131
being a secular Jew and, 131, 360
business success and, 47, 131, 171, 368
childhood synagogue attendance and, 22–23
desire to do good in the world and, 19, 132
financial settlement with Mrs. Logan and,
260, 261
Frank case and, 127, 129, 130, 132, 133,
142, 171
friendship with Harding and, 202
Hutchins at University of Chicago and,
360–362
joking by Lasker and awareness of, 202, 255
Lasker on Jews and, 132, 363
Lasker's experience of, 131–132, 378
legacies of father Morris and uncle Eduard
and, 10, 18, 19, 132, 142
outsider status related to, 378–379
pride in his Jewish heritage and, 131
Shipping Board appointment and, 202
trip to Israel and, 362–363
Johns Hopkins hospital, Baltimore, 153, 261–262

Johnson, B. J., 105
Johnson, Ban, 161, 162, 165, 166
Johnson, Hiram, 163, 181–182, 184, 194, 207, 234,
235, 236, 295
Johnson, Jack, 27–28
Johnson Soap Co., 104–107
Jones, Wesley, 211, 223
Joseph Campbell Soup Company, 90
Journal of Commerce, 224
Judicious Advertising (Lord & Thomas house
journal), 58, 61, 62–63
Jungle, The (Sinclair), 78, 296

Kalamazoo Pure Food Company, 51
Kalamazoo Tuberculosis Remedy Company, 99
Katz, Eugene, 52
Kearney, Dennis, 294–295
Kearneyism, 294, 296
Kellogg, W. W., 77
Kelvinator, 283
Kennedy, John E., 8, 55–58
business generated by, 63
contradictory aspects of work style of, 64–65
copyediting department and, 64
departure from Lord & Thomas, 65
as father of modern advertising, 66
fundamentals of advertising and, 376
half-time status of, 62–63
Lasker on, 65, 66
mail-order business and, 62
New York office of Lord & Thomas and, 65
Nineteen Hundred Washer Company
campaign and, 59–60, 61
Van Camp account and, 89, 90–91
writing by, 65–66
Kennedy, Joseph P., 324
Kenyon, Doris (second wife), 328–330
divorce from Lasker, 330, 335, 338, 348, 371
initial meeting between Lasker and, 178,
328–329
marriage to Lasker, 4, 329–330
prenuptial agreement with, 329, 330
keyed advertising, 60–61
Killifer, William Jr., 160
Kimberly-Clark, 264
Kleenex and, 5, 247
Kotex and, 5, 243–244, 247
King Coal (Sinclair), 296
Kleenex, 5, 247, 281–282, 326, 377
Kline, Nathan, 357
Knox, Philander C., 182
Knox, William Franklin ("Frank"), 345
Ku Klux Klan, 141, 142
Kotex, 5, 243–246, 247, 326, 377

Ladies' Home Journal, 42–43, 91, 91, 107, 124, 245
La Follette, Robert, 223–224
LaGuardia, Fiorello H., 230–231

Acknowledgments

First, we owe special thanks to the many libraries, archives, museums, and repositories that gave us access to their collections, as detailed in our "Note on Sources." Books like this are not possible without resources like theirs. We are also indebted to the many people who forwarded Lasker-related materials to coauthor Schultz over the years, including his colleagues at Foote, Cone & Belding (today's Draftfcb).

David Sicilia, Chloe Kline, and Lauren Schug all made major contributions to one or more chapters. Chloe, in particular, dug deep to make this book happen, organizing our primary and secondary materials into an accessible collection and regularly engaging in spirited arguments with the noisy ghost of Albert Lasker. Liza Rogerson investigated several archives and pulled together decades' worth of newspaper clippings.

We thank the many, many individuals—including several members of the Lasker family—who looked at chapters in progress and made suggestions as to how to improve them. The late Francie Lasker Brody, Albert's younger daughter, gave us an interview in March 2004; we're happy to have had that opportunity.

We thank the companies that permitted us to reprint their ads, logos, and other copyrighted materials. There is no better way to understand Lasker's contributions to advertising than to look at ads before and after Lasker.

There are too many great people at the Harvard Business Review Press to thank individually, but Jeff Kehoe—our editor—is in a class by himself. Nearly a decade ago, he said that he hoped the Press could do more high-quality business biographies aimed at a broader audience. That is what we tried to deliver.

We end with our agent, Helen Rees, who one day, way back at the turn of the century, said, "Why don't you try a biography? That might play to your strengths."

About the Authors

JEFFREY L. CRUIKSHANK is a writer, editor, and communications consultant. The cofounder (in 1989) of The Cruikshank Company (www.cruikshank.org), he is the author or coauthor of several dozen books, including a murder mystery (*Murder at the B School*); books on commercial real estate and venture capital; and histories of Cummins, New England Electric, Herman Miller, Perdue Farms, the Harvard Business School, and the United States Merchant Marine Academy. He lives and works in Milton, Massachusetts.

ARTHUR W. SCHULTZ is a preeminent and respected authority on the founding of modern advertising. He was CEO of Foote, Cone & Belding—the successor agency to Albert Lasker's Lord & Thomas—from 1971 to 1982. He met Albert Lasker, has known many members of the Lasker family, and has worked with many of Lasker's senior executives and key clients. His access to the Lord & Thomas files, reports, and correspondence facilitated the creation of this book. A graduate of the University of Chicago, Schultz served on the university's board of trustees and has also served as a trustee and chairman of the Art Institute of Chicago. He is the author of *In Praise of America's Collectors* and lives in Southern California.